Robert Milligan

Reason and revelation

The province of reason in matters pertaining to divine revelation defined and

illustrated

Robert Milligan

Reason and revelation
The province of reason in matters pertaining to divine revelation defined and illustrated

ISBN/EAN: 9783337280413

Printed in Europe, USA, Canada, Australia, Japan

Cover: Foto ©Andreas Hilbeck / pixelio.de

More available books at **www.hansebooks.com**

REASON AND REVELATION.

REASON AND REVELATION:

OR,

THE PROVINCE OF REASON

IN MATTERS PERTAINING TO

DIVINE REVELATION DEFINED AND ILLUSTRATED;

AND THE PARAMOUNT AUTHORITY OF

THE HOLY SCRIPTURES VINDICATED.

By R. MILLIGAN,

PRESIDENT OF THE COLLEGE OF THE BIBLE IN KENTUCKY UNIVERSITY.

"All Scripture is given by inspiration of God; and is profitable for doctrine, for reproof, for correction, for instruction in righteousness, that the man of God may be perfect, thoroughly furnished for every good work."—2 TIMOTHY iii: 16.

CINCINNATI:

R. W. CARROLL & CO., PUBLISHERS,

117 WEST FOURTH STREET.

1868.

FOURTH EDITION.

GENERAL CONTENTS.

(v)

CHAPTER V.

CHAPTER VI.

CHAPTER VII.

CHAPTER VIII.

PART II.

PART III.

CHAPTER II.

CHAPTER III.

CHAPTER IV.

INTRODUCTION.

It is painful to see the popular indifference that is every-where manifested for the Word of God. I do not mean to say, with some, that this indifference is increasing; or that it is even as great now as it was a hundred years ago. I am fully persuaded that it is not. Indeed, I feel entirely confident, that the Holy Scriptures had never before so great an influence over the masses of mankind as they have at present. But, nevertheless, their influence is very little in comparison with what it ought to be. Very few persons seem to believe the Bible with their whole hearts. And hence but few tremble at its solemn precepts and warnings: very few seem to feel and to acknowledge its paramount claims and authority. Most unconverted men have, of course, but little regard for it: and even in the Church, its laws and its institutions are, by many, treated with more indifference than the petty rules and regulations of a borough police.

It would be an interesting problem, to inquire into the

(xi)

cause or causes of this wide-spread indifference with respect to the laws, and ordinances, and institutions of Jehovah. And it might, moreover, have a bearing for good, in many ways. But for this, I have not time, at present. My object, in the following pages, is not so much to inquire into the origin and history of this popular skepticism, as to remove it. I wish, as far as possible, to enlighten the popular understanding; to assign to Reason her proper province; and to arouse to a sense of feeling and activity, the slumbering conscience. In this way, and by these means, I hope to sweep away some of the false refuges in which men are prone to trust; and to help, it may be in a very humble way, to restore the Bible to its proper position, *as the only safe and all-authoritative rule of faith and practice.*

The work is designed for *all classes of readers;* and I have therefore written it with all possible simplicity and plainness. The occasional introduction of Greek and Hebrew words need not discourage any one from reading the book. Their English equivalents are always given, as far as the nature of the case will permit: so that the mere English student can use the work with as much freedom and satisfaction as if it contained no foreign words of any kind; while the classical student will not unfrequently be assisted by having the original words expressed in their proper connection.

To all students of the Bible, then, and especially to young men preparing for the work of the Christian Ministry, the following pages are respectfully and affectionately dedicated. If they in any measure serve the purpose for which they were written, I will not regret, that in great physical weakness and suffering, I have, at the request of many brethren, prepared them for the press. That God may graciously sanctify them to his own glory, and make them eminently instrumental in promoting truth and righteousness among men, is my earnest and sincere prayer, for Christ's sake.

R. MILLIGAN.

KENTUCKY UNIVERSITY,
October 1, 1867.

REASON AND REVELATION.

PART FIRST.

DIVINE ORIGIN OF THE BIBLE.

CHAPTER I.

PRELIMINARY.

My theme is The Province of Reason in matters pertaining to Divine Revelation. On this, as on most other questions of great practical importance, mankind have long been divided. Some run to one extreme, and some to another. The Mystics, for example, constrained by their false system of philosophy, have generally assigned to Reason a very low and subordinate place in the investigation and discovery of truth. With them, the *Inner Light*, (lumen internum,) produced by the immediate and direct operation of the Spirit of God on the sensibilities of the human soul, is the guide of life. Without this, Reason, in their estimation, is blind; and the Bible is a sealed book, an inexplicable enigma.

The Rationalists, on the other hand, give to Reason all authority. Whatever they can explain rationally, *i. e.*, according to their approved system or

General scope of the Treatise.

Two extremes on this question.

Views of the Mystics.

Views of the Rationalists.

(15)

systems of philosophy, they receive as true; but whatever they can not so explain and comprehend, they reject as false and absurd. And hence it follows that the Bible has no more authority with them than a heathen classic. Its mira-- cles are all either wholly ignored as false, or treated as myths. And its remaining portions are constantly tortured and per- verted in the ever-varying crucible of whatever may happen to be the popular system of philosophy.

How these two extremes meet in reference to the Bible.

Here, then, as in many other cases, extremes meet. The tendency of both Mysticism and Rationalism is to greatly diminish, if indeed not to wholly destroy, the authority and influence of Divine Revelation. The former does this, by degrading Reason; the latter, by unduly exalting her. The former makes her the mere slave of feeling: the latter deifies her, and makes her the sovereign arbiter in all things pertaining to human life and human destiny.

Where the truth lies.

But here also, as in most similar cases, the truth occupies medium ground. The fundamen- tal principle of Mysticism is a fundamental error. Every

Refutation of the Mystical hypothesis.

man who looks narrowly into his own con- sciousness, knows full well that subjective truth originates not in the feelings or sensibilities, as Swedenborg and his school would have us believe, but in the understanding or the intellect. Through the medium of the intellect, it pervades the sensibilities; through the sensibili- ties, it influences the will; and through the will,-it controls the life. Even the conscience itself is subject to the dictates and teachings of the understanding. It is always a faithful moni- tor. But its office is not to judge, but to execute. It is the sheriff that faithfully carries out the decisions of Reason, whether they be right or wrong; whether they be true or false; whether they be just or unjust. Paul had always a good conscience; that is, an approving conscience; because he always acted conscientiously; but, nevertheless, he was a very great sinner, because his reason erred.

Reason, then, has something to do, even in religious matters. But it does not follow that her influence here is absolute, or that she is at liberty to reject as spurious or absurd whatever she can not herself fully explain and comprehend. Not at all. Her powers and functions are limited. She must have the necessary evidence before she can decide on the truth or falsity of any proposition. She may, it is true, form an opinion on any subject; but even this opinion will be found, on examination, to depend on the implied probabilities or improbabilities of the case. The uninstructed youth, for example, would not hesitate for a moment to answer in the negative the question whether or not the planet Jupiter is inhabited. As he looks up into the heavens, he sees there, under the name of Jupiter, but a bright spot, apparently not near so large as the small sunflower in his father's garden. And hence, from the evidence in his possession, he can not think that it would be a suitable residence for such beings as are men and women. But let him now be informed that the earth was made for man; that its vast mineral, vegetable, and animal resources were all designed for the comfort and happiness of beings formed in the image and likeness of their Creator; let him be further told or made to understand, on reliable evidence, that Jupiter is about fourteen hundred times larger than the earth; that it has four times as many satellites; that it revolves on its axis and in its orbit, like the earth; and that, on the whole, it has a much greater influence in the Solar system than our own little planet, and soon his doubts will begin to change, and his reason will finally decide in favor of the probability of its being inhabited by some such rational and accounta-

Reason limited in her operations.

She depends on the evidence submitted.

Illustration from the planet Jupiter.

2

ble beings as man.   I say *probability*, because, the evidence

being only probable, the conclusion must also
be probable.   But let the evidence be conclusive or demonstrative, and so, also, will be
the conclusion.   Concede, for example, that all
men are mortal, and that Socrates is a man, and then Reason will, of necessity, draw the conclusion that Socrates is
mortal.   If she is not satisfied with the conclusion, she may
review the premises.   But let their correctness be conceded,
and then *Reason has no alternative left but to draw the conclusion and to acquiesce in it, whether she fully comprehends*

it or not.   This, then, is her province in every
department of truth to which the human mind
has access.   It is simply by a process of abstraction, comparison, and generalization to draw from the
data otherwise furnished, the proper inferences and conclusions.

And hence it is obvious that her relations to Divine Rev-

elation are most intimate and important.   The
very first question that naturally arises in the
mind of every man concerning the Bible respects
its origin.   Is it of human, or is it of Divine
origin?   Is it the word of man's wisdom, or is it, as it

claims to be, the word of the living God?   To
answer this question, therefore, on the ground
of all the evidence variously furnished, is the
first province of Reason in matters pertaining
to Divine Revelation.

God requires no man to believe without sufficient evidence.   He did not require even Pharaoh and the Egyptians to do this.*   Nor did
Christ require this of the Jews.   "If," said he,
"I had not come and spoken unto them, they had not had

· *Exodus vii: 9.

sin; but now they have no cloak for their sin." And again, he adds, in the second verse following: "If I had not done among them the works which no other man has done, they would have had no sin; but now they have both seen and hated both me and my Father."*

In such a treatise as this, in which brevity is a primary object, it will not, of course, be expected that I should furnish even a general outline of the evidences of Christianity. For this, I must refer the reader to the works of Lardner, Paley, Butler, Blount, Horne, Chalmers, Hengstenberg, Mansell, Rogers, Taylor, McCosh, Ullmann, Auberlen, Schaff, and other writers on the genuineness and Divine authenticity of the Holy Scriptures. But a matter so fundamental as this should not be passed over in silence. Reason demands that, even in this brief treatise, *we should have a sufficient and satisfactory reason for our faith in the Word of God.* Without this, indeed, my object in writing this book would be in a great measure defeated. And I will, therefore, as briefly as I can, present and illustrate *one* of the many chains of evidence that serve to prove the Divine origin of the Holy Scriptures. It all depends on the universally-acknowledged *relation that exists between cause and effect.* {.marginnote Works on the evidences of Christianity.} {.marginnote The chain of evidence presented in this treatise.}

It is now every-where conceded, and received as an axiomatic truth, that every effect must have its own adequate and sufficient cause. It is not enough that it have merely *a* cause. The common sense of mankind demands and requires that the cause shall be adequate and sufficient. Otherwise, we know intuitively, as well as experimentally, that the effect can not and will not follow in any case. {.marginnote The fundamental principle of this chain of argument is universally conceded.}

Thus, for instance, all sane persons would reject as absurd

* John xv: 22 and 24.

the allegation that a clock or a watch is the result of

Illustration.   chance; that it was made in some way without
a maker, and that it was designed without a

designer. Such an idea is wholly inconsistent with even our earliest intuitions, and the first developments of Reason.

And hence, you see why it is that the dogmas of Athe-

Why Atheism   ism have always been regarded as so very ab-
is so very ab-   surd by all men of sobriety and reflection. Con-
surd.   cede that there is a God who made, preserves,

and governs all things, and then all is plain, simple, and rational. We have, then, a cause that is adequate and sufficient to account for all the varied phenomena of nature. We can, then, understand how it is, and why it is, that the heavens are so beautiful, and that the earth is so well adapted to all the wants and circumstances of man.

But to deny, with most modern Atheists, that the uni-

Fundamental   verse has any marks of design or intelligence,
truth denied by
Modern Athe-   is to deny the evidence of our own senses.
ists.   And to say, with ancient Atheists, that evi-

dence of design does not of necessity imply the existence

Fundamental   and agency of a designer, *is to ignore the funda-*
truth denied by
Ancient Athe-   *mental laws of human belief, and to deprive rea-*
ists.   *son of her most reliable data.*

And just so it is with respect to the Divine authenticity

Concede that   of the Holy Bible. Concede that this wonder-
God is the au-   ful volume is the inspired Word of God, and
thor of the Bi-
ble, and what   then all that follows is plain, simple, and ra-
follows?   tional. The facts and other recorded phenom-

ena are just such as we might reasonably anticipate.

Deny this   But deny this fundamental truth, assume that
fundamental
truth, and   the Bible is not the inspired Word of God, but
what *facts* can   that it is a work of uninspired men, however
not be account-   great and however learned, and then how will
ed for?

you account,

I. For the Unity and the Harmony of this wonderful book?

II. How will you account for its great Simplicity, and, at the same time, for its absolute Incomprehensibility?

III. How will you account for its unparalleled Theology?

IV. How will you account for its superior code of Morality, and its ameliorating influence on society?

V. How will you account for the Supernatural Character of Christ?

VI. How will you account for the Existence, History, and Prevalence of Christianity?

VII. How will you account for the many plain and unmistakable instances of Fulfilled Prophecy?

VIII. And, finally, how will you account for the Harmony of the Bible with the Progress and Discoveries of Modern Science and Philosophy?

It seems to me that this Chapter of Christian Evidences has never yet been fairly and satisfactorily investigated. And I have, therefore, selected it, for the double purpose of proving the Divine origin of the Holy Scriptures, and showing that God still requires no man to believe without sufficient evidence.

Reason for selecting this Chapter of Evidence.

CHAPTER II.

THE UNITY AND HARMONY OF THE BIBLE.

My present subject is the Unity and Harmony of the

Subject of Chapter Second.

Holy Bible. This will be best understood by referring, for illustration, to the unity and harmony of the Book of Nature.

It has been often said, and truly said, that nature is a

Proof that Nature is a unit:

unit. With this important truth most of my readers are, no doubt, more or less familiar. Many of you have learned from your Chemistry that the whole mineral kingdom is composed of about sixty-four

From Chemistry.

different kinds of atoms, united together in the most exact and definite proportions. And from your text-books on Natural History, some of you, at

From Natural History.

least, have also learned that there is a very close connection between the Mineral, Vegetable, and Animal Kingdoms; that, as the mineral is the basis of the vegetable, so, also, is the vegetable the stay and support of the animal; and the animal, again, of the spiritual. So that the earth, though composed of millions of atoms, and occupied by innumerable species, is really but one perfect and harmonious whole.

Nor is this all. Under the mysterious influence of attrac-

From Astronomy.

tion, the Earth and several other planets, primary and secondary, are bound to the Sun, forming one Solar system. And by the same mysterious forces, the Solar system is linked to another; and this again to another, and another, until all are finally united in one glorious, sublime, and boundless universe.

True, indeed, there are, in this vast and boundless scheme of nature, many *apparent* discrepancies and irregularities. Acids and alkalies have very unlike properties. Some vegetables are poisonous, and others are nutritious. Some animals are rational, and others are irrational. Some of the planets move westward, and some eastward; some in orbits that are nearly circular, and others in orbits that are extremely elliptical But all such cases of *apparent* discord are really essential elements of unity and harmony. They are all necessary parts and links of

Apparent discrepancies in nature.

These are all essential elements of harmony.

—— " that golden, everlasting chain,
Which in its strong embrace holds heaven, and earth, and main,"

and which really serves to unite in one harmonious whole all parts and parcels of the entire physical universe.

And just so it is, with respect to the Bible. It, too, has its links and its chains of Divine harmony, extending from its Alpha to its Omega; and from its center to all parts of its circumference.

Evidence that the Bible is also one harmonious whole.

Take, for example, the chain of Divine promises concerning the coming, the reign, and the triumphs of the Messiah. The first of these is given in the sentence that God pronounced on the Old Serpent, immediately after the fall of man. " I will," said Jehovah, " put enmity between thee and the woman, and between thy seed and her seed. It shall bruise thy head, and thou shalt bruise his heel."* He did not say seeds, as if he were speaking of many; but he said, " *Her Seed,*" which is Christ.†

From the promises concerning Christ.

Again it was said to Abraham, " In thy seed shall all the

* Genesis iii: 15.   † Galatians iii: 16.

nations of the earth be blessed."* And again, Jacob said
to his twelve sons, "The scepter shall not depart from
Judah, nor a lawgiver from his offspring, till Shiloh come;
and to him shall the gathering of the people be."† And
again, Moses said to the children of Israel, "A prophet shall
the Lord your God raise up to you of your brethren, like
unto me: him shall ye hear in all things. And it shall
come to pass, that whosoever will not hear that prophet,
shall be cut off from among the people."‡ And still again,
Isaiah, speaking in vision, says, "Unto us a child is born;
unto us a son is given; and the government shall be upon
his shoulder; and his name shall be called Wonderful, Coun-
sellor, the mighty God, the Father of the everlasting age,
the Prince of Peace. Of the increase of his government
and peace, there shall be no end; upon the throne of David,
and upon his kingdom; to fix it, and to establish it, with
justice and with judgment from henceforth and forever.
The zeal of the Lord of hosts will do this."||

Similar promises were afterward frequently and variously
repeated by other prophets. But when the fullness of time
was come, the Seed of the woman, the Seed of Abraham, the
promised Shiloh, the long-expected Prophet, the Messenger
of the Covenant, and the Founder of the everlasting age,
all appeared in the person of Jesus of Nazareth. This chain
of evidence has been so often and so fully illustrated by
others, that to say more concerning it at present is unnecessary.

Another very good illustration of the unity and harmony
of the Holy Bible, we have given in the institution of sacrifice. This was a very ancient ordi-
nance. For many centuries, sacrifices were daily,
and I may say blindly, offered on both Jewish and Gentile

Illustration taken from the Institution of sacrifice.

* Genesis xxii: 18.   † Genesis xlix: 10.   ‡ Deut. xviii: 15–19.
|| Isaiah ix: 6 and 7.

altars. A lamb was selected from the flock; it was then killed; its flesh was burned on the altar, and its blood was sprinkled on and about the altar. But for what purpose? *There was not found on earth a Jewish Rabbi or a Gentile philosopher that could answer this question.* It was all mystery—dark as the original chaos, and inexplicable as a shadow without a substance—until Christ came as the Lamb of God to take away the sin of the world. Then, and not till then, it was manifest that the institution pointed clearly, distinctly, and exclusively to Him who was to be wounded for our transgressions and bruised for our iniquities.

The same may be said of the Levitical Priesthood, and most of the other types of the Old Covenant. Evidence drawn from They all directly or indirectly pointed to Him other legal who is the Alpha and the Omega, the beginning types. and the end, the center and the circumference of the whole Bible. And hence it is evident that *the Holy Scriptures are a unit;* that there is thus formed between all their parts a connection, which is at once plain, clear, and unmistakable.

If any thing more is necessary on this subject, it may be found in *the oneness of sentiment and doctrine* Proof drawn from the one- *which pervades the whole Bible.* But I presume ness of doctrine that enough has been said to establish clearly and sentiment. and fully the unity and harmony for which we plead.

I do not, of course, mean to say that there are not in the Bible, as there are in nature, some *apparent* dis- Apparent dis- crepancies. Even the great and good Luther crepancies; how accounted once thought that the teachings of James were for. irreconcilably opposed to the teachings of Paul. Luther's mis- And hence, for a time, he rejected the Epistle take. of James as an uninspired document. But a more careful and critical study of both James and Paul finally convinced the great Reformer that the error was in himself; that the alleged discrepancy was only apparent; and that James and Paul not only perfectly agree with each other, but also with all the other writers of both the Old and the New Testament.

How, then, is this very remarkable unity of doctrine, and sentiment, and plan to be accounted for?

If the Bible had been all written by one and the same

Diversity of circumstances under which the Bible was composed.

author, this might serve to account for it in part, though it would by no means account even partially for many other characteristics of this wonderful volume. But as my readers all know, even this much can not and must not be conceded. The Bible consists of sixty-six books, composed by about thirty different authors, during a period of about sixteen hundred years, and under the most diverse circumstances conceivable. Moses wrote the Pentateuch in the wilderness, when science, literature, and the arts were in their infancy. David composed most of his odes under the exciting, distracting and embarrassing influences of a regal court. Daniel and Ezekiel prophesied in captivity. Paul dictated several of his most important epistles while he was a prisoner at Rome, and under the care and vigilance of a Roman guard. And John wrote the Apocalypse while he was banished to Patmos, for the word of God and the testimony of Jesus Christ.

Whence, then, I again ask, is this remarkable unity,

Nevertheless, its unity and harmony are without a parallel, save in nature.

this unparalleled harmony that pervades the whole Bible? We find nothing like it in the ancient or modern systems of philosophy; nothing like it in the traditions of the Jews; and nothing like it in the creeds and confessions of modern Christendom. *The only parallel case is found in the book of nature.*

The necessary and only legitimate conclusion, then, from all these premises, is, that *the Author of Nature is also the Author of the Bible; and that holy men of old composed this most wonderful book as they were moved by the Holy Spirit.*

Conclusion.

CHAPTER III.

THE UNITED SIMPLICITY AND INCOMPREHENSIBILITY OF THE BIBLE.

THE second argument that I shall submit in proof of the Divine Origin of the Holy Bible, is taken from its great simplicity associated with a length, and breadth, and depth of meaning that far transcends the range and capacity of the most profound uninspired genius.

Scope and source of the second argument.

That the way of life is plain and accessible to every one who honestly seeks after honor, and glory, and immortality, may be very easily and very clearly proved in several ways. And,

Proof that the way of life is very plain to every honest student of the Bible.

I. By a reference to *the pilgrimage of the children of Israel, from Egypt to Canaan.* So long as the traveler kept his eye on the pillar of the cloud, and followed its movements, all was well. There was no danger of his being misled or misdirected by any one. Nothing short of a *willful* neglect of the line of march, and of the places of rest marked out by that supernatural symbol of Jehovah's presence, could cause any one to wander from the way that would have inevitably led all Israel, if obedient, into the enjoyment of the Promised Land. It was their obstinate refusal to follow

Argument first: from the types of the Old Covenant.

the cloud, or a persistent determination to anticipate its movements, that caused them to wander so long in the wilderness. Had they been obedient, the way was open, and they might all, without the loss of one, have marched directly from Kadesh Barnea into Canaan.

Now, be it remembered that all these things happened unto them as Types, (τυποι*), and they were written for our admonition. The Hebrews were delivered from bondage, and so are we. Their march was through a great and terrible wilderness, and so is ours. Their guide was supernatural, and so is ours. So long as they followed it with the humble, confiding disposition of little children, all was well; and just so it has ever been with Christians. So long as they have faithfully followed God's directions, so long their way has always been plain and prosperous. But whenever they have laid aside the Word of God, and taken reason, or feeling, or any invention of their own as the guide of life, then, just as uniformly, have followed shame, misery, and disappointment.

Argument and Illustration from Prophecy.   II. The great plainness and simplicity of the way of duty, life, and happiness may be further illustrated *by prophecy.*

In one of Isaiah's most vivid, clear, and interesting visions concerning the times and reign of the Messiah, he saw a beautiful highway cast up for the redeemed. It was called "*The Way of Holiness.*" It was, moreover, entirely free from all the dangers and annoyances of ravenous beasts. And, at the same time, it was *so perfectly plain that the wayfaring men, though simpletons, were in no danger of being misled on their march to the everlasting Zion.*† This, I need hardly say, was all designed to illustrate the way of eternal blessedness under the peaceful and glorious reign of the Messiah.

*1 Corinthians x: 1–12.   †Isaiah xxxv: 8–9.

III. The same important truth is also very clearly taught in *the actual developments of the Gospel.* Its requirements are all so very plain that no honest man can well misunderstand his duty. For the sake of method and perspicuity, I will simply request my readers to consider, by and for themselves,

Argument from the actual requirements of the Gospel.

1. What is required in order to admission into the Kingdom of Christ here on earth, such as faith, repentance, confession, and baptism; and,

2. The conditions of continued membership, and of admission into God's everlasting Kingdom. For a summary of these, see 2 Peter i: 1–11.

But connected with this wonderful simplicity of the Gospel plan of salvation, there is also in it a *depth* of meaning which no finite or uninspired mind can ever fully comprehend.

Great depth and comprehensiveness of the Bible.

Let me here appeal to the consciousness of my readers. Have you ever attempted to study a work of mere human genius, that, after making the necessary preliminary preparations, you have really felt that you could not master? Take, for instance, the writings of Plato or Aristotle; or, if you please, take the philosophy of Lord Bacon, or the Principia of Sir Isaac Newton, or any other work of like character. Have you ever really, and with due preparation, tried to master such works of human genius? If so, are you not conscious of success, or, at least, of the ability to succeed? The effort may have cost you much labor, and, for a time, you may, perhaps, have given up the task as hopeless, for want of the necessary preliminary preparations. But, having made these, have you ever, after due and proper effort, really failed to understand any work of human genius? I presume that most of you can truthfully answer this question in the negative. You feel conscious that you perfectly un-

Argument from our own consciousness.

derstand your grammar, your rhetoric, your logic, your philosophy, your arithmetic, your geometry, and even your calculus.

But can you say the same of the Holy Bible? Have you ever fathomed its depths? Have you ever risen from the study of this wonderful volume feeling conscious that you fully comprehend the entire range of thought that underlies the very plain but expressive words of its Author? Or have you not, rather, discovered, by every such effort, that beneath what at first seemed to be the lowest depths, there are still others, opening wide and deep, that lie far beyond the grasp and compass of the human intellect?

Just, for instance, as it is in the study of nature. When *In this respect the Bible is like Nature.* you begin to study the Book of Nature, the whole truth seems to lie on the surface, or, at least, very near the surface. In fact, the mere child can understand and enjoy whatever of nature is most useful and most practical. But the greatest philosopher on earth has never sounded the depths of the immense ocean of truth that lies beneath its surface.

Now, how is this wonderful combination of simplicity and *Only way of accounting for this very remarkable characteristic of the Holy Bible.* *incomprehensibility in the Bible to be accounted for?*

Concede that the Author of Nature is also the Author of the Bible, and then all is plain, clear, and satisfactory. Every thing then follows just as we might reasonably anticipate. But how utterly unsatisfactory is every other conceivable hypothesis! For eighteen hundred years, infidels of all schools have labored to explain this and other similar characteristics of the Holy Bible on the assumption that the whole Book is of human origin. But hitherto they have given us no solution of the problem that is even satisfactory to themselves.

And, hence, we are again brought to the alternative that we must either ignore an axiomatic and funda- Conclusion. mental law of human belief, or, otherwise, *we must conclude that the Author of Nature is also the Author of the Bible.*

CHAPTER IV.

THE UNPARALLELED THEOLOGY OF THE BIBLE.

THAT the Bible is of Divine origin, may also be proved from its *unparalleled theology.* There is in hu- *Scope of third* man nature a very marked and characteristic *argument.* proneness to make itself the *standard* by which *Characteristic tendency of hu-* to judge of every thing else. This is seen, *man nature.*

I. In the disposition and habit of most persons *to estimate the motives and conduct of others by their* *Illustrated by* own. The mean, low, selfish man, for example, *our proneness to judge of the* can never properly appreciate a generous and *motives of oth-* benevolent action. He finds nothing in his *ers by our own.* own little, narrow, contracted, and selfish soul that corresponds with it. And this is, perhaps, after all, the main reason why the Gospel seems to be so very absurd to most infidels. It is entirely too benevolent for their standard of comparison.

II. This same characteristic of human nature is also seen in all *the theological systems of the heathen world.* *Illustrated also* "*Like people, like gods,*" is true to every earth- *by the theology of heathen na-* born system of theology. Take, for example, *tions.*

1. The theology of the ancient Greeks, the most enlightened, elevated, and refined heathen nation *Theology of the* known in history. They excelled in all *Greeks.*

"Those polished arts that humanized mankind,
    Softened the rude, and calmed the boisterous mind."

But, nevertheless, their theology was but a transcript of depraved and fallen humanity. In it is clearly seen every
element of man's sinful nature. Uranus, the most ancient
of their gods, is said to have hated and imprisoned his own
children. Saturn made war against his father Uranus, and
also attempted to devour his own male children. But his
son Jupiter drove him from Crete into Latium, where, for
a long time, he remained concealed from his ambitious and
revengeful offspring. In Greece was also worshiped Venus,
the goddess of licentiousness; Bacchus, the god of drunkenness; and many other gods and goddesses of like character.

2. The ancient Scythians were cruel in the extreme. And
hence their gods, Odin, Thor, and other chief
divinities are said to have delighted in nothing
so much as in scenes of blood.

Theology of the Scythians.

3. In Central Africa it is said that the idols
are all made black, and with flat noses, like
their worshipers.

Idols of Africa.

Now how infinitely removed from all such human weak-
nesses, follies, and sinful passions and propensities, is the God of the Bible! I will not
attempt to describe his character. This no uninspired man
can do properly. But a few citations from the Holy Bible
will sufficiently illustrate the great contrast of which I now
speak. Read, for instance, the following passages, and carefully compare what is therein said of Jehovah with the
most favorable accounts that are anywhere given of the
heathen deities:

The theology of the Bible.

Illustrations from the Old Testament.

I.   Genesis i—ii: 3.
II.   Exodus xx: 1–11.
III. Deuteronomy xxxii.
IV.   Job xxxviii—xli.

V.   Psalm l and cxxxix.

VI.   Isaiah xl: 12–31.

VII. Habakkuk iii.

Illustrations from the Old Testament.

But it is in the Scheme of Redemption, as it is fully developed in the New Testament, that the perfections of God are most gloriously displayed and illustrated. Read, for example, the following passages:

I.   Matthew vi: 24–34.

II.   Luke xv: 11–32.

III. John i: 1–14, and iii: 16, 17.

IV.   Acts xvii: 16–31.

Illustrations from the New Testament.

V.   Romans iii: 21–31, and xi: 33–36.

VI.   Philippians ii: 5–11.

VII. Revelation, *passim.*

These passages are sufficient to prove that the theology of the Bible is *infinitely superior* to that of any heathen nation, ancient or modern.

Infinite superiority of the Bible theology.

How, then, is this great difference to be accounted for? How does it happen that the gods of Homer, Hesiod, and all other heathen writers, are characterized by every conceivable degree and kind of selfishness, ambition, pride, envy, jealousy, revenge, and all other degrading lusts, passions, and propensities of the human heart;

This difference not owing to any natural or acquired superiority of the Old and New Testament writers.

and that the God of the Bible is the only Divinity that is every-where represented as being infinite in power, knowledge, wisdom, justice, holiness, mercy, truth, and benevolence?, It can not be owing to the superior logical and inventive powers of the Jews; for in this respect they certainly did not excel the Greeks. Nor can it be accounted for on the hypothesis that the writers of the Old and the New Testament had a more active and fruitful imagination than the Greeks and Romans. Even if this were true, it would in no respect serve to remove the difficulty. For, be

3

it remembered, the imagination *creates* nothing. It simply forms, shapes, moulds, and modifies. It depends on perception, memory, judgment, and other faculties for all the *materials* and the elements of its so-called creations. If the elements so furnished are corrupt and impure, so likewise will be all its productions. See, for illustration, Ovid's Metamorphoses.

The conclusion, then, is irresistible and unavoidable, that

Conclusion. *the Holy Scriptures are the Revelations of God himself, through that Spirit which searches all things; yea, the deep things of Jehovah.*

CHAPTER V.

SUPERIOR MORALITY OF THE BIBLE.

THE Divine origin of the Bible may be still further

Scope of the fourth argument. proved and illustrated by its *superior morality.* This may be demonstrated in four ways:

I. By a comparison of the Heathen and Christian standards of morality.

Four sources of proof: II. By the superior motives of the Christian system.

III. By contrasting the actual state of morals in Heathendom and Christendom.

IV. By the still more elevating *tendencies* of the Christian system.

SECTION I.—STANDARDS OF MORALITY.

The Bible standard of right and wrong. It will, I presume, be generally conceded that *the will of God is the natural and only proper standard of all that is right, and pure, and vir-*

tuous. If God is our Sovereign King and Lawgiver, it is of course his right to command, and it is our duty to obey. And hence the Scriptures require that all our actions shall be in harmony with God's will. "You are not your own," says Paul; "for you are bought with a price; therefore glorify God in your body and in your spirit, which are God's."* And again, Christ says, "My meat is to do the will of Him that sent me, and to finish his work."†

The ancient heathen philosophers generally admitted the correctness of this principle; they conceded that mortals should serve and obey the immortals. But the trouble was that Polytheism furnished no consistent and uniform standard of right. What was supposed to be according to the will of one god, was often inconsistent with the will of another. Ormudz and Ahriman were irreconcilably opposed to each other. So, too, were Osiris and Typhon. And even Jupiter, Neptune, Pluto, Juno, Minerva, and other superior gods and goddesses of Greece and Rome, had their frequent wars and altercations. So testifies Homer, as well as most of the later Greek and Roman poets. Take, for instance, the following illustration from the twentieth book of the Iliad:

Why the same standard could not be adopted by the heathen.

Illustration from the Iliad.

> "But when the Powers descending swelled the fight,
> Then tumult rose; fierce rage and pale affright
> Varied each face; then Discord sounds alarms,
> Earth echoes, and the nations rush to arms.
> Now through the trembling shores Minerva calls,
> And now she thunders from the Grecian walls.
> Mars, hovering o'er his Troy, his terror shrouds
> In gloomy tempest and a night of clouds:
> Now through each Trojan heart he fury pours
> With voice Divine from Ilion's topmost towers;
> Now shouts to Simois from the beauteous hill;
> The mountain shook, and rapid streams stood still.

* 1 Cor. vi: 19 and 20.   † John iv: 34.

> Above the sire of gods the thunder rolls,
> And peals on peals redoubled rend the poles.
> Beneath, stern Neptune shakes the solid ground;
> The forests wave and mountains nod around.
> Through all her summits tremble Ida's woods,
> And from their sources boil her hundred floods.
> Troy's turrets totter on the rocky plain;
> And the tossed navies beat the heaving main.
> Deep in the dismal regions of the dead,
> The infernal monarch reared his horrid head,
> Leaped from his throne, lest Neptune's arm should lay
> His dark dominions open to the day,
> And pour in light on Pluto's drear abodes,
> Abhorred by men, and dreadful e'en to gods.
> Such wars the immortals wage; such horrors rend
> The world's vast concave, when the gods contend."

From such discordant elements, then, it would, of course, be impossible to construct any thing like a consistent and uniform standard of rectitude.

The heathen philosophers felt and acknowledged this difficulty, and hence some of them proposed to make *expediency* the standard of rectitude. This was generally adopted by the Platonic school. But this was also found to be very defective. For,

Standard of the Platonic school.

1. The people, as a matter of course, thought it very expedient to worship and placate all their acknowledged divinities. The Persians, for instance, thought it necessary to worship Ahriman, as well as Ormudz, and the Egyptians worshiped Typhon, as well as Osiris. In like manner, the Zabians worshiped their Shammael, and the Greeks and Romans worshiped and served the Diræ or Furies.

Objections to it as a standard of rectitude.

2. A second objection to this as a standard of rectitude is, that *its legitimate and necessary tendency is to make mankind extremely selfish.* This must ever, of necessity, be the effect of every system of ethics that makes self-interest the criterion by which to judge of every moral action. I need

only add, on this point, that history fully sustains this *à priori* conclusion.

Perceiving these difficulties and objections, some of the other schools of ancient philosophers proposed to follow *nature* as the only proper standard of rectitude. But the difference between this and the preceding is only nominal. Nature, as she is now defiled and perverted by sin, would inevitably lead all her votaries into the same errors and inconsistencies. Thus, for instance, it is natural for all men to gratify their desire for wealth, power, and every thing else that in any way serves to administer to their depraved lusts, and passions, and appetites. *Nature an imperfect standard of rectitude.*

And hence we are brought to the conclusion that *Christianity furnishes the only proper and correct standard of morality.* *Conclusion.*

SECTION II.—MOTIVES OF DIFFERENT ETHICAL SYSTEMS.

The various systems of heathen morality were as deficient in their *motives to virtue* as they were with respect to their standards of rectitude. *Heathen systems deficient in motives.*

The motive of future rewards and punishments was almost wholly wanting in their schemes and systems of morality. The Cynics, Cyrenaics, and Epicureans rejected the doctrine as absurd. *Heathen views of a future State* Their chief maxim was, "Let us eat and drink, for to-morrow we die." The Peripatetics and Stoics had no settled and well-defined views on this subject. And the same may be said of the Chinese. Indeed, Confucius, the great corypheus of Chinese philosophy, seems to have had no faith whatever in the doctrine of a future state. He regarded the soul as a sort of subtle, refined, and attenuated matter, that forever perishes with the dissolution of the body.

It is true that Pythagoras, Socrates, Plato, Cicero, and some others, believed in a state of future rewards and punishments. But it is also true that they always failed in all their attempts to prove it to the conviction and satisfaction of the people. Their arguments were without the force of authority, and hence they accomplished but little for the good of the masses.

But take away from mankind their belief in a state of Insufficiency of any and all other motives. future rewards and punishments, and then all remaining motives to virtue are utterly insufficient to restrain their propensities to evil. So testifies all history, as well as all sound philosophy.

How wonderfully, then, Christianity contrasts, in this The superior motives of the Christian system illustrated. respect, with all other schemes of religion and philosophy. It begins by revealing to us, as our Creator, Preserver, Redeemer, Guide, and Exemplar, a Being of infinite justice, holiness, and benevolence. This is wisdom. We all feel the need First, by the character of our Leader. of such a leader, and we have, doubtless, all felt the power and influence of the motives that prompt us to merit his love and approbation. If an illustration is wanting, I need only refer my readers to the influence of an Alexander, a Cæsar, and a Napoleon, over the many thousand admirers who cheerfully followed them to death or to victory.

But this is not all. Christianity has brought life and Secondly, by the clearly-revealed doctrine of a future state. immortality to light. It gives to us, beyond all peradventure, the full assurance of a future state of rewards and punishments, and it offers to us eternal life, on the condition of our living soberly, and righteously, and godly. This is as an anchor to our souls, reaching within the veil. It serves to elevate our thoughts and aspirations above all the perishing things of time and sense. We feel that this world is not our home—that we are here but pilgrims, traveling to a better country.

SECTION III.—ACTUAL STATE OF MORALS.

Such, then, being the great difference between the motives of these systems, we need not wonder that there should also exist *so great a difference in the actual state of morality in Heathendom and Christendom.* *(Actual state of morals.)*

It would be a shame to speak of the many abominable and degrading vices that have ever been tolerated, and even legalized, in the heathen world. Every student of ancient history is familiar *(1. Among the Ancient Heathen.)* with the scenes of debauchery, intemperance, and impurity that were always practiced in the Dionyssia of Bacchus, the Aphrodisia of Venus, the Lupercalia of Pan, the Thesmophoria of Ceres, the Ludi Florales of Flora, the Kottitia of Kotis, and other similar obscene rites and ceremonies of the ancient Greeks and Romans.

And all who are acquainted with the present condition of the heathen world know perfectly well that the state of morals is even now no better than it was among the ancients. Indeed, it has been *(2. Among the Modern Heathen.)* clearly proved by the testimony of missionaries, as well as by the acknowledgements of the heathen themselves, that Paul's description of the moral state of the Gentile world, given in the first chapter of his epistle to the Romans, is still a true and faithful picture of the moral condition of all nations that are without the light and influence of a revelation from God.

Now, it must be confessed that, in all parts of Christendom, the standard of practical morality, as well as the standard of practical piety, is entirely *(3. Among Christians.)* too low. But, nevertheless, who will presume to say that

the cause of virtue has not been promoted by the influence of Christianity wherever the Bible has been read?
Contrast, for example, these United States with ancient
Greece, and mark the difference between their state of
morals.

SECTION IV.—Superior and more Elevating Tend-
    encies of the Christian System of Morality.

The contrast, then, between the existing moral condition
of Christendom and Heathendom is very great.
Tendencies to a much greater difference in practical morality. But, nevertheless, the practical difference is not
near so great as is the theoretical. And hence
it is, that *there is a constant tendency to a still
greater difference in their practical ethics.* The reason of this
The reasons of this. is obvious. There is nothing in any scheme
of heathen morality that can possibly serve to
make mankind much, if any, better than they are. The
natural and necessary tendency of all heathen systems is to
selfishness and impurity. But let Christianity be carried
out to perfection in the lives of its professors, and very
soon we would have a heaven upon earth.

How, then, is this superiority of Christian morality over
all heathen systems to be accounted for? It
These moral distinctions not owing to any difference of natural endowments. can not be owing to any natural superiority in
the mental and moral endowments of Christians.
In this respect they certainly do not excel the
ancient Greeks and Romans. Nor can it be
Nor can they be owing to any difference of human culture. owing to any superiority of our education, so far
as it respects any thing of merely human origin.
The ancient heathen philosophers spared no
pains in getting the very best education that they possibly
could. They traveled wherever they thought they could enjoy superior advantages. And hence the conclusion follows,

as a logical necessity, that *the morality of the Bible, and of course the Bible itself, is from God.* Conclusion.

How careful then we should all be to study and to practice this Divine scheme of morality and virtue. As we have the will of God so very clearly revealed to us in the Holy Bible, how very diligent we should all be in perfecting our characters according to this Divine standard. Practical inference.

CHAPTER VI.

THE SUPERNATURAL CHARACTER OF CHRIST.

"What think you of Christ? Whose son is he?"—Matthew xxii: 42. Scope of the sixth chapter.

It is evident that Matthew, Mark, Luke, and John all wrote for the purpose of proving that Jesus of Nazareth is the promised Messiah and Son of the living God. And if we accept without abatement the facts which they have severally recorded concerning him, the evidence is entirely conclusive; and we have, in their united testimony, a very clear and satisfactory answer to the proposed question. For as Nicodemus once said, No man could do the miracles that Jesus is said to have done, unless God were with him. But if God were with him, he must have honored God by speaking the truth. And if he spoke the truth he was the Messiah. Testimony of Matthew, Mark, Luke, and John concerning Christ.

But many so-called Rationalists of the nineteenth century are wont to reject and eliminate from this evidence all that is miraculous. This they do on various grounds, and for various reasons. Strauss and other German *Pantheists* reject all miracles as a spe- Part of this testimony rejected by Rationalists.

cies of absurd impossibilities. To this conclusion they are,
Grounds of their objections to Miracles. of necessity, brought by their own false system
of philosophy. For, if God is the universe,
and the universe is God, then indeed the supernatural is wholly out of the question. The French school
of Rationalists do not go quite so far in their opposition to
miracles as the German. Renan, for instance, does not say
that a miracle is either an impossibility or an absurdity.
He simply denies the credibility of the evidence. He alleges that there is no satisfactory evidence that a miracle
has ever been wrought.

But nearly all modern skeptics of any pretensions to either
Concession of modern skeptics. learning or candor concede the *general truthfulness and credibility* of the Gospel narratives.
Renan compares them to the memoirs that four
of Napoleon's old soldiers would write concerning the deeds
and exploits of their admired and almost adored hero. We
would all, he says, naturally expect that their narratives
would contain many very great exaggerations. But no one
would think of calling into question their general truthfulness. And just so he thinks of the four narratives of Matthew, Mark, Luke, and John. In his estimation, all the
miracles reported are to be regarded as exaggerations or
perversions of the real facts. But that they are, in the
main, trustworthy, he assumes and maintains for the following reasons:

1. Because they contain all the *internal* marks and other
His reasons for regarding the Gospel narratives as in the main authentic. evidences of authentic history. Such, for instance, as the minuteness and particularity of
their details; their unaffected air of candor
and naturalness; their many undesigned coin-
cidences; and their general harmony with the well-known
customs, manners, literature, and other circumstances of the
age and country in which they were written.

2. Because many of the main facts recorded in these narratives are also given by Philo, Josephus, Tacitus, the authors of the Talmud, and other contemporary and later historians.

For these and other similar reasons the authenticity and general fidelity of the four Gospel narratives are now conceded by Renan and many others who deny their inspiration, and who reject as spurious, or as an exaggeration, every thing in them that claims to be miraculous.

But is their position tenable? Can we consistently receive as true that which is natural in these narratives; and reject as false all that claims to be supernatural? I think not, for several reasons: *The natural and the supernatural of the Gospel narratives can not be separated.*

I. *Because the natural and the supernatural are so related and so blended together in these narratives, that they must both either stand or fall together.* The miracles recorded are not a sort of mere episode or appendix, like the fine rhetorical *First, because they are too intimately blended together as cause and effect.* speeches that were often introduced into their narratives, by ancient historians, for the sake of ornament, or for the purpose of producing a sensation. They are an *essential* part of the narrative itself, and are absolutely necessary to account for most of the other events with which they stand connected. How, for instance, can we account for the almost unbounded influence that Christ had over the multitudes, save on the hypothesis that he wrought many real miracles among them? Renan concedes the wonderful extent of this influence; and he further admits that in order to this, he must have been a man of colossal proportions. But he thinks that the people were deceived. *Renan's explanation of Christ's reputed miracles.* He alleges that the captivating influence of Jesus over the multitudes was so overwhelming that they were perfectly overcome by it, and that, as a

consequence, they were often led to mistake the natural for
the supernatural. A man, for instance, prostrated by nerv-
ous debility, would be relieved and the demon cast out by
the mere presence, or look, or word, or touch of Jesus. And
by working a few such cures, his fame would soon spread
abroad as a wonderful Thaumaturgist.

Objections to Renan's explanation. This hypothesis is objectionable chiefly for two
reasons:

It is incon- 1. It is not to be supposed that a person of
sistent with Christ's unostentatious and truth-loving disposi-
Christ's char- tion would have indulged the people in so false
acter. an impression of his true character and pretensions. That the people believed he wrought real miracles is
evident. This much Renan concedes. That Christ, moreover, knew they entertained such an opinion of him is also
evident. And that he would have corrected this impression, had it been erroneous, is just as evident.

2. In this hypothesis the objector assumes that the
It is inconsist- people were incapable of undeceiving them-
ent with the selves, by properly testing the nature and char-
known facts of acter of the wonders wrought by Christ. This
the case. is a purely groundless assumption. It has not even the
shadow of evidence for its support. For most of the
miracles of Christ were of such a nature that any man
of ordinary intelligence and capacity could decide as to
their real character, as well as the most learned sage or
philosopher. Take, for example, the healing of Peter's
mother-in-law, the curing of many lepers, the feeding of
the multitudes, the healing of cripples, and the giving of
sight to those who had been blind from their birth. To
judge of such plain and palpable facts, wrought openly,
and in the presence of thousands, certainly required no
extraordinary degree of either logical skill or philosophical acumen.

II. To separate the natural from the supernatural, in such cases, is further impossible; because, even on the concessions of Renan and his school, *Christ is, really, himself the greatest of all miracles.* This is evident from the following considerations:

The natural can not be separated from the supernatural in these narratives, because Christ is himself the greatest of all miracles.

1. These men concede that *Christ had not in his whole nature one particle of selfishness.* On page 90 of Renan's "Life of Jesus," the author says, in substance, as follows: "He was free from all selfishness, the source of our sorrows; and he thought only of his work, of his race, and of

This is implied, first, in his entire freedom from selfishness.

humanity." This testimony is evidently true. But how can we account for this very remarkable characteristic of Jesus? If we examine the history of all past ages, and narrowly scrutinize and investigate the character of the living age, we will find that selfishness is invariably one of the first developed characteristics of the infant mind. But what is thus universal must be natural. So we reason in reference to all the powers, characteristics, and susceptibilities of the human soul. But Christ had no selfishness, Mr. Renan himself being judge. And hence we conclude, of necessity, that he was not a *natural,* but a *supernatural,* personage.

2. Another very marked characteristic of Christ was *his entire freedom from all Jewish prejudices, and from all other partisan feelings of every kind.* Even on Renan's representation of the case,

Secondly, in his freedom from all party prejudices.

he was a philanthropist without an equal in the entire history of our race. Rising not only above every thing that is selfish, but also above every thing that is merely national or sectional, he embraced the world in his sympathies and in his schemes of benevolence.

This is evident from his memoirs, and also from the scope and character of the religion that he came to establish. But how is all this to be accounted for? He was born and educated among a people of as strong party prejudices and

sectional jealousies and antipathies as any other people of
ancient or modern times.   How, then did it happen that
he alone of all the great and good of earth rose above all
such influences, and embraced within the scope of his benevolence not only every nation, but even every individual
of our poor fallen race? Does not this, of itself, clearly
demonstrate his supernatural character? Why, then, ask
for another sign from heaven, when we have, in the person
of Jesus, so many evidences of the miraculous?

3. *Christ was also, as Renan concedes, free from all*
worldly ambition. He aimed, it is true, at universal dominion, but his empire was an empire of souls. It was an empire for the liber-
ation, and emancipation, and salvation of the spirits of all
men. It was as far above the political and selfish monarchies
of Nebuchadnezzar, and Cyrus, and Alexander, and Cæsar,
and, I may add, the politico-ecclesiastical monarchy that
the Jews themselves anticipated, as the benevolence of God
is above the selfishness of men.

Thirdly, in his freedom from all worldly am-bition.

And here, as the author of " Ecce Homo" very justly remarks, " we scarcely know which to admire most, the prodigious originality of his conceptions, or his entire freedom
from all worldly ambition in the execution of his plans." *
Both, however, alike serve to demonstrate his own Divinity;
and hence to present him to the world as the greatest of all
miracles. Nothing strictly identical with either of these
characteristics of Jesus has ever distinguished a fallen son
of Adam. Even after his scheme has been conceived, and
his kingdom established among men, there is not found,
among all the followers of Christ, enough of his Spirit to
preserve his original plan from the degrading influences of
a selfish and worldly ambition. For the proof and illustration of this, I need only refer to the past history of

* This is not designed as a general commendation of *Ecce Homo.* Its
tendencies are *rationalistic.*

the Church, and to the present ambitious and semi-political schemes of most Papal and Protestant parties.

4. Renan furthermore concedes, what is indeed evident from the united testimony of the four Evangelists, that *Christ never expressed a doubt on any subject,* and that *his speeches and addresses cost him no effort.* Other great men labored much, and were, nevertheless, always in doubt; and very frequently expressed their doubts. Even the teachings of Socrates abound with such expressions as the following: "*If* death is a removal hence to another place, and *if* what is said of death be true, etc., then those who live in Hades are henceforth immortal." Among the last words of Socrates are the following: "But the hour of separation has come. I go to die; you to live. But which of us is destined to an improved being is concealed from every one except God."* How very unlike these are the last words of Jesus to the dying thief that was perishing at his side: "To-day shalt thou be with me in Paradise."†

Fourthly, in his freedom from all doubt and hesitation, on even the most difficult questions.

Compared in this respect with Socrates and other philosophers.

How, then, shall we account for this perfect consciousness of knowing the truth on all occasions, and which gave to the discourses of Christ an air of authority and certainty which is without a parallel in the history and literature of the world? It can not be explained on the ground of his superior learning and education. For he was probably never at school in his life; and it is evident he read very little except what is contained in the Old Testament.

This difference not owing to Christ's superior education.

Nor can it be explained on the ground of his greater experience. Socrates was about seventy years of age when he drank the fatal cup, and Christ was only thirty-three and a half years old when

Nor to his greater experience.

---

* Apol. vol. I, p. 79.   † Luke xxiii: 48.

he was crucified. Plato, Pythagoras, and many other ancient philosophers traveled over the civilized world in quest of wisdom and knowledge; but Christ very seldom went beyond the narrow limits of his own native Palestine. Plato, Aristotle, Zeno, Epicurus, and other ancient sages did little else from their youth than study books and listen to the wisdom of the learned; but Christ worked at the carpenter business until he was about thirty years of age; and then he entered at once on his public ministry, and commenced the discussion of the most difficult subjects, without books, without instructors, without the advantages of fortune and the patronage of the great; and, in a word, without any of those extraneous aids and helps that serve to give confidence, and authority, and success to most public instructors.

Nor, again, can this remarkable difference between Christ

Nor can it be accounted for on the ground of his superior talents as a man.

and all other public teachers be explained on the ground of Christ's superior talents and abilities as a man. Nothing short of *infinite* wisdom and knowledge will fully meet and satisfy the demands and requirements of the case. No elevation of mere *finite* intelligence can give to any man the confidence and the authority with which Christ always spoke of God, of the human soul, and of the spiritual universe generally. To the most exalted human genius the discovery of any truth always reveals one or more mysteries. And hence it is that the greatest sages have always been the greatest doubters. But Christ never doubted. Why, then, among all the many millions of our race, does he stand alone in this respect? We search in vain for any other satisfactory

Conclusion.

explanation of this matter than that which has been given by the sacred writers, viz., that *Jesus of Nazareth was himself God manifest in the flesh.* Why, then, should it be thought incredible that HE should raise the dead, cast out demons, heal the sick, feed the hungry, and clothe the naked?

Here, then, we might safely rest the whole controversy. For, if Christ was without selfishness, without party prejudices, without worldly ambition, and without doubt and hesitation on any and all subjects, he must have been infinitely perfect in every respect; for the possession of any one perfect virtue implies, of necessity, the possession of every other. *The foregoing concessions are virtually an end of the controversy.*

But this is going a little further than any of the skeptical authors referred to are willing to go. Renan, Newman, and others freely concede that Jesus was the greatest and best of his race.* But, at the same time, they allege that he was far from being sinless.† *Further allegations of skeptical writers.*

It may, therefore, be well to look a little further into this matter, in order that we may see whether there really is, in the whole life and character of Christ, a single spot, or blemish, or imperfection of any kind. If there is, it seems to me that it would be an easy matter to discover it; for his was a life of entire publicity. He ever taught in the synagogues and on the streets, so that whatever he did, and whatever he said, was subject to the scrutiny and investigation of his enemies, as well as of his friends. And if his confident and authoritative manner was, as most skeptics now allege, the result and offspring of an ardent and boundless enthusiasm, it would certainly not be long until he would commit a series of blunders and mistakes that would have to be corrected. This, I need not say, is the history, not only of all *Christ's course of life not to be explained on the ground of his ardent enthusiasm.*

---

* "All ages will proclaim that, among the sons of men, there were none born greater than Jesus."— *Renan's Life of Christ,* p. 376. See also pp. 90, 102, 106, 241, and 367.

† Renan, p. 375.

4

enthusiasts, but also of even the most calm and deliberate sages that have ever attempted the reformation of any part or portion of our race.

How, then, was it with Jesus? Did he ever, like Socrates, Plato, Aristotle, and other great philosophers and reformers, confess that he had made a mistake or committed an error of any kind? Did he ever change his plans and purposes in consequence of the opposition of his enemies, the force of circumstances, or from any other consideration whatever? *Never! never!* Had he done so, his foes might well have triumphed. It would at once have betrayed a weakness and an imperfection inconsistent with his high claims as the Messiah, the Son of the living God. But, thank God! no such indication of imperfection is found in his entire history. During his whole life, he never took back a single word that he had uttered, nor did he ever attempt to correct any thing that he had ever done.

But it may, perhaps, be said that this was owing to his pride of consistency; that great men never like to expose their weakness by confessing their mistakes. This is, no doubt, to some extent, true of all erring men, and especially of those who desire to maintain their authority and influence with the people. But this does not prevent others from discovering their mistakes, and exposing their errors. Has any one, then, discovered an error in the whole life and teachings of Christ? His purposes and his doctrines have been before the world for eighteen hundred years. During all this long period, then, has any one discovered an error in his manner 'of teaching, or in his principles of morality, or in his scheme of philanthropy? Not one. His style of speaking and teaching is still the wonder and admiration of the world. And every honest skeptic is still compelled to exclaim, with the officers that were once

Nor on the ground of his love of consistency.

No defect in his manner of teaching.

sent by the Sanhedrim to apprehend Jesus, "*Never man spake like this man.*"

His principles of morality are also acknowledged to be faultless. Since his coronation in the heavens, Seneca, Cudworth, Paley, Mackintosh, and many other profound thinkers, have given to the world their systems of ethics and codes of morality. But the imperfections of all these are now manifest. How, then, does it happen that in the morality of Jesus not a single error has ever been detected?

No error in his principles of morality.

And what shall I say of his scheme of philanthropy? It, too, has had many rival systems, some of them devised by men of profound learning and of towering genius. But they, too, have been mostly buried with their authors. And Christianity is, really, the only scheme of reformation worthy of the name that now challenges the sympathies and suffrages of mankind. True, indeed, it has often been most grossly perverted by its nominal friends and supporters. But for this Jesus was not responsible. Nor does it imply any defect in Christianity itself. In this respect it has only suffered like all the other best gifts of God to man. But, nevertheless, it still stands as an abiding and ever-living monument of the infinite knowledge, and wisdom, and benevolence of its Divine Author. Even the skeptical Renan is constrained to admit, in substance, that all that is now necessary to convert the world into a paradise, and all mankind into one glorious and happy brotherhood, is the universal adoption of primitive Christianity.*

None in his scheme of philanthropy.

Renan's concessions.

If, then, we may judge the tree by its fruit, the character of Jesus is certainly, in all respects, pure and spotless. But no, says Renan, "He was far from being sinless." I find, however, in his en-

Conclusion from the premises.

*Renan's Life of Jesus, pp. 365–367.

tire " Life of Jesus " but two specifications of what he seems to regard as imperfections in Christ's character.　The first of these is an expression of mingled grief, pity, and compassion, and, as Renan thinks, of *impatience*, with respect to the multitude, when, on one occasion, he exclaimed, with deep emotion, " *O faithless and perverse generation! how long shall I be with you? how long shall I bear with you?* "* And the second he regards as a manifestation of *vain pleasure*, when on his entry into Jerusalem, on the Monday before his crucifixion, he heard from the surrounding multitudes shouts and hosannas addressed to himself as the Son of David.†

Renan's specifications of alleged imperfections in the life and character of Christ.

But in these two instances is the imperfection in Christ, or is it in Mr. Renan's own judgment and imagination?　Why does he not also find fault with God as the Governor of the Universe, when, in his righteous indignation, he hurls upon the unbelieving and disobedient the thunderbolts of his wrath and the fires of his indignation?　And why does he not also censure the same infinitely-glorious and perfect Being, because he too hears with pleasure and complacency the songs and supplications of his adoring children?　Manifestly, the error is in Mr. Renan himself, and not in Jesus.　Had he looked upon Christ as he really was and is, *God manifest in the flesh*, he would have seen, in these manifestations of feeling, no indications of weakness or imperfection.

Refutation of these charges.

How pure and spotless, then, must be the character of our blessed and adorable Redeemer!　For eighteen hundred years argus-eyed infidelity has scrutinized it most carefully and most diligently, without finding in it a single blemish or imperfection!　How vain a thing it is, then, for infidels to object to the miracles of Christ, while he himself stands before us the greatest mira-

Conclusion.

* Matthew xvii: 17.　　　† Matthew xxi: 8–16.

cle that the universe has ever beheld, and, at the same time, the greatest blessing that God has ever bestowed on man. Without him what is life, and what is every thing else besides? Take away his name and his influence from our race, and who can describe its wretchedness! But let him only be received into every heart, and then all is glory to God in the highest, and on earth, peace and good-will among all men.

But if Jesus is Divine, then indeed the Bible is certainly of Divine origin; for the testimony of Jesus is its scope from its alpha to its omega.

CHAPTER VII.

EXISTENCE AND PREVALENCE OF CHRISTIANITY.

SECTION I.—TRIUMPHS OF THE GOSPEL A PROOF OF ITS DIVINE ORIGIN.

THE next argument that I shall introduce to prove the Divine origin of the Bible is derived from the existence, progress, and prevalence of Christianity. *Scope of the seventh chapter.*

That Christianity is now an existing reality of great power and influence in the world, no one will deny. And, moreover, that it owes its origin, progress, and triumphs to some adequate and sufficient cause, no one will presume to deny. And hence the whole argument is simply reduced to the question, What is that cause? Is it human, or is it Divine? *Conceded facts.* *Gist of the controversy.*

Admit the claims of Christianity, and then all follows as a matter of course. We have then embraced within our premises all the power, the wisdom, and the benevolence that are necessary to account for every thing pertaining to it as a scheme and *The claims of Christianity furnish a cause fully adequate and sufficient.*

system of religion. For Divine power and wisdom are, of course, sufficient to accomplish any thing that is really great and good.

But deny the claims of Christianity; assume that it is of human origin, and then how shall we account for such facts as the following:

No other cause adequate to explain the change of habits among the primitive Christians.

I. *The great change of habits and new modes of life to which the primitive Christians very generally submitted.*

The force of habit is very great. And hence there is in every people a strong inclination to adhere to the religion of their fathers.* Indeed, the history of the world clearly proves that extraordinary

Difficulty of changing the religious habits of any people.

power has always been necessary to effect a religious change or revolution in any portion of the human race; and hence we find that the Greeks and Romans very wisely permitted the several tribes and nations that they conquered to worship their own gods.

But a change from one false religion to another is a small matter compared with the change from any sys-

Still greater difficulty of converting them to Christianity.

tem of false religion to Christianity. In the former case it is a mere change of forms and ceremonies. The *heart* is not affected. Its evil passions and propensities all remain, and are all gratified as before. But in the latter case it is wholly different. One of the very first things required of every Christian is to deny himself, to take up his cross, to crucify the flesh with its affections and its lusts, and henceforth to live soberly, and righteously, and godly. This is a change that has never yet been effected by mere human power and authority.

Actual change of life and habits among the primitive Christians.

But the primitive Christians very generally submitted most willingly and cheerfully to these extraordinary claims. Their former habits were abandoned, and new rules of life were at once

* Jeremiah ii: 10, 11.

adopted. For the proof of this, I need only refer my readers to the historians of the first, second, third, and fourth centuries. And, for the present, I will trouble you with but a single quotation from the infidel but accomplished Lucian. He was born in Samosata, in Syria, Testimony of about A. D. 120. He was first a sculptor, Lucian. then an advocate, then a teacher of rhetoric and philosophy, and after that he was appointed to some political office in Egypt. He traveled extensively through Syria, Greece, Gaul, Italy, and Northern Africa, and had, therefore, the very best opportunities of becoming acquainted with the lives and habits of Christians living in all these countries during the second century. Concerning them he writes as follows:

"It is incredible," he says, "what expedition they use when any of their friends are known to be in trouble. In a word, they spare nothing on such an occasion. For these miserable men have no doubt that they will be immortal, and live forever. And, therefore, they contemn death, and surrender themselves to sufferings. Moreover, their first Lawgiver has taught them that they are all brethren when they have once turned and renounced the gods of the Greeks and worship this Master of theirs, who was crucified, and when they engage to live according to his laws. They have also a sovereign contempt for all things of this world, and look upon them as common."*

Now, I ask, How is all this to be accounted for? Concede that the Bible is the Word of God, that Cause of this the miracles recorded in it really occurred, and extraordinary change. that all the writers of the Old and the New Testament spoke as they were moved by the Holy Spirit, and then all is plain, simple, and natural. But on any other hypothesis, how can these great changes be accounted

---

* Lucianus de Morte Perigrini, tome i, p. 565, ed. Graev.

for? I will leave the reader to reflect on this matter while I proceed to notice,

Patience of the Christians under persecutions.

II. *The persecutions that these primitive Christians patiently endured from both Jews and Gentiles.*

The Jews opposed and persecuted the Christians because

Why the Jews were opposed to Christ and his followers.

they felt sure that Christianity, as it was proclaimed and taught by the Apostles, was opposed to all their schemes and theories of religion, and they knew, therefore, that its success would soon put an end to all their hopes and expectations as Jews. They were all looking for a great politico-ecclesiastical leader who would free them from every foreign yoke, and extend their religion and empire to the ends of the earth. And hence their deep hatred and uncompromising hostility to Him who refused to wear an earthly crown; who was the man of sorrows, and acquainted with grief. And hence, too, their deadly hatred of all his followers.

The Gentiles were also violently opposed to the Chris-

Twofold ground of Gentile hostility and opposition.

tian religion because it was opposed to all their schemes of religion and philosophy, and also on account of its own inflexible and uncompromising character. And hence, for about three hundred

Persecutions under the heathen Roman emperors.

years, most of the Roman emperors, statesmen, philosophers, priests, and populace endeavored to suppress it. From A. D. 64 to A. D. 313, it is generally conceded that ten persecutions were waged against the Christians by the authority of the Roman government.* But all these afflictions were patiently endured by the Christians.

How, then, I ask again, is all this to be accounted for?

* Waddington's Church History, pp. 58–69; and Lardner's Credibility, vol. viii, p. 335, Lond. edit.

We might here allow this question to take a very wide range, and call in to our aid many witnesses. But it is generally best to bring every question within as narrow limits as possible. And I therefore propose the following trilemma as a plain, simple, and yet strictly logical statement of all the points at issue. I affirm, then, that the Apostles and the other early propagators of Christianity were, *The question limited, and stated in the form of a trilemma.*

1. *Either deceivers;*

2. *Or they were themselves deceived;*

3. *Or they were true men, and spoke as they were moved by the Holy Spirit.*

But they could not have been deceivers:

1. Because they had no conceivable motive or inducement to be such. Many of them gave *They were not deceivers.*
up all their property, and willingly died as martyrs to the truth.

2. Because all their teachings were directly opposed to to every thing like falsehood and deception.

Nor could they be deceived. For, *They were not deceived.*

1. The miracles and other facts recorded were generally of such a nature that all men might easily judge of them by their senses. Such, for example, was the miracle of Christ's resurrection, the healing of lepers, giving sight to the blind, and, indeed, most of the other miracles wrought by Christ and his Apostles.

2. These miracles were performed publicly, and in the presence of many witnesses, so that thousands of the enemies, as well as of the friends and supporters of Christianity, had every conceivable opportunity of judging for themselves in these matters.

3. It is positively absurd to suppose that the Apostles and others, who wrought those miracles, could be deceived in the exercise of their spiritual gifts.

And hence we are constrained, by a logical necessity, to
Conclusion.   *conclude that the Apostles and the other early pro-*
                      claimers and propagators of Christianity spoke
the truth as the Spirit gave them utterance; and, consequently,
that the Bible is of God, and that the Gospel is the power of
God for the salvation of every one that believeth.

SECTION II.—CHRISTIANITY AND MAHOMETANISM COMPARED.

Just here we are met with an objection arising out of the
Objection aris- successes and triumphs of Mahometanism. It
ing out of the   is alleged that Mahometanism is also an exist-
successes of
Mahometan-   ing reality; that its votaries are nearly half as
ism.   numerous as are the advocates of Christianity;
and yet that it is, nevertheless, nothing more than a splen-
did ·falsehood. And hence it is inferred that Christianity
may also be false, notwithstanding all its triumphs over the ·
world, and the flesh, and the devil.

This is plausible, but wholly fallacious. The objection is
Fallacious   founded on an assumed parallelism which has
ground of this   no existence in fact. This is obvious from the
objection.   following considerations:

I. Christianity requires of all her votaries that they deny
Points of differ- themselves all ungodliness and worldly lusts,
ence between   and that they live soberly, and righteously,
Christianity
and Mahomet-   and godly in this present world; but Mahometanism.   anism grants to her disciples the almost unbridled and unrestricted gratification of their lusts and appetites.*

II. Christianity never drew the sword, either offensive-
ly or defensively. She depends wholly and solely on the
power of truth. But Mahometanism never made much

* Sale's Koran, chap. iii, p. 54; Gibbon, vol. vi, p. 322.

progress till the sword was drawn in its behalf. During the first three years of his public ministry, Mahomet made only fourteen proselytes.* And during the twelve years that he labored to accomplish his ends through diplomacy and moral suasion, he accomplished but little. But then the sword was drawn, and the terrible alternatives of death, tribute, or Islamism were offered to the conquered.†

III. The early opposition of the Arabians to Mahometanism was nothing in comparison with that which Christianity had to encounter. True, indeed, from A. D. 613 to A. D. 622, Mahomet was opposed to the Koreish of Mecca; and in A. D. 622 he was forced to flee to Medina. But what was all this compared with the losses and persecutions of the primitive Christians? During the first month of the Dioclesian persecution, it is estimated that about one hundred and eleven thousand Christians perished without resistance; and during the entire ten years of its continuance, it is supposed that about seven hundred thousand perished in Egypt alone. Such opposition would have crushed Mahometanism at once.

IV. Christianity has always flourished most in the light, and Mahometanism in darkness. So teaches the entire history of the two institutions.

Other points of difference might easily be stated. But these are abundantly sufficient to expose the fallacy of the objection. For, as the learned and thoughtful Paley remarks, in speaking on this very subject, "The success of Mahometanism bears so little resem- Remarks of Paley. blance to the early propagation of Christianity, that no inference whatever can be justly drawn to the prejudice of the Christian argument. For what are we comparing? A Galilean peasant, accompanied by a few fishermen, with a conqueror at the head of an army. We compare Jesus

---

* Gibbon, vol. vi, p. 324, Lond. edition.   † Gibbon, vol. vi, p. 333.

without force, without power, without support, without one external circumstance of attraction or influence prevailing against the prejudices, the learning, the hierarchy of his country; against the ancient religious opinions, the pompous religious rites, the philosophy, the wisdom, the authority of the Roman empire in the most polished and enlightened period of its existence; we compare him with Mahomet making his way among Arabs, collecting followers in the midst of conquests and triumphs in the darkest ages and countries of the world, and when success in arms not only operated by that command of men's wills and persons which attends prosperous undertakings, but was also considered as a sure testimony of Divine approbation. That multitudes, persuaded by this argument, should join the train of a victorious chief; that still greater multitudes should, without any argument, bow down before irresistible power, is a course of conduct in which we can not see much to surprise us—in which we can see nothing that resembles the causes by which the establishment of Christianity was effected.

The success, therefore, of Mahometanism stands not in the way of our conclusion: that the propagation of Christianity, in the manner and under the circumstances in which it was propagated, is a *unique* in the history of our species. A Jewish peasant overthrew the religion of the world.*

And hence it follows that we must either ignore the law of Conclusion. *causality as an axiomatic and fundamental law of human belief, or otherwise we must concede that the Bible is from God. Reason furnishes no other alternative.*

* Paley's Evidences, p. 410, Nairne's edit.

CHAPTER VIII.

FULFILLED PROPHECY.

SECTION I.—NEBUCHADNEZZAR'S VISION OF THE STONE AND THE IMAGE.

ABOUT the year 607, B. C., Nebuchadnezzar being then associated with his father Nabopolassar, in the <small>Introductory circumstances.</small> government of Babylon, came up against Jerusalem, made Jehoiakim, king of Judah, his vassal, and carried many of the Jews captive to Babylon, among whom were Daniel, Hananiah, Mishael, and Azariah. Two years after this Nebuchadnezzar became sole monarch of the empire;* and in the second year of his reign, that is, about 603, B. C., he had, according to Daniel, the following vision: *"Thou, O king, sawest, and behold a great image. This great image, whose likeness was excellent, stood* <small>The vision.</small> *before thee; and the form thereof was terrible.*
This image's head was of fine gold, his breast and his arms of silver, his belly and his thighs of brass, his legs of iron, his feet part of iron and part of clay. Thou sawest till that a stone was cut out without hands, which smote the image on its feet that were of iron and clay, and brake them to pieces. Then was the iron, the clay, the brass, the silver, and the gold broken to pieces together, and became like the chaff of the summer threshing-floors; and the wind carried them away, that no place was found for them: and the stone that smote the image

* See Jahn's History of the Hebrew Commonwealth, p. 134.

became a great mountain, and filled the whole earth."—Daniel ii: 31–35.

Of this vision, Daniel also gave the following interpreta-
Its interpreta- tion: "*Thou, O king, art a king of kings: for*
tion.   *the God of heaven has given thee a kingdom,*
*power, and strength, and glory. And wheresoever the chil-
dren of men dwell, the beasts of the field and the fowls of
heaven hath he given into thy hand, and hath made thee ruler
over them all. Thou art this head of gold. And after thee
shall arise another kingdom, inferior to thee; and another
third kingdom of brass, which shall bear rule over all the
earth. And the fourth kingdom shall be strong as iron: forasmuch as iron breaketh.in pieces and subdueth all things:
and as iron that breaketh all these, shall it break in pieces
and bruise. And whereas thou sawest the feet and toes, part
of potters' clay, and part of iron, the kingdom shall be divided;
but there shall be in it the strength of the iron, forasmuch
as thou sawest the iron mixed with miry clay. And as the
toes of the feet were part of iron, and part of clay, so the kingdom shall be partly strong, and partly broken. And whereas
thou sawest iron mixed with miry clay, they shall mingle themselves with the seed of men: but they shall not cleave themselves
one to another, even as iron is not mixed with clay. And in
the days of these kings shall the God of heaven set up a kingdom, which shall never be destroyed: and the kingdom shall
not be left to other people, but it shall break in pieces and
consume all these kingdoms, and it shall stand forever. ·For-
asmuch as thou sawest that the stone was cut out of the
mountain without hands, and that it brake in pieces the iron,
the brass, the clay, the silver, and the gold; the great God
hath made known to the king what shall come to pass hereafter. And the dream is certain, and the interpretation thereof
sure.*"—Daniel ii: 37–45.

From the preceding record it appears,

I. That the image described was but a symbol of four universal monarchies, of which the Babylonian or Chaldean was the first in order. *Symbolical meaning of the Image.*

II. That the stone cut out of the mountain without hands was also a symbol of another monarchy, which is here called the Kingdom of Heaven; but which was of an order very different from the four preceding. *Symbolical meaning of the Stone.*

More than twenty-four centuries have passed away since this vision was revealed and interpreted by Daniel. What, then, does history record concerning it? Have intervening events served to place Daniel among the true or the false prophets? Let us inquire. And observe,

I. That the epoch from which the chronology of this vision is reckoned is by the interpretation fixed at the beginning of Nebuchadnezzar's reign. *The head of gold represents the Chaldean Monarchy.* "*Thou art this head of gold.*" Here the emperor is, by a common figure of prophecy, put for the empire; and this, therefore, clearly identifies the first kingdom.

II. The second was the Medo-Persian. This is evident, (1.) Because it immediately succeeded the Chaldean empire, 538 B. C. (2.) It, too, was universal. (3.) It was inferior to the Chaldean in morality, unity, and energy. *The silver portion of the Image represents the Medo-Persian.* "The Persian kings," says the learned Prideaux, "were the worst race of men that ever governed an empire." (4.) It was by its silver plate, shields, etc., distinguished as "*The silver empire.*"

III. The third was the Macedonian. This is obvious, (1.) Because it immediately succeeded the Medo-Persian, 334 B. C. (2.) It was universal. (3.) Because the Greeks were distinguished for their brazen armor. *The Brass, the Macedonian.* Χαλκοχίτωνες Ἀχαιοι, *brazen-coated Greeks*, was one of their common appellations.

IV. The fourth was the Roman empire. It, and it alone,
The iron and clay represent the Roman empire. fulfills all the conditions and specifications of
this part of the prophecy. (1.) Because it suc-
ceeded the Greek empire. (2.) It was uni-
versal. (3.) It was, on account of its great strength, most
properly represented by the iron. (4.) But the Romans
were weakened by their admixture with foreigners. And
hence theirs was an empire composed of iron and clay. The
other three kingdoms were comparatively homogeneous.
They were all oriental in their language, laws, customs, *et
cetera*. But the Roman empire embraced all the peculiarities of Europe, Asia, and Africa.

We have now clearly identified the image as a whole, and
also in its several parts; and it only remains, therefore, to
consider the stone, or, rather, the kingdom of God, of
which the stone is here used as an emblem. Concerning
Four particu-
lars predicated
of the King-
dom of God. this kingdom, then, four things are clearly and
distinctly predicated:

I. That it should be set up in the days of
these kings or kingdoms; that is, during the existence of
this image, or the prevalence of universal monarchy.

II. That it should break these kingdoms into pieces, and
consume them like the chaff of the summer threshing-
floors.

III. That it should itself become a great mountain, and
fill the whole earth. And,

IV. That it should not pass away like the four monarchies preceding it; but that it shall stand forever, the
fifth and last universal monarchy of the world.

Let us consider these four points briefly in order. And,
first, is it true that at any epoch between the reign of Nebuchadnezzar and the fall of the Roman empire God did
set up a kingdom on earth? On this point, it gives me
pleasure to say, the evidence is clear, convincing, and in all

respects satisfactory. That the kingdom of Christ, otherwise called the kingdom of heaven or of God, was set up on or about the day of Pentecost, A. D. 34, is as clearly and as fully established as any other event in the history of the world. *The first of these fulfilled in the setting up of the Kingdom of Christ, A. D. 34.*

To this effect Pagans, Mahometans, Jews, and Christians all bear witness. And as this was about four hundred and forty-two years before the fall of the Roman empire, we conclude that the first point is satisfactorily made out: that in the days of these kings the God of heaven did set up his kingdom among men.

The second point is equally well sustained by evidence, but its meaning is not quite so obvious to most readers. The difficulty consists in seeing and comprehending how the kingdom of heaven, which *Difficulty of understanding the second point.* was not set up till the day of Pentecost, A. D. 34, could have any influence over empires which had fallen centuries before that ever-memorable epoch. But this is all owing to the very abstract nature of the conception on which the image was founded and constructed; *Its explanation.* for be it observed that in this vision the Holy Spirit does not attempt to identify these empires in their outward or material organizations. In the vision there is no commingling of the gold, and the silver, and the brass, and the iron. But, nevertheless, *all these were animated by one and the self-same spirit.*

Here, then, is the true bond of union. Here is the link that unites all these heterogeneous and discordant elements. Here is to be found the personal identity of the image. Here we discover that *The identity of the Image in the spirit that animated it.* living principle which moved and governed the world from the days of Nebuchadnezzar till the fall of the Roman empire. Daniel, it seems, was not a materialist. He knew that a man has a soul as well as a body; and, moreover, that

5

no physical elements, however discordant, can have power to destroy our personal identity so long as our bodies are severally animated, sustained, and governed by one and the self-same spirit.

The spirit of this image is well illustrated by the common maxim of all these empires that " *Might makes* *right.*" It consisted in all those feelings and passions of pride, and envy, and malice, and revenge, and ambition, and selfishness that have ever characterized the unrenewed and unsanctified heart of fallen and depraved humanity. What but such a spirit of inordinate ambition, pride, and selfishness could have moved Nebuchadnezzar to lead his armies against the nations of Western Asia? What else moved Cyrus to make war on many of the tribes of the East, and of the West, and of the North, and finally to lead his victorious army against Babylon itself, the pride and glory of the Chaldean monarchy? What but this principle moved Alexander the Great to undertake the conquest of all Asia, and Cæsar to lead his victorious legions throughout the provinces of Gaul and Britain?

Attributes and characteristics of the spirit of this image.

Between all such governments and the kingdom of heaven there must ever exist a war of uncompromising hostility. Its king is the Prince of Peace. Its fundamental principle consists in love and benevolence. Its laws are such as the following: " *Thou shalt love the Lord thy God with all thy heart, and with all thy soul, and with all thy strength, and with all thy mind; and thou shalt love thy neighbor as thyself.*" And again: " *Whatsoever ye would that men should do to you, do ye even so to them: for this is the law and the prophets.*"

Laws and constitution of the kingdom of heaven.

These principles, emanating from the highest authority in the universe, were first proclaimed to the whole world, in all their fullness, during the last days of the Iron empire. They spread like leaven

Their influence on the Roman empire.

among the masses. Even the Roman army felt their all-subduing power and sanctifying influence; and the consequence was that many, like the devout Cornelius, beat their swords into plowshares and their spears into pruning-hooks, and solemnly declared, before their emperors and generals, that they would learn and practice the art of war no more.

The image was then smitten on its *feet*. But the wound was mortal to the whole body. The tyrant that had governed the world from the days of Nebuchadnezzar to that hour was slain. His spirit was vanquished, and his whole physical organization, consisting of gold, and silver, and brass, and iron, and clay, was then broken into many fragments.

Dissolution and destruction of the Image.

Since that time, Charlemagne, Napoleon, and many others of like ambition, have attempted to revive the spirit and reunite the scattered fragments of this fallen image. But all such attempts have been in vain. The most powerful nations on earth acknowledge their allegiance to the Prince of Peace, and their obligations to the claims of the kingdom of heaven.

Impossibility of ever establishing another universal political monarchy.

It is true that the spirit of war still exists. Blood is often shed for the most trivial causes. But let any king, prince, or potentate now attempt to revive the spirit of this fallen image; let him, like Nebuchadnezzar, Cyrus, Alexander, and Cæsar, attempt to subdue the world, and to govern it on the principle that "*might makes right*," and if not treated as a maniac by his own subjects, he will, at least, soon find arrayed against him all the combined powers of Christendom. In this country, we can not even talk of the conquest of Cuba, or any other portion of territory, however small and insignificant, without exciting in millions of our fellow-citizens feelings of the most inveterate opposition to every such act of injustice and oppression. And the same spirit of Gospel benev-

Spirit of opposition to this in America and in Europe.

olence prevails, also, to a very considerable extent, in all the nations of modern Europe. The principles of Christianity are prevailing every-where. The scattered fragments of the fallen image are daily becoming more and more like the chaff of the summer threshing-floors, and every thing seems to indicate that the time is not far distant when the stone that smote the image will become a great mountain and fill the whole earth.

Conclusion.

And this brings me to the third item concerning this kingdom. On the day of Pentecost, A. D. 34, the number of Christ's faithful subjects was very small. The kingdom might then be well compared to a grain of mustard-seed; or, as David says in the seventy-second psalm, it was like a handful of corn on the tops of the mountains; or, in the expressive language of Daniel, it was like a stone cut out of the mountain without hands. But, during the first three centuries, its increase was marvelous. Nothing could withstand the Divine energy and power with which it spread in all directions. The prejudices, the superstitions, the philosophies, the learning, the wealth, the pomp, the pride, and the politics of the world were all arrayed against it. The sword was unsheathed, and bathed in the blood of its subjects. The fires of persecution were kindled, and thousands of the followers of Christ perished at the stake for no other reason than that they would not renounce their birthrights and immunities as citizens of the kingdom of heaven. But all opposition was in vain. Its boundaries were constantly enlarged, the number of its citizens was daily multiplied, and in less than three centuries after the coronation of the Messiah, his kingdom embraced the most enlightened and influential citizens of the Roman empire. In A. D. 312, the emperor Constantine became a vassal of the King of kings, and in A. D. 384, the Roman Senate

Small begin-ning of the kingdom of heaven.

Its rapid in-crease during the first three conturies.

abolished Paganism, and made Christianity the religion of the empire.

This is certainly strong evidence of the inherent energy and previous triumphs of Christianity. But the alliance was unnatural, and hence it became a great curse instead of a blessing to the Church. *"My kingdom,"* said Christ, *"is not of this world."* There was no affinity between the Stone that was cut out of the mountain without hands and that symbol of human wickedness which it was designed to crush into atoms. No wonder, then, that after this unnatural alliance the old landmarks of the kingdom of heaven were soon obliterated, and that its glory was henceforth very greatly obscured. *(Effect of the union between the Church and the State.)*

About the same time, the barbarians of the North spread like a storm of hail and fire, mingled with blood, over the Roman empire. The lights of literature and science were extinguished, and the *"dark ages"* followed, during which Mahometanism and many other abominations deluged the earth. *(Effect of the incursions of the Northern barbarians.)*

At length the world's midnight came, in the eleventh century. Darkness that might be felt then sat brooding upon the nations. This was the reign of terror—of Satanic terror. And, no doubt, to many a poor, despised and persecuted follower of Jesus, it did appear as if the gates of Hades were about to prevail against the kingdom of the Messiah. *(Further progress of error.)*

But man's extremity is God's opportunity. There were still living a few noble spirits who had not bowed the knee to the image of Baal. These rose, in the spirit and power of Elijah, to repair the altar of God that was broken down. Heaven sustained and blessed their noble efforts. Every thing began to wear a more encouraging and promising aspect. New elements of hope and success were providentially developed. Learning be- *(Change for the better.)*

gan to revive in the fourteenth century; the art of printing was discovered in the fifteenth; and the great leaders
of the Protestant Reformation appeared in the sixteenth.

That was a remarkable era in the growth and prosperity
What was ac-
complished by
the Reforma-
tion of the 16th
century. of the kingdom of heaven. Much was then
done to restore the apostolic order of things.
The Bible was translated and put into the hands
of the people; men were taught to read, and
think, and act for themselves; and the power of the everlasting Gospel was again felt in every province of Europe.

But the most active and practical elements of the Gospel
Wherein it was
deficient. were not then fully restored. The missionary
spirit of the Church still slumbered. The fol-
lowers of Luther and Calvin became too much engaged in
political and *metaphysical* discussions; and the progress of
the reign of heaven among men was again very much retarded, till about the beginning of the nineteenth century.

Then the Ancient of Days came, and judgment was given
Spirit and prog-
ress of the 19th
century. to the saints of the Most High, and the time
came that the saints should possess the king-
dom. Then commenced the era of Modern
Missions. Then was formed the benevolent design of supplying the world with the Word of Life. Then a new
spirit of zeal, energy, and activity was developed and manifested throughout all Protestant Christendom.

I need not dwell on the results and consequences that
have followed. The reader sees them in his own church
and community. He sees them in the progress that Christianity has made in America, in Europe, in Asia, in Africa,
and even in many of the most remote islands of the Atlantic and the Pacific. He sees them in the multiplication of
Bibles, of schools and colleges, and of the arts and sciences.
He sees them in the decline of Catholicism, Mahometanism, Brahmanism, Buddhism, and all the other abominations

that have so long opposed the progress and the interests of the kingdom of heaven.

What need, then, have we of further testimony? Is it not as plain as evidence can make it, that God *Conclusion.* is now making every thing tributary to the spread of the Gospel? *And hence we infer that the day is not far distant when the Stone that smote the image will become a great mountain and fill the whole earth.*

It now only remains to consider briefly the duration of this kingdom. The prophet says, "*It will stand* *Duration of* *forever;*" that is, as long as the world stands, *the kingdom* or until the judgment shall sit and the books *of heaven.* be opened. Then, of course, the kingdom will be delivered up to God the Father, that God may be all and in all.*

As this part of the prophecy extends far into the future, it can not, of course, like the first and second *What history* items considered, be proved and illustrated his- *and the signs* torically. But in view of its past history and *of the times in-* its present increasing influences on the nations, who can *dicate.* doubt that this kingdom will endure forever? Does any man of intelligence, whatever may be his religious belief or his party prejudices, really and soberly think that Christianity will ever pass away, as did the Chaldean, Medo-Persian, Grecian, and Roman empires? I think not. I know of no intelligent person who really entertains notions so chimerical and so utterly opposed to all the indications of our present rapidly-increasing civilization; and hence I think we are fully warranted in the conclusion that the kingdom of heaven will stand while time endures.

How clearly, then, this prophecy, with its ful- *Bearing of this* fillment, serves to prove the Divine origin of *prophecy on* *the question* the Holy Bible. It was uttered more than two *respecting the* *origin of the* thousand years ago, in the open court of the *Bible.*

* Rev. xx: 11–15; 1 Cor. xv: 24–28.

greatest monarch then living. It was aimed against the
pride, and vanity, and ambition of all earthly princes. It
was, of course, watched with an eye of heathen jealousy by
all the kings, and princes, and priests, and philosophers of
Babylon and the three succeeding empires. It was sacredly
guarded by the Jews and rigorously scrutinized by the Gentiles till the coming of the Messiah. It is, therefore, no
Christian fabrication, as some have supposed. It is found
in the sacred archives of those who are most hostile to the
Christian system. And yet, wonderful to be told, it is now
being fulfilled before our own eyes, and also in the presence

Conclusion. of the most enlightened Jews, Turks, and Pagans. How true it is, then, that Daniel and
other holy men of old spake as they were moved by the
Holy Spirit.

SECTION II.—DANIEL'S VISION OF THE FOUR BEASTS.—
Daniel vii.

The main scope of the vision recorded in the seventh

General scope chapter of Daniel is to illustrate the origin,
of the vision. progress, and fortunes of the Little Horn of the
fourth beast, especially in its relations to the kingdom of
the Messiah. But for the sake of consistency and harmony,
the whole subject of universal monarchy is again introduced, as in the first vision of Nebuchadnezzar.

The scene is laid on the Mediterranean Sea, and Daniel

The scene or sees four wild beasts rising up out of the agi-
place of the tated waters. For the symbolical import of
vision. these waters, see Rev. xvii: 15.

I. The first beast, we are told, resembled a lion; had

Characteristics eagle's wings; the wings were plucked; the
of the first beast was made to stand upright like a man;
beast. and a man's heart was given to it.

These characteristics all serve to mark out this beast as a symbol of the Chaldean empire.

II. The second beast was like a bear; it seemed to be raising itself up on one side, as a bear when about to pounce upon his prey; it had three ribs in its mouth, and it was commanded to devour much flesh.

This was a symbol of the Medo-Persian empire. The three ribs in its mouth most likely represent the three principal kingdoms subdued by it, viz.: Lydia, Babylonia, and Egypt.

III. The third beast was like a leopard; had four wings, representing the great celerity of its motions; four heads, representing its four principal divisions; and great dominion.

These are all symbolical of the Grecian or Macedonian empire.

IV. The fourth beast was a monster, and had great iron teeth; it trampled down every thing before it; it had ten horns, symbolical of ten kingdoms; and from among these sprung up another little horn, or kingdom.

This beast was evidently a symbol of the Roman empire. The ten kingdoms into which it was divided, according to Machiavel, an Italian politician and historian, are as follows. The chronology is given by Bishop Lloyd: (1.) The Huns in Hungary, A. D. 356; (2.) The Ostrogoths in Moesia, A. D. 357; (3.) The Visigoths in Pannonia, A. D. 378; (4.) The Franks in France, A. D. 407; (5.) The Vandals in Africa, A. D. 407; (6.) The Sueves and Alans in Spain, A. D. 407; (7.) The Burgundians in Burgundy, A. D. 407; (8.) The Heruli and Rugians in Italy, A. D. 476; (9.) The Saxons and Angles in Britain, A. D. 476;

(10.) And the Lombards first in Northern Germany, A. D. 483, and afterward in Italy, A. D. 562.

THE LITTLE HORN.

Characteristics of the Little Horn.

From the record given in this seventh chapter of Daniel concerning the Little Horn it appears,

I. That its locality would be among the other ten horns or kingdoms; that is, in some part of the Western Roman empire.

II. That it would be a *little* horn, or, as the angel explains it, a little kingdom.

III. That it would be diverse or different in kind from the other ten horns.

IV. That it would in some way overcome and subdue three of the ten.

V. That it would have eyes like the eyes of a man; that is, that it would be remarkable for its knowledge, cunning, and sagacity.

VI. That it would utter blasphemies against the Most High.

VII. That its bearing would be more arrogant and presumptuous than the other ten.

VIII. That it would arrogate to itself authority to change times and laws.

IX. That it would make war upon the Saints and prevail against them for a time, times, and a dividing of time; that is, for three years and a half, or according to the year-day theory, by which a day is put for a year in the short-hand writing of prophecy, one thousand two hundred and sixty years.*

X. That at the close of this period the Ancient of

---

* See Ezekiel iv: 6.

Days would sit in judgment upon it and take away its *dominion*.

XI. That it would not at that time be wholly destroyed, but that *from that epoch it would be gradually consumed even to the time of its final ruin*.

Compare with all this what is said of the Man of Sin in 2 Thessalonians ii: 1–12, and the description of the two-horned beast in Revelation xiii: 11–18. *Other references to the same power.*

In order to identify this Little Horn it is necessary to find a kingdom *that will answer to all the given characteristics.* Such a one we find in the Roman Catholic hierarchy, and nowhere else. This will appear more evident as we proceed with the several particulars specified. And, *Requisites in order to identify this kingdom. The conditions all fulfilled in the Roman Catholic Hierarchy.*

I. All concede that Popery had its origin in the Western Roman empire, among the ten horns of the fourth beast. *Its birthplace.*

II. It is also evident that Popery has always been, *intrinsically*, a weak and feeble power. True, indeed, in one aspect, it was for a time very powerful; but it was so, not by its own, but by borrowed power. It has generally accomplished its ends and purposes through the agency and instrumentality of some other political power; and hence to John it appeared as a lamb, but it spake like a dragon. *Its intrinsic feebleness.*

III. It was diverse from all the other kingdoms of the empire. They were all purely secular in their character, but it was a politico-ecclesiastical despotism. *Its diverse character.*

IV. It is a well-known historical fact that through the influence of the Catholic party the Vandals, the Ostrogoths, and the Lombards were all subdued and removed out of the way. The following *The three Horns plucked up by the Little Horn.*

facts are taken, *in substance*, from Gibbon's "Decline and Fall of the Roman Empire:"

The Arian controversy was the occasion of much enmity The Arian controversy. between nations as well as between individuals and churches. The Romans and the Greeks were generally Athanasians or Trinitarians; but the cause of Arius was, for the most part, espoused by the Vandals, the Ostrogoths, the Lombards, and other tribes hostile to the Quarrels between the Catholics and Vandals of Africa Romans. Religion was carried into their secular and political differences; and for many years the political leaders of the respective parties were among their most violent religious partisans. But about A. D. 530, Hilderic, king of the Vandals, became more friendly to the Trinitarians, or Catholic party of Northern Africa. He restored two hundred deposed Athanasian bishops to their churches, and allowed the free profession of the Athanasian Creed. This, of course, gave great offense to his Arian subjects. His clergy charged him with having renounced the faith of his fathers. He was finally deposed, and Gelimer, a violent Arian partisan, was placed on the throne.

This, again, greatly offended the Catholics in the East, as Subjugation of the Vandals. well as in Africa and in Italy, and as the emperor Justinian was then the political representative of the Catholic party, all looked to him to defend the faith and to chastise the Vandals. His consent was easily obtained. Having himself, about the same time, acknowledged the Bishop of Rome to be the head over all the churches, and having asked his services in the settlement of an Eastern controversy, he seemed anxious to prove his faith by his works, and readily consented to undertake the subjugation of the Vandals.* An army was sent into Af-

---

* The following letter from Justinian to John, Bishop of Rome, A. D. 533, sufficiently explains the purposes and designs of the Emperor, and his great obsequiousness to the See of Rome:

rica, under Belisarius, A. D. 533, and in the course of that and the following year the Vandals were subdued and almost exterminated.*

The same fate befel the Ostrogoths of Italy in A. D. 539.† Thus two of the ten original horns were subdued and vanquished through the influence of this Little Horn. Subjugation of the Ostrogoths in Italy.

In A. D. 568 the Lombards got possession in Italy. They, too, were uncompromising Arians, and their political and religious controversies with the Catholics became more and more frequent and violent. Appeals were again made to the East, but in vain. At Subjugation of the Lombards.

"Rendering honor to the Apostolic See and to your holiness, as always was and is our desire, and, as it becomes us, honoring your blessedness as a father, we have laid without delay before the notice of your blessedness all things pertaining to the state of the Church. Since it has always been our earnest study to preserve the unity of your Holy See, and the state of the holy churches of God which has hitherto obtained, and will remain without any interfering opposition. *Therefore we hasten to subject and to unite to your holiness all the priests of the whole East.* Justinian's letter to the Bishop of Rome.

"As to the matters which are at present agitated, although clear and undoubted, and, according to the doctrine of the Apostolic See, held assuredly resolved and decided upon by all the priests, we have yet deemed it necessary to lay them before your holiness. Nor do we suffer any thing which belongs to the state of the Church, however manifest and undoubted, that is agitated, to pass without the knowledge of your holiness, *who are the head of all the holy churches.* For in all things, as had been said or resolved, we are prompt to increase the honor and authority of your See."—*Bower's History of the Popes*, vol. ii, pp. 335, 336.

The same supremacy is ascribed to the Bishop of Rome by Justinian in his celebrated code of Roman laws, published about the same time. In the 131st Novella, the Emperor says: "*We therefore decree that the Most Holy Pope of Rome is the first of all the priesthood*, and that the most blessed Archbishop of Constantinople, the new Rome, shall be second in rank after the Holy Apostolic Chair of the elder Rome." Decree of Justinian.

* See Gibbon, vol. v, pp. 127–158. † Ibid, vol. v, pp. 178–210.

length Pope Stephen called on Pepin, king of France, who came in person, subdued the Lombards, and, in A. D. 755, conferred on the Pope the Exarchate of Ravenna and Pentapolis. Thus fell the third of the ten horns.*

V. The cunning, sagacity, and far-reaching policy of the *Its sagacity and foresight.* Catholics, and especially of the Order of the Jesuits, are proverbial.

VI. The following quotation from Bishop Newton's " Dissertations on the Prophecies" will sufficiently *Its blasphemous character and pretensions.* illustrate this characteristic of Popery: "At all times he (the Pope) exercises Divine authority in the Church, showing himself that he is God; affecting Divine titles and attributes, such as holiness and infallibility; assuming Divine powers and prerogatives, in condemning and absolving men, in retaining and forgiving sins, in asserting his decrees to be of the same or greater authority than the Word of God, and commanding them to be received under the penalty of the same or greater condemnation. Like another Salmoneus, he is proud to imitate the state and thunder of the Almighty, and is styled and pleased to be styled, 'Our Lord God the Pope; another God upon earth; King of kings and Lord of lords.' The same is the dominion of God and the Pope. To believe that our Lord God the Pope might not decree as he decreed, is heresy. The power of the Pope is greater than all created power, and extends itself to things celestial, terrestrial, and infernal. The Pope doeth whatsoever he listeth, even things unlawful, and is more than God. Such blasphemies are not only allowed, but are even approved, encouraged, and rewarded, in writers of the Church of Rome, and they are not only the extravagances of private writers, but are the language even of public decretals and acts of councils."†

* See Gibbon, vol. v, pp. 213–219.　　† Disser. xxii: pp. 404–5.

VII. It was not enough for this little horn to uproot three of its ten predecessors; it also claimed ju- *His arrogant bearing toward kings and princes.* risdiction over the remaining seven, as well as over all other kings and potentates. On the necks of some the Pope placed his foot, in token of his absolute sovereignty. Others were required, after the manner of slaves, to hold his stirrup, while he mounted on horseback; and others again were, through his influence, reduced to such a degree of degradation, that they were glad of the opportunity to kiss his toe, in token of their absolute subjection to his holiness.* Such facts very clearly indicate that "*his looks were more stout than his fellows.*"

VIII. The power to change times and laws, even the laws of the Most High, has always been claimed *His claimed-authority to change times and laws.* as one of the prerogatives of the Pope of Rome. This is made sufficiently clear by the previous citation from Bishop Newton.

IX. It is well to observe here that *the term of twelve hundred and sixty years does not refer, as some have alleged, to the entire period of the Little Horn's existence, but only to the period of his dominion* *Period of his dominion over the saints.* *over the saints.* That this commenced as early as A. D. 533, is, I think, evident from what is given under the fourth characteristic. That many of the Vandals were ignorant, superstitious, and hypocritical formalists, is of course conceded; but that some of them were also sincere followers of our Lord Jesus Christ admits, I think, of no doubt. And be it remembered, that the war which resulted in their complete subjugation was really a religious war, *undertaken and prosecuted for the sake of the Catholic party.* This is evident from many passages in Gibbon, as well as from what has been said and written by many other historians.

* See Ranke's "History of the Popes," and Dowling's "History of Romanism."

Take, for instance, the following brief extract from the " Decline and Fall of the Roman Empire." After a free conference with his Council of State, in reference to undertaking
the war, the emperor hesitated; and Gibbon adds, "The
design of the war would perhaps have been relinquished, if
Justinian's courage had not been revived by a voice which
silenced the doubts of profane reason. 'I have seen a
vision,' cried an artful or fanatic bishop of the East. 'It is
the will of Heaven, O Emperor, that you should not abandon
your holy enterprise for the deliverance of the African Church.
The God of battles will march before your standard, and dis-
perse your enemies, who are the enemies of his Son.' "*

This appeal to the emperor was decisive. There was no
longer room either for doubt or for hesitation. The war was
resolved on *for the sake of the Catholic Church.* During that
and the following year much blood was shed in the name of
Religion; and the persecution was continued, without much
interruption, for a period of one thousand two hundred and
sixty years, during which the Church fled into the wilderness. The two witnesses prophesied in sackcloth, and many
of the saints suffered martyrdom for the Word of God and
the testimony of Jesus Christ. But in A. D. 1793, just one
thousand two hundred and sixty years from the commencement of the African war, the breaking out of the French
revolution *put a stop to all religious persecution throughout
Europe.*

X. But this was not all that followed. It was not a mere
suspension of Papal power and Papal tyranny.
God's judg-
ments on the
Little Horn.
*Then the Ancient of Days sat in judgment on
this monster of iniquity. His power was broken,
his dominion was then taken away, and the kingdom was soon
given to the saints of the Most High.*

On the 21st of September, 1792, the French National

* Gibbon, vol. v, chap. xli, p. 131, Lond. edit.

Convention abolished royalty and proclaimed the French nation a free republic. On the 19th of Novem- Acts of the French National Assembly. ber following, they passed the "*Decree of Fraternity*," promising aid to all people who were willing to contend for the principles and enjoyment of liberty. These measures were preparatory to the solemn and extreme issues of the next year, during which king Louis, "The Eldest Son of the Church," was beheaded, vast numbers of the royalists put to death, the republican era proclaimed, and all ecclesiastical connection with Rome publicly renounced. The events of the two following years were of the same type. While they were characterized by the most wild, reckless, and lawless spirit of unbridled democracy, they were, at the same time, a terror to Popery as well as to every other surviving horn of the fourth beast. Thus it is that God makes even the wrath and wickedness of man praise him.

But it was reserved especially for Napoleon to humble the pride of Rome, and to completely sever the ec- Napoleon's success in Italy. clesiastical and political ties that bound all Western Europe to the throne of the Papacy. *This was his mission*, and while he confined himself within its proper limits, no hero was ever more successful. On the third of February, 1796, when only twenty-six years of age, he was appointed commander-in-chief of the army in Italy. The battle of Lodi is a monument of his military greatness. All Northern Italy then felt and acknowledged his power. The Pope was forced to purchase the forbearance of the republicans by ceding to them Bologna and several other towns, paying a heavy ransom, and sending three hundred precious manuscripts and pictures to enrich the National Museum of Paris. Other important events followed in quick succession, and, on the 15th of February, 1798, General Berthier, the commander of the French forces, entered the gates of the

6

Eternal City. The conquest was easy and rapid. *He soon abolished the Papal Government, proclaimed Rome a republic, dragged Pope Pius VI from the altar of the Vatican, sent him first into Tuscany, and thence to Valence, in France, where, after an illness of ten days, he expired in captivity.*

XI. This was an end of the administration of Pius VI, but not of Popery. The prophet foresaw that after the terminus of the one thousand two hundred and sixty years of Papal supremacy this once persecuting power would itself pass through a period of consumption, until it would be finally destroyed. *And this is now being fulfilled before our eyes in all parts of Christendom.*

Popery in a state of consumption.

The French had freed themselves from the evils of monarchy, but not from their own religious blindness and fanaticism. They never understood the spirit and genius of pure Christianity; and hence when their own experience had convinced them that even superstition is better than atheism, they were not prepared for any thing better than a modified species of Roman Catholicism; and this was, therefore, re-established as the religion of the republic. This was certainly making some concession to the Roman Catholic Hierarchy. But all the powers of earth can never restore what it lost by the French revolution and the victories of Napoleon. True, indeed, its numbers are still very great, and, it may be, that they are even increasing; but, nevertheless, *its spirit is broken, its dominion over the saints has ceased, its power to persecute has been taken away, and for several years the intervention of foreign bayonets has been necessary to preserve its head from ruin.*

In the mean time the kingdom has been given to the saints of the Most High. From the day that the Papal scepter was broken by Napoleon, the cause of primitive Christianity has been onward and up-

The kingdom given to the saints.

ward. Then commenced the work of modern missions. Then was conceived the benevolent design of supplying the destitute and dying millions of our race with the Word of Life. And never before, since the days of the Apostles, was so much done for the conversion of the world and the restoration of primitive Christianity as has been accomplished within the last sixty years. The Bible has, during this short period, been translated into all the principal languages and dialects of the earth, the number of its copies has been multiplied more than tenfold, and all things seem to indicate the speedy triumphs of the Gospel throughout the whole world.

From all these premises, then, we conclude,   Conclusion

1. That Daniel was a true prophet, and spoke as he was moved by the Holy Spirit.

2. That the days of Zion's mourning are past; that her warfare is almost accomplished; that the two witnesses will no more prophesy in sackcloth; and that the bottomless pit will hereafter be opened only to receive the enemies of the Church.

SECTION III.—The Mahometan Dominion; or, The Little Horn of the Goat.—*Daniel viii.*

The scope of Daniel's second vision is very similar to that of his first. It is evidently to illustrate the origin, exploits, and destiny of a Little Horn. But whether the Little Horns of the two visions are identical, the sequel will show.   *Scope of Daniel's second vision.*

The scene is laid on the banks of the river Ulai. While there Daniel saw a Ram pushing westward, and northward, and southward. This Ram, according to Gabriel, was a symbolical representation of the Medo-Persian empire, and to   *Its locality.*

Characteristics and symbolical meaning of the Ram.

it all the marks and characteristics of the Ram evidently refer.

While Daniel was admiring the Ram for his great strength *Characteristics of the He-Goat.* and prowess, a He-Goat came rapidly and sweepingly from the west, and completely vanquished the Ram. But when the Goat became very powerful, his great horn was broken, and in its stead came up four other notable horns toward the four winds of heaven.

This Goat, according to the same authority, was a symbol *Their symbolical meaning.* of the Greek or Macedonian empire. The great horn denoted Alexander the Great, and the four notable horns that succeeded it, represented Greece, Thrace, Syria, and Egypt: the four principal divisions of the Greek empire.

Out of one of these came up afterward the Little Horn, *Criteria and characteristics of this Little Horn.* which is evidently the principal subject of the vision. From the vision of the prophet, and Gabriel's interpretation, we learn the following particulars concerning it:

I. That this Little Horn would have its origin in one of the four divisions of Alexander's empire.

II. That the time of its rise would be when the dominion of the four kingdoms of the goat had passed away, and the transgressors had come to the full.

III. That its character would be exceedingly unique and paradoxical. For instance,

1. That it would be a little horn, but that it would also be a king of fierce countenance.

2. That it would be skillful in understanding dark sentences.

3. That one of its characteristic crimes would be the transgression of desolation.

IV. That it would wage war, and exercise its hostility,

1. Upon the South, the East, and the Pleasant Land.

2. Against the host of heaven; or, as Gabriel explains it, against the mighty and holy people.

3. Against the Prince of the Host.

4. Against the Daily.

V. From the same sources we also learn by what means it would succeed in its ambitious and unholy purposes. These are,

1. Not by its own, but by borrowed power.

2. By a crafty and cunning policy.

3. By offers of peace.

VI. Finally, we have an account of the manner and time of its end. It is to be broken without hands, and within a period of twenty-three hundred prophetic days.

There is a very striking analogy between some of these characteristics and those of the Little Horn described in the seventh chapter of Daniel; and hence some have inferred that the horns are themselves identical. But this opinion is evidently erroneous. In some respects these two horns differ very essentially, as, for instance, *Analogy between the Little Horns of the 7th and 8th chapters of Daniel. Points of difference.* with respect *to the place of their origin and the sphere of their influence.* It has been demonstrated, I hope to the satisfaction of all my readers, that the Little Horn of the seventh chapter is a symbol of the Roman Catholic Hierarchy. But this power did not grow up in any one of the four divisions of Alexander's empire; nor did it ever exercise very much influence over them. The seat of its dominion has always been in Western Europe, a territory over which Alexander's empire never extended. And hence it follows that these two Little *Hence not identical.* Horns are essentially different. The one has long been the curse of Western Europe, and the other of Western Asia. The former represents Popery, and the latter represents Mahometanism. To this power, *What these two horns severally symbolize.*

and to this alone, belong all the characteristics of the Little

Identification of the latter. Horn described in the eighth chapter. Let us notice them all very briefly in order.

I. The first characteristic mark which serves to identify

Its locality. this Little Horn is its locality or birth-place. It was to grow up in one of the four divisions of Alexander's empire; that is, in Macedonia, Thrace, Syria, or Egypt. To some there may be an apparent difficulty in applying this part of the prophecy to Mahometan power. But the difficulty is only apparent. It is true that Mahometanism had its origin in Arabia, and it is also true that Arabia was never perfectly subjugated by any one of Alexander's successors. But, nevertheless, it was for a long time nominally subject to the kings of Egypt, just as Philistia and Phœnecia were always reckoned among the possessions

Divisions of Alexander's empire. of the twelve tribes. "After the battle of Ipsus," says Rollin, " the four confederate princes divided the dominions of Antigonus among themselves, and added them to those already possessed. *The empire of Alexander was then divided into four kingdoms, of which Ptolemy had Egypt, Lybia, Arabia, Coele-Syria, and Palestine; Cassander had Macedonia and Greece; Lysimachus had Thrace, Bithynia, and some other provinces beyond the Hellespont, with the Bosphorus; and Seleucus had all the rest of Asia to the other side of the Euphrates, and as far as the river Indus.** It appears, therefore, that the birth-place of this Little Horn exactly corresponds with the birth-place of Mahometanism.

II. The chronology of this Little Horn serves also to

Time of its birth. identify it with the ecclesiastical system of Mahomet. Two circumstances serve to fix the time of its birth. Gabriel says that it would stand up in the end of the kingdoms of Greece, Thrace, Syria, and

---

* Rollin's Anc. Hist., book xvi, chap. 2, sec. 1.

Egypt; or, more exactly, after the time of these four kingdoms, when the transgressors were come to the full.* These
transgressors were evidently the nominal Christians of Western Asia, and particularly of Arabia, who had very generally
departed from the faith before the rise of Mahometanism.
The following very brief extract from Taylor's "Manual of
History" is sufficient to illustrate this point: "Unfortunate-
ly" says the historian, on page 356, "*Christianity, when introduced into the Peninsula, had been deeply sullied* Religious char-
by man's devices. The different tribes were im- acter of the
bued with a fierce sectarian spirit, and hated each Arabians.
*other more bitterly than Jews or Pagans. The vivid imagina-
tions of the Arabs led them to investigate questions beyond the
powers of man's understanding, and the consequence was so
abundant a supply of new doctrines, that one of the early
fathers described Arabia as the land most fruitful in heresies.*"†

This might be further illustrated and confirmed by the testimony of St. John.‡ Had not the star first Illustration
fallen from heaven, the bottomless pit would not from the Apoc-
have been opened, and, consequently, the smoke John.
and the darkness and the locusts would never have covered
the provinces of Western Asia. But the Asiatic churches
had then very generally filled the cup of their iniquity; and
hence God permitted these very heavy and severe judgments
to come on them. Darkness has since covered that once favored portion of the earth, and gross darkness has brooded
over those towns and cities that were first illuminated by the
Sun of Righteousness.

III. The character of this Eastern Power is also very dis-

* אַחֲרִית is from, אָחַר, to remain behind or to be after. And hence it
primarily denotes that which is after or posterior, as Psa. cix: 13; and
Amos iv: 2.

† See also Sale's Koran, Prelim. Discourse, Sec. II.

‡ Revelation ix: 1–11.

tinctly marked. It seems that *it was to be a little horn, a*

Its character.

king of fierce countenance, and interpreter of dark sentences, and a mighty desolator of the earth. All these points have been very clearly and strikingly fulfilled in the politico-ecclesiastical system of Mahomet. In its origin, Mahometanism very much resembled the Little Horn

Evidence of its intrinsic feebleness.

of the Western monster. For several years its progress had been very slow. It was not until the civil power was associated with the ecclesiastical that it gained much influence either at home or abroad.

But though in its origin and ecclesiastical capacity it was

Severe and revengeful character of Mahometanism.

a little horn, it nevertheless soon became a king of fierce countenance. Every man's religion has an effect on his intellectual, moral, and even physical constitution. Christianity, whose very essence is love, renders its subjects mild, amiable, gentle, and forgiving in their disposition. It changes the raven to the dove, the lion to the lamb. But Mahometanism breathes out vengeance and slaughter against and upon all who oppose the Koran. Death, tribute, or Islamism were the terms which the caliphs offered to their most favored opponents. What a contrast between the ambassadors of the Cross and the vicars of the False Prophet!

Skill in the interpretation of dark sentences is another

Their knowledge and love of literature.

characteristic of this politico-ecclesiastical despotism. And it is well known that the Arabians have always been distinguished for the love of parables, riddles, and enigmas. The Koran itself abounds in all the dark parabolical forms of the Eastern style; and besides, Gabriel may also have had reference to their superior knowledge of the arts, sciences, and literature during the middle ages.

But though these polished arts have generally had a softening and refining influence on mankind, they had but little effect on these locusts of the desert, whose characteristic crime was "*the transgression of desolation.*" In the day of their power they were, therefore, "the abomination of desolation." This seems to have been a common name, applicable to any power distinguished for the crime of desolating large portions of the world. Thus the Chaldean army was once "the abomination of desolation." To it succeeded the Medo-Persian. Then followed the Grecian, and then the Roman. The last is evidently intended in Daniel xi: 31, and to it our Savior refers in Matthew xxiv: 15. But the Saracen army also became "the abomination of desolation," and it is evidently so designated in Daniel xii: 11. This was so very manifest, even to Sophronius, the last patriarch of Jerusalem, that when the Caliph Omar entered the city, to take possession of it in the name of the False Prophet, "*Sophronius bowed before his new master, and secretly muttered, in the words of Daniel, 'The abomination of desolation is in the holy place.'*" *

The abomination of desolation.

IV. The objects of its dislike and resentment are next enumerated by the prophet: "*It waxed exceeding great toward the South, and toward the East, and toward the Pleasant Land. And it waxed great even to the host of heaven, and it cast down some of the host and of the stars to the ground, and stamped on them. Yea, he magnified himself even to (or against) the Prince of the host. And by him the Daily was taken away, and the place of his Sanctuary was cast down. And a host was given him against the Daily by reason of transgression, and it cast down the truth to the ground.*"

Objects of its hatred.

Any map or geographical chart of the Saracenic empire is a sufficient proof and illustration of the correctness of Daniel's topography in this connection. The western conquests of the caliphs,

Geography of the Saracenic empire.

* Gibbon, vol. vi, chap. li, p. 430, Lond. edit.

though extending even to the Atlantic Ocean, were nevertheless comparatively small, and were, by the Mahometans
themselves, called *"The sleeve of the robe."*   ,

The host of heaven, or, as the phrase is interpreted by the
Mahomet's
opposition to
Christ, to his
disciples, and
to his cause. angel, "the mighty and holy people," and the
Prince of the host, were the next objects of its
resentment.   By the former we are evidently to
understand the Christians, who, at that time,
were the only holy people on earth; and, consequently, by
the latter is meant the Messiah himself.   All this was literally fulfilled in the conquests and exploits of Mahomet,
who greatly magnified himself against both Christ and his
disciples.   He taught that Adam, Noah, Abraham, Moses,
Christ, and himself were all true prophets, rising in just
and regular gradation above each other, and that whoever
hates or rejects any one of them must be numbered among
the infidels.   But by placing himself above them all, he of
course stood up against the Prince of the host; and by
placing the Koran above the Bible, and the Crescent above
the Cross, he cast down the truth to the ground, and practiced and prospered.

"By it also the Daily was taken away, and the place of
Meaning of the
Daily in this
prophecy. the Sanctuary was cast down."   In interpreting
any ancient documents it is very necessary to
consider the historical meaning of terms.   There
was a time when the word *temple* was used in the Sacred
Canon to denote the building erected by Solomon for the
worship of Jehovah; but this word has since been transferred from the type to the antitype, from the edifice on
Mount Moriah to the Christian Church, which, since the
ever-memorable day of Pentecost, in A. D. 34, has been a
habitation of God through the Spirit.   Thus says Paul, 1
Corinthians iii: 16–17: "Know ye not that ye are the temple of God, and that the Spirit of God dwells in you?   If

any one destroy the temple of God, God will destroy him; for the temple of God is holy, which temple ye are."

And just so there was a time when *the Daily* signified the daily services of the Tabernacle, or of the Temple made with hands. But this term has also been transferred from the type to the antitype. It has no longer reference to the sacrifices and the incense that were daily offered by the priests under the Law. It now refers to the daily services of the Christian temple, the Sanctuary of the Living God, which is the pillar and the support of the truth. And it is a very remarkable fact, that while the Little Horn of the fourth beast has deluged all West- *By whom this was taken away.* ern Europe with the blood of the saints, it has never taken away the daily services of the Sanctuary; but the Little Horn of the Goat has removed both the altar and the incense from nearly all the churches of the East.

V. " *His power,*" says Gabriel, " *shall be mighty, but not by his own power.*" At first Mahomet appeared *Its means of success.* merely as a prophet or teacher of religion. But his system was in itself utterly impotent. It very soon be- came manifest that if the world were ever converted to Is- lamism, it must be done by extraneous means, and, there- fore, the sword was brought in as an auxiliary *Use of the sword.* to the Koran. "The sword," said Mahomet, " is the key to heaven and hell. A drop of blood shed in the cause of God, or a night spent in arms, is of more avail than two months of fasting and prayer. Whosoever falls in battle, his sins are forgiven. At the day of judgment his wounds shall be resplendent as vermilion, and odoriferous as musk, and the loss of his limbs shall be supplied by the wings of angels and cherubim."[*]

But the sword was not his only means of suc- *Crafty and cunning policy.* cess. " *Through his policy,*" said the angel,

---

[*] Gibbon, vol. vi, chap. l, page 334, Lond. edit. of eight volumes.

"*he shall cause craft to prosper in his hand.*"   The following brief extract from the "Decline and Fall of the Roman Empire," will show how very applicable all this is to the followers of Mahomet: "In the prosecution of the war, their *policy* was not less effectual than their sword.   By short and separate truces they dissolved the union of the enemy; accustomed the Syrians to compare their friendship with their enmity; familiarized the idea of their language, religion, and manners; and exhausted, by clandestine purchase, the magazines and arsenals of the cities which they returned to besiege.   They aggravated the ransom of the more wealthy or the more obstinate; and Chalis alone was taxed at five thousand ounces of gold, five thousand ounces of silver, two thousand robes of silk, and as many figs and olives as would load five thousand asses. But the terms of truce or capitulation were faithfully observed; and the lieutenant of the caliph, who had promised not to enter the walls of the captive Baalbec, remained tranquil and immovable in his tent, till the jarring factions solicited the interposition of a foreign master."*

Another means of success was peace.   "*By peace he shall destroy many.*"   The terms generally proposed to the vanquished were death, tribute, or peace on condition that they would embrace the Mahometan faith. Thousands embraced this last condition to their present disgrace and their eternal ruin.

How very different from all this is the religion of the Prince of Peace, which, in less than three centuries, by its own intrinsic power, subdued the Roman empire, and took possession of the palace and the throne of the Cæsars.

VI. But notwithstanding the temporary triumphs of this Little Horn, its doom is sealed,

*Gibbon, vol. vi, chap. li, pp. 423–4.

its destiny is determined. *"It shall be broken,"* says Gabriel, *"without hands;"* that is, I presume, by Divine power. The Lord will consume it, as he is now consuming the Little Horn of the West, by the spirit of his mouth, and he will destroy them both by the brightness that will anticipate his coming.

The period of two thousand three hundred years, or prophetic days, has been assigned as the terminus *ad quem* of its existence. The Sanctuary or Church will then be cleansed from every stain and pollution of both Eastern and Western abominations. But as this still relates to the future, it does not properly fall within our prescribed limits.

Enough, however, has been said for our present purpose. Here is a chain of prophecy extending from the days of Daniel to the present time, every link — Conclusion. — of which has its counterpart in the well-authenticated events of profane history. And hence it follows that we must either wholly ignore all connection between cause and effect, or otherwise concede that these are the revelations of that Spirit that searches all things, yea the deep things of Jehovah.

Note.—The reader should be extremely cautious in adopting any theory of unfulfilled prophecy. It was never God's purpose to gratify our curiosity in this respect by giving us any thing more than a mere *outline* of future events, and hence there is great danger of falling into error in our — Necessity of caution in the study of unfulfilled prophecy. — attempts to fill up the details. It is just here that most writers on prophecy forget their proper office as interpreters of the Word of Life, and become prophets themselves.

We all, however, feel that there is a great pleasure in looking into the chapter of unfulfilled prophecy, as to a light that shines in a dark place. And there is certainly no harm in endeavoring to understand it, *provided*, only, that we do not become dogmatists, nor wrest the Scriptures by our own theories and speculations.

With this caution to the reader, I will add a few words here touching the *probable* time when the Sanctuary will be cleansed. The principal difficulty consists in fixing — Terminus a quo of the 2,300 years. — the terminus *a quo*, or the epoch from which the two thousand three

SECTION IV.—THE SEVENTY WEEKS OF DANIEL.—
Chapter ix.

This chapter consists of three parts. In the first we have
Daniel's dis- given Daniel's discovery respecting the duration
covery. of the captivity. By referring to the prophecies
of Jeremiah, he had learned that it would continue during
a period of seventy years.* This period had now almost
expired. Sixty-eight years had elapsed since Daniel and his
companions had been carried to Babylon, and still nothing
in the events and signs of the times seemed to favor their
deliverance, nor even to indicate that the day of their emancipation was near at hand.

hundred years are to be reckoned. It seems most probable, however,
that this period is to be reckoned, not from the rise or birth of the Ram,
as some writers have alleged, (for he was in his full strength and vigor
when Daniel first saw him,) but *from the time when he was first attacked by*
Terminus ad *the He-goat.* If this assumption is warranted by the con-
quem of the text, it fixes the beginning of this period to the spring
same period. of the year 334 B. C., and consequently it will terminate
in the spring or about the middle of A. D. 1967.

And this conclusion seems to be sustained by the chronology of the
Confirmation twelfth chapter. The reader will observe that in that
of this from the chapter the future history of the Israelites is summed up
12th chapter. in three leading events. These are, first, their restoration to Palestine; second, their general conversion to Christ; and, third,
the conversion of the world through their agency and instrumentality.
Three leading Now each of these events seems to be marked and defined
events and pe- by the terminus of a distinct period, the first consisting
riods of this of 1260 years, the second of 1290, and the third of
chapter. 1335.

If this be so, then we have only to inquire, when did these periods
commence? And this seems to be settled, as a question of fact, by the
Terminus a quo angel himself. He says, at least in reference to the sec-
of each period. ond of these periods, that its terminus *a quo* is to be reckoned from the taking away of the Daily. And that this

* Jeremiah xxv: 8–11, and xxix: 10.

This seems to have greatly distressed him. Probably he thought that, on account of the great wickedness of the nation, God was about to protract the period of their sufferings, and he therefore betook himself to prayer, with fasting, and sackcloth, and ashes. *His own probable reflections.*

In the second part we have given the prayer of Daniel. It consists, *Daniel's prayer.*

1. Of an acknowledgement of God's fidelity. V. 4.
2. Of an humble confession of Israel's sins. V. 5–15.
3. Of supplications for Jerusalem. V. 16–19.

The third part contains God's answer to this prayer. It was communicated to Daniel through Gabriel, and it embraces the following particulars. *God's answer to this prayer.*

I.   That a period of seventy weeks had been determined

Daily of the twelfth chapter is the same as that of the eighth, just considered, is evident, because this word, in its restricted meaning, has never had but two senses in the Holy Scriptures: the typical and the antitypical. The Romans took away the Daily in the typical sense when they destroyed Jerusalem, in A. D. 70, (see Daniel xi: 31,) and the Saracens took it away in its antitypical sense when they subjugated Palestine, the conquest of which was *commenced* in A. D. 632.

Now that it can not relate to the former of these events is evident, because if to A. D. 70 we add the three numbers given in the twelfth chapter, we are brought down to A. D. 1330, 1360, and 1405. But nothing in the history of these years corresponds with the leading events of the prophecy, which seem to mark out prominently three important epochs, and hence we conclude that the Daily in the twelfth chapter refers not to the type, but to the antitype.

If, then, to A. D. 632 we add 1260, 1290, and 1335, we have, as the result, A. D. 1892, A. D. 1922, and A. D. 1967. The first of these, most probably, designates the time when the Israelites will return to the Holy Land; the second, the time *Terminus ad quem of each.* when they will be generally converted to Christ; and the third, the time when, through their instrumentality, the Sanctuary will be cleansed, and the kingdoms of this world will become *Conclusion.* the kingdoms of our Lord and of his Anointed.

on Israel, during which they would continue to enjoy their then covenanted relation to God for the accomplishment of the following ends and purposes:

1. *To restrain the transgression,* or, more particularly, to
prevent the universal spread of idolatry. (See Gal. iii: 19.)

2. *To seal or shut up sins.* This and the first clause constitute a parallelism. The object expressed in the first clause is specific; that in the second is more generic.

3. *To cover iniquity;* that is, to cover it with the typical blood of the Old Covenant until He would come whose blood cleanses from all sin.

4. *To bring in or introduce everlasting righteousness;* that is, God's everlasting scheme of justification.

5. *To seal or to confirm and ratify vision and prophecy.* At the close of these seventy weeks God was about to fix, as it were, the seal of heaven on all the predictions of the Old Testament, by the introduction of the Gospel and the fulfillment of his many promises to the fathers; but, in the mean time, the agency of the Jews, in their covenanted relations to God as his peculiar people, was necessary to the accomplishment of this end.

6. *To anoint the Most Holy.* This title may refer to any person or thing that is peculiarly sacred, or that has been especially consecrated to God. Here it evidently refers to Christ himself, who, about the close of this period, was anointed with the Holy Spirit and with power.*

It is evident, from the context, that a considerable length
of time would be necessary for the accomplishment of all these ends and purposes—much more, certainly, than that which is included within a period of seventy literal weeks—and hence it is evidently

---

* Acts x: 38.

implied that a day is here put for a year, as in Ezekiel;* and that this is, therefore, a period of four hundred and ninety years.

II. The second point embraced in this response to the prayer of Daniel is *the division of this period* Three divisions *into three subordinate periods of seven weeks, six-* of this period. *ty-two weeks, and one week, or, rather, half a week;* or, according to the year-day rule of interpretation, into periods of forty-nine years, four hundred and thirty-four years, and three and a half years. The terminus of each of these is pretty clearly marked by an important event in How each di- Jewish history. The first is designated as a marked or des- period of very great trouble, during which Jeru- ignated. salem was to be restored; the close of the second is marked by the advent of the Messiah, and that of the third by his death.

III. The third general topic contained in this answer re-lates chiefly to *the destruction and desolations of* Predictions *Jerusalem.* The following particulars are ex- second destruc- pressed with more or less clearness and full- tion of Jerusa- ness: lem.

1. That soon after the death of the Messiah the city would be destroyed by a foreign prince.

2. That its destruction would be very great, even as the ruin caused by a deluge.

3. That it would also be of long continuance, even till the consummation of God's purposes in reference to it.

Such then is, in brief, the meaning of this prophecy. Has it ever been fulfilled? Let us inquire.

Our first object must be to ascertain the *beginning* of the period here designated by the seventy weeks. Beginning of And here great caution is necessary. True, in- the 490 years. deed, we are told very distinctly that it is to be reckoned *"from the going forth of the commandment to restore and to build Jerusalem."* But history records no less than four decrees or commandments, all of which had some reference to the restoration of the Jewish Commonwealth.

1. The first of these was issued by Cyrus, B. C. 536. It is recorded in Ezra i: 2–4.

Four decrees concerning Jerusalem.

2. The second was made by Darius Hystaspes, B. C. 519. (Ezra vi: 1–12.)

3. The third by Artaxerxes Longimanus, B. C. 457. (Ezra vii: 1–26.)

4. The fourth by the same monarch, about thirteen years later, B. C. 444. (Nehemiah ii: 1–8.)

From which of these epochs, then, is this period to be reckoned? Evidently not from the first, for that had special reference to the building of the Temple; nor from the second, for that was but a reënactment of the first. But to Ezra belongs the honor of restoring and rebuilding Jerusalem in its most important sense. And hence he is to this day called by the Jews *"The Restorer of the Law."* The commission of Nehemiah referred chiefly to the secular affairs of Jerusalem, and it

The year 457 B. C. to be taken as the beginning of this period.

may therefore be very properly regarded as a mere appendix to that given by Artaxerxes to Ezra; and hence we think that the year 457 B. C. is to be taken as the beginning of the four hundred and ninety years.

If, then, from 457 B. C. we reckon forty-nine years, we find that the events of that period correspond very exactly with the specifications of the prophecy. For,

Extent and scope of the first period.

1. It was a period of great trouble. (See the fourth chapter of Nehemiah.)

2. It was a period distinguished especially as the era of restoration and reformation. The events recorded in the thirteenth chapter of Nehemiah occurred about forty-

nine years after Ezra received his commission from Artaxerxes.

The second period begins with the year 408 B. C.; and if to this we add four hundred and thirty-four years, it brings us down to the year A. D. 26. *Extent of the second period.* But, according to Archbishop Usher and other distinguished writers on Chronology, Christ was born four years before the epoch which Dionysius Exigüs fixed as the beginning of the Christian Era, and consequently A. D. 26 would exactly correspond with the thirtieth year of the life of Christ. And according to Luke this was the year in which Christ commenced his public ministry.*

The third period is the shortest and most intensely interesting of the three; but, nevertheless, its chronology is not defined with absolute certainty. *Duration of the third period.* It is very remarkable that neither the day of our Savior's birth, nor the day of his baptism, nor the day of his death, is known with absolute certainty. Neither do we know the exact number of days during which his ministry lasted; but in the prophecy it is given at about three and a half years, for it is said that he would be cut off in the midst of the week. And this corresponds very exactly with the testimony of the four Evangelists: for it appears, from the record of John, that Christ's baptism took place sometime—probably about six months—before he attended the first Passover that occurred during his public ministry.† And according to the same Apostle, Christ attended just four Passovers during his ministry.‡ And as this festival occurred but once a year, it follows that Christ's ministry, so far as we can learn from history, must have continued about three years and six months, which is in exact harmony with the words of the prophecy.

* Luke iii: 23.　　　　　† Compare John, chaps. i and ii.
‡ See John ii: 13–17; v: 1–9; vi: 4; and xiii: 1–30.

Here, then, is certainly a most wonderful harmony be-

Harmony of this prophecy with the events of history. tween the various specifications of this prophecy. and the corresponding dates and events of history. *Observe, there is not a single discrepancy in the case.* There are, it is true, some omissions in the minute details of history. But there are no contradictions

Now add to all this the following well-authenticated facts:

1. That from the time of Daniel to the death of Christ, Specifications. the law of Moses was God's chief means of restraining sin and transgression.

2. That Judaism was about that time very greatly weakened, and soon after abolished.

3. That the Christian Church was about that time established, and that it has since become by far the most powerful means of civilization, infidels themselves being judges.

4. That about thirty-six years after the death of Christ, the Roman general Titus did actually destroy Jerusalem, as if by an overflowing deluge; and,

5. That since that time it has been in a state of comparative desolation. Place, I say, alongside of this prophecy all these indubitable facts, and then say, gentle reader, what Conclusion. is your conclusion from the premises. Who but a Being of infinite knowledge could have foreseen these events, fixed these dates, and foretold with such unerring certainty all the various particulars of this eventful prophecy? Concede that the claims of the Bible are just and true, and then all this is plain, simple, and perfectly rational. But deny this; ascribe the book of Daniel to any uninspired man, however learned, and you have, on this hypothesis, an enigma that is far more wonderful and perplexing than the greatest miracle recorded in the Bible. In the one case you have a cause fully adequate to the effect; but in the other, you have an effect without a cause. If, then, thy faith is weak, why choose the harder side?

SECTION V.—PROPHETIC HISTORY OF THE ISRAELITES.—
Daniel x, xi, and xii.

In the tenth, eleventh, and twelfth chapters of the book of Daniel we have the prophet's last recorded vision. It occurred in the third year of the reign of Cyrus, and probably also in the last year of Daniel. *Date of Daniel's last vision.*

It appears that from the beginning of the first month, Abib, till after the feast of unleavened bread, Daniel had been fasting on the banks of the Tigris. The special reasons for this are not given, but it is probable that it was on account of the very discouraging condition and prospects of his people. *The occasion of this vision.*

While he was fasting, an angel appeared to him, very much resembling Jesus Christ, as he appeared to John on the island of Patmos.† He received his commission to go and wait on the afflicted prophet when the latter first began to pray; but it seems that he was detained twenty-one days, in some way and for some reason, by the Prince of Persia. *An angel commissioned to wait on, and comfort Daniel.*

The effect of this vision on Daniel and his companions is next given. (V. 7–9.) And then we have an account of Daniel's being strengthened and encouraged by this heavenly messenger. (V. 10–12.) *Effect of this vision on Daniel and his companions.*

In the fourteenth verse, we have given the general scope of all that follows. *"And now I am come,"* said the angel, *" to make thee understand what shall befall thy people in the latter days; for yet the vision is for many days."* The reader should never forget this in all his attempts to comprehend the several parts of the following prophecy. *General scope of the prophecy.*

In the next four verses following, we have an account of

*Rev. i: 13–16.

Further
strength and
encouragement
to Daniel.
Daniel's further prostration, and of his being again strengthened and encouraged.

Finally, the introductory chapter closes with
God's ambassa-
dors at the
court of Persia.
an account of God's angelic ambassadors at the court of Persia.

After these preliminaries, the angel commenced his pro-
The narrative
given indirect-
ly.
phetic narrative concerning the Israelites. But as there was much in it to distress the aged prophet, and perhaps also for other reasons, the narrative is given, for the most part, *indirectly*, through the history and fortunes of those nations with whom God foresaw the Israelites would be associated, and to whom they would generally be in subjection.

For the sake of perspicuity, I will first quote each section
Proposed order.
of the prophecy, and then explain and illustrate it as briefly as I can.

I. *"Behold there shall stand up yet three kings of Persia. And the fourth shall be far richer than they all. And by his strength, through his riches, he shall stir up all against the realm of Grecia."* (xi: 2.)

The Israelites were at that time subject to the Persians;
Scope and par-
ticulars of the
first section.
and with these, therefore, the angel begins his narrative. The four kings referred to are Cambyses, or Ahasuerus I, Smerdis the usurper, Darius Hystaspes, and Xerxes the Great. In the reign of Xerxes the revenue of the empire, according to Herodotus, was sixty-four million dollars annually. India alone, the twentieth province of the empire, paid into the royal treasury one Euboic talent of gold, or about eighty pounds avoirdupois, every day.*

According to the same historian, the army led by Xerxes against Greece consisted of two millions six hundred and forty-one thousand six hundred and ten fighting men, and

---

* Herodotus, Book iii.   See, also, Diodorus Siculus, x: 3.

at least as many more servants and workmen, making in all about five millions two hundred and eighty-three thousand two hundred and twenty persons.*

II. *"And a mighty king shall stand up, that shall rule with great dominion, and do according to his will. And when he shall stand up, his kingdom shall be broken, and shall be divided toward the four winds of heaven; and not to his posterity, nor according to his dominion which he ruled; for his kingdom shall be plucked up, even for others besides those."* (V. 3, 4.)

After the death of Xerxes nine other kings reigned over Persia. But the angel evidently aims at brevity, and as the invasion of Greece by Xerxes suggests the conquest of Asia by Alexander the Great, he passes immediately from the former to the latter. From the given prophecy we learn,

Scope of the second section.

1. That the principal subject of it would be a mighty king. *Specifications.*

2. That his dominion would be very great.

3. That he would do according to his own will.

4. That his kingdom would be broken.

5. That it would be finally divided into four parts.

6. That it would not be left to his posterity.

7. That none of his successors would have equal power.

All this is clearly applicable to Alexander the Great and his successors. He was himself but twenty years of age when his father, Philip, fell by the hand of Pausanius. Many then tried to throw off the Macedonian yoke. But he very soon brought them all to subjection, and in the spring of 334 B. C. he crossed the Hellespont at the head of thirty thousand infantry and five thousand cavalry, and immediately commenced his career of conquest in Asia. He conquered an army of one hundred and ten thousand Persians on the banks of the river Gran-

Evidence of Alexander's greatness.

* Herodotus, Book vii.

icus, and another of six hundred thousand near the Bay of
Issus. He then captured Tyre, after a siege of seven months,
took Egypt, and again overcome Darius, at the head of an
army of one million soldiers, on the plains of Arbela; and
soon after this he subjugated all the northern and eastern
provinces of the empire, and extended his conquests even beyond Indus. He was, therefore, certainly a mighty king.

His dominion was also a great dominion. In less than ten
Extent of his   years he extended his empire from Ethiopia and
dominion.   the Indian Ocean, on the south, to the Danube
and the Imaus Mountains, on the north, and from the Adriatic,
on the west, to the utmost bounds of civilization on the east.

He was, moreover, extremely self-willed, putting to death
His stubborn-   many of his most intimate friends simply because
ness.   they would not yield implicitly to his own arbitrary dictation; such, for example, as Parmenio, Clitus, Ca-
listhenes, and Orsines.

He died 323 B. C., and after a conference of seven days,
Division of his   it was agreed to by his generals that Alexander's
kingdom.   half-brother, Philip Aridæus, should be invested
with the shadow of royalty, and that each of them should
take charge of a province. Thus his kingdom was at first
divided into thirty-three parts or provinces.

But in less than fifteen years his mother Olympias, his
Fate of his pos-   wife Roxana, his brother Philip Aradæus, his
terity.   son Alexander, his son Hercules, and all his remaining relatives were put to death, and the empire was then
divided into four kingdoms, viz.: Greece, Thrace, Syria, and
Egypt. These were severally governed by Cassander, Lysimachus, Seleucus Nicator, and Ptolemy Lagus, all of them
great princes, but none of them equal to Alexander.*

---

*For a confirmation of all these facts, and many other interesting de-
Works of refer-   tails of this important section of history and prophecy,
ence.   the reader is referred to the original works of Diodorus

III. " *And the king of the south shall be strong, and one of his princes: and he shall be strong above him, and have dominion; his dominion shall be a great dominion.*" Or, as I think the passage might be more clearly and more properly rendered, " *And the king of the south, even one of his (Alexander's) princes, shall be strong: and (another) shall be strong above him, and have dominion; his dominion shall be a great dominion.*" (V. 5.)

In the investigation of this prophecy, it is important to remember that its entire scope has reference to the seed of Abraham, according to the flesh. The narrative, as I before said, is *indirect;* but, nevertheless, it all relates to the fortunes of the twelve tribes, and hence you see why it is that the kingdoms of Macedonia and Thrace are henceforth passed over in silence. These constituted the western portion of Alexander's dominions, and the Jews were, therefore, in no way influenced by either their fortunes or their misfortunes. *Future omission of the kingdoms of Greece and Thrace.*

But it was very different with the kingdoms of Syria and Egypt. For about two hundred and thirty-five years the Israelites were almost constantly harrassed by their mutual jealousies and intrigues. Dependent, as they were, sometimes on the former and sometimes on the latter; and being always situated near the intervening boundaries of these kingdoms, they were compelled, by the force of circumstances, to sympathize and suffer with them in all their wars and revolutions. This is why the angel describes these so very minutely in the following *Minute details of the kingdoms of Syria and Egypt.*

Siculus, Justin, Arrian, and Plutarch. But if these can not be conveniently procured, he will find a very interesting outline and illustration of all these points in Prideaux's Connection, vol. i, Book viii, and also in Rollin's Ancient History, vol. iii, Books xv and xvi. The work of Dean Prideaux is especially valuable to the student of the Bible, and it should have a place in every Bible library. Harper's edition is the one referred to in these notes.

narrative. He could not cheer the heart of the aged prophet by any thing very pleasing and encouraging in the fortunes of his people during this eventful period, and he therefore very benevolently casts a vail over their sufferings and their afflictions, by indirectly describing their condition and circumstances through the history of those nations with which he foresaw they would be politically and geographically associated.

It is also very important to observe, just here, *that Jerusalem is made the stand-point of comparison in all the following geographical allusions.* The king of the North is simply that monarch, or rather succession of monarchs, that ruled over those provinces and districts that lay north of Jerusalem, and the king of the South is used, in like manner, for all those kings that reigned south of Jerusalem.

Geographical stand-point of comparison.

King of the North and king of the South.

The first king of the South was Ptolemy Lagus, called also Ptolemy Soter. He was one of Alexander's princes, and was strong in wealth, in men, and in territory. In the division of the empire he received as his portion Egypt, Libya, Arabia, Cœle-Syria, and Palestine. To these he afterward annexed Cyprus, Phœnicia, part of Lesser Asia, several cities of Greece, and some of the Ægean islands. He also established a college of learned men in Alexandria, founded the famous Alexandrian Library, and did much in many ways to promote the prosperity, power, and influence of Egypt.

First king of the South.

His greatness

But another of Alexander's princes was stronger than Ptolemy. This was Seleucus Nicator, who was at the same time king of the North. After the battle of Ipsus he reigned over most of the provinces of Asia Minor, all Syria proper, Armenia, Mesopotamia, Assyria, Chaldea, Babylonia, Susiana, Media, Persia, Carmania, Aria, Parthia, Gedrosia, Arachosia, Drangi-

First king of the North.

Evidence of his superiority.

ana, Bactriana, Sogdiana, and a portion of India; and having defeated and slain Lysimachus, 281 B. C., he then added to his former possessions the kingdoms of Thrace and Macedonia. His dominion was, therefore, a great dominion.*

IV. "*And in the end of years they shall join themselves together; for the king's daughter of the south shall come to the king of the north to make an agreement; but she shall not retain the power of the arm; neither shall she stand, nor his arm; but she shall be given up, and they that brought her, and he whom she brought forth, and he that strengthened her in these times.*" (V.6.)

The angel here passes over the events of several years, and next notices an attempt that was made to consolidate the two belligerent kingdoms. About the year 256, B. C., Antiochus Theos declared war against Ptolemy Philadelphus, and for six years it was carried on with great violence. But a revolt of nearly all the provinces east of the Tigris made it necessary for Antiochus to conclude a treaty of peace with Ptolemy, and direct all his forces to the suppression of this rebellion. After much court intrigue and political management, it was Treaty between Ptolemy Philadelphus and Antiochus Theos. agreed that Antiochus should put away his wife Laodice, and her two sons; that he should marry Berenice, the daughter of Ptolemy, and that he should entail on her male offspring the crown of Syria

These conditions were all ratified, and faithfully observed during the reign of Ptolemy. Laodice was divorced, and the marriage of Berenice was celebrated with great pomp and solemnity. But as soon as Violation of this treaty. Antiochus heard of the death of his father-in-law, he put

---

* For further details on this section, see Prideaux's Connection, vol i, book viii, pp. 393–425, and vol ii, book i, pp. 1–23; also Rollin's Ancient History, vol. iii, book xvi, chap. ii.

away Berenice, and recalled Laodice. This was the beginning of an awful tragedy. Laodice, knowing
the fickle temper of her husband, and being apprehensive that she and her children might be again sup-
planted, resolved to improve the present opportunity, and
to secure the crown for her own son. She therefore caused
Antiochus to be poisoned; and when she saw him expir-
ing, she placed in his bed, to personate him, a man named
Artemon, who very much resembled the king, both in his
features and in his tone of voice. Artemon performed his
part of the play admirably. He recommended his dear
Laodice and her children to the care and sympathies of the
people, and gave orders that his oldest son by Laodice, Seleucus Callinicus, should be his successor. His death was
then publicly announced, and Seleucus peaceably ascended
the throne, which he enjoyed for the space of twenty years.

What followed.

Laodice, not thinking herself safe while Berenice and her
son were living, concerted measures with Seleucus to destroy them also. Berenice, hearing of
this, fled with her infant son to Daphne, a town
about five miles south of Antioch, where she shut herself up
in an asylum built by Seleucus Nicator; but being at last
betrayed by the guards, first her son and then herself, with
all her Egyptian attendants, were murdered in the basest
and most inhuman manner. Such was the end of Berenice,
and of her husband, and of her son, and of those that accompanied her from her native land; and such was the exact fulfillment of this very remarkable prophecy.*

*Death of Bere-
nice and her
son and attend-
ants.*

V. *"But out of a branch of her roots shall one stand up
in his estate; who shall come with an army, and shall enter
into the fortress of the king of the North, and shall deal
against them, and shall prevail: and shall also carry captives
into Egypt their gods with their princes, and with their precious*

* See Prideaux's Connection, vol. ii, pp. 49–60.

vessels of silver and of gold. And he shall continue more years than the king of the North. So the king of the South shall come into his kingdom, and shall return into his own land." (V. 7–9.)

While Berenice was besieged in Daphne, a report of her misfortune reached Egypt, whereupon her brother, Ptolemy Evergetes, immediately collected a formidable army and hastened to her rescue. Other troops were sent from Asia Minor for the same purpose. But they all came too late. Berenice was murdered before either army reached the place of her confinement. Ptolemy, however, determined to avenge her death. He united his forces with those from Asia Minor, put Laodice to death, and made himself master of Syria and Cilicia. Thus he entered into the fortress of the king of the North. After this he crossed the Euphrates and conquered all the provinces as far as the Tigris; and if the progress of his arms had not been arrested by a sedition, which required his attention in Egypt, he might have subdued the whole Syrian empire. But he left the conquered provinces under the care of two of his generals, and hastened to Alexandria, carrying back with him forty thousand talents of silver, with a prodigious quantity of gold and silver vessels, and two thousand five hundred statues, part of which were the Egyptian idols that Cambyses had carried from Egypt into Persia.

On his way to Egypt he passed through Jerusalem, where he offered many sacrifices to the God of Israel, to whom he seems to have ascribed his great victories, rather than to his own acknowledged idols. It is difficult to account for this extraordinary conduct on any other supposition than that, like Cyrus and Alexander, he had read this remarkable prophecy, which so perfectly accords with the leading events of his life that no one,

properly instructed, can fail so to apply it. Even the four
years that he outlived Seleucus are here made a subject of
prophecy.*

VI. *"But his sons"* (i. e., *the sons of Seleucus Callinicus*)
*" shall be stirred up, and shall assemble a multitude of great
forces. And one of them shall certainly come"* (i. e., *into
Judea*) *" and overflow and pass through. Then shall he return and be stirred up even to his fortress"* (*fortress of the
king of the South*). *" And the king of the South shall be moved
with choler, and shall come forth"* (*toward Judea*), *" and fight
with him, even with the king of the North. And he* (*Antiochus*) *shall set forth a great multitude; but the multitude shall
be given into his* (*Ptolemy's*) *hand."* (V. 10–11.)

These and the following verses, as far as the twentieth,
relate chiefly to Antiochus the Great. Seleucus Callinicus
died a prisoner in Parthia. He left two sons, Seleucus and
Antiochus. The former succeeded his father, and assumed
the title of Ceraunus (*the Thunderer*), though he was very
weak both in mind and body; but weak men most need titles
to support their dignity. His reign was short
and inglorious. At the head of a great army,
he attempted to regain the provinces lost by
his father, but was soon afterward poisoned by two of his
own soldiers, leaving the throne to his brother Antiochus.
The remark of the angel at this point is very significant,
and well illustrates the remarkable precision of the whole
prophecy. Observe, both of the sons of Seleucus were stirred
up; but only one of them was successful. Antiochus having suppressed a rebellion in the
east, turned his forces against Ptolemy Philopater, a most vain, luxurious, and profligate debauchee, who
was then king of Egypt. He first took Seleucia, and then

*Inglorious
reign of Seleu-
cus Ceraunus.*

*First successes
of Antiochus
the Great.*

---

* Prideaux's Connection, vol. ii, pp. 60–70, and Rollin's Ancient History, vol. iii, pp. 856–361.

recovered all Syria, making himself master of some places by treaty, and of others by force of arms.

During the next campaign he defeated Nicholas, the Egyptian general, on the Straits of Mount Lebanon, conquered all Galilee and Persia, and threatened to invade Egypt and attack Ptolemy even in his own fortress; but this, at length, roused from his lethargy this profligate king of the South, and early in the spring of 217 B. C. Ptolemy collected an army of seventy thousand infantry, five thousand cavalry, and seventy-three elephants, and marched to Raphia, a town on the Mediterranean Sea, near the southern borders of Judea. Here he met Antiochus with an army which Rollin estimates at seventy-two thousand infantry, twelve thousand cavalry, and one hundred and two elephants. The result of the battle there fought was the defeat His defeat at of Antiochus, with the loss of ten thousand men Raphia. killed and four thousand taken prisoners. Antiochus fled to Gaza, and thence to Antioch. Soon after this, all Palestine and Cœle-Syria again voluntarily submitted to the conqueror.*

VII. *" And when he hath taken away the multitude, his heart shall be lifted up; and he shall cast down many ten thousands; but he shall not be strengthened by it.* (V. 12.)

Ptolemy, through the aid of his Greek generals, knew better how to gain a victory than to profit by Ptolemy's sub- it. Had he taken advantage of his late success, sequent indis- and of the rebellion that was then actually going cretions. on in Asia Minor, it is generally conceded that he might, in all probability, have deprived Antiochus of his whole empire. But his heart was lifted up by his success, and his love of ease and desire for carnal pleasure, moved him to

* Polybius, Book V; Prideaux's Connection, vol. ii: pp. 70–77; Rollin's Ancient History, vol. iii: pp. 399–408.

agree first to a truce for one year, and afterward to the terms of peace which his enemy proposed.

After the retreat of Antiochus, Ptolemy visited several cities of Cœle–Syria and Palestine. While at Jerusalem he offered many sacrifices, and expressed a desire and intention to go into the Most Holy Place. This produced great excitement and alarm throughout Jerusalem. The High Priest informed him of the sacredness of the place, and of the law of God which forbade his entrance. The Priests and Levites were gathered together to oppose his rash design, and the people besought him to abandon it; but all their entreaties and expostulations only inflamed his excited curiosity. He forced his way as far as the sacred court; but, if we may credit the · author of the third book of Maccabees, just as he was about to enter the temple, God struck him with such a terror and confusion of mind, that he was carried out of the court half dead. Soon after, he left the city greatly exasperated against the whole Jewish nation, on account of what had befallen him, and threatening them with his displeasure and vengeance.

His attempt to enter the Holy of Holies.

When he returned to Alexandria, he began a cruel persecution against the Jews in that city, in which, according to Jerome, sixty thousand of them suffered martyrdom. Thus did he cast down many ten thousands. But neither did his late treaty with Antiochus nor his persecution of the Jews serve to strengthen him.*

His persecution of the Jews.

VIII. "*For the king of the North shall return, and shall set forth a multitude greater than the former; and shall certainly come (into Judea) after certain years, with a great army and with much riches. And in those times there shall many*

* Prideaux's Connection, vol. ii, pp. 77–83; Rollin's Ancient History, vol. iii, pp. 408–411. See also Polybius and other original authorities cited by Prideaux.

stand up against the king of the South; also the robbers (re-volters) of thy people shall exalt themselves to establish the vision, but they shall fall." (V. 13–14.)

For about fourteen years after the battle of Raphia there was peace between Syria and Egypt. In the mean time Antiochus, having taken and beheaded Achæus, the leader of the rebellion in Lesser Asia, and having reduced to subjection Media, Parthia, and some other Eastern provinces, had returned to Antioch with great riches and an immense army. *Successes of Antiochus after the battle of Raphia.*

As soon as he heard of the death of Ptolemy Philopater, and the ascension of his son Ptolemy Epiphanes, who was then but five years of age, he forgot, or rather disregarded, the obligations of the existing treaty, and resolved to extend his dominions by the conquest of Egypt. And in this design Antiochus was not alone. He and Philip, king of Macedon, entered into a league, in which it was stipulated that the latter should have the provinces of Caria, Libya, Cyrene, and Egypt, and that the former should have all the rest of Ptolemy's dominions. At the same time there prevailed in nearly all the provinces of the king of the South a very seditious spirit, owing to the maladministration of Agathocles, his prime minister. Many of the Jews also then revolted from Ptolemy. It was, no doubt, the general expectation that the confederated Syrians and Macedonians would, under the circumstances, very soon take possession of the whole empire, and hence all Cœle-Syria and Palestine submitted to Antiochus with very little opposition. *League between Antiochus and Philip of Macedon.* *Their partial success.*

But the decrees of the Roman Senate soon gave a new aspect to the war. The Egyptians, being greatly distressed on account of the league made against their infant king, sent an embassy to the Romans, soliciting *Interference of the Romans.*

8

their protection, and offering them the guardianship of the king and the regency of the kingdom during his minority. The Romans very willingly accepted this, and sent three ambassadors to Philip and Antiochus, requiring them to desist from any further interference in the affairs of Egypt.

Soon after, while Antiochus was engaged in a war with Attalus, king of Pergamos, the Egyptian ministry sent Scopas, with a great army, into Palestine and Cœle-Syria for the recovery of these provinces. He soon conquered all Judea, put a garrison in the castle at Jerusalem, and returned to Alexandria covered with glory and the spoils of victory. During this campaign many of the revolting Jews were put to death. Josephus says the Jews submitted to Scopas by force, but to Antiochus they submitted willingly.*

(margin: Recovery of Cœle-Syria and Palestine by the Egyptians.)

IX. "*So the king of the north shall come* (*into Judea again*), *and cast up a mount, and take the most fenced cities. And the arms of the south shall not withstand; neither his chosen people; neither shall there be any strength to withstand. But he that cometh against him shall do according to his own will; and none shall stand before him. And he shall stand* (*stand firm, or establish his dominion*) *in the glorious land* (*Judea*) *which by his hand shall be consumed.*" (V. 15, 16.)

On the remonstrance of the Roman Senate, Antiochus withdrew his forces from Pergamus, and again lead them into Cœle-Syria and Palestine. Scopas was sent against him with a choice army. They met at Paneas, near the source of the river Jordan, where the Egyptians were defeated with great slaughter. Scopas fled with ten thousand men to Sidon; but he was so closely and so strongly besieged by Antiochus that, although the government at Alexandria sent for his relief three of their

(margin: Defeat of Scopas by Antiochus.)

* Prideaux's Connection, vol. ii, pp. 83–87; Rollin's Ancient History, vol. iii, pp. 451–454; also, vol. iv, pp. 7–20.

best generals and their most reliable troops, (*chosen people,*) he was forced to surrender, on the condition of life only. He and his troops were then stripped and sent back to Egypt.

Antiochus then took all the most fenced cities and strongholds of Palestine. From this time the king of the North reigned over Judea, *the glorious land,* by whose hand it was consumed, till driven Palestine retaken and held by Antiochus. to desperation by the cruelty and inhumanity of Antiochus Epiphanes, the Jews threw off the Syrian yoke and maintained a nominal independence, until they were subjugated by the Romans, 63 B. C.*

X. "*He shall also set his face to enter with the strength of his whole kingdom, and upright ones with him; thus shall he do: and he shall give him the daughter of women, corrupting her: but she shall not be on his side, neither be for him.*" (V. 17.)

Having conquered Cœle-Syria and Palestine, Antiochus was ready to enter Egypt with the strength of his whole kingdom, composed now of upright Israelites as well as idolatrous Gentiles. But the aspect of affairs in Asia Minor and Greece His purpose to take Egypt, first by arms and then by strategy. seems to have suddenly changed his designs, and, therefore, what he was not prepared to do by force he attempted to accomplish by stratagem and diplomacy. With a fraudulent design, as Jerome informs us, he sent an ambassador to Alexandria, with proposals of marriage between Ptolemy and his own beautiful daughter Cleopatra. The conditions were accepted, and the marriage afterward consummated. But the promised dowry, and all the other attempts of Antiochus to *corrupt* his daughter, could not alienate her from the interests of her husband. Faithful to his cause, she even accompanied an embassy sent to Cleopatra true to the interests of her husband. congratulate the Romans after they had defeated her father at

* Prideaux, vol. ii, pp. 87, 88; Rollin, vol. iv, p. 20.

Thermopylæ, and to exhort them not only to drive him out of Greece, but also to carry the war into Asia.*

XI. *"After this, he shall turn his face in to the isles, and shall take many: but a prince for his own behalf shall cause the reproach offered by him to cease; without his own reproach he shall cause it to turn upon him."* (V. 18.)

When Antiochus thought he had secured the favor of Ptolemy by the proposed marriage, he turned his face to the islands of the sea. With a fleet of one hundred large ships of war and two hundred smaller vessels, he subdued some of the most important maritime places on the coasts of Greece, Thrace, and Asia Minor, and took Samos, Euba, and several other islands in the Ægean and Mediterranean Seas. But the Romans soon turned the tide of his fortune. Acilius routed his army at Thermopylæ, Livius and Æmilius defeated his fleet in two successive engagements, and, finally, Lucias Cornelius Scipio gained a decisive victory over him in Asia Minor, near the city Magnesia, at the foot of Mount Siphylus. Antiochus lost fifty thousand infantry and four thousand cavalry slain on the field of battle; one thousand four hundred more were taken prisoners, and he himself escaped with difficulty to Sardis.†

Conquests of Antiochus in the Ægean and Mediterranean.

His subsequent reverses and defeat by the Romans.

XII. *"Then he shall turn his face toward the fort of his own land: but he shall stumble and fall, and not be found."* (V. 19.)

From Sardis Antiochus went to Celænæ, in Phrygia, to join his son Seleucus, and thence made all possible haste to "the fort of his own land." As soon as he arrived at Antioch he sent his nephew, Antipater, and Zeuxis, former governor of Lydia and Phrygia, to desire peace with the Romans. A treaty was made at Sar-

His treaty with the Romans.

---

* Prideaux, vol. ii, pp. 88–92; Rollin, vol. iv, pp. 20 21.

† Prideaux, vol. ii, pp. 92–96; Rollin, vol. iv, pp. 45–76.

dis, and afterward ratified by the Roman Senate, in which it was agreed that Antiochus should deliver up Hannibal, the Carthagenian, and Thoas, the Etolian, who were the chief instigators of the war; that he should defray all its expenses, which were estimated at fifteen thousand Euboic talents; that he should quit all Asia Minor west of Mount Taurus, and that he should give twenty hostages for the faithful performance of the stipulated conditions of the treaty.

Soon after this, five hundred talents were paid to the consul at Ephesus, two thousand five hundred more were to be paid as soon as the Senate would ratify the treaty, and the rest in twelve annual installments. Antiochus was greatly perplexed to make these payments. He made a tour through his eastern provinces to collect his revenues. When he arrived at Elymais he was informed that there was a great amount of treasure in the temple of Jupiter Belus. This temptation was too strong for a prince pressed as he then was for money, and, at the same time, destitute of moral principle, and, therefore, *he stumbled and fell.* Under a false pretense, he entered the temple by night, and carried away all the wealth that had been treasured up there for many years; but when the people heard of it, they were so greatly exasperated that they immediately slew him and all his attendants, 185 B. C.* Death of Antiochus.

XIII. "*Then shall stand up in his estate a raiser of taxes in the glory of the kingdom. But within a few days he shall be destroyed, neither in anger nor in battle.*" (V. 20.)

This is a perfect miniature of Seleucus Philopater, the son and successor of Antiochus the Great. The annual payment of one thousand talents to the Romans, besides meeting the expenses of his own government, rendered the taxes of the provinces very oppressive during his entire reign. He sent his treasurer, Heliodorus, Reign of Seleucus Philopater.

---

* Prideaux, vol. ii, pp. 97, 98; Rollin, vol. iv, pp. 79–87.

to rob the temple at Jerusalem, but the God of Israel inter-
fered to prevent this sacrilege. After a feeble and ignomin-
ious reign of eleven years, or prophetic days, he was cut off,
neither in anger nor in battle, but by the secret treachery of
his own treasurer, Heliodorus, 175 B. C.*

XIV. "*And in his estate shall stand up a vile person, to
whom they shall not give the honor of the kingdom; but he
shall come in peaceably, and obtain the kingdom by flatteries.*"
(V. 21.)

The subject of this section is Antiochus Epiphanes, son of
Antiochus the Great, and brother of the late
king. He was one of the twenty hostages chosen
and delivered for the faithful performance of all
the conditions and terms of the treaty which his father had
made with the Romans after the battle of Magnesia. In
this capacity he remained in Italy thirteen years; but for
some reason his brother Seleucus wished him to return to
Antioch, and, in order to obtain him, he sent to Rome, as
a substitute, his only son, Demetrius, who was then about
twelve years of age. Antiochus was set at liberty, and had
returned as far as Athens, when he heard that Heliodorus,
having poisoned Seleucus, was endeavoring to usurp the
throne, and, moreover, that a strong party had declared in
favor of his own sister, Cleopatra, queen of Egypt. He
also knew that Demetrius, who was then a hostage at Rome,
was the lawful heir and successor of Seleucus. But, notwithstanding all these obstacles, he resolved that he would,
if possible, be the next king of Syria, and what he could
not obtain by the right of birth or by the choice of the
people, he determined to secure by his flatteries. Accordingly, by flattering speeches and fair promises, he gained the
assistance of Eumenes, king of Pergamos, against Heliodorus. At the same time he greatly flattered the Syrians,

How Antiochus Epiphanes se-cured the throne of Syria.

* Prideaux, vol. ii, pp. 102–105: Rollin, vol. iv, pp. 87–121.

so that, by a show of clemency, he secured their favor, and thus, without very much opposition from any of his competitors, he came in peaceably, and obtained the kingdom by flatteries.

He afterward assumed the title of Epiphanes, *i. e.*, the *Illustrious.* But Daniel here calls him a vile His character. person, and many of his contemporaries called him *Epimanes,* or *the madman,* on account of his low, base, and lascivious demeanor. We learn, from the writings of Polybius, Philarchus, Livy, and other heathen historians, that he would often leave his palace, with two or three of his domestics, and ramble up and down the streets of Antioch; that he would visit the shops of goldsmiths, and dispute with them about the merest trifles of their art; that he would associate, drink, and carouse with the very dregs of the people; that he would go uninvited to parties of pleasure, and indulge in all the vanities, follies, and wanton fooleries of the young; that he would often lay aside his royal dress, put on a Roman gown, and assume the character of a Roman politician; that he would spend large portions of his revenue in fits of drunkenness, revelry, and debauchery; that he would sometimes leave his palace and walk about the streets in a Roman dress, with a crown of roses on his head, and stones under his garments to pelt any who would attempt to follow him on such occasions; that he would bathe in the public baths, and disgust all present by his obscene behavior; and, in short, that his general demeanor proved him to-be a vile and despicable person.*

XV. "*And with the arms of a flood shall they be overflown before him, and shall be broken; yea, also the Prince of the Covenant. And after the league made with him he shall work deceitfully: for he shall come up and become strong with a small people. And he shall enter peaceably, even upon*

---

*Prideaux, vol. ii, pp. 97–107; Rollin, vol. iv, pp. 71, 121.

the fattest places of the province. And he shall do that which his fathers have not done, nor his fathers' fathers; he shall scatter among them the prey, and spoil, and riches." (V. 22–24.)

Notwithstanding Antiochus's eccentricities and the debasing idiosyncrasies of his character, the prophet foresaw that he would succeed in his ambitious designs, and become powerful. All his competitors for the crown were swept away

His treacherous dealing with the High Priest.

from before him as if by a flood; and Onias, the Prince of the Covenant, or High Priest of the Jews, was also deposed, and his office was sold to his brother Jason for three hundred and sixty talents of silver. But after the contract was made with Jason, Antiochus worked deceitfully: for three years afterward, he again sold the High Priesthood to his younger brother, Menelaus, for three hundred talents more.

What follows, as far as the last clause of the twenty-fourth verse, is a mere recapitulation and amplification of what precedes. From Rome Antiochus came up to Antioch with only a few attendants, and for a short time he had but a few

His means of success.

adherents in Syria; but through the favor of Eumenes, the influence of his own insinuating manner, and the prodigality of his gifts, he soon became strong, and took possession of the eastern as well as most of the western provinces, for he did that which neither his fathers nor his fathers' fathers had done. With a profuseness before unknown, he scattered among the people the prey of his enemies, the spoils of their temples, the riches of his friends, and even the surplus of his own revenues. Jose-

Evidence of his extravagance and liberality.

phus says, "In his gifts he was magnanimous and munificent." The author of the first book of Maccabees says, that "in the liberality of his gifts he abounded above the kings that were before him." And Polybius mentions several instances of his extravagance. Among other things, he says that Antiochus would sometimes bestow very large gifts on entire strangers, and that at other times, standing in the public streets, he would throw handfuls of money among the people, saying, "Let him take it to whom fortune sends it."[*]

XVI. "*And he shall forecast his devices against (upon) the strongholds (fortifications) for a time.*" (V. 24.)

Ptolemy Epiphanes died 180 B. C., and was succeeded by his son, Ptolemy Philometor, who was then only six years of age. His first guardian was his mother, Cleopatra, the sister of Antiochus Epiphanes, king of Syria. During her life peace continued between the king of the North and the king of the South; but after her death, and until the young prince reached his majority, the affairs of Egypt were administered by Lennæus, an Egyptian nobleman, and Eulæus, one of Ptolemy's pedagogues. Soon after these men entered upon the duties of their office, they demanded of Antiochus the provinces of Cœle-Syria and Palestine, on the ground that they belonged to Ptolemy Soter, according to the distribution that was made of Alexander's empire after the battle of Ipsus, and also because that Antiochus the Great had promised to restore them to Ptolemy, as the dower of his daughter Cleopatra; but Antiochus denied the justice of both these claims, and in anticipation of war, he, for a time, forecast his devices by repairing and strengthening the strongholds and fortified cities of these provinces.[†]

Ground of diffi-culty and dis-pute between Antiochus and Ptolemy Philo-metor.

XVII. "*And he shall stir up his power and his courage against the king of the South with a great army. And the king of the South shall be stirred up to battle with a great and mighty army; but he shall not stand, for they shall forecast devices against him. Yea, they that feed of a portion of his*

---

[*] Prideaux, vol. ii, pp. 107–110; Josephus, vol. i, p. 407.
[†] Prideaux, vol. ii, pp. 109, 110; Rollin, vol. iv, p. 122.

meat shall destroy him; and his army shall overflow, and many shall fall down slain. And both these kings' hearts shall be to do mischief; and they shall speak lies at one table; but it shall not prosper, for yet the end shall be at the appointed time. Then shall he return into his land with great riches." (V. 25–28.)

Antiochus, having made all necessary preparations for a

Success of Antiochus during the first campaign. war with Ptolemy, resolved not to wait for the enemy, but to attack him in his own fortress. The first battle was fought between Mount Casius and Pelusium, in which Antiochus was victorious. Early the next spring, 171 B. C., he lead another army against Ptolemy, routed his forces on the frontiers of Egypt,

His gains during the second. took Pelusium, Memphis, and all the other fortified cities of Egypt, except Alexandria. Ptolemy also fell into his hands, in some way which history does not record; but it is generally conceded that the misfortunes which at that time befell Egypt were not owing so much to the cowardice and incapacity of her king as to the injudicious and malicious conduct of those who fed upon a portion of his meat, and especially to the corrupting influence of Eulæus, his instructor and guardian. This man had purposely led his royal pupil into every extreme of lux-

Defect in Ptolemy's education. ury and effeminacy, to render him the more incapable of managing his own affairs and the concerns of his kingdom, and thereby to secure for himself, during the king's majority, the same office which he had so much abused during his minority. Ptolemy was therefore wholly unfit for the crisis. While in the field he always kept himself as far out of danger as possible, and by his very effeminate demeanor he so disgusted many of his friends and other citizens of Alexandria that they forsook

Party formed against him. him, and the following year, made his younger brother, Evergetes, king in his stead. In this dilemma, it is most probable that he voluntarily surrendered himself to his uncle Antiochus for protection.

Be this as it may, of this we are certain, that for some time the uncle and the nephew were associated together as guardian and ward in the interests of Egypt. They ate at the same table, and professed for each other the most cordial friendship. Antiochus expressed much concern for the welfare of Philomator, and the latter acknowledged his very great obligations to his uncle, and laid the whole blame of the war on Eulæus, his prime minister. But all this was a mere game of deception and falsehood; for Ptolemy embraced the very first opportunity of freeing himself from the restraints and guardianship of his uncle; and as soon as Antiochus had secured the peaceable possession of the country, he seized upon whatever he saw fit, and enriched himself and his soldiers with the spoils of the Egyptians. Thus did he return to his own land with great riches.*

Mutual false pretensions of both Antiochus and Ptolemy.

XVIII. *"And his heart shall be against the holy covenant, and he shall do exploits, and return to his own land."* (V. 28.)

While Antiochus was in Egypt, a false report of his death was spread throughout Palestine, and Jason thought this a fit opportunity to regain the High Priesthood. He therefore collected together about one thousand men, and marched against Jerusalem. Many of the citizens joined him, with whose aid he easily overcame the rest, drove out Menelaus, and unmercifully put to death all who fell into his hands, and whom he regarded as his enemies.

Report of the death of Antiochus.

When Antiochus heard this, he supposed that the Jews had made a general insurrection, and he therefore set out immediately to quell it.

His barbarous treatment of the Jews.

* Prideaux, vol. ii, pp. 113, 114; Rollin, vol. iv, pp. 124, 125.

What most exasperated him was his being informed that the inhabitants of Jerusalem greatly rejoiced when they heard the report of his death. He therefore besieged the city, took it by storm, and for three days gave it up to the fury and avarice of his soldiers, in which time eighty thousand men were inhumanly butchered, forty thousand were made prisoners, and as many more were sold into slavery.

After this Antiochus entered the Temple, explored the Holy and the Most Holy Place, offered swine's flesh on the altar of burnt offerings, contemptuously sprinkled broth, made of the same, on the Temple, carried away the altar of incense, the table of shew-bread, the candlestick, and the other golden vessels, to the value of one thousand eight hundred talents of gold. He then robbed other parts of the city, and returned to Antioch loaded with the immense spoils of both Egypt and Judea.*

XIX. *"At the appointed time he shall return and come to the south; but it shall not be as the former or as the latter (invasion). For the ships of Chittim shall come against him; therefore shall he be grieved, and return, and have indignation against the Holy Covenant. So shall he do; he shall even return, and have intelligence with them that forsake the Holy Covenant."* (V. 29, 30.)

The next spring, 169 B. C., Antiochus returned into Egypt with a determination to finish the work of its
His purpose to entire subjugation, and especially to vanquish
reduce Egypt
by civil wars. the party that was now becoming powerful under Ptolemy Evergetes, the younger brother of Philometor. He first led his army against Alexandria; but this fortress was found to be impregnable. He then changed his plan of conquest, and resolved to weaken Egypt, and thereby to secure it the more readily by keeping up a civil war between the two brothers, who were then contending for the crown;

* Prideaux, vol. ii, p. 115; Rollin, vol. iv, pp. 124, 125.

and he therefore raised the siege of Alexandria, led his army to Memphis, and invested Philometor with such power and authority as he thought would enable him to withstand the forces of Evergetes; and he himself then returned to Antioch.

But, to his great mortification, he soon learned that Philometor had played the hypocrite as well as him- His disappoint-self; that he had been fully reconciled to his ment.
brother Evergetes, and that the two were then reigning jointly in Alexandria.

He then laid aside the mask, and publicly proclaimed his intention to take Egypt by force. The winter Resolution to was spent in making preparations for the war. take all Egypt by force. Early the next spring, 168 B. C., he sent his fleet to Cyprus, and, at the same time, he himself led a powerful army into Egypt. But this invasion was not like either the first or the second; for while he was breathing vengeance against Alexandria, within four miles Roman inter-of the city, he was met by ambassadors who had ference.
just arrived in ships from Chittim or Italy, and who, at the request of Ptolemy, had been sent by the Roman Senate to forbid his further interfering with the affairs of Egypt. With one of them, Caius Popilius, Antiochus had formed a very pleasant and familiar acquaintance at Rome, and, therefore, as soon as he recognized him, he offered to embrace him as his old friend; but Popilius declined the compliment, saying that his country's interests should be placed before private friendships, and that he must, therefore, know whether he was an enemy or a friend to the Roman people. He then handed to him the written decree of the Senate. Antiochus read it, and said he would consult with his friends, and speedily give him such an answer as they would advise. But Popilius, with the wand that he had in his hand, drew a mark around Antiochus, and,

in a very firm and decided manner, said, "Answer the Senate before you stir out of that circle!" This was certainly a very haughty demand, but Antiochus had lived long enough at Rome to understand it, and, in a few minutes, he said, " I will act according to the request of the Senate."

This put an end to the war, but not to the evil temper and malicious disposition of Antiochus. He left Egypt in great wrath, on account of his disappointment, breathing vengeance against the unoffending Jews. When he came to Palestine, he sent Apollonius, with twenty-two thousand men, to destroy Jerusalem. For a few days after his arrival, this general concealed his diabolical purpose; but, on the next Sabbath, when the people were all collected in their synagogues for social worship, he ordered his troops to execute his bloody commission. The men were butchered, the women and children were taken captives, and the city was plundered, and much of it consumed by fire.

Revengeful spirit of Antiochus against the Jews.

Diabolical conduct of Apollonius.

Apollonius then built a strong tower on an eminence in the city of David, and filled it with soldiers and military stores for the further execution of the will of his majesty. The temple worship was then wholly suspended, and the entire city was given up to these idolaters.

This was but a part of the malicious purpose of Antiochus. He was resolved to execute the same summary vengeance on all the Jews throughout his dominions. As soon, therefore, as he returned to Antioch, he published a decree in which he required all the people of his empire to worship the same gods that he worshiped, and to observe exclusively the same religious ceremonies. As he anticipated, the Gentiles submitted to this decree without much opposition. Many of the Jews also apostatized, and became the most zealous ex-

Intolerant decree of Antiochus.

ecutioners of the king's decree. Thus had he intelligence with them that forsook the Holy Covenant. Others patiently suffered martyrdom, "not accepting deliverance that they might obtain a better resurrection."

But in Modin, a town in the inheritance of Dan, the standard of opposition was raised by Matta- Fidelity of Mattthias and his five sons, Johannan Kaddis, five sons. Simon Thassi, Judas Maccabæus, Eleazar Avaran, and Jonathan Apphus. They were priests of the course of Jehoiarib, and all zealously devoted to the laws and institutions of Moses. Mattathias, seeing a Jew offering sacrifice on a heathen altar, ran upon the apostate and slew him. At the same time, Apelles, the Syrian commander, and all his retinue, were put to death. This was the first of a series of heroic exploits that once more secured to Israel for a time their national independence. Mattathias did not live to see the issue. Worn down with the fatigues of the first campaign, he died 166 B. C., having appointed his son Judas Maccabæus his successor.

Judas was eminently qualified for the crisis. With a comparatively small force, he defeated the armies Exploits and of Antiochus, first under Apollonius, governor Judas Maccaof Samaria, then under Seron, deputy-governor bæus. of Cœle-Syria, afterward under Nicanor, lieutenant of Ptolemy Macron, who was then acting as governor of Cœle-Syria and Phœnicia. Soon after this he routed the army of Timotheus, governor of the country beyond the Jordan, and, finally, that of Lysias, a nobleman of the royal family, to whom the king had committed the government of all the provinces west of the Euphrates, with special orders to destroy the whole Jewish nation and distribute their land to others, while he was himself attempting to restore order in the eastern portions of his empire. After these victories, Judas led his army to Jerusalem, pulled down the heathen altar, cleansed the temple, supplied it with new furniture, and restored the Mosaic laws and ordinances of worship.

Antiochus was at Ecbatana, in Media, when he heard of the defeat of Nicanor and Timotheus. He immediately set out for Judea, threatening vengeance and utter ruin to the whole Jewish nation. When near Babylonia, he received further intelligence that Judas had also defeated Lysias, retaken Jerusalem, cast down the images and altars that he had set up, and fully restored the worship of the God of Israel. When he had received this message he became perfectly furious, and commanded his charioteers to double their speed, that he might the sooner satiate his vengeance on the devoted Israelites, declaring that he would make Jerusalem the burying-place of the whole nation, and that he would not leave within it a single inhabitant. But while he was uttering these boastful words the hand of God smote him. He was immediately seized with the most excruciating agony, and, after suffering indescribable torments of both mind and body, he expired at Tabae, on the borders of Babylonia, an object of disgust to all spectators. Such was the awful and monumental end of this "*vile person,*" according to the united testimony of Polybius, Josephus, and the author of the first book of Maccabees.*

Death of Antiochus.

XX. "*And arms shall stand on his part, (or in his place,) and they shall pollute the sanctuary of strength, and shall take away the daily sacrifice, and they shall place the abomination that maketh desolate.*" (V. 31. Compare Matthew xxiv: 15.)

All this evidently refers to the Roman army. From the death of Antiochus Epiphanes, 164 B. C., to the time of the Roman invasion, the Jews, though greatly harassed by the Syrians, maintained in some measure their national independence, and the services

Independence of the Jews after the death of Antiochus.

* See on this section Prideaux, vol. ii, pp. 116–136; Rollin, vol. iv, pp. 128–140; and Josephus, vol. i, pp. 410–419.

of the temple were daily and regularly performed. But in the year 65 B. C., the Roman armies stood up and were firmly established in the place of Antiochus. At that time Pompey the Great reduced all Syria to a Roman province, and two years after that, having been requested to decide upon the claims of Hyrcanus and his brother Aristobulus to the miter and the crown of Israel, Pompey led a great army into Judea, took Aristobulus captive, slew twelve thousand of his party, who had taken refuge in the temple, broke down the walls of Jerusalem, restored Hyrcanus to the office of high priest, and made him prince over the whole country, on condition that he should pay an annual tribute to the Romans; but he took away his crown, and confined his jurisdiction to the old limits of Judea.

Roman conquest of Syria and Palestine.

In A. D. 8, Archelaus, son of Herod the Great, was condemned for maladministration, and banished to Gaul, and Judea was then reduced to a Roman province.

Judea reduced to a Roman province.

From that time the power of life and death was taken away from the Jews, and their bill of rights was, in many other respects, very much restricted. But the scepter had not yet wholly departed from Judah, because Shiloh had not yet come in his official capacity. The Jews still had their Sanhedrim and inferior courts of judicature, and still they continued to worship God according to their own laws and institutions.

The scepter not yet wrested from Judah.

But when they crucified the Lord of life and glory, the cup of their iniquity was full. Anarchy, disorder, and rebellion rapidly increased among the people till Titus set up the Roman ensigns, or symbols of abomination and desolation, around Jerusalem, demolished its walls, dug up its foundations, slew one million one hundred thousand of its inhabitants, polluted and

Destruction of Jerusalem by the Romans.

9

afterward destroyed the temple or sanctuary of strength, and put an end to the daily sacrifices, A. D. 70.*

XXI. *"And such as do wickedly against the covenant shall be corrupt by flatteries."* (V. 32.)

The change of number here, from the plural to the singular, is very significant. The Roman army first invaded Judea in the days of the republic. No one *will* then governed all the provinces. The Roman army, under the consuls, was the terror of nations, and the proper subject of prophecy relating to the conquest of kingdoms; and hence, even in the destruction of Jerusalem, the eye of the angel still rests on the desolating army. But now there is a change from the army to the emperor. A new system of religion and philosophy was now threatening to desolate the temples of the Romans, to break down their altars, destroy their images, change their literature, and revolutionize the manners and customs of the whole empire. To prevent this the most dreadful penalties were threatened, and the highest rewards were offered by the successive emperors; and these, in many cases, were quite effectual. The temptations offered were too strong for all who could be influenced by a time-serving policy. Multitudes of converted Jews, as well as Gentiles, were corrupted or caused to dissemble by these imperial flatteries. They transgressed the Covenant, renounced Christianity, and sacrificed to the statues of the emperor and the images of his gods.

Agency and policy of the Roman emperors.

XXII. *"But the people that do know their God shall be strong and do exploits: and they that understand among the people shall instruct many."* (V. 32, 33.)

Exploits of the Apostles and other primitive teachers of Christianity.

There is not on record, within the same compass, a more graphic description of the lives and labors of the Apostles and other primitive teachers of Christianity, than we have given here in

*Josephus, vol. ii, pp. 870–442.

these prophetic words. That most of the early proclaimers of the Gospel were of the seed of Abraham according to the flesh is universally conceded; and that they performed a series of exploits unparalleled in the history of the world, can easily be proved by the united testimony of Jews and Pagans, as well as Christians. Never since time began was there a more unequal contest, so far as it respects human power, than was the war between Christianity and the combined systems of Jewish and Gentile superstition. The advocates of the former were generally without learning, without wealth, and without political influence. They had to contend against prejudices strengthened by the growth of ages; against the learning, wealth, power, and secular interests of all the proud Rabbis, philosophers, and political despots of the world; and more than all that, had to overcome and hold in abeyance all the sinful propensities of man's unsanctified nature. But they shrunk not from the contest. Enlightened by the Spirit of God, and clothed with the power of Omnipotence, they commenced their holy warfare, according to prophecy, in the city of Jerusalem. Thence the tocsin was sounded throughout Judea, Syria, Asia Minor, and all other parts of the Roman empire. Every-where the cry was heard, "These that have turned the world upside down are come hither also." Philosophers were confounded, tyrants trembled, idols fell, temples decayed, altars moldered, and vast multitudes in all parts and from all the sects of the known world became obedient to the faith. Such were the effects produced, the revolutions wrought, and the victories won by the Holy Twelve and their coadjutors in the proclamation of the everlasting Gospel. "While the Roman empire," says Gibbon, "was invaded by open violence, or undermined by slow decay, a pure and humble religion gently insinuated itself into the minds of men, grew up in silence and obscurity, derived new vigor from opposition, and, finally, erected the triumphant banner of the Cross on the ruins of the capitol."*

XXIII. " *Yet they shall fall by the sword, and by famine, and by captivity, and by spoil, many days.*" (V. 33.)

For about three hundred years after the death of Christ, all Christians, and especially the converted He-brews, were objects of both Jewish and Gentile persecution. Sometimes, as in the case of Ste-phen, they were put to death through the mere envy, malice, and popular fury of the multitude; but more frequently their martyrdom was sanctioned by the laws of the empire. The emperors Nero, Domitian, Trajan, Marcus Antoninus, Sep-timus Severus, Maximinus, Decius, Valerian, Aurelian, and Dioclesian, according to Augustine, all published decrees au-thorizing the persecution of the saints. It is not in harmony with my purpose to enter much into details, but the follow-ing brief extract from Gibbon, touching the ten years' per-secution of Dioclesian and his two colleagues, Maximian and Galerius, will be interesting to the reader: " The next day the *general edict* of persecution was published, in which it was enacted that the Christian churches in all the provinces of the empire should be demolished to their foundations, and the punishment of death was denounced against all who should presume to hold any secret assemblies for the purpose of religious worship. It was further decreed that the bishops and presbyters should deliver all their sacred books into the hands of the magistrates, who were commanded, under the severest penalties, to burn them in a public and solemn manner. By the same edict the prop-erty of the church was at once confiscated, and the several parts of which it might consist were either sold to the high-est bidder, united to the imperial domain, bestowed on the cities and corporations, or granted to the solicitations of

Persecution of the primitive Christians.

Extract from Gibbon.

---

* Gibbon, vol. i, p. 66, Lond. edit.

rapacious courtiers. After taking such effectual measures to abolish the worship and dissolve the government of Christians, it was thought necessary to subject to the most intolerable hardships the condition of those who should still reject the religion of nature, of Rome, and of their ancestors. Persons of a liberal birth were declared incapable of holding any honors or employments, slaves were forever deprived of the hopes of freedom, and the whole body of the people were put out of the protection of the law. The judges were authorized to hear and to determine every action that was brought against a Christian; but the Christians were not permitted to complain of any injury which they themselves had suffered, and thus those unfortunate sectaries were exposed to the severity, while they were excluded from the benefits, of public justice." Other decrees followed. The same historian adds: "The resentment or the fears of Dioclesian at length transported him beyond the bounds of moderation, which he had hitherto preserved, and he declared, in a series of cruel edicts, *his intention of abolishing the Christian name.* By the first of these edicts, the governors of the provinces were directed to apprehend all persons of the ecclesiastical order, and the prisons destined for the vilest criminals were soon filled with a multitude of bishops, presbyters, deacons, readers, and exorcists. By a second decree, the magistrates were commanded to employ every method of severity which might reclaim them from their odious superstitions, and oblige them to return to the established worship of the gods. This rigorous order was extended, by a subsequent edict, *to the whole body of Christians,* who for ten years were exposed to a violent and general persecution."*

The effect of these edicts may be better imagined than

---

* Gibbon, vol. ii, chap. xvi. See, also, Waddington's Church History pp. 58–69; Mosheim, vol. i, pp. 51–59, 97, 105, 156–160, 208–211, etc.

described. The number of Christians that suffered death under their influence was so great that at one time Diocle- sian and his colleagues seem to have thought that they had really accomplished their diabolical purpose, and, in a pom-
pous inscription, they announced to the world that they had "extinguished the Christian name and superstition, and every-where restored the worship of the gods to its former purity and luster." But these were vain words, for Christ had said, "On this rock I will build my Church, and the Gates of Hades shall not prevail against it."

XXIV. "*Now when they shall fall, they shall be helped with a little help; but many shall cleave to them with flatter- ies.*" (V. 34.)

These words evidently relate to the help which the *con-*
verted Hebrews, as well as all other Christians, received from the Emperor Constantine. In A. D. 306 he was proclaimed Emperor of the West by the army of Gaul and Britain, and immediately he granted full liberty of worship to all his subjects. After his victory over Maxentius, A. D. 312, he became master of the whole Western empire, and in connection with Licinius, the emperor of the eastern provinces, he published a decree of universal toleration. This was soon followed by the special edict of Milan, in wh'n it was required that all places of worship and public lands which had been confiscated should be restored to the church without dispute, without delay, and without expense. In A. D. 324, Constantine became sole emperor, and the edict of Milan was then republished as the law of the whole empire.*

Had Constantine properly comprehended the true genius

---

* Murdock's Mosheim, vol. i, pp. 211–213; Waddington's Church His- tory, p. 105. See, also, Gibbon, vol. ii, chaps. 14–16, and Lardner's Credi- bility, vol. viii, p. 335, Lond. edit.

of the Christian religion, and merely, as in these United States, granted to all his subjects the right to worship God according to the dictates of their own reason and conscience, he would have rendered Their advantages and disadvantages. very important service to the cause of Christianity, and very greatly helped the Hebrew Christians. In this way the earth may still do much to help the woman. But by the union of church and state, by abolishing paganism and making Christianity the religion of the empire, and himself the arbiter of all ecclesiastical controversies, he has left it doubtful, in the estimation of many, whether, on the whole, his course was really a benefit or an injury to the church. It is certain that the aforesaid edicts of Constantine gave some temporary relief and advantages to Christians; and hence the Angel said that, after a long period of persecution, the converted Israelites would receive *a little help*. But he anticipated the evils that would soon result from this political interference, and, therefore, immediately added, *"But many shall cleave unto them with flatteries."*

"It is evident," says Mosheim, "that the victories of Constantine the Great, and both the fear of punishment and the desire of pleasing the Roman emperors, were cogent reasons, in view of whole Extracts from Mosheim and Gibbon. nations as well as of individuals, for embracing the Christian religion."* And the skeptical but eloquent Gibbon adds: "By the edicts of toleration, he (Constantine) removed the temporal disadvantages which had hitherto retarded the progress of Christianity, and its active and numerous ministers received a free permission, a liberal encouragement, to recommend the salutary truths of revelation by every argument which could affect the reason or the piety of mankind. The exact balance of the two religions continued but for a moment, and the piercing eye of ambition and avarice soon

---

* Murdock's Mosheim, vol. i, p. 227.

discovered that the profession of Christianity might contribute to the interests of the present as well as of a future life. The hopes of wealth and honors, the example of an emperor—his exhortations, his irresistible smiles—diffused conviction among the venal and obsequious crowds which usually fill the apartments of a palace. The cities which signalized a forward zeal by the voluntary destruction of their temples were distinguished by municipal privileges and rewarded with popular donations; and the new capital of the east gloried in the singular advantage that Constantinople was never profaned by the worship of idols. As the lower ranks of society are governed by imitation, the conversion of those who possessed any eminence of birth, of power, or of riches, was soon followed by the dependent multitudes."*

XXV. "*And some of them of understanding shall fall, to try them, and to purge, and to make them white even to the time of the end; because it is yet for a time appointed.*" (V. 35.)

Scarcely had persecution ceased from without when it be-

Internal perse-
cutions of the
Church.

gan to rage from within. The edicts of Constantine were far more potent in restraining the diabolical fury of the heathen than in enlightening, humbling, and sanctifying the minds and hearts of either the ruled or the rulers of a sectarian church. Controversies arose about Arianism, Pelagianism, Nestorianism, Eutychianism, Monophysitism, Monothelitism, the worship of images, and various other heresies, in all of which imperial favor and the terrors of martyrdom had much more influence than the inspired oracles of the Old and the New Testament. The testimony of Gibbon is again in point. He says: "The simple narrative of intestine divisions, which distracted the peace and dishonored the triumph of the church, will confirm the remark of a pagan historian, and justify the complaint of a venerable bishop. The experi-

---

* Gibbon, vol. ii, pp. 465, 466. Lond. edit.

ence of Ammianus convinced him that the enmity of the Christians toward each other surpassed the fury of savage beasts against men. And Gregory Nazianzen most pathetically laments that the kingdom of heaven was converted by discord into the image of chaos, of a nocturnal tempest, and of hell itself."*

In this protracted warfare, as in most similar cases, the most intelligent, virtuous, and godly men were often the victims of persecution. The same Divine wisdom that permitted the Apostles to seal their testimony with their own blood, and the dying martyrs of the west to bear witness to the truth, was also pleased to allow many in the east, and especially of the *Hebrew converts*, to fall, to try them, and to purge them, and to keep them white, even from the reign of Constantine to the end of the Greek empire.

God's design in permitting these.

XXVI. "*And the king shall do according to his will. And he shall exalt himself and magnify himself above every god; and he shall speak marvelous things against the God of gods, and shall prosper till the indignation be accomplished. For that that is determined shall be done. Neither shall he regard the God of his fathers, nor the desire of women, nor regard any god; for he shall magnify himself above all. But in his estate he shall honor the god of forces. And a god whom his fathers knew not shall he honor with gold, and silver, and precious stones, and pleasant things. Thus shall he do in the most strongholds with a strange god whom he shall acknowledge and increase with glory. And he shall cause them to rule over many, and shall divide the land for gain. And at the time of the end the king of the South shall push at him, and the king of the North shall come against him like a whirlwind, with chariots and with horsemen, and with many ships; and he shall enter into the countries, and shall overflow and pass over.*" (V. 36-40.)

* Gibbon, vol. iii, p. 70.

It may be proper to remind the reader that the closing *General scope of this prophetic narrative.* scenes of the book of Daniel relate chiefly to the seed of Abraham according to the flesh. "Now I am come," said the Angel, " to make thee understand what shall befall thy people in the latter days." Sometimes the narrative is wholly indirect, and, very often, it is partially so. But the Angel never takes his eye off Palestine. The governments of Persia, Macedonia, Egypt, Syria, and Rome are all successively introduced by the heavenly messenger, but always with some reference to Canaan, and to the Jews as its rightful possessors.

Keeping this in mind, then, we have given the follow- *Criteria and characteristic marks of this king.* ing criteria by which to distinguish and identify the king who is made the principal subject of this section. It seems evident from the narrative:

I. That he would be king over Judea and all the surrounding countries. It is not the king of the North nor the king of the South; it is "*The King*" that appears to the Angel in vision.

II. That he would be an absolute monarch, and rule according to his own will.

III. That he would be extremely vain and presumptuous, even to the assumption of Divine prerogatives.

IV. That for a time he would succeed in his arrogant, ambitious, and irreligious designs.

V. That he would in some way disregard or discourage marriage.

VI. That forsaking the God of his fathers, he would introduce a strange divinity and new objects of worship.

VII. That he would divide the land for gain.

VIII. That in the latter part of his reign the king of the South would make an assault on him.

IX. And that he would be finally vanquished, and his

whole empire completely subjugated by the king of the North.

These characteristics all apply to the successors of Constantine the Great, who reigned at Constantinople over the eastern Roman empire. For,

I. It is universally conceded by infidels, Jews, and Christians that from the banishment of Archelaus, *Period of Roman and Byzantine rule over Palestine.* A. D. 8, to the conquests of the Saracens in the seventh century, Judea was a province of the Roman empire, and that from the removal of the seat of government from Rome to Constantinople, A. D. 330, it was subject to the will, and under the administration of, the emperors of the east.

II. That the Byzantine or eastern Roman emperors were also extremely self-willed and despotic is also *The Byzantine emperors self-willed.* generally known and conceded. Should any, however, be skeptical on this point, I refer them ιo Gibbon's "Decline and Fall of the Roman Empire."

III. They were also exceedingly vain and presumptuous. No civil rulers ever assumed more authority *Their arrogant assumptions.* over their subjects than did the unworthy successors of the great Constantine. The decisions of the ecclesiastical councils were but the echo of the imperial voice, and the plain, moral, and positive precepts of the God of heaven were often set aside by the edicts of these earthly monarchs. Thus did they magnify themselves above every god, and thus did they speak marvelous things against the God of gods.

The following historical extracts will sufficiently illustrate this characteristic of these Greek or Byzantine *Extracts from Neander.* emperors. Neander says: "The coöperation of the emperors having once become so necessary in order to the assembling of these councils and the carrying out of their decisions, it could, of course, no longer remain a matter of indifference to them which of the contending parties they should sustain with their power. ‘However emphatically they might

Influence of the Greek emperors in ecclesiastical matters.

declare in theory that the bishops alone were entitled to decide in matters of doctrine, still human passions proved mightier than theoretical forms. Although these councils were to serve as the organs to express the decisions of the Divine Spirit, yet *the Byzantine court had already prejudged the question,* as to which party should be considered pious and which impious, wherever it could be contrived to gain over the court in favor of any particular doctrine or interest; or in case the court persecuted one of the contending doctrinal parties, merely out of dislike to the man who stood at the head of it, then the doctrinal question must be turned into a means of gratifying personal grudges. The emperors were under no necessity of employing *force* against the bishops. By indirect means they could sufficiently influence the minds of all those with whom worldly interests stood for more than the cause of truth, or who were not yet superior to the fear of man. It was nothing but the influence of the Emperor Constantine which induced the eastern bishops, at the council of Nice, to suffer the imposition of a doctrinal formula which they detested, and from which, indeed, they sought immediately to rid themselves. * * * Now, as so much depended on the fact whether a party had the emperor's vote on his side, consequently every art was employed to secure this. All that was corrupt in the Byzantine court found its way into the bosom of the church. Court parties became doctrinal parties, and the reverse. Imperial chamberlains, eunuchs, directors of the prince's kitchen, disputed on formulas of faith, and affected to set themselves up as judges in doctrinal disputes. That which must pass current for sound doctrine in the church was subjected to the same fluctuations with the parties at court. At length, A. D. 476, Basaliscus, who enjoyed a brief authority, set the example, wholly in accordance with the spirit of the Byzantine court, *of effecting changes in the ruling doctrines of the church by imperial decrees, and of settling dogmatic controversies by a resort to the same expedient.* And this example was soon after but too eagerly followed by other emperors, such as Zeno and Justinian."*

Their arrogant claims to change the laws and doctrine of the Bible.

The same author further adds: "The rage for dogmatizing among the Greek emperors had, from the earliest times, been the cause of many checks and disorders in the Greek Church, and the same thing proved true under Manuel Comnenus, who reigned from A. D. 1143 to 1180. The historian Nicetas Choniates was doubtless right in saying the Roman emperors were not satisfied to rule and to deal with freemen as slaves, but they took it quite amiss if they were not also recognized *as wise and infallible dogmatists, as lawgivers, called to decide on all matters human and divine.*"†

The following is from the learned Gieseler: "Notwithstanding these great privileges," says this very critical historian, "the hierarchy became more and more dependent on the state. *The emperors sent their ecclesiastical laws to be promulgated by the bishops, as they did their civil laws to the pretorian prefects.* Their right to do this was unquestioned as long as they confined themselves to the external relations of the church, or even to subjects connected with its internal government; but hardly so *when they began to decide questions of faith by edicts, and to assemble squads only to adopt articles which they had prescribed.* The Greek bishops, indeed, became more and more confirmed in the habit of sacrificing their convictions to their interests; but the bishops of the Latin Church, favored by

Extract from Gieseler.

---

* Neander's History of the Christian Religion and Church, vol. ii, pp. 183–185.

† Vol. iv, p. 533.

the political condition of their country, were more successful in preserving their independence.*

On this point we will finally hear from the skeptical Gibbon, whom no one will accuse of an intention to confirm and illustrate the truth of prophecy. He says: "Such were the rise and progress, and such were the natural revolutions of these theological disputes which disturbed the peace of Christianity under the reigns of Constantine and his sons. But as these princes presumed to extend their despotism over the faith as well as over the lives and fortunes of their subjects, the weight of their suffrage sometimes inclined the ecclesiastical balance, and *the prerogatives of the King of heaven were settled, or changed, or modified in the cabinet of an earthly monarch.*"†

Further illus-trations from Gibbon.

Note also the following remarks of the same author concerning the emperor Justinian. He says: "The reign of Justinian was a uniform yet various scene of *persecution*, and he appears to have surpassed his indolent predecessors, both in the contrivance of his laws and the rigor of their execution. The insufficient term of three months was assigned for the conversion or exile of all heretics; and if he still connived at their precarious stay, they were deprived, under his iron yoke, not only of the benefits of society, but of the common birthright of men and Christians."‡

Intolerant character of Justinian.

That nothing may be wanting in our attempts to prove and illustrate the vain and blasphemous assumptions of these Greek emperors, the reader will indulge us in making one more quotation from the "Decline and Fall of the Roman Empire." The learned and eloquent author says: "The most lofty titles and the most humble postures which devo-

---

* Geiseler's Ecclesiastical History, vol. i, p. 385.

† Gibbon, vol. iii, p. 32.

‡ Gibbon, vol. vi, p. 50. Lond. edit.

tion has applied to the Supreme Being have been prostituted by flattery and fear to creatures of the same nature with ourselves. The mode of *adoration*, of falling prostrate on the ground and kissing the feet of the emperor, was borrowed by Dioclesian from Persian servitude; *but it was continued and aggravated till the last age of the Greek monarchy, excepting only on Sundays,* when it was waived from a motive of religious pride. This humiliating reverence was exacted from all who entered the regal presence, from the princes invested with the diadem and purple, and from the ambassadors who represented their independent sovereigns, the caliphs of Asia, Egypt, or Spain, the kings of France and Italy, and the Latin emperors of ancient Rome.

Adoration required by the Greek emperor.

" In his transactions of business, Liutprand, bishop of Cremona, asserted the free spirit of a Frank and the dignity of his master Otho; yet his sincerity can not disguise the abasement of his first audience. When he approached the throne, the birds of the golden tree began to warble their notes, which were accompanied by the roarings of two lions of gold. With his two companions, Liutprand was compelled to bow and fall prostrate, and thrice he touched the ground with his forehead. He rose; but in the short interval the throne had been hoisted by an engine from the floor to the ceiling, the imperial figure appeared in new and more gorgeous apparel, and the interview was concluded in haughty and majestic silence."*

Case of Liutprand.

From these extracts, it is evident that the Greek emperors did according to their own will; that they exalted and magnified themselves above every god; that they often spoke marvelous things against the God of gods, and did not regard the God of their fathers; and, in a word, that if the Pope of the West was the

Inference from the preceding extracts.

---

* Gibbon, vol. vii, pp. 100 101.

veritable man of sin, the emperor of the East was his twin brother.

IV. It is further evident, from the preceding citations, that absolute authority in all matters, human and divine, was claimed and exercised by these Byzantine or Greek emperors for about one thousand years, and hence the given testimony of Neander, Gieseler, and Gibbon sufficiently illustrates also the fourth point of our analysis.

V. Paul said and taught that " marriage is honorable ir.
Marriage discouraged and degraded under the rule of the Greek emperors. all ;" but, from a very early period, the notion of greater purity and sanctity was associated with celibacy in the Greek Church under the emperors, as well as in the Latin Church under the popes; and hence the marriage of the clergy was discouraged, as polluting and dishonorable, in both the east and the west. "The Council of Elvira, in
Decree of the Council of Elvira. Spain," says Neander, "which met in A. D. 305, and was governed by the ascetic and hierrarchal spirit which prevailed particularly in the Spanish and North African Churches, was the first to announce the law that the clergy of the first three grades should abstain from all marriage intercourse or be deposed."*

The same subject was also warmly discussed in the Coun-
Decree of the Council of Nice. cil of Nice, A. D. 325, in which, according to the same learned author, it was finally agreed that the ecclesiastics of the three first grades, when once ordained, should no longer be permitted to marry, and the rest was left to the free choice of each individual. "And this," he says, " was not a thing altogether new. The
Of the Council of Neocæsarea. Council of Neocæsarea, in the year 314, had already decreed that the presbyter who married
Of the Council of Ancyra. should forfeit his standing; and the Council of Ancyra, in the same year, that the deacons who,

* Ecclesiastical History, vol. ii, p. 147.

at the time of their ordination, should declare that they could not tolerate the life of celibacy, might subsequently be allowed to marry; while those who said nothing on this point at their ordination, and yet afterward married, should be deposed from their office. How much the ascetic spirit of the moral system which then prevailed in many portions of the *Eastern Church*, first giving rise to monasticism, and then receiving support from the same system, contributed to spread the erroneous notion of the necessity of celibacy to the sacred character of the priesthood, is made evident by the decisions of the Council of Gangra in Paph- Decree of the lagonia, about the middle of the fourth century, Council of Gangra. which council, at the same time, deserves notice as being opposed to this spiritual tendency and to this delusion. Its fourth canon pronounces sentence of condemnation on those who would not hold communion with married ecclesiastics. *But the practice became continually more prevalent in the Eastern Church, for the bishops, at least, if they were married, to abandon the marriage relation."*

But, " like priests like people," is an old proverb. What was dishonorable in the former could not long Effect of these be regarded as wholly unobjectionable in the decrees. latter; and hence we find that under the Greek emperors marriage was not honored and respected as a Divine institution of elevating and purifying tendencies, but it was merely tolerated as a necessary evil, on account of the weakness and depravity of human nature.

VI. The worship of new divinities is another marked characteristic of this subject of prophecy. That the Worship of new Greek emperors, though professing Christianity, divinities. had really but little reverence and respect for its Divine Founder, and for the laws and institutions of his kingdom, is quite evident from the testimony already submitted. "But,"

* Neander's Ecclesiastical History, vol. ii, p. 147.

10

says the Angel, "In his estate he shall honor the god Mauzzim; even a god whom his fathers knew not shall he honor with gold, and silver, and with precious stones and pleasant things." The word *Mauzzim*, taken abstractly, signifies *munitions, bulwarks, fortresses;* but taken concretely, it may denote *protectors, defenders,* and *guardians.* This is evidently its meaning in this connection, and in this sense it is applicable to the theological systems of both Rome and Constantinople. In the Eastern and Western churches, departed saints were worshiped as the *guardians* and *protectors* of the living. This is so generally conceded by all parties that witnesses in the case may be regarded as unnecessary; but the following brief extracts from Mosheim and Gibbon will, I hope, not be unacceptable to the reader: "The aid of departed saints," says the former, "was implored with supplications by vast multitudes, and no one censures this absurd devotion."* And, again, the same author adds: "The temples erected in memory and to the honor of the saints were immensely numerous, both in the East and in the West. There had long been enough houses of worship to accommodate the people, but this age (the sixth century) courted the saints by offering them these edifices as a kind of presents. *Nor did they doubt at all that the saints took under their immediate protection and care the provinces, cities, towns, and villages in which they saw such residences prepared for them.*"† To the same effect is also the following testimony of Gibbon: "Without approving the malice," (of Eunapius,) says this infidel histotorian, "it is natural enough to share the surprise of the sophist, the spectator of a revolution which raised these obscure victims of the laws of Rome to *the rank of celestial and invisible protectors of the Roman empire.*"‡ .

Illustrations from Mosheim.

From Gibbon.

---

* Mosheim's Ecclesiastical History, vol. i, p. 342.   † Ib., vol. i, p. 414.
‡ Decline and Fall of the Roman Empire, vol. iii, p. 530.

VII. That these celestial and invisible protectors were also honored with gold, and silver, and precious Division of the land for gain. stones, and pleasant things; that the whole Roman empire was divided among them for gain, each country having its own patron saint; and that, from the same mercenary motives, it was also subdivided among the monks, bishops, and other clerical orders, are facts too well known to require any special proof or illustration.

VIII. From the subjugation of Syria and Egypt by the Romans till the decline of the eastern Roman No king of the North or South during the Roman dominion. empire, no mention is made of the king of the North or the king of the South. The reason of this is obvious. During all this period the Romans had possession not only of Judea, but also of all the countries both north and south of it. The geographical distinction so often referred to in that part of this prophecy which relates to Syria and Egypt had, therefore, no existence while Rome or Constantinople governed all western Asia; but this distinction was afterward revived by the Saracens The Saracens became king of the South. of Arabia and the Turks of Asia Minor and northern Syria. Under the banners of the False Prophet, the former left the sandy deserts of the peninsula, conquered all Persia, Syria, Palestine, Egypt, northern Africa, parts of Europe, and, in forty-six years after the flight of Mahomet from Mecca, his followers appeared in arms under the walls of Constantinople. "During many Their attempts to take Constantinople. days, from the dawn of light to the evening, the line of assault was extended from the Golden Gate to the eastern promontory, and the foremost warriors were impelled by the weight and effort of the succeeding columns. But the besiegers had formed an insufficient estimate of the strength and resources of Constantinople. The solid and lofty walls were guarded by numbers and discipline, the spirit of the Romans was rekindled by the last danger of their religion and empire, the fugitives from the conquered provinces more successfully renewed the defense of Damascus and Alexandria, and the Saracens were dismayed by the strange and prodigious effects of artificial fire. This firm and effectual resistance diverted their arms to the more easy attempts of plundering the European and Asiatic coasts of the Propontis, and after keeping the sea from the month of April to that of September, on the approach of winter they retreated fourscore miles from the capital to the isle of Cyzicus, in which they had established their magazine of spoils and provisions. So patient was their perseverance, or so languid were their operations, that they repeated, in the six following summers, the same attack and retreat, with a gradual abatement of hope and vigor, till the mischances of shipwreck and disease, of sword and fire, compelled them to relinquish their fruitless enterprise."* In like manner ended all subsequent attempts of the Saracens to take Constantinople. For many years this new king of the South continued to *push* at the Greek emperors.

IX. It was reserved for the Turks, the revived king of the North, to put an end to the eastern Roman empire. Othman was the founder of the Ottoman or Turkish empire. In 1299 he established a kingdom in Bythinia, of which Bursa, at the foot of Mount Olympus, was made the capital. His successors, Orchan, Amurath I, Bajazet I, Mahomet I, Amurath II, and Mahomet II, greatly extended the Ottoman dominions in both Asia and Europe. Bajazet reigned from the Euphrates to the Danube, all being subject to him but Constantinople.

The king of the North revived in the Turks.

To take this was the work of Mahomet II. At the head of an army of three hundred thousand men, and supported by a fleet of three hundred sail, he laid siege to this celebrated metropolis on the sixth

Siege and capture of Constantinople.

* Gibbon, vol. vii, pp. 3, 4.

of April, A. D. 1453, and on the twenty-ninth of May following the Turks stormed the walls. The last Constantine fell as he boldly disputed every inch of ground. Multitudes of his subjects were massacred in the first outburst of Turkish fury; the rest were sold into slavery; and when Mahomet made his triumphal entry into the city he found it a vast solitude.*

The conquest of Constantinople was soon followed by that of Servia, Bosnia, Albania, and Greece, including the Peloponnesus, several islands in the archipelago, and the Greek empire of Trebizond. Thus did the king of the North come against the Greek emperor like a whirlwind, with chariots, and with horsemen, and with many ships; and thus did he enter into the countries and overflow and pass over.

XXVII. "*He shall enter also into the glorious land, and many countries shall be overthrown; but these shall escape out of his hand, even Edom, and Moab, and the chief of the children of Ammon. He shall stretch forth his hands also upon the countries, and the land of Egypt shall not escape; but he shall have power over the treasures of gold, and of silver, and over all the precious things of Egypt, and the Libyans and Ethiopians shall be at his steps.*" (V. 41–43.)

All this applies clearly to the Turkish sultans, and to them only. In A. D. 1481, Mahomet II was succeeded by his son Bajazet II, a prince of mild and amiable temper. He, however, subdued Bessarabia and some important provinces in Asia. After a reign of thirty years, he was forced to resign his throne to his son Selim, surnamed Gavuz the Savage. This most cruel of the Ottoman monarchs commenced his reign with the murder of his brothers, his nephews, and forty thousand dissenters from the orthodox faith. Having removed all competitors for the crown, he turned his arms

Further evidence that the king of the North and the Turkish sultans are identical.

---

* Gibbon, vol. viii, chap. lxviii.

against the Persians, over whom he gained several important victories, and from whom he wrested large portions of territory beyond the Tigris.

He then marched against Gauri, the Mameluke sultan of Egypt, who, in the late Persian wars, had fought against the Turks. The two armies met near Aleppo, a town in northern Syria. The engagement was fierce and sanguinary, but Gauri was slain, his army defeated, and all Syria added to the dominions of the conqueror. Judea was included in this conquest, and from that time, A. D. 1516, *"the glorious land"* has been subject to the Sublime Porte.

Conquest of Syria and Palestine.

"But these shall escape out of his hand, even Edom, and Moab, and the chief of the children of Ammon." These countries were all overrun and pillaged by the Turks, but never conquered by them; and now any map of the Turkish Empire is a sufficient proof and illustration of the correctness of this prediction.

Escape of the Arabian tribes.

But the land of Egypt was not so fortunate. Selim met and defeated the new sultan, Tuman Bey, near the walls of Cairo. He afterward stormed the city, hung Tuman before its principal gate, put to death fifty thousand of its inhabitants, sent five hundred of the most influential families and a vast amount of gold and silver and other treasures to Constantinople, and finally reduced Egypt to a Turkish province, in which condition it remained for about three hundred years.

Conquest of Egypt, Libya, and Ethiopia.

After the conquest of Egypt, several of the neighboring tribes on the west and south sent ambassadors to Selim, and voluntarily became his subjects. Others were subdued by Solyman, the son and successor of Selim, in whose reign the Turkish empire attained to its greatest extent and the height of its power. He headed his armies in thirteen campaigns, took parts of Hun-

Other conquests of the Sultans.

gary and northern Africa, captured Rhodes and other islands in the Mediterranean, defeated the Persians, and added Tebreez and Bagdad to his dominions. Thus did the Sultan of Constantinople stretch forth his hand upon the countries, thus had he power over all the treasures of Egypt, and thus did the Libyans and the Ethiopians serve him according to the most authentic records of mediæval and modern history.*

The next section relates to the future—to the final ruin of the Turkish empire—and hence it transcends our prescribed limits. But we have said enough on the subject of prophecy for our present purpose. We have now examined from the one book of Daniel alone, several hundred predictions, extending over a period of more than twenty-four centuries, and relating to the most influential and enlightened nations of the world during that period, and in every case we have found an exact agreement between the prophetic specifications and the corresponding events of profane history. In a few instances we have failed to find in history as full and as detailed an account of particulars as we could have desired, but in not a single instance have we found any discrepancy between the prophetic specifications and the historic events. *[Harmony of these prophetic specifications with historic events.]*

How, then, is all this to be explained and accounted for? It will not do to say, with Porphyry, that these so-called prophesies were written after the events occurred to which they relate. Many of these predictions refer to events that are just now occurring, whereas the book of Daniel was written more than twenty-four hundred years ago. Of this we have very clear and satisfactory evidence; for, *[Absurdity of Porphyry's allegation. Age of the book of Daniel.]*

1. The book of Daniel is found in all copies of the Hebrew Bible, and was shown to Alexander the Great as

---

* See, on all these points, Anquitil's Universal Hist., vol. vi, pp. 105–174, and Mavor's Univ. Hist., vol xii, chap. xiii.

one of the sacred books of the Old Testament, when he
passed through Judea, on his way to Persia, 332
B. C. So Josephus testifies in the following
brief extract : " And when he (Alexander) went
up into the temple he offered sacrifice to God,
according to the High Priest's directions, and magnificently
treated both the High Priest and the priests. *And when the
book of Daniel was shown him*, wherein Daniel declared that
one of the Greeks would destroy the empire of the Persians,
he supposed that himself was the person intended. And
as he was then glad, he dismissed the multitudes for the
present; but the next day he called them to him, and bid
them ask what favors they pleased of him. Whereupon, the
High Priest desired that they might enjoy the laws of their
forefathers, and that they might pay no tribute on the seventh
year. He granted all they desired."* And hence the allegation of Porphyry and his school is absurd and preposterous.

2. The book of Daniel is found in all copies of the Septuagint. This oldest version of the Hebrew
Scriptures into Greek was made under Ptolemy
Philadelphus, king of Egypt, about 280 B. C.,
and from that time to the present it has been in the hands
and libraries of the learned world, both of Jews and Gentiles; and hence it follows that the book of Daniel was certainly in existence before the date of this translation.

But most of the prophecies examined have reference to
events that occurred long after the times both of
Alexander the Great and of Ptolemy Philadelphus. The coming of the Messiah, the setting
up of his kingdom, the destruction of Jerusalem,
the persecutions of the saints, the internal cor-
ruptions and divisions of the church, the arrogant assumptions and blasphemous pretensions of both the Roman Cath-

---

* Antiquities, book xi, chap. viii.

olic Hierarchy and the Byzantine emperors, the rise and exploits of the Saracens and the Turks, the great revival and rapid progress of primitive Christianity in the nineteenth century, these and many other events foretold by Daniel have all occurred since the Old Testament Canon was closed and sealed in the sacred literature of both the Hebrews and the Greeks. And as no finite Conclusion respecting Daniel and his writings. intelligence could, by any possibility, have foreseen these matters, it follows, of necessity, that Daniel spoke all these oracles as he was moved by that Divine Spirit that searches all things; yea, even the deep counsels and purposes of Jehovah.

And when it is remembered that the prophecies examined are not the tithe of all that are contained in General conclusion in reference to the whole Bible. the Old and the New Testament; that evidence equally strong and convincing is also furnished by Isaiah, Jeremiah, Ezekiel, and other prophets, the entire argument from fulfilled prophecy becomes absolutely overwhelming and there is really left no rational way of avoiding the conclusion that THE BIBLE IS THE WORD OF GOD.

NOTE.—It would be an easy matter to extend this course of argument indefinitely; and, in some respects, it would certainly be very desirable to devote at least another chapter to the consideration of the very remarkable and unprecedented harmony that subsists between the teachings of the Bible and even the latest discoveries of science and philosophy; but the argument has already been protracted much beyond my prescribed limits, and as I think enough has been said to satisfy any and every candid inquirer after truth that the Bible is of Divine origin, I will hereafter regard this as an established fact.

PART SECOND.

THE CANON OF THE HOLY SCRIPTURES.

THE second province of Reason in matters pertaining to Divine Revelation, *is to decide on the Canon of the Holy Scriptures.*

<small>Second province of Reason.</small>

The word *canon* (καυων) literally means a straight rod or carpenter's rule, and hence it has long been used to denote the entire catalogue or list of inspired books which God has himself given to the Church as the only proper and authoritative rule of both our faith and our practice.

<small>Meaning of the word Canon.</small>

It is not enough to prove simply that the Bible, as a whole, is of Divine origin. It is further necessary to examine the claims of the several books that compose it, and also to decide on the merits of all the other books for which inspiration has been claimed by any portion of Christendom. Here, then, we again clearly need the aid of enlightened Reason in our attempts to settle this important question. We simply ask and require, that in this, as in all other cases, she shall render a verdict according to the nature and weight of the evidence submitted. To do this is her proper province; and to this no reasonable man will object.

<small>The aid of reason necessary in deciding on the Canon of Scripture.</small>

(154)

CHAPTER I.

CANON OF THE OLD TESTAMENT.

First of all, then, we affirm that the thirty-nine books of the Old Testament are all canonical. This may be clearly and satisfactorily proved from the following considerations: The thirty-nine books of the Old Testament are canonical.

I. *These books were all so regarded and so classified by the last of the inspired Jewish writers.* First source of evidence.

For the truth of this proposition we have the united and unbroken testimony of all the Jews who have ever written on this subject from the days of Malachi to the present time. They all testify in substance as follows: that the Old Testament Canon was completed by Ezra, Nehemiah, Zechariah, Malachi, and other inspired members of the Great Synagogue, or last School of the Prophets, founded by Ezra.* Testimony of later Jewish writers.

This unity of sentiment is a very remarkable and significant fact, and should have very great weight in settling this question. Especially is this the case, when it is remembered that on most other points they were very much divided; as, for instance, on the weight and authority of their own traditions. The Pharisees insisted on the binding obligations of the Oral as well as of the Written Law. But the Sadducees as earnestly protested against this, and insisted on making the Written Law their only rule of faith and practice. This was the great dividing Weight of this testimony.

* Buxtorf's Tiberias, book i, chap. x.

question of these sects. So Josephus testifies.   He says:

"Their" (the Sadducees) "custom was to regard nothing except the Laws," (that is, the
Written Laws, the Old Testament); "for they
reckon it as a virtue to dispute against the doctors, in favor
of the wisdom which they follow.* And again he says:
"The Pharisees inculcated many rules upon the people, received from the fathers, which are not written in the law of
Moses; and on this account, the Sadducees reject them, al-
leging that those things are to be regarded as rules which
are written" (in the Scriptures); but that the traditions of
the fathers are not to be observed; and concerning these
things it is that great disputes and differences have arisen
among them."†

But notwithstanding their great zeal for the traditions of

Reverence and
respect of all
Jews for the
books of the
Old Testament. their fathers, the Pharisees never presumed to
place any of them in the same category with the
thirty-nine books of the Old Testament.   On
this point the testimony of Josephus is also very
clear and satisfactory.   He says: "We have not an innu-

merable multitude of books among us, disagree-
ing from and contradicting one another, as the
Greeks have, but only twenty-two books, which contain the
records of all the past times, which are justly believed to be
Divine.   And of them, five belong to Moses, which contain
his laws and the traditions of the origin of mankind till
his death.   This interval of time was little short of three
thousand years; but as to the time from the death of Moses
to the reign of Artaxerxes, king of Persia, who reigned after
Xerxes, the prophets who were after Moses wrote down what
was done in their times in thirteen books.   The remaining
four books contain hymns to God and precepts for the con-

---

* Antiquities, book xviii, chap. i: 4.
† Antiquities, book xiii, chap. xi: 6.

duct of human life. It is true, our history has been written since Artaxerxes, very particularly, but has not been esteemed of like authority with the former by our forefathers because there has not been an exact succession of prophets since that time. And how firmly we have given credit to these books of our own nation is evident by what we do, for, during so many ages as have already passed, *no one has been so bold as either to add any thing to them, to take any thing from them, or to make any change in them, but it is become natural for all Jews, immediately and from their very birth, to esteem these books to contain Divine doctrines*, and to persist in them, and, if occasion be, to die for them ; for it is no new thing for our captives, many of them in number, and frequently in time, to be seen to endure racks and deaths of all kinds upon the theaters, that they may not be obliged to say one word against our laws or the records that contain them." * On this one point, then, be it observed, the Jews were unanimous. Much as were the Pharisees wedded to the traditions of their fathers, not one of them had ever dared to incorporate any of these traditions into the Canon which, they all say, they had received from the inspired prophets of the Great Synagogue.

The reader will observe that Josephus here reckons but twenty-two inspired books. And this is still the custom of many Jewish Rabbis. Their reason for this enumeration is because there are but twenty-two letters in the Hebrew alphabet. "According to this classification, Judges and Ruth make but one book; the two books of Samuel, two of Kings, and two of Chronicles, make but three in all ; Ezra and Nehemiah are one, Jeremiah and Lamentations are one, and the twelve Minor prophets are but one." † Some of the Jewish doctors, however, as

Rabbinical classification of the thirty-nine books of the Old Testament.

---

* Against Apion, book i, sec. 8.

† New Am. Cyclopædia, vol. iii, p. 225; Horne's Introduction, vol. i, chap. ii, sec. i, 5; and Bundt's Apparatus Biblicus, book ii, chap. ii, p. 281.

in the Talmud and the Massorah, separate Judges and Ruth, and Jeremiah and the Lamentations, and thus make in all twenty-four sacred books; "And, in order to accommodate this number to that of the letters of the Hebrew alphabet, they repeat the *Yod* three times, as they say, in honor of the great name *Jehovah,* of which Yod is the first letter; and, in the Chaldee language, three Yods together express this sacred and adorable name." *

Hence it seems that there has never been any important

What follows from this extraordinary agreement of the Jewish sects. difference of opinion among the Jews with regard to the Old Testament. The Thirty-nine books of our modern Hebrew Bibles are the same that have ever been received by the Pharisees,

the Sadducees, and the Essenes. In the common consent of these several parties, we have, therefore, the most convincing evidence that the Canon of the Old Testament rests on the authority of Ezra, Zechariah, Malachi, and other prophets of the Great Synagogue. On no other hypothesis can we satisfactorily account for this extraordinary unity of sentiment on a question of so much intrinsic difficulty and perplexity.

When these books were all collected into one volume is not

Formation and close of the Old Testament Canon. known with absolute certainty, but it is probable that this was done for the sake of convenience, as was the custom before the captivity,†

very soon after the last book was written by Malachi; after this the work of revision probably continued, as the Jews say, till the spirit of prophecy ceased with Simon the Just, the last member of the Great Synagogue and last School of

---

* Bundt's Ap. Crit., book ii, chap. ii, p. 281, and Stuart on the Canon of the Old Test., p. 278.

† Compare Deut. xxxi: 9 and 26; Joshua i: 8, and xxiv: 26; 1 Samuel x: 25; 2 Kings xxii: 8; Isa. xxxiv: 16; Dan. ix: 2; Josephus, book v, chap. i, 17.

the Prophets, about 300 B. C.* Of the truth of this, the Scriptures themselves furnish strong evidence. In Nehe-miah xii: 22, for example, there is mention made of Jad-dua the High Priest, and also of Darius Codomannus, king of Persia, both of whom lived at least one hundred years after the time of Ezra, and a short time before Simon the Just; and in the third chapter of the first book of Chron-icles the genealogy of the sons of Zerubbabel is brought down to about the same period; and hence the year 300 B. C. is the approximate time that is now most generally assigned, by both Jewish and Christian writers, as the closing period of the Old Testament Canon.

Soon after that the entire Hebrew Bible, consisting of the aforesaid thirty-nine books, was translated into Greek, under the auspices and patronage of Ptolemy Philadelphus, for the famous Alexan-drian Library, and from that important epoch in sacred lit-erature, the Old Testament Scriptures have been in the hands of both Jews and Gentiles; *so that it has ever since been abso-lutely impossible to make any change in these sacred books with-out detection.*

Its first trans-lation into Greek.

If any thing is still wanting to prove that the Canon of the Old Testament was completed about the time aforesaid, it is found in the fact that the same threefold division of the books that is now found in our Hebrew Bibles, is known to have existed soon after that period. It is first mentioned in the Pro-logue to the apocryphal book of Ecclesiasticus, or The Wisdom of Jesus, the Son of Sirach. The Prologue was written by the grandson of Jesus about 132 B. C.; but according to our best chronologers, the book itself was writ-

Threefold di-vision of the Old Testament.

First mention of this.

* In the Talmud, Simon the Just is called "one of the *remnants* of the Great Synagogue," which indicates that he had outlived it.—*Kitto's Cyclo-pedia,* vol. i, p. 378.

ten about one hundred years earlier. And it is evident, from the following words of the grandson, that this threefold division of the Old Testament Scriptures was *current* among the Jews at that time; that is, about 232 B. C. He says: " My grandfather, Jesus, when he had much given himself to the reading of *the Law* and *the Prophets* and *other books* of our fathers, and had gotten therein good judgment, was drawn on also himself to write something pertaining to learning and wisdom, to the intent that those who are desirous to learn, and are addicted to these things, might profit much more in living according to *the Law;* wherefore, let me entreat you to read it with favor and attention, and to pardon us wherein we may seem to come short of some words which we have labored to interpret, for the same things uttered in Hebrew, and translated into another tongue, have not the same force in them; and not only these things, but *the Law* * itself, and *the Prophets*, and *the rest of the books* have no small difference when they are spoken in their own language."

Here, then, we have evidently the same general divisions of the Old Testament Canon that are given by Josephus in the citation already made from his writings, and by Christ in the forty-fourth verse of the twenty-fourth chapter of Luke, and by the Rabbis in the Talmud and the Hebrew Bible. What it implies respecting the close of the Canon. But the division of any thing implies, of course, the previous existence of the thing itself, and hence it is reasonable to suppose that the Canon of the Old Testament was completed before the year 232 B. C.†

* The word Law is also used in a more general sense, to denote the entire Canon of the Old Testament, because the thirty-nine More comprehensive meaning of the word Law. books of which it is composed, taken together as one whole, were regarded by all the Jews as their rule of life. See, for example, John x: 34, and xii: 34; also Romans iii: 19.

† The various names applied to the third division in no way militates against this conclusion. The Canon itself was called by different names at different periods. The name *Bible* was first given to it by Chrysos-

II. *The thirty-nine books of the Old Testament were all frequently indorsed as canonical by Christ and his Apostles.* This is evident from the following passages: "Jesus said unto them, Did ye never read in the *Scriptures*, The stone which the builders rejected, the same is become the head of the corner; this is the Lord's doing, and it is marvelous in our eyes?" (Matthew xxi: 42; Psalm cxviii: 22, 23.) "Jesus said unto them, Ye do err, not knowing the *Scriptures*, nor the power of God." (Matthew xxii: 29.) "But how then shall the *Scriptures* be fulfilled?" (Matthew xxvi: 54; Isaiah liii, etc.) "But all this was done that the *Scriptures* of the prophets might be fulfilled." (Matthew xxvi: 56.) "I was daily with you in the temple teaching, and ye took me not; but the *Scriptures* must be fulfilled." (Mark xiv: 49.) "And the *Scripture* was fulfilled which saith, And he was numbered with the transgressors." (Mark xv: 28; Isaiah liii: 12.) "And he closed the book, (of Isaiah,) and he gave it again to the minister,

Second proof that the thirty-nine books of the Old Testament are canonical.

Citations from the New Testament.

tom in the fifth century; previous to that it was called the *Scripture*, the *Scriptures*, the *Holy Scriptures*, the *Divine Scriptures*, etc.; and just so it was with the various books that compose it; they too have been called by different names at different periods and in different languages. The Hebrews commonly named the sacred books from the first word or words with which they severally begin; but the Greeks named them from their subject-matter, and hence the Hebrews called their first book *Bereshith*, in the beginning; but the Greeks called it *Genesis*, creation. The Hebrew name of the second book is *Veelleh Shemoth*, and these are the names; but its Greek name is *Exodus*, a going out. The name of the third book in Hebrew is *Vaiyikra*, and he called; its Greek name is *Leviticus*, because it treats chiefly of the Levites. But these different names imply no want of identity; and just so it is with respect to the names of the three principal divisions of the Hebrew Bible. "*The rest of the books*" in the Prologue of Ecclesiasticus; "*The remaining books*" in Josephus; "*The Psalms*" in Luke xxiv: 44; and "*The Hagiographa*" in our more modern literature, evidently all refer to the same general division of the sacred books.

Different names given to the Bible and its various parts.

11

and sat down.   And the eyes of all them that were in the
synagogue were fastened on him.   And he began to say unto
them, This day is this *Scripture* fulfilled in your ears."
(Luke iv: 20, 21.)   "And beginning at Moses and all the
prophets, he expounded unto them in all the *Scriptures* the
things concerning himself."   (Luke xxiv: 27.)   "And they
said one to another, Did not our hearts burn within us while
he talked with us by the way, and while he opened to us
the *Scriptures!*"   (Luke xxiv: 32.)   "And he said unto
them, These are the words which I spake unto you while I
was yet with you, that all things must be fulfilled which are
written in *the Law of Moses*, and in *the Prophets*, and in *the
Psalms* concerning me.   Then opened he their understanding, that they might understand the *Scriptures.*"   (Luke
xxiv: 44, 45.)   " He that believeth on me, as the *Scripture*
hath said, Out of his belly shall flow rivers of living water."
(John vii: 38; Proverbs xviii: 4.)   "Others said, This is
the Christ.   But some said, Shall Christ come out of Galilee?   Hath not the *Scripture* said that Christ cometh of
the seed of David, and out of the town of Bethlehem, where
David was?"   (John vii: 41, 42; Psalm lxxii; Jeremiah
xxiii: 5, 6; Micah v: 2, etc.)   "Jesus said unto them, Is
it not written in your *Law*, I said, ye are gods?   If he
called them gods unto whom the word of God came, and the
Scripture can not be broken; say ye of Him whom the Father
hath sanctified and sent into the world, Thou blasphemest;
because I said, I am the Son of God?"   (John x: 34–36;
Psalm lxxxii: 6.)   "I speak not of you all; I know whom
I have chosen; but that the *Scripture* may be fulfilled, He
that eateth bread with me has lifted up his heel against
me."   (John xiii: 18; Psalm xli: 9.)   " While I was with
them in the world, I kept them in thy name.   Those that
thou gavest me I have kept, and none of them is lost but
the son of perdition, that the *Scripture* might be fulfilled."

(John xvii: 12; Psalm cix: 8.) "They said therefore among themselves, Let us not rend it, (the tunic,) but cast lots for it, whose it shall be; that the *Scripture* might be fulfilled which saith, They parted my raiment among them, and for my vesture they did cast lots." (John xix: 24; Psalm xxii: 18.) "After this, Jesus, knowing that all things were now accomplished that the *Scripture* might be fulfilled, said, I thirst." (John xix: 28; Psalm lxix: 21.) "For these things were done that the *Scripture* should be fulfilled. A bone of him shall not be broken. And again another Scripture saith, They shall look on him whom they pierced." (John xix: 36, 37; Exodus xii: 46; and Zechariah xii: 10.) "For as yet they knew not the *Scripture*, that he must rise again from the dead." (John xx: 9; Psalm xvi: 9; Isaiah liii: 10–12, etc.) "Men and brethren, this *Scripture* must needs be fulfilled which the Holy Spirit, by the mouth of David, spake before concerning Judas, who was guide to them that took Jesus." (Acts i: 16; Psalm cix: 8.) "The place of the *Scripture* which he read was this, He was led as a sheep to the slaughter, and like a lamb dumb before his shearer, so opened he not his mouth." (Acts viii: 32; see, also, v. 35; Isaiah liii: 7, 8.) "And Paul, as his manner was, went in unto them, and three Sabbath days reasoned with them (the Jews) out of the *Scriptures*." (Acts xvii: 2.) "These (the Bereans) were more noble than those in Thessalonica, in that they received the word with all readiness of mind, and searched the *Scriptures* daily, whether these things were so." (Acts xvii: 11.) "And a certain Jew named Apollos, born at Alexandria, and mighty in the *Scriptures*, came to Ephesus." (Acts xviii: 24.) "For he mightily convinced the Jews, and that publicly, showing by the *Scriptures* that Jesus is the Christ." (Acts xviii: 28.) "And when they had appointed him a day, there came many to him into his lodging, to whom he expounded and testified the kingdom of God, persuading them concerning Jesus, both out of the *Law* of Moses, and out of the *Prophets*, from morning till evening." (Acts xxviii: 23.) "Which (Gospel) he had promised before by his prophets, in the *Holy Scriptures.*" (Romans i: 2.) "For what saith the *Scripture?*" (Romans iv: 3; Genesis xv: 6.) For the *Scripture* saith unto Pharaoh, even for this same purpose have I raised thee up, that I might show my power in thee, and that my name might be declared throughout all the earth." (Romans ix: 17; Exodus ix: 16.) "For the *Scripture* saith, Whosoever believeth on him shall not be ashamed." (Romans x: 11; Isaiah xxviii: 16; and xlix: 23.) "For *whatsoever things were written aforetime* were written for our learning, that we, through patience and comfort of the *Scriptures*, might have hope." (Romans xv: 4.) "Now to him that is of power to establish you according to my Gospel and the preaching of Jesus Christ, according to the revelation of the mystery which was kept secret since the world began, but now is made manifest, and by the *Scriptures* of the prophets, according to the commandment of the everlasting God, is made known to all nations for the obedience of faith : to the only wise God, through Jesus Christ, be glory forever." (Romans xvi: 25–27.) "For I delivered unto you first of all that which I also received, that Christ died for our sins, according to the *Scriptures*, and that he was buried, and that he rose again the third day according to the *Scriptures.*" (1 Corinthians xv: 3, 4; Psalm xxii; Isaiah liii; Daniel ix: 26; Zechariah xiii: 17; Psalm ii: 7; xvi: 10, etc.) "And the *Scripture*, foreseeing that God would justify the heathen through faith, preached before the Gospel unto Abraham, saying, In thee shall all nations be blessed." (Galatians iii: 8; Genesis xii: 3, etc.) "But the *Scripture* has concluded all under sin, that the promise by faith of Jesus Christ might be given to them that believe." (Galatians iii: 22.) "Nevertheless, what saith the *Scripture?* Cast out the bond-woman and her son; for the son of the bond-woman shall not be heir with the son of the free woman." (Galatians iv: 30; Genesis xxi: 10, 12.) "For the *Scripture* saith, Thou shalt not muzzle the ox that treadeth out the corn; and, The laborer is worthy of his reward." (1 Timothy v: 18; Deuteronomy xxv: 4; and Leviticus xix: 13.) "But continue thou in the things which thou hast learned and hast been assured of, knowing of whom thou hast learned them, and that from a child thou hast known the *Holy Scriptures,* which are able to make thee wise unto salvation, through faith which is in Christ Jesus. All *Scripture* is given by inspiration of God, and profitable for doctrine, for reproof, for correction, for instruction in righteousness, that the man of God may be perfect, thoroughly furnished for all good works." (2 Timothy iii: 14–17.) "If ye fulfill the royal law according to the *Scripture,* Thou shalt love thy neighbor as thyself, ye shall do well." (James ii: 8; Leviticus xix: 18.) "And the *Scripture* was fulfilled which saith, Abraham believed God, and it was imputed unto him for righteousness; and he was called the friend of God." (James ii: 23; Genesis xv: 6; 2 Chronicles xx: 7, etc.) "Do ye think that the *Scripture* saith in vain, The spirit that dwelleth in us lusteth to envy?" (James iv: 5; Genesis vi: 5; viii: 21; Proverbs xxi: 10, etc.) "Wherefore also it is contained in the *Scripture,* Behold I lay in Zion a chief corner-stone, elect, precious; and he that believeth on Him shall not be confounded." (1 Peter ii: 6; Psalm cxviii: 22; and Isaiah xxviii: 16.) "Knowing this first, that no prophecy of the *Scripture* is of any private interpretation; for the prophecy came not in old time by the will of man, but holy men of God spake as they were moved by the Holy Spirit." (2 Peter i: 20.) "And account that the long-suffering of God is salvation, even as our be-

loved brother Paul, also according to the wisdom given unto
him, hath written unto you, as also in all his epistles, speaking in them of these things, in which are some things hard
to be understood, which they that are unlearned and unstable wrest, as they do also the other *Scriptures,* unto their own
destruction." (2 Peter iii : 15, 16.)

It is evident that in all these passages the word *Scripture*
Meaning of the (γραφη) or *Scriptures* (γραφαι) is used like the
word Scripture
or Scriptures in word *Bible,* in a limited and specific sense, to
these citations. denote all those books that were then received
by the Jews as canonical. But these, according to Josephus
and other Rabbinical writers, were the same identical thirty-
nine books that now compose the Hebrew Bible. Indeed,
it is preposterous to talk of any material change having been
made in the Hebrew Scriptures since the time of Christ ; and
hence, these thirty-nine books were all indorsed by Christ
and his Apostles. But these, as I have shown in the first
part of this treatise, were severally God's inspired ambassadors sent forth to proclaim to the world Heaven's own ap-
Conclusion   pointed scheme of justification, and sanctifica-
from all the   tion, and redemption. *And hence it follows, of*
premises.
               necessity, that the aforesaid thirty-nine books of
the Old Testament are each and all canonical. So reason un-
hesitatingly decides in view of all the premises.

It may be well to observe, just here, that it is the original
The original   Hebrew, and not any translation of it, that
Hebrew only
indorsed as   Christ and his Apostles have indorsed as canon-
canonical.   ical. It is true that they often quote from the
Septuagint or Alexandrian Version of the Original, especially
Quoting is not when they are addressing either the Greeks
indorsing.   or the Hellenists; but this is no proof that
it was their intention thereby to indorse that version as
canonical. They evidently referred to it, for the sake of
convenience, just as we now refer to our common English

version. When it expresses the mind of the Spirit clearly and definitely, they quote it *verbatim*. But when it fails to do this, then they either correct its errors by making the necessary changes in its phraseology; or, otherwise, they wholly disregard it, and make their appeal directly to the original Hebrew.

This whole subject has been ably treated by Thomas Hartwell Horne in his very excellent "Introduction to the Critical Study of the Bible." Under the general head of "Quotations in the New Testament from the Septuagint," he reckons seventy-five that agree with said version *verbatim;* forty-seven that vary from it but slightly; thirty-two that agree with it in sense, but not in form; eleven that differ from it materially and agree with the Hebrew; and nineteen that differ from both it and the Hebrew.

Summary of quotations given by Horne.

The reader will, of course, receive this remark with caution. It is scarcely necessary to remind him that every apparent discrepancy is not a real discrepancy. The accomplished teacher varies his words, and phrases, and illustrations to suit the attainments, habits, and capacities of his pupils. Sometimes it is best to convey his meaning in very generic,

Explanation of apparent departures from the Hebrew in quotations found in the New Testament.

abstract, and highly-figurative forms of expression. And sometimes, again, it may be necessary to use nothing but the very plainest and most specific words and phrases. All such considerations were, of course, a matter of care to the inspired writers of the New Testament; and hence, we may reasonably expect to find in their writings and quotations many apparent departures from the original Hebrew, but nothing that really contradicts it.

III. *The canonical authority of the thirty-nine books of the Old Testament may, if necessary, be still further proved and supported by their own internal evidence and the testimony of the Christian fathers.**   But as I aim at brevity in all these

Third source of evidence in support of the Old Testament Canon. discussions, and as the evidence submitted on this point is entirely sufficient, I will add no more, but simply refer the reader to what has been said in Part First on the unity, harmony, and other internal evidences of the Divine Origin of the whole Bible.

CHAPTER II.

CANON OF THE NEW TESTAMENT.

THE Canon of the New Testament, consisting of twenty-

On what the canonical authority of the New Testament rests. seven books, rests, in like manner, *on the authority of the Apostles and other inspired members of the Primitive Church.* This is evident,

I. *From the entire unanimity with which all the*

---

* The first catalogue of the books of the Old Testament given by any of the Christian fathers, is that of Melito, Bishop of Sardis, in Lydia, about A. D. 170. He was a man of great learning and piety, and commonly called a *prophet* by his Christian brethren; it may, therefore, be interesting to the reader to hear from him what was the number and the order of the books of the Old Testament in his day. His catalogue is reported by Eusebius as follows: "The five books of Moses: Genesis, Exodus, Leviticus, Numbers, Deuteronomy; then Joshua of Nun, Judges, Ruth, four books of Kings, two of Chronicles; the Psalms of David, the Proverbs of Solomon (also called Wisdom), Ecclesiastes, the Song of songs, Job. Prophets: Isaiah, Jeremiah, the Twelve in one book, Daniel, Ezekiel, Ezra."

The books of Nehemiah and Esther seem to be omitted in this catalogue; but at that time Ezra and Nehemiah were always reckoned as but one book by both the Jews and the Greeks; and critics are still divided on the question whether Esther was also included under the same general head, or omitted, through mistake, by Eusebius. It is frequently referred to by Josephus. (See Stuart on the Canon of the Old Testament, pp. 257–261.)

primitive Christians received and adopted these books as their only infallible and all-authoritative rule of faith and practice. For, be it remembered, First source of evidence.

1. That on all speculative questions resting on mere human authority the disciples of the first and second centuries were exceedingly prone to differ in their opinions. This was a necessary consequence growing out of their previous education. Tendency of the Primitive Church to divide on speculative questions. They had been collected into the Christian Church from all the religious and philosophical parties of the then known world, and, as a matter of course, they brought into their new relations many of their old habits and modes of thought. Some of them were inclined to Platonism, some to Aristotelianism, some Epicureanism, some to Stoicism, some to Pharisceism, and some to Sadducceism. This old leaven soon began to work throughout the entire body. One began to say, I am of Paul; and another, I am of Apollos; and another, I am of Cephas; and another, I am of Christ. Sectarianism was, in fact, the necessary tendency in all the congregations, and nothing but *Apostolic authority* could have prevented a division of the primitive church into a great number and variety of contending sects and parties; this is evident from nearly all of Paul's epistles, as well as from the united testimony of ecclesiastical historians. See, for instance, the first volumes of Mosheim, Gieseler, and Neander.

2. But on the question of the Canon there were some additional and special reasons that must have inevitably led to divisions in the primitive church, had it in any sense or in any measure Special tendency to divide on the question of the Canon. been a speculative question. On this assumption every one would have been inclined to receive those books as canonical which most fully coincided with his own philsophical opinions and religious prejudices—just as it now is with those who practically disregard the authority of God's word; so

that in a short time the church would have been hopelessly divided, and every little sect and party would have had its own favorite canon.

3. But, notwithstanding these plain and inevitable ten-
Unity of the
Church on this
question. dencies to strife, and division, and sectarianism in the primitive church, and especially on the question touching their rule of faith and prac-
tice, it is, nevertheless, a remarkable and well-authenticated historical fact, that *on no other question has any body of men ever been more fully and firmly united.* Indeed, the unity of the Israelites on the question of the Old Testament Canon, is the only parallel case known in history. During the first three centuries, the twenty-seven books of the New Testa-ment, and the thirty-nine of the Old, were the only ones that were quoted as canonical by any Christian writer.* And at no period of the Christian Church were any of these twenty-seven books rejected by any Christian writer or teacher after a fair examination of the evidence. It is true, that for a time, the Epistle to the Hebrews, the Epistle of James, the Second of Peter, the Second and Third of John, that of Jude, and the Apocalypse, were by some regarded as of *doubtful* authority. But this only proves that the forma-tion of the New Testament Canon, was a matter of great care and concern among all true Christians. For as soon as they had fully investigated the matter, and had clearly as-certained from the testimony of competent witnesses, that these books had been written and indorsed by inspired men, that was with them an end of the controversy. They then no longer hesitated to regard and receive them as ca-nonical.

Here, then, we might perhaps safely rest the whole ques-

---

* Paley's Evidences, p. 195, Nairne's edition. Paley speaks only of the historical books. But I am persuaded that his remarks may be made general, so as to include books of all classes.

tion; for even from the premises now before us, it evidently follows that the canonical authority of these books rests on the authority of the Apostles and other inspired teachers of the primitive church. But,

Conclusion from the premises submitted.

II. This conclusion is greatly confirmed and strengthened by the consideration that *these twenty-seven books were all in existence, and most of them extensively circulated in the churches, and actually quoted as canonical by the Apostolic Fathers, and others, for more than fifty years before the cessation of miraculous gifts.* The evidence on this point is full and satisfactory; and I think that a few observations will make it plain and obvious to all. Be it remembered, then,

Second source of evidence in proof of the canonical authority of the books of the New Testament.

1. That the Apostles were all fully endowed with these supernatural gifts. Through them they were enabled to understand the great scheme and mystery of redemption, to reveal it to others, and also to demonstrate to all who sought to know the truth, that the Gospel is the power of God for salvation to every true believer. This is evident from such passages as the following: Matthew x, and also xxviii: 18–20; Luke xxiv: 48, 49; John xiv: 26 and xvi: 13; and the entire book of Acts.*

Extraordinary gifts bestowed on the Apostles.

* I here transgress no rule of logical propriety by introducing these witnesses. When a mathematician has once demonstrated the truth of a proposition, he may ever afterward use it as he would a definition or an axiom in any other demonstration. And just so in the present case. We have already proved, in Part First, that the Bible is from God; and hence we have now a right to use its facts and its precepts as the testimony and teachings of the Holy Spirit. True, indeed, it is still, to some extent, an open question with us in this discussion, what books belong of right to the Bible: and hence, to some, it may appear irrelevant and improper to

Propriety of here introducing New Testament witnesses

2. That the Apostles had power to bestow these gifts on
Their power to bestow like gifts on others. other persons, and that they often actually did this for the double purpose of converting the world and of edifying the church. See, for instance, Acts viii: 14–25; Romans i: 11; and 2 Timothy i: 6. See also 1 Corinthians xii and xiv.

3. But as God is no respecter of persons or of churches, and
Extent to which these gifts were bestowed. as the primitive churches were all equally needy in this respect before the books of the New Testament were written, it is but fair to conclude, that what was done for Timothy, was also done for Mark, and Luke, and all others who were called to labor in word and doctrine; and, moreover, that whatever gifts were bestowed on the Samaritans and the Corinthians, would, in like manner, be bestowed on all other churches, under similar circumstances, and hence that *most, if not all, of the first evangelists and bishops of the Christian Church were, like Timothy, endowed with these extraordinary spiritual gifts.**

4. Many of these would of course outlive the Apostles,
Period of their continuance. and it is but reasonable to suppose that some of them would continue to minister to the wants of the churches, until at least the middle of the second century. Polycarp, for example, one of John's disciples, and bishop of the church of Smyrna for about eighty years, suffered martyrdom in A. D. 166. And if Polycarp's ministry continued so long in Asia Minor, it is fair to presume that some other evangelists and bishops who had seen the Apostles, and who had received from their hands these extraor-

---

use any of these books in order to prove that they are really a part of the Canon. But the reader will observe that the facts here used in evidence can not be denied without rejecting the whole Bible as the Word of God. But this can not be done, as we have before proved; and hence it follows, that the use we here make of these facts, is entirely legitimate.

* See 1 Cor. xii: 28–31, and Ephes. iv: 7–16.

dinary gifts, would also continue to labor for other churches in other parts of Christendom, till at least A. D. 150.

I have here purposely cut off all ground of debate by limiting these spiritual gifts to the very shortest presumable period, on the supposition that they were conferred on evangelists, pastors, and teachers, solely through the agency of the Apostles. But every student of the Bible knows very well that these gifts were *Modes of conferring these gifts.* not always so bestowed. Christ gave them sometimes to his disciples directly, without any human instrumentality in the case. He did so, on the day of Pentecost, when the Christian Church was first established; he did so seven years after this, when the first fruits of the Gentiles were received into the fold and family of God; and he may have done so in a thousand other cases, whenever and wherever the interests of his Church required it. And if so, it is by no means necessary to suppose that these gifts were confined to the first and second centuries; they may have extended to the *Their duration according to ancient writers.* third, and, if need be, even to the fourth. And this is just what all ecclesiastical historians of the first centuries testify. The learned translator of Mosheim's Ecclesiastical History says "That what are called the *miraculous* gifts of the Holy Spirit were liberally conferred not only in this (the second), but also in the following century, especially on those engaged in propagating the Gospel, all who are called Christians believe, *on the unanimous and concordant testimony of all the ancient writers.* Nor do we, in my opinion, hereby incur any just charge of departing from sound reason; for, as these witnesses were all grave men, fair and honest, some of them philosophers—men who lived in different countries, and relate not what they *heard*, but what they *saw*, call God to witness the truth of their declarations (see Origen Contra Celsum, book i, p. 35, Spencer's edit.), and do not claim for themselves, but attribute to others these miraculous powers, what reason can there be for refusing to believe them?*

If, then, there is any reliance to be placed on "the unanimous and concordant testimony of all the ancient writers," we might safely extend the period of these miraculous gifts to at least the middle of the third century; but it is not necessary to do this in our present argument, and I wish, in this whole discussion, to occupy nothing but the safest and most reliable ground.

No debatable ground claimed in this discussion.

5. However these gifts were received and imparted, one thing is certain, *that those who possessed them were divinely qualified to judge of the character of any document, and to decide infallibly whether it was of God and had any just claims to a place in the Canon or not.* This is evident from such passages as the following: "If any man think himself to be a prophet or a spiritual man, let him acknowledge that the things that I write unto you are the Commandments of the Lord." (1 Cor. xiv: 37.) "But ye have an *unction* (a spiritual gift) from the Holy One, and ye know all things." (1 John ii: 20.) And in the twenty-seventh verse of the same chapter, John adds: "But the anointing which ye have received of him abides in you, and ye need not that any man teach you; but as the same anointing teaches you of all things, and is truth, and is no lie; and even as it hath taught you, ye shall abide in him."

Qualifications of these spiritual men to judge of the Canon.

The only remaining question, therefore, to be considered is simply this: Whether the aforesaid twenty-seven books were in existence long enough to be thoroughly examined and approved by inspired men before the cessation of miraculous gifts in the churches? for I do not think it necessary to pause here in order to prove that while these gifts continued they were

The only remaining question.

* Murdock's Mosheim's Ecclesiastical History, vol. i, p. 102.

constantly exercised in the defense of the truth; nor is it necessary to prove that the whole church would receive and respect the accredited decisions of her inspired men as the voice of God in such matters. It is enough to show that the aforesaid books were all in the hands of at least some of the churches for a number of years before the age of miracles had passed away; and on this point it gives me pleasure to say the evidence is full and satisfactory. True, indeed, it is now difficult, perhaps impossible, to determine, with absolute certainty, the precise time when some of these books were written; but all writers who have any claim on our respect for their learning and candor concede that they were all in existence before the close of the first century. *Fullness of the evidence on this point.*

I regret that my prescribed limits will not allow me to make any thing like a full statement of the evidence that might be brought forward in favor of this allegation. For this and many other interesting details relating to the genuineness and authenticity of these books, I must refer the reader to Lardner's Credibility of the Gospel History, Horne's Introduction to the Critical Study of the Bible, Davidson's Introduction to the New Testament, and Dean Alford's Prolegomena to the the last edition of his Greek Testament. *Works of reference.*

But some proof on so important a point is essential to the proposed plan and object of this work, and I will, therefore, endeavor to present as briefly and plainly as I can a mere outline of the evidence, confining myself chiefly to the Scriptural quotations and allusions of the Apostolic fathers. *Kind and source of evidence selected for this work.*

We will begin with the Epistle of Barnabas. And here it is proper to say that some doubts have been entertained respecting both the authorship and the date of this epistle: *"But the external evidence is unani-* *The Epistle of Barnabas.*

mous in ascribing it to Barnabas, the companion of Paul." It was quoted as such by Clement of Alexandria, in the second century, and by Origen, in the beginning of the third; and hence Lardner, after weighing all the evidence relating to

Its date and author. both its date and its authorship, comes to the conclusion that Barnabas, the companion of Paul, was most likely its author, and that it was certainly written soon after the destruction of Jerusalem, probably about A. D. 71 or 72.†

For the sake of convenience in comparing the quotations and allusions with the Scriptures themselves, I will place them in parallel columns; and for the sake of brevity, I will ordinarily use but one quotation from each of the several books to which the authors refer. In the Epistle of Barnabas we have but few *quotations*, but many *allusions*. The following may be taken as a specimen:

NEW TESTAMENT.	BARNABAS.
I. So the last shall be first, and the first last, *for many are called, but few chosen.* (Matt. xx: 16.)	I. Let us, therefore, beware, lest it should happen to us *as it is written: There are many called, few chosen.* (Ch. iv.)
II. *Give to every man that asketh thee.* (Luke vi: 30.)	II. *Give to every one that asketh thee.* (Ch. xix.)
III. Know ye not that *ye are the temple of God*, and that the Spirit of God dwells in you? (1 Cor. iii: 16.)	III. For, my brethren, *the habitation of our heart is a holy temple to the Lord.* (Ch. vi.)
IV. Redeeming the time, because *the days are evil.* Wherefore be ye not unwise, but understanding what the mind of	IV. Seeing, then, *the days are exceeding evil, and the adversary has the power of this present world,* we ought to give diligent

Five books quoted and indorsed by Barnabas.

* Donaldson's History of Chris. Literature and Doct., vol. i, p. 201.
† Lardner's Credibility, vol. ii, p. 14.

NEW TESTAMENT.

the Lord is. (Eph. v: 16, 17.) *The Prince of the power of the air, the spirit that now worketh in the children of disobedience.* (Eph. ii: 2.)

V. I charge thee before God *and the Lord Jesus Christ, who shall judge the quick and the dead.* (2 Tim. iv: 1.)

BARNABAS.

heed to inquire into the righteous judgments of the Lord. (Ch. ii.)

V. If, therefore, *the Son of God, who is the Lord of all, and shall judge the quick and the dead, hath suffered——.* (Ch. vii.*)

THE EPISTLE OF CLEMENS ROMANUS.

The next document that I will introduce, is a letter addressed by the Church of Rome to the Church of Corinth. The name of the writer is not attached to the epistle, but it was unanimously ascribed by the ancients to Clemens Romanus,† of whom honorable mention is supposed to be made in Philippians iv: 3. It was written about A. D. 96,‡ and contains many references to the books of the New Testament. The following will suffice for our present purpose:

Its date and author.

NEW TESTAMENT.

I. But *woe to that man by whom the Son of Man is betrayed! It had been good for that man if he had not been born.* (Matt. xxvi: 24. See also Matt. xviii: 6, and Mark ix: 42.)

CLEMENT.

I. Remember the words of the Lord Jesus. *For he said: Woe to that man by whom offenses come. It were better for him that he had not been born,* than that he should offend one of my elect.

Eighteen books quoted and indorsed by Clement.

* Lardner's Credibility, vol. ii, pp. 11–22.
† Donaldson's Hist. of Christian Literature and Doctrine, vol. i, p. 90.
‡ Donaldson, vol. i, p. 108, 109, and Lardner, vol. ii, p. 28.

NEW TESTAMENT.	CLEMENT.

It were better for him that a millstone were hanged about his neck, and he cast into the sea, than that he should offend one of these little ones. (Luke xvii: 2.)

II. How he said: *It is more blessed to give than to receive.* (Acts xx: 35.)

III. Being filled with *all unrighteousness, fornication, wickedness, covetousness, maliciousness; full of envy, murder, debate, deceit, malignity, whisperers, backbiters, haters of God, despiteful, proud, boasters, who, knowing the judgment of God, that they who do such things are worthy of death, not only do the same, but have pleasure in them that do them.* (Rom. i: 29–32.)

IV. Now this I say, that every one of you saith, *I am of Paul, and I of Apollos, and I am of Cephas, and I of Christ.* (1 Cor. i: 12.)

V. But he that glories, let him glory in the Lord. *For not he that commendeth himself is approved, but whom the Lord commendeth.* (2 Cor. 17–18.)

It were better for him that a millstone should be tied about his neck, and that he should be drowned in the sea, than that he should offend one of my little ones. (Ch. xlvi.)

II. Ye were all of you humble-minded, *more willingly giving than receiving.* (Ch. ii.)

III. Casting off from us *all unrighteousness and iniquity, covetousness, debates, malignities, deceits, whisperings, backbitings, hatred of God, pride, boasting, and vain-glory, and ambition. For they that do these things are hateful to God, and not only they that do them, but they also who have pleasure in them.* (Ch. xxv.)

IV. Take into your hands *the epistle of the blessed Paul the Apostle.* What did he at first write to you in the beginning of the Gospel ? *Verily he did by the Spirit admonish you concerning himself, and Cephas, and Apollos;* because that even then you did form parties. (Ch. xlvii.)

V. *Let our praise be in God, not of ourselves, for God hates those that commend themselves.* (Ch. xxx.)

NEW TESTAMENT.

VI. *Of the Jews received I forty stripes, save one. Thrice was I beaten with rods; once was I stoned.* (2 Cor. xi: 24.)

VII. *Who gave himself for our sins, that he might deliver us from this present evil world, according to the will of God and our Father.* (Gal. i: iv.)

VIII. *There is one body and one Spirit; even as ye are called with one hope of your calling. One Lord, one faith, one baptism. One God and Father of all.* (Eph. iv: 4.)

IX. Let this mind be in you which was also in Christ Jesus, who being in the form of God, thought it not robbery to be equal with God; but made himself of no reputation, and took upon him the form of a servant, and was made in the likeness of men: and being found in fashion as a man, he humbled himself, and became obedient unto death, even the death of the cross. (Philippians ii: 5–8.)

X. *In every thing give thanks.* (1 Thess. v: 18.)

XI. I will, therefore, that men pray every-where, *lifting*

CLEMENT.

VI. *Seven times was he (Paul) in bonds. He was whipped, was stoned.* (Ch. v.)

VII. *For the love which he had for us, Christ our Lord gave his blood for us, by the will of God; his flesh for our flesh; his soul for our soul.* (Ch. xlix.)

VIII. *Have we not one God and one Christ? And is there not one Spirit poured out upon us; and one calling in Christ?* (Ch. xlvi.)

IX. For Christ is theirs who are humble. The scepter of the majesty of God, our Lord Jesus Christ, came not in the show of pride and arrogance, though he could have done so, but in humility. Ye see, beloved, what is the pattern which has been given us. If the Lord thus humbled himself, what should we do who are brought by him under the yoke of his grace? (Ch. xvi.)

X. Having, therefore, all these things from him, *we ought in all things to give thanks to him.* (Ch. xxxviii.)

XI. Let us, therefore, come to him in holiness of soul, *lift-*

up holy hands without wrath and doubting. (1 Tim. ii: 8.)

XII. Who hath saved us, and called us *with a holy calling.* (2 Tim. i: 9.)

XIII. *To be ready to every good work.* (Titus iii: 1.)

XIV. *Who being the brightness of his glory, and the express image of his person*——. *Being made so much better than the angels, as he has by inheritance obtained a more excellent name than they. For unto which of the angels said he at any time, Thou art my Son, this day have I begotten thee? And of the angels he saith, Who maketh his angels spirits, and his ministers a flame of fire. But to which of the angels said he at any time, Sit on my right hand, until I make thy enemies thy footstool?* (Heb. i: 3, 4, 5, 7, 13.)

XV. *As also Moses was faithful in all his house. And verily Moses was faithful in all his house.* (Heb. iii: 2, 5.)

XVI. *And is a discerner of the thoughts and intents of the heart.* (Heb. iv: 12.)

XVII. *That by two immuta-*

ing up to him chaste and undefiled hands. (Ch. xxix.)

XII. *And let us come up to the glorious and venerable rule of our holy calling.* (Ch. vii.)

XIII. *Ye were ready to every good work.* (Ch. ii.)·

XIV. *Who being the brightness of his majesty, is by so much greater than the angels, as he has obtained a more excellent name than they. For so it is written, Who maketh his angels spirits, and his ministers a flame of fire. But unto his Son thus saith the Lord, Thou art my Son, this day have I begotten thee. Ask of me, and I will give thee the heathen for thine inheritance, and the uttermost part of the earth for thy possession. And again he saith unto him, Sit on my right hand, until I make thine enemies thy footstool.* (Ch. xxxvi.)

XV. *When also Moses, that blessed and faithful servant in all his house*——. *Moses was called faithful in all his house.* (Chs. xliii, xviii.)

XVI. *For he is a searcher of the intents and thoughts.* (Ch. xxi.)

XVII. *For nothing is impos-*

NEW TESTAMENT.

ble things, in which it was impossible for God to lie. (Heb. vi : 18.)

XVIII. *They wandered about in sheep-skins and goat-skins.* (Heb. xi : 37.)

XIX. *Was not our father Abraham justified by works, when he had offered Isaac his son upon the altar?* (Jas. ii : 21.)

XX. *And he was called the friend of God.* (Jas. ii : 23.)

XXI. *Who is a wise man and endued with knowledge among you? Let him show out of a good conversation his works with meekness of wisdom.* (Jas. iii : 13.)

XXII. *For charity shall cover a multitude of sins.* (1 Pet. iv : 8. Comp. Jas. v : 20.)

XXIII. *Yea, all of you be subject one to another, and be clothed with humility : for God resisteth the proud, and giveth grace to the humble.* (1 Pet. v : 5.)

XXIV. *A double-minded man is unstable in all his ways.* (Jas. i : 8.) ——*And saying, When is the promise of his coming? For since the fathers fell asleep,*

CLEMENT.

sible with God but to lie. (Ch. xxvii.)

XVIII. Let us be imitators of those *who went about in goat-skins and sheep-skins preaching the coming of Christ.* (Ch. xvii.)

XIX. For what was our father Abraham blessed? *Was it not, because that through faith, he wrought righteousness and truth?* (Ch. xxxi.)

XX. Abraham has been greatly witnessed of; *and was called the friend of God.* (Ch. xvii.)

XXI. *Let the wise man show forth his wisdom, not in words, but in good works.* (Ch. xxxviii.)

XXII. *Charity covers the multitude of sins.* (Ch. xlix.)

XXIII. *And let every one be subject to his neighbor.* (Ch. xxxviii.) *For God, saith he, resisteth the proud, but giveth grace to the humble.* (Ch. xxx.)

XXIV. Let that be far from us *which is written : Miserable are the double-minded, who are doubtful in their minds, and say, These things have we heard even*

NEW TESTAMENT.	CLEMENT.
all things continue as they were from the beginning of the crea-tion. (2 Pet. iii: 4.)	*from our fathers; and, behold, we are grown old, and none of these things have happened to us.* (Ch. xxiii.*)

THE SHEPHERD OF HERMAS.

The author of this highly-allegorical production is sup-
Author, date, and character of this docu-ment. posed by Origen, Eusebius, and some other ancient writers, to be the same Hermas to whom
Paul refers in Romans xvi: 14: "Salute Asyn-
critus, Phlegon, *Hermas*, Patrobas, Hermes, and the brethren
who are with them." Its date is fixed by Lardner at about
A. D. 100.† It consists of three books, the first of which
contains four visions, the second twelve commands, and the
third ten similitudes. The nature of the composition is not
such as to admit of any *direct quotations*, but it contains
many *allusions* to the books of the New Testament. The
following will suffice for illustration:

NEW TESTAMENT.	HERMAS.
I. Verily I say unto you, ex-cept ye shall be *Fourteen books referred to and indorsed by Hermas.* converted, and be-come as little chil-dren, ye shall not enter into the kingdom of God. Whosoever, therefore, shall humble himself as this little child, the same is the greatest in the kingdom of heaven. (Matt. xviii: 3, 4.)	I. Whosoever, therefore, says he, shall continue as little chil-dren, free from malice, shall be more honorable than all these of whom I have yet spoken. For all little children are hon-orable with the Lord, and es-teemed the first of all. (Simil. ix.)

* Lardner's Credibility, vol. ii, pp. 22–46.   † Ibid, p. 51.

NEW TESTAMENT.	HERMAS.
II. *And have peace one with another.* (Mark ix: 50.)	II. *Now, therefore, hearken unto me, and have peace one with another.* (Vis. iii.)
III. *I am the door; by me if any man enter in he shall be saved, and shall go in and out, and find pasture.* (John x: 9.) *I am the way, and the truth, and the life; no man cometh unto the Father but by me.* (John xiv: 6.)	III. *The gate is the only way of coming to God. For no man shall go to God but by his Son.* (Simil. ix.)
IV. *If any man defile the temple of God, him shall God destroy.* (1 Cor. iii: 17. See also 1 Cor. vi: 9.)	IV. *For if thou defile thy body, thou shalt also at the same time defile the Holy Spirit. And if thou defile thy body thou shalt not live.* (Simil. v.)
V. *And grieve not the Holy Spirit of God.* (Eph. iv: 30.)	V. *Grieve not the Holy Spirit that dwelleth in thee, lest he ask of God and depart from thee.* (Com. iii.)
VI. *Who is the first-born of every creature.* (Col. i: 15.)	VI. *The Son of God is more ancient than any creature.* (Vis. ii.)
VII. *For he found no place of repentance.* (Heb. xii: 17.)	VII. *For these there is no place of repentance.* (Simil. viii.)
VIII. Submit yourselves therefore to God. *Resist the devil, and he will flee from you.* (James iv: 7.)	VIII. *For if ye resist him (the Devil) he will flee from you with confusion.* (Com. xii.)
IX. Though now for a season, if need be, ye are in heaviness through manifold temptations. That the trial of your	IX. The golden part are ye who have escaped from this world. For as gold is tried by the fire and made profitable, so

faith, being much more precious than of gold that perisheth, though it be tried with fire, might be found unto praise, and honor, and glory, at the appearing of Christ. (1 Peter i: 6.)

are ye also tried who dwell among them (the men of this world.) They, therefore, who shall endure to the end, and be proved by them, shall be purged. And as gold is cleansed and loses its dross, so shall ye also cast away all sorrow and trouble, and be made pure for the building of the tower. (Vis. iv.)

X. *Who have forsaken the right way.* (2 Pet. ii: 15.)

X. They are such as have believed indeed, but through their doublings *have forsaken the true way.* (Vis. iii.)

XI. Hereby know we *the Spirit of Truth,* (1 John iv: 6,) because *the Spirit is truth.* (1 John v: 6.)

XI. For they received *the Spirit of Truth,* and became habitations of *the true Spirit.* (Com. iii.)

XII. I rejoice that I found of, thy children *walking in truth.* (2 John, verse 4.)

XII. For thou oughtest, as the servant of God, *to walk in the truth.* (Com. iii.)

The whole of the third commandment of Hermas is very analogous to the Second and Third Epistles of John. (Lardner, vol. ii, 61.)

XIII. *Keep yourselves in the love of God, looking for the mercy of our Lord Jesus Christ unto eternal life. Others save with fear, pulling them out of the fire: hating even the garment spotted by the flesh.* (Jude, verses 21 and 23. See also 24.)

XIII. *Because the elect of God should be pure, and without spot, unto life eternal.* (Vis. iv.)

The allusions to the Apocalypse are very many; and hence Lardner is of the opinion that Hermas had not only read the book of Revelation, but that in his visions he also attempts to imitate it. The following brief extract is given as an illustration:

"In Revelation ch. xii, *the Church is represented under the figure of a woman, as we have already seen the Church to be in Hermas.* In the Revelation *the woman is persecuted by a dragon.* Hermas also sees *a great and terrible beast, which he is informed is the figure of the trial which was coming.* John saw *the Holy City, the New Jerusalem, coming down from God out of heaven prepared as a bride adorned for her husband.* (Ch. xxi: 2.) Hermas says, *Behold, there met me a virgin, well adorned, as if she were just come out of the bride-chamber, clothed in white. And I knew by my former visions, that it was the Church.* John sees *a city, the foundations of the walls of which were garnished with all manner of precious stones.* (Ch. xxi: 19.) Hermas sees *a tower built with bright, square stones.* In the Revelation, *the city lies four-square. The tower in Hermas is likewise built upon a square.* In Revelation vii: 9, John says, *After this I beheld, and lo, a great multitude which no man could number, stood before the throne, and before the Lamb, clothed with white robes and palms in their hands.* And Hermas says, *Then the angel of the Lord commanded crowns to be brought, made as of palms. And the angel crowned these men, and commanded them to go into the tower.* The writer of the Revelation is soon after informed who these are. Ver. 14. *He said to me: These are they who came out of great tribulation, and have washed their robes and made them white in the blood of the Lamb.* In Hermas we have a like explanation. *But who then, Lord, said I, are they who enter into the tower crowned? He says to me: All who, having striven with the Devil, have overcome him; these are crowned. And these are* *they who have suffered hard things that they might keep the law."**

THE EPISTLES OF IGNATIUS.

Ignatius was an overseer of the Church of Antioch during
Their date, address, and author. the latter part of the first and the beginning of the second century. He suffered martyrdom at Rome, according to Du Pin, Lardner, and others, in A. D. 107.† While on his way from Antioch to Rome, he wrote seven epistles, viz. : one to the Church of Ephesus ; one to the Church of Magnesia ; one to the Church of Trallium ; one to the Church of Philadelphia ; one to the Church of Smyrna ; and one to Polycarp, who was then president of the eldership of the Church of Smyrna. The following are some of the many references that he makes to the books of the New Testament :

NEW TESTAMENT.	IGNATIUS.
I. *For thus it becomes us to fulfill all righteousness.* (Matt. iii: 15.) Seventeen books quoted and indorsed by Ignatius.	I. *Baptized of John that all righteousness might be fulfilled by him.* (Smyrn.)
II. *Behold my hands and my feet, that it is I myself: handle me and see, for a spirit has not flesh and bones as ye see me have.* (Luke xxiv: 39.)	II. *He (Christ) said to them, Take, handle me, and see that I am not an incorporated demon.* (Smyrn.)
III. *I am the door: by me if any man enter in, he shall be saved.* (John x: 9.)	III. *He (Christ) is the door of the Father,* by which enter in Abraham, and Isaac, and Jacob, and the Apostles, and the Church. (Philad. ix.)
IV. Satan is called, *The*	IV. *The prince of this world*

* Lardner's Cred., vol. ii, pp. 50–65.   † Ibid, p. 66. See also pp. 67–85.

prince of the world, in John xii: 31; xiv: 30; and xvi: 11.

would fain carry me away. (Rom.)

Avoid the ambushes of the prince of this world. (Philad.)

V. *Who did eat and drink with him, after he arose from the dead.* (Acts x: 41.)

V. *But after his resurrection, he did eat and drink with them.* (Smyrn.)

VI. *Concerning his Son Jesus Christ our Lord, who was made of the seed of David, according to the flesh ; and declared to be the Son of God with power.* (Rom. i: 3, 4.)

VI. *Our Lord was truly of the race of David, according to the flesh; the Son of God, according to the will and power of God.* (Smyrn.)

VII. *Purge out, therefore, the old leaven, that ye may be a new lump, as ye are unleavened. For Christ our Passover is sacrificed for us. Therefore let us keep the feast, not with old leaven, neither with the leaven of malice and wickedness.* (1 Cor. v: 7.)

VII. *Cast away, therefore, the evil leaven which is waxen old and sour: and be transformed into the new leaven, which is Jesus Christ.* (Magnes.)

VIII. And that he died for all, that they who live should not henceforth live unto themselves but unto him who died for them, and rose again. (2 Cor. v: 15.)

VIII. Him I seek who died for us: him I desire who rose again for us. (Rom. vi.)

IX. Christ is become of none effect unto you; *whosoever of you are justified by law, ye are fallen from grace.* (Gal. v: 4.)

IX. *For if we still live according to Judaism, we confess we have not received grace.* (Magnes.)

X. *Husbands, love your wives, even as Christ also loved the Church.* (Eph. v: 25.)

X. In like manner, exhort my brethren, in the name of Jesus Christ, *to love their wives, as the Lord the Church.* (Polycarp.)

NEW TESTAMENT.

IGNATIUS.

XI. Wherefore take unto you *the whole armor of God.* Stand therefore *having your loins girt about with truth, and having on the breast-plate of righteousness. Above all taking the shield of faith: and take the helmet of salvation, and the sword of the Spirit, which is the word of God.* (Eph. vi: 13.)

XI. Let none of you be found a deserter, *but let your baptism remain as your arms; faith as a helmet; love as a spear; patience as whole armor.* (Polycarp, sec. v.)

XII. For me to live is Christ; *and to die is gain.* (Phil. i: 21.)

XII. *He* (Christ) *is the gain that is laid up for me.* (Rom., sec. vi.)

XIII. *Let nothing be done through strife. Let this mind be in you which was also in Christ Jesus.* (Phil. ii: 3.)

XIII. *I beseech you, that ye do nothing through strife, but according to the instruction of Christ.* (Phila., sec. vii.)

XIV. *Pray without ceasing.* (1 Thess. v: 17.)

XIV. *Be at leisure to pray without ceasing.* (Polyc. i.)

XV. *No man that warreth, entangleth himself with the affairs of this life, that he may please him who hath chosen him to be a soldier.* (2 Tim. ii: 4.)

XV. *Please Him under whom ye war, and from whom ye receive your wages.* (Polyc. vi.)

XVI. The aged women, that they be in *behavior,* as becometh godliness. (Titus ii: 3.) · This is the only place in which χαταστημα (behavior) occurs in the New Testament.

XVI. Whose very *behavior* is an excellent instruction. (Trall. iii.)

XVII. *Yea, brother, let me have joy of thee in the Lord.* (Philem., ver. 20.)

XVII. *And may I always have joy of you.* (Ephes., sec. ii.) This phrase of St. Paul to Philemon, occurs in several epistles of Ignatius.

NEW TESTAMENT.	IGNATIUS.
XVIII. *Yea, all of you be subject one to another.* (1 Pet. v: 5.)	XVIII. *Be ye subject to the bishop, and to one another.* (Magnes. xiii.)
XIX. And the life was manifested—and—we show unto you that eternal life, which was with the Father, and was manifested unto us. (1 John i: 2.)	XIX. Jesus Christ who was with the Father before the world was, and in the end appeared. (Magnes. vi.)
XX. *Beloved, I wish above all things, that thou mayest prosper, and be in health, even as thy soul prospereth.* (3 John, ver. 2.)	XX. *That whatsoever ye do, ye may prosper in the flesh and spirit.* (Magnes. xiii.)

POLYCARP'S EPISTLE TO THE PHILIPPIANS.

Finally, I invite the attention of the reader to a few of the quotations and scriptural allusions contained in Polycarp's letter to the Philippians. It was written, according to Lardner, about A. D. 108.* _{Its date, address, and author.}

NEW TESTAMENT.	POLYCARP.
I. *The spirit indeed is willing; but the flesh is weak.* (Matt. xxvi: 41. See also Mark xiv: 38.)	I. As the Lord hath said: *The spirit indeed is willing; but the flesh is weak.—* (Ch. i.)
II. *Judge not, and ye shall not be judged. Forgive and ye shall be forgiven. For with the measure that ye mete, it shall be measured to you again.* (Luke vi: 37, 38. See also Matt. vii: 1.)	II. But remembering what the Lord said teaching: *Judge not that ye be not judged: forgive, and ye shall be forgiven: be ye merciful, that ye may obtain mercy: with what measure ye mete, it shall be measured to you again.* (Ch. ii.)

Eighteen books quoted and indorsed by Polycarp.

* Lardner's Cred., vol. ii, p. 89.

III. *Whom God hath raised up, having loosed the pains of death.* (Acts ii: 24.)

IV. *We shall all stand before the judgment-seat of Christ. So then every one of us shall give an account of himself to God.* (Rom. xiv: 10, 12.)

V. *Do ye not know that the saints shall judge the world?* (1 Cor. vi: 2.)

VI. *By the armor of right-eousness.* (2 Cor. vi: 7.)

VII. *Providing for honest things, not only in the sight of the Lord, but also in the sight of men.* (2 Cor. viii: 21.)

VIII. *Be not deceived, God is not mocked.* (Gal. vi: 7.)

IX. *Be ye angry and sin not: let not the sun go down on your wrath.* (Eph. iv: 26.)

X. *That at the name of Je-sus, every knee should bow, of things in Heaven, and things in Earth, and things under the Earth. And that every tongue should confess.* (Philip. ii: 10.)

XI. That we may present

III. *Whom God hath raised, having loosed the pains of Ha-des.* (Ch. i.)

IV. *And must all stand be-fore the judgment-seat of Christ; and every one give an account of himself.* (Ch. vi.)

V. *Do ye not know, that the saints shall judge the world,* as Paul teaches? (Ch. xi.)

VI. *Let us arm ourselves with the armor of righteousness.—* (Ch. iv.)

VII. *Always providing what is honest in the sight of God and men.* (Ch. vi.)

VIII. *Knowing therefore, that God is not mocked.* (Ch. v.)

IX. For I trust that ye are well exercised in the Holy Scriptures—as in these Scrip-tures it is said: *Be ye angry, and sin not. And, Let not the sun go down on your wrath.* (Ch. xii.)

X. *To whom all things are made subject that are in Heaven, and that are in Earth; whom every living creature serves.—* (Ch. ii.)

XI. That your fruit may be

every man *perfect in Christ.*
(Col. i: 28.)

XII. *Pray without ceasing.*
(1 Thess. v: 17.)

XIII. *Abstain from all appearance of evil.* (1 Thess. v:
22.)

XIV. *Yet count him not as
an enemy; but admonish him
as a brother.* (2 Thess. iii: 15.)

XV. *For we brought nothing
with us into this world, and it
is certain that we can carry nothing out. For the love of money
is the root of all evil.* (1 Tim.
ii: 1, 2.)

XVI. It is a faithful saying—*If we suffer we shall also
reign with him.* (2 Tim. ii: 11.)

XVII. *And is a discerner of
the thoughts and intents of the
heart. Neither is there any creature, that is not manifest in his
sight; but all things are naked
and open unto the eyes of Him,
with whom we have to do.* (Heb.
iv: 12.)

XVIII. *Whom having not*

manifest in all; and ye may be
perfect in him. (Ch. xii.)

XII. *Praying without ceasing for all.* (Ch. iv.)

XIII. *Abstain from all evil.*
(Ch. ii.)

XIV. Giving advice about
one who had offended, Polycarp says: Be ye also moderate
in this; *and do not count such
as enemies; but call them back
as suffering and erring members.* (Ch. xi.)

XV. *But the love of money
is the beginning of all troubles.
Knowing therefore that we
brought nothing into the world,
so neither can we carry any
thing out.*

XVI. According as he has
promised us, that he will raise
us up from the dead; *and that
if we walk worthy of him, we
shall also reign with him.* (Ch.
v.)

XVII. *Knowing that he sees
all things, and that nothing is
hid from him, not the reason-
ings, nor the intents, nor any
secrets of the heart.* (Ch. iv.)

XVIII. *In whom, though ye*

NEW TESTAMENT.	POLYCARP.
seen ye love: in whom, though now you see him not, yet believing, ye rejoice with joy unspeakable, and full of glory. (1 Pet. i: 8.)	*see him not, ye believe; and believing, ye rejoice with joy unspeakable, and full of glory.* (Ch. i.)
XIX. *Not rendering evil for evil; or railing for railing.* (1 Pet. iii: 9.)	XIX. *Not rendering evil for evil; or railing for railing.* (Ch. ii.)
XX. *And every spirit that confesseth not that Jesus Christ is come in the flesh, is not of God. And this is that spirit of Antichrist, whereof ye have heard.* (1 John iv: 3.)	XX. *For whosoever confesseth not, that Jesus Christ is come in the flesh is Antichrist.* (Ch. vii.)
XXI. *Earnestly contend for the faith once delivered to the saints.* (Jude, ver. 3.)	XXI. *To edify yourselves in the faith delivered to you.* (Ch. iii.)*

The number of these quotations and allusions might, if

Number of references to the books of the New Testament.

necessary, be very greatly increased. I have not given even half of those that are contained in the few short epistles referred to; and by extending our inquiries to the works of Papias, Justin Martyr, Irenæus, and other writers of the second century, the number of Scripture references might be almost indefinitely multiplied.

But this, I think, is wholly unnecessary. One clear and

The number necessary to our present argument.

indubitable reference or allusion to each of the twenty-seven books of the New Testament, before the cessation of miracles in the churches, is enough for our present purpose. Take, for illustration, the following reference that Paul makes to the book of Deuteronomy:

* Lardner's Cred., vol. ii, pp. 91–100.

MOSES.	PAUL.
For this commandment which I command thee this day, is not hidden from thee; neither is it far off. It is not in heaven, that thou shouldst say, *Who shall go up for us to heaven, and bring it unto us?* Neither is it beyond the sea, that thou shouldst say, *Who shall go over the sea for us, and bring it unto us, that we may hear it and do it?* *But the word is very nigh unto thee, in thy mouth, and in thy heart*, that thou mayest do it. (Deut. xxx: 11–14.)	But the righteousness which is of faith speaketh on this wise: Say not in thy heart, *Who shall ascend into heaven?* (that is, to brnig Christ down from above): or *Who shall descend into the deep?* (that is, to bring up Christ again from the dead). But what saith 'it? *The word is nigh thee, even in thy mouth and in thy heart:* that is, the word of faith which we preach, that if thou shalt confess with thy mouth the Lord Jesus, and shalt believe in thy heart that God hath raised him from the dead, thou shalt be saved. (Rom. x: 6–9.)

Illustration.

This can scarcely be regarded as a *direct quotation* from Moses; it is rather an *allusion* to a sentiment which Moses very beautifully and very happily expressed concerning the Law; and which Paul perceived could, with but a slight change of the phraseology, be applied even more appropriately to the Gospel. But nevertheless it clearly indicates and proves the following particulars:

What this allusion implies.

1. That the book of Deuteronomy was extant in the time of Paul.

2. That Paul regarded it as an inspired work.

3. That it was then also well known to the Roman brethren; and looked upon by them with the same feelings and sentiments of reverence and respect.

13

Now it is evident, that the same or analogous things are also implied in each of the preceding allusions that Barnabas, Clement, Hermas, Ignatius, and Polycarp make to the several parts of the New Testament. In them, these authors seem to refer to every one of the twenty-seven books that compose our present Canon; and if so, then it follows of necessity,

Things implied in the preceding quotations and allusions of the Apostolic Fathers.

1. That these books were all extant before the epistles were written in which they are severally referred to. That is, that some of them were certainly in existence before A. D. 72; others before A. D. 96; and all of them before A. D. 108.

2. That they were severally regarded by Barnabas, Clement, Hermas, Ignatius, and Polycarp as works of Divine authority. They are quoted by these writers just as they are now quoted by those who receive and respect them as the word of God.

3. That these books were then also well known to the several churches addressed, as the books and writings of inspired men. In no instance, are they introduced as novelties that required to be explained before their true character could be known and appreciated; but always as the acknowledged word of God, and divinely-appointed rule of faith and practice.

The only remaining ground of doubt, then, is simply this: Whether, in the citations made from the aforesaid authors, there is certain reference to every one of the twenty-seven books that now compose the New Testament Canon. Some of these allusions are confessedly indefinite: and it is therefore possible, that in a few instances the reference may be to some other part of the Scriptures than that which I have supposed.

The only ground of doubt in relation to the canonical authority of these twenty-seven books.

But such a doubt, if it exists at all, can exist only in reference to Mark, Colossians, 2 Thessalonians, Philemon, 2 John, 3 John, and Jude. The references Limit of this doubt. to all the other books, are I think clear and indisputable; and their canonical authority is therefore fully established. For there is scarcely any room to Qualifications of the aforesaid Apostolic Fathers to judge of such matters. doubt that Barnabas,* Clement, Hermas, Ignatius, and Polycarp were all possessed of the miraculous gifts of the Holy Spirit; and that they were therefore divinely qualified to judge of all manner of writings. At any rate, they were certainly the grave, sober, and discreet companions of the Apostles and many other inspired men: and could not fail to understand their views on a matter that concerned their own daily instructions; and which was, at the same time, of vital importance to the edification and welfare of all the churches. And hence I conclude that *the canonical authority of Mat-* Conclusion concerning twenty of the twenty-seven books. *thew, Luke, John, Acts, Romans, 1 Corinthians, 2 Corinthians, Galatians, Ephesians, Philippians, 1 Thessalonians, 1 Timothy, 2 Timothy, Titus, Hebrews, James, 1 Peter, 2 Peter, 1 John, and Revelation, rests on the authority of inspired men.*

And we are also, I think, fully warranted in placing the canonical authority of the remaining seven books on the same ground. For, be it observed,

1. That there is a strong presumption in favor of this, implied in the previously given allusions. While it Reasons for placing the remaining seven books on the same ground. is not absolutely certain, it is nevertheless highly probable, that these are the identical books referred to by Hermas, Ignatius, and Polycarp.

2. It is a conceded fact, depending on the unequivocal testimony of the Christian fathers and the internal evidence of these books, that they were all extant and in the hands

* Barnabas seems to be ranked among the Prophets in Acts xiii: 1.

of the churches before the close of the first century;* and hence that for more than fifty years, I might, perhaps, truthfully say one hundred and fifty, they were subject to the inspection and scrutiny of inspired men.†

3. That although doubts were for a while entertained concerning some of these, as well as concerning the Hebrews and the Revelation, yet that after a full and fair examination of all the evidence in the case, *the twenty-seven books that now compose the New Testament Canon were all finally received by the whole church, without a dissenting voice.*‡

*It is now generally conceded by our best authorities that Matthew was written about A. D. 42; *Mark*, A. D. 64; Luke, A. D. 61; John, A. D. 90; Acts, A. D. 63; Romans, A. D. 58; 1 Corinthians, A. D. 56; 2 Corinthians, A. D. 56; Galatians, A. D. 55; Ephesians, A. D. 62; Philippians, A. D. 62; *Colossians*, A. D. 62; 1 Thessalonians, A. D. 51; 2 *Thessalonians*, A. D. 51; 1 Timothy, A. D. 65; 2 Timothy, A. D. 66; Titus, A. D. 56; *Philemon*, A. D. 62; Hebrews, A. D. 63; James, A. D. 62; 1 Peter, A. D. 63; 2 Peter, A. D. 64; 1 John, A. D. 96; 2 *John*, A. D. 97; 3 *John*, A. D. 97; *Jude*, A. D. 64; Revelation, A. D. 96. (See Davidson's Introduction.)

Date of the several books of the New Testament.

†There is a plain reference made to the Gospel of Mark by Papias, about A. D. 116; to Colossians, and 2 Thessalonians by Justin Martyr, A. D. 140; to Mark, Colossians, and 2 John, by Irenæus, A. D. 178; to Mark, Colossians, 2 John, and Jude, by Clement of Alexandria, A. D. 194; to Mark, Colossians, Philemon, and Jude, by Tertullian, A. D. 200; and to all these seven books, as well as to every other book in the New Testament, by Origen, A. D. 230. (Lardner's Credibility, vol. ii.)

‡Much of the doubt expressed by ancient writers concerning some of these books had reference, not to their *authenticity*, but merely to their *genuineness*. These, however, are two very different matters, and should never be confounded. To this day many of our ablest critics are in doubt whether the Epistle to the Hebrews was written by Paul, or Apollos, or Barnabas, or Luke, or Silas, or Clement of Rome; but no Christian man now doubts its authenticity and canonical authority.

Doubt of genuineness implies no doubt of authenticity.

It is enough for us to know that the Epistle to the Hebrews and all the other books of the Old and New Testaments were indorsed by inspired men, and received into the Canon on their authority. The question of authorship is of minor importance: and for wise reasons, the Holy Spirit

When this was done can not now be ascertained with absolute certainty. Some time would necessarily Causes of delay in forming the Canon. intervene before the churches could all be made acquainted with the inspired books; and with the evidence on which their claims severally rested. That was not an age of printing-presses, steam-engines, railroads, and telegraphs. It was then a very tedious, laborious, and expensive work to transcribe and circulate such a book as the New Testament. And hence it is probable, that for some time, most of the churches would be satisfied with those books that were looked upon as the most important; and that such as were of a more personal and private character, as, for instance, Philemon, and the Second and Third Epistles of John, would be comparatively unknown, especially in those churches and provinces that were most remote from the place of their origin.

But that most, if not all, of these inspired books, were collected together into one volume, and received as Evidence that most of these twenty-seven books were soon collected into one vol. the Word of God, at a very early period, by the most enlightened and influential churches of Christendom, is evident,

1. *From what we find in the most ancient versions.* The Peshito or Old Syriac version, for instance, con- First, from the ancient versions. tains all the books of the New Testament, except the Second Epistle of Peter, the Second and Third of John, the Epistle of Jude, and the Revelation. And of this version the learned Horne says: "There is every reason to believe that it was made, if not in the first century, at least in the beginning of the second century."[*]

2. *From sundry expressions found in the writings of the Apostolic and Christian Father.* Igna- Secondly, from the writings of the Fathers.

may leave forever concealed the names of the authors, just as it has designedly concealed the genealogy of Melchisedec.

[*] Horne's Introduction, vol. ii, p. 203, Littell edit.

tius, in his epistle to the Church of Philadelphia, written as
Remarks of Ig- we have seen about A. D. 107, speaks of the
natius. Gospels and the Apostles, in terms that evidently imply a *collection* of the historical and epistolary
Of Polycarp. writings of the New Testament.* Polycarp, in
his letter to the Philippians, written A. D. 108,
calls the books of the New Testament, *" The Scriptures ;
the Holy Scriptures."*† And as these were the names then
commonly used to denote all the collected inspired writings
of the Old Testament, it is most likely that Polycarp used
the same words to denote a *collection* of the inspired books
of the New Testament. In the same letter he calls them
Of Melito. the *Oracles* of God.‡ About A. D. 170, Melito,
bishop of Sardis, in writing to his friend Onesi-
mus, spoke of the Old Testament.‖ But the *Old* Testament
is a relative term, and implies also the existence of a *New*
Testament. Soon after this, about A. D. 178, Irenæus con-
Of Irenæus. nects *" The Evangelic and Apostolic Writings "*
with *" The Law and the Prophets ;"§* clearly in-
dicating that by the latter he meant a *collection* of the inspired books of the Old Testament; and by the former, a
similar collection of the books of the New Testament. And

* His words are: "Fleeing to the Gospel as the flesh of Jesus, and to
the Apostles as the presbytery of the Church ;" that is, as he is generally
understood, "In order to understand the will of God, he fled to the Gospels, which he believed no less than if Christ in the flesh had been
speaking to him: and to the writings of the Apostles, whom he esteemed
as the presbytery of the whole Christian Church." (Lardner's Cred., vol.
ii, p. 81.)

In his letter to the Church of Smyrna, Ignatius says: "Ye ought to
hearken to the Prophets, but especially to the Gospel." And again:
"Whom neither the Prophecies nor the Law of Moses have persuaded ;
nor yet the Gospel even to this day." (Lardner's Cred., vol. ii, p. 82.) Observe that Ignatius here gives to the Gospel a pre-eminence over even
the Law and the Prophets.

† Lardner's Cred., vol. ii, p. 91.   ‖ Ibid, p. 148.
‡ Ibid, p. 99.   § Ibid, p. 171.

about sixteen years later, A. D. 194, Clement of Alexandria
says: "There is a consent and harmony between Of Clement of
the *Law and the Prophets, the Apostles and the* Alexandria.
Gospel." It is evident from this citation, that the *Gospel*
and the *Apostles* were the two names then commonly used to
designate the collected writings of the New Testament. In
the two following citations he uses the word *Gospel* to denote
the whole of the New Testament, just as the word Law is
often used for the entire Old Testament. "There is," he
says, "one God who is preached by the Law, the Prophets,
and the Gospel." And again he says: "The *Scriptures* which
we believe have been confirmed by *Almighty authority;* one
God, and Almighty Lord, is taught by the Law, and the
Prophets, and the *blessed Gospel."* Finally, he calls the
books of the New Testament, *" The Scriptures of the Lord,
the true Evangelical Canon."**

3. *From the most ancient published catalogues of the books
belonging to the New Testament.* These were not Thirdly, from
necessary in the primitive age of the Church; the ancient
nor until spurious and apocryphal books began catalogues.
to be circulated by false teachers and heretics. And hence
they do not appear so early as some other kinds of witnesses.
But when they do appear, their testimony is very full and
satisfactory.

(1.) The first regular catalogue is that of Origen, the disciple of Clement of Alexandria, in Egypt, and Origen's cata-
whom Jerome calls "The greatest doctor of the logue.
Church since the Apostles."† He was born in Egypt, A. D.
185, was well educated in the school of Alexandria, and
afterward traveled extensively through Greece, Italy, and
Palestine; so that he was in all respects well qualified to
make out a catalogue of the books that were then received
as canonical by the first and most enlightened churches of

---

* Lardner's Cred., vol. ii, p. 231.   † Ibid, p. 457.

Christendom. This he did, as is generally supposed, near the beginning of the third century, or a little more than one hundred years after the death of the Apostle John. The original document is now lost; but a copy of it is given by Eusebius in his Ecclesiastical History.*

In this catalogue are contained all the books of the New

Whether it was clean and complete. Testament, except the Epistles of James and Jude; and these were evidently omitted in some way by mistake and not by design; for, in his other works, Origen frequently refers to these books and quotes them as canonical. Thus, in the Greek edition of his works, published by Huet, we find the following direct quotation from the Epistle of James. Origen says: *"For though it be called faith, if it be without works, it is dead; as we read in the epistle ascribed to James."*† And in the Latin edition of his works by Rufinus, the same book is called, *" the Epistle of James, Apostle and brother of the Lord."* And again, it is called *" Divine Scripture."*‡ Concerning the Epistle of Jude, he thus speaks: *"And Jude wrote an epistle, of a few lines indeed, but full of powerful words of the heavenly grace, who at the beginning says: Jude the servant of Jesus Christ, and brother of James."*‖ His writings contain also several other direct quotations from the same epistle.

Origen's catalogue is therefore complete. And it is worthy of special remark, that while it contains all the books of our present canon, it contains nothing more. Nothing spurious or apocryphal is found in it. And hence it is evident that in or before the time of Origen, there was a broad and distinct line drawn between these inspired books and all the writings of men, by at least many of the most enlightened and influential churches of Christendom.

(2.) The next catalogue in order is that of Eusebius,

* Book vi, ch. 25.
† Lardner's Cred., vol. ii, p. 478.
‡ Ibid, p. 476.
‖ Ibid, p. 482.

bishop of Cæsarea, in Palestine. It was published about A. D. 315, and contains all the books of the Catalogue of
Eusebius. New Testament, and no others.*

(3.) The third is that of Athanasius, bishop of Alexandria, in Egypt. Its date is given by Lardner Of Athanasius. at about A. D. 326. It has all the books of the New Testament and no others, with this significant remark, "Let no man add to them or take away any thing from them."†

(4.) About A. D. 348, Cyril, bishop of Jerusalem, published a catalogue of the New Testament Scrip- Of Cyril. tures, which is in all respects identical with our present received Canon, except that it omits the Revelation.‡

(5.) That of the Council of Laodicea, about Of the Council
of Laodicea. A. D. 363, is identical with that of Cyril.||

(6.) After that what are called *clean* catalogues (that is, such as contain all the books of the New Testa- Other cata-
logues. ment and no others) became numerous. Such, for instance, was that of Epiphanius, bishop of Cyprus, about A. D. 368;§ and that of Basil, bishop of Cæsarea in Cappadocia, A. D. 370;¶ and that of Gregory Nazianzen, bishop of Constantinople, A. D. 370;** and that of Jerome of Bethlehem, A. D. 392;†† and that of Rufinus, bishop of Aquileia,

---

* Eusebius, Eccl. Hist. B. iii, ch. 25; comp. with ch. 3.

† Lardner's Cred., vol. iv, pp. 283–289.

‡ Ibid, p. 300. In the fourth century, some doubts were expressed about the book of Revelation, chiefly on account of its great obscurity and its supposed tendency to favor the doctrine of the Chiliasts. But it was received about the close of the first century by Hermas; in the second century by Justin Martyr, Irenæus, Clement of Alexandria, and Tertullian; in the third, by Hippolytus, Origen, Dionysius, Cyprian, and Victorinus; and in the fourth, by Athanasius and many others. After that it was generally received as an inspired book.

|| Ibid, p. 309.   ** Ibid, p. 408, 409.

§ Ibid, p. 313.   ¶ Ibid, p. 370.   †† Ibid, vol. v, pp. 31, 32, 55.

A. D. 397;* and that of Augustine, bishop of Hippo in Africa, A. D. 395;† and that of the third Council of Carthage, composed of forty-four bishops, A. D. 397;‡ and many others afterward published in Europe, Asia, and Africa.

Now, courteous reader, how is all this to be accounted for? Concede that these books were all written by inspired men; that they were afterward read, examined, and indorsed by other inspired men during a period of five, ten, fifty, one hundred, or one hundred and fifty years, as the case may be; and that, *on their authority*, they were all received by the fathers, and handed down from generation to generation;—concede this, and all that follows is then plain, reasonable, and natural. On this hypothesis, we can then easily account for such facts as the following:

1. That the most sacred names were given to these books by the companions of the Apostles and their immediate successors: and that from the very beginning they were placed on an equality with the inspired books of the Old Testament.

Summary of facts, explicable only on the ground of Apostolic authority.

2. That these, and these only, in connection with the Old Testament, were read as books of Divine authority in the primitive churches.‖

3. That these, and these only, were quoted by primitive Christians as books of Divine authority in all their religious controversies.§

4. That the primitive Christians esteemed these books as they esteemed their own lives: and that many of them actually suffered death rather than give them up to be destroyed by their persecutors.¶

5. That at a very early period, they were collected into

---

* Lardner's Credibility, vol. v, pp. 76, 77.   † Ibid, pp. 85–87.

‡ Ibid, pp. 79, 80.

‖ Ibid, pp. 259, 262, 271, 283, 308, 312, 337.

§ Ibid; also ibid, vol. ii, pp. 489, 490.

¶ Murdock's Mosheim's Eccl. Hist., vol. i, pp. 208, 209.

one volume, and translated into different languages and dialects.

6. That though doubts were, for a time, very naturally entertained in reference to some of them; yet that, after a full and fair examination of the evidence, they were all finally received as the word of God by the whole Christian world.

7. That since the Canon was finally settled by the authority of the Apostles and other inspired men, no one has dared to add any thing to it, or to subtract any thing from it.

8. That however Christians may differ on other matters, they nevertheless all receive the New Testament as the word of God.

These and many other similar facts are all plain and perfectly natural, if we receive the testimony of Clement and other Christian fathers, that the claims of these books are sanctioned and sustained " by *Almighty authority*."

But how can they be explained on any other hypothesis? Concede, for a moment, that this chain of Almighty authority which connects our present Canon with the Apostles, were broken; and let us suppose that the most learned and pious men *Evidence that they can not be accounted for on any other hypothesis.* of all Christendom were assembled in council for the purpose of forming a new Canon out of all the religious literature of the world—what kind of a book, kind reader, do you suppose they would give us as a rule of faith and practice?! What have they already given us in the multiplied, jarring, and inconsistent creeds of modern Christendom?! Evidently, this is a question that far transcends the limits of our poor, weak, and erring reason. There is need here of *Almighty authority*, as the fathers said, to secure and maintain that unity of faith and practice for which Christ and his Apostles so fervently prayed. But the Holy Spirit assures us that in these Scriptures we have all things per-

taining to life and godliness.* And hence we infer, *à priori*
and *à posteriori*, that *the Canon of the New Testament rests on the infallible authority of the Apostles and other inspired men.*

Conclusion.

III. *The third argument in support of the New Testament
Canon is drawn from the internal evidence of the
books themselves.* This, by itself, without any
reference to the preceding argument, would be
very unreliable and unsatisfactory; owing, not
to the weakness of the evidence (for it is very strong), but
simply to our inability to judge of it correctly.
But in connection with the former, and as a
means of corroborating and sustaining it, the latter is of
very great weight; *for such is the connection between the
several books of the New Testament that they must all stand
or fall together.* It is folly to receive some of them as inspired books, and to reject others as uninspired. The same
God and Father; the same Lord and Redeemer; the same
Holy Spirit; the same scheme of religion and morality; the
same evidences of superhuman wisdom, power, justice, truth,
grace, mercy, and benevolence, are plainly and unequivo-
cally revealed in them all. And hence if we can prove historically, that some of these books were written
or indorsed by the Apostles, it may then be
easily demonstrated by a proper analysis of the books themselves that they were all so written or indorsed; and that
they therefore *all rest on the same infallible authority of
Divine inspiration.*

The third
source of evi-
dence in sup-
port of the Can-
on of the New
Testament.

Strength of
this evidence.

Course of the
argument.

But I design to do nothing more here than simply to indicate the course and process of the argument. The reader
can now analyze these books for himself, collect together the
evidence, and construct an argument as long or as short as
he pleases.

* 2 Peter 1: 3.

CHAPTER III.

THE APOCRYPHAL WRITINGS

THE proper canonical test of any book, is *the evidence of its inspiration.* If we have sufficient evidence, either that it was written, or that it was fully indorsed, by an inspired man, we should not hesitate to receive it as a part of the Canon. But without this evidence, it should of course be rejected.

Proper test or criterion of canonical books.

On this ground, we have received the thirty-nine books of the Old Testament and the twenty-seven books of the New. That these were all written and frequently indorsed by inspired men, we have, as given in the two preceding chapters, the most reliable evidence. But according to this rule, we are compelled to reject,

Books received and rejected according to this rule.

I. All the Apocryphal Books, sometimes connected with the Old Testament. Of these the Council of Trent, in A. D. 1546, received as canonical, Tobit, Judith, Wisdom of Solomon, Ecclesiasticus or the Wisdom of Jesus the son of Sirach, Baruch, and the first and second books of Maccabees. "And besides these, they include under the name Esther and Daniel, certain additional chapters which are not found in the Hebrew copies. The book of Esther is made to consist of sixteen chapters : and prefixed to the book of Daniel is the history of Susannah ; the Song of the Three Children is inserted in the third

Apocryphal books received by the Council of Trent.

chapter; and the History of Bel and the Dragon is added at the end of this book."*

Reasons for re-
jecting them.   But these are justly rejected by all Protestants, for the following reasons:

1. Because they are not found in the Hebrew Bible; or the Canon composed by Ezra and other inspired members of the Great Synagogue.

2. Because they were never received as canonical by the Jews.

3. Because they were never quoted, nor in any way indorsed by Christ and his Apostles.

4. Because they were rejected by the most eminent of the Christian Fathers; such as Origen, Athanasius, and Jerome. Augustine was the first that was in favor of canonizing them.

5. Because they contain many false and contradictory statements.

The Talmud.   II. We reject the Talmud (לָמַד to teach) or Supplementary Law of the Jews.

The Mishna.   Besides the Written Law, or the thirty-nine books of the Old Testament, the Jews say that God gave to their fathers, through Moses, an Unwritten Oral Law. This is called the *Mishna* (שָׁנָה to repeat,) or repetition. It is the first part of the Talmud: and was first reduced to writing by Judah Hakkadosh, about A. D. 150.†

The second part of the Talmud is called the *Gemara* (גְּמַר

The Gemara.   to finish,) or completion. In the Jerusalem Talmud, the Gemara consists of but one volume, and was composed about A. D. 370. In the Babylonish Talmud, the Gemara consists of twelve volumes, and was

---

* Alexander on the Canon, p. 39, and Appendix, Note A. See also Townley's Bib. Lit., vol. ii, p. 155.

† Lardner's Cred., vol. vii, pp. 138–140. See also Townley's Bib. Lit., vol. i, p. 151.

completed about A. D. 450.* The Jews say that the *Mishna* is the text and the *Gemara* the comment.

The Jews have never dared to *canonize* the Talmud, or to place it among the thirty-nine books of the Old Testament. But, nevertheless, the Rabbis frequently prefer it to the Scriptures. "They compare the Scriptures to water; the Mishna to wine; and the Gemara to aromatic spices. The Oral Law, say they, is the foundation of the Written Law; and they exhort their disciples to attend rather to the words of the Scribes, than to the words of the Law. The words of the Scribes, say they, are lovely, above the words of the Law: for the words of the Law are weighty and light; but the words of the Scribes are all weighty."† *Jewish estimation of the Talmud.*

This, if true, is indeed a high commendation of the Talmud. But, nevertheless, we are constrained to reject it for the following reasons:

1. Because neither the existence of such a law, nor its authority, is in any case recognized in the whole Bible. *Reasons for rejecting the Talmud.*

2. Because all the traditions that compose it, are rejected by Christ, as the precepts and commandments of men.‡

3. Because it has none of the internal evidences of inspiration.

III. "Besides the Mishna, the Jews pretend to have received from the Divine Author of the Law, another and more mystical interpretation of it. This mystical interpretation, they call the *Cabbala* or *Reception*, (קבל to receive as a law:) by which they design to intimate that this mystical comment was *received* from God by Moses, who transmitted it orally to posterity. *Rabbinical views of the Cabbala.*

* Davidson's Bib. Crit., pp. 115, 116.
† Townley's Bib. Lit., vol. i, p. 152.
‡ Mark vii: 1–18.

The *Mishna*, say they, explains the manner in which the rites and ceremonies of the Law are to be performed; but the *Cabbala* teaches the mysteries couched under these rites and ceremonies, and hidden in the words and letters of the Scriptures. They give us, as an instance, the precepts relating to the phylacteries. The *Mishna* teaches the *materials* of which they are to be prepared; the *form* in which they are to be made; and the *manner* in which they are to be worn: but the Cabbala shows the mystical *reasons* for these directions, and informs them why the slips of parchment are to be inclosed in a *black* calf-skin, in preference to any other color; why the phylacteries for the head are to be separated into four divisions; and why the letters written upon them are to be of such a particular form. They divide this mystical science into thirteen different species, and by various transpositions, abbreviations, permutations, combinations, and separations of words, and from the figures and numerical powers of the letters, they imagine the law sufficient to instruct *Cabalistic* adepts in every art and science.*

I need scarcely say, that these Rabbinical views of the Cabbala are wholly imaginary; and that its claims to be of Divine origin are not supported by any show of reason whatever.

Why rejected.

IV. The Targums (תַּרְגּוּם R. רָגַם to cast stones) are translations of portions of the Hebrew Bible into Chaldee. Eleven of these are now extant:† the most important of which are the Targums of Onkelos and Jonathan. The former is a translation of the Pentateuch; and the latter is a paraphrase of Joshua, Judges, Samuel, Kings, Isaiah, Jeremiah, Ezekiel, and the Twelve Minor Prophets. Their date is uncertain. Some refer them

Jewish Targums.

---

* Townley's Bib. Lit., vol. i, p. 153.
† Kitto's Cyclop. Bib. Lit.

to the first or second century of the Christian era: but they are generally supposed to have been written a short time before the birth of Christ.[*]

They are both held in very high esteem by the Jews; the latter of which, they say, was written down from the mouth of Haggai, Zechariah, and Malachi.[†]   But of this, there is not the slightest evidence.   And that they are the productions of uninspired men, is sufficient- Not inspired. ly obvious from their numerous errors compared with the original Hebrew.

For similar reasons we reject as uncanonical, the Septua- gint translation of the Old Testament; and the The Septuagint. Vulgate translation of the whole Bible: the former of which was by many of. the Jews and The Vulgate. Christian fathers, thought to be inspired;[‡] and the latter was canonized by the Council of Trent, A. D. 1546.[||]

V. The Masorah is a work containing critical notes and observations on the Hebrew Scriptures.   Some Origin, nature, of the Jews attempt to trace its origin to Moses; and scope of the Masorah. and others, to Ezra and the Great Synagogue. But these views have been fully exploded; and it is now commonly referred to a succession of learned Rabbis, who lived between the beginning of the sixth and the close of the eleventh century.[§]

These notes are *grammatical, exegetical,* and *philological.* They are called by the Jews, "*The fence or hedge of the law;*" and were at first transmitted from generation to gen- eration, *orally.*   Hence the name *Masorah,* .(מְסוֹרָה, *tradi- tion*).   Afterward they were written on parchment: and from the immense mass of observations so collected, extracts of what was supposed to be most useful, were made and

---

[*] Davidson's, Bib. Crit., p. 224–239.   [†] Ibid, p. 232.
[‡] Ibid, pp. 168, 194.   [||] Townley's Bib. Lit., vol. i., p. 135.
[§] Davidson's Bib. Crit., p. 120.

14

transferred to the margin of the Old Testament manuscripts.

The professed object of these Masorites, was to deliver to

Care and regard of the Masorites for the purity of the Text. posterity the Old Testament Scriptures in their original purity. And for this purpose, "they not only numbered every verse, word, and letter of the text; but even went so far as to ascertain *how often each letter of the alphabet occurred in the whole Bible.*"* At the same time, they adopted many other rules and regulations for preserving the purity of the Hebrew Text; most of which are still observed by the Jews in copying the original Scriptures for the use of their synagogues. "It is still a constant rule with them," says Butler, "that whatever is considered as corrupt, shall never be used; but shall be burned or otherwise destroyed. A book of the law, wanting but one letter, or with one letter too much, or with an error in a single letter; written with any thing but ink, or written on parchment made of the hide of an unclean animal, or on parchment not purposely prepared for that use, or prepared by any one but an Israelite, or on skins of parchment tied together by unclean strings, shall be holden to be corrupt: that no word shall be written without a line first drawn on the parchment; no word written by heart; or without having been first pronounced orally by the writer; that before he writes the name of God, he shall wash his pen; that no letter shall be joined to another; and that if the blank parchment can not be seen all around each letter the roll shall be corrupt. There are settled rules for the length and breadth of each sheet of parchment; and for the space to be left each letter, each word, and each section."†

In all this, we have abundant evidence of the great care

---

* Townley's Bib. Lit., vol. i, p. 54.

† Ibid, p. 56, 57.

of the Masorites for the Sacred Text; but none whatever of their inspiration. And hence we must regard all the Masoretic notes, points, etc., as we regard the suggestions and criticisms of Griesbach, Scholz, and Tischendorf.

No evidence of their inspiration.

VI. The *Traditions* of the Roman Catholic Church, are also to be excluded from the Sacred Canon. "The religion which Rome would have men regard as the only true religion, and which she enjoins on all Christians universally," says the learned Doctor Mosheim, "is derived, as all their writers tell us, from two sources, *the written word of God*, and *the unwritten;* or *the Holy Scriptures* and *tradition*."* But as these traditions are often inconsistent with each other, as well as contradictory of the Holy Scriptures, it is absurd to canonize them as Rome has done.

The traditions of Rome not canonical.

VII. To the same category belongs that collection of Apocryphal writings first published by Fabricius, about the beginning of the eighteenth century, and commonly known as the Apocryphal Gospels. Fabricius gives the titles of about fifty such spurious works; but most of these are now regarded as but different editions and recensions of the same original narratives. And hence Thilo, in his edition of 1832, reduces the original number of these Apocryphal books to twelve; and Tischendorf, in his Leipsic edition of 1854, gives us the titles of twenty-two.

Apocryphal Gospels.

Of these the following are the most important.

1. *The Protevangelium of James the brother of the Lord;* or, a "Declaration and History how the most holy mother of God was born for our salvation."

2. *The Greek Gospel of Thomas.*

3. *The Greek Gospel of Nicodemus.*

* Mosheim's Eccl. Hist., vol. iii, p. 99.

4. *The Latin Gospel of the Nativity of Mary.*

5. *The Latin History of the Nativity of Mary, and of the Infancy of the Savior.*

6. *The Arabic History of Joseph the Carpenter.*

7. *The Arabic Gospel of the Childhood of the Redeemer.*

It is enough to say of these Apocryphal books, that there is no evidence whatever, that they were ever given by inspiration; and that they differ as widely from the inspired Narratives of Matthew, Mark, Luke, and John, as does the basest counterfeit from the original genuine coin.

VIII. There are also extant, Apocryphal Acts, Apocryphal Epistles, and Apocryphal Revelations. Such, for instance, are the Acts of Peter and Paul; the Acts of Paul and Thecla; the Acts of Barnabas and Mark; the Epistles of the Apostolic Fathers; and the Revelations of Moses, Ezra, and Paul. But of these, only the Epistles are genuine; and none of them have any just claims to be regarded as canonical.

Other Apocryphal Books.

It is unnecessary to extend our inquiries any further in this direction. We have laid in the scale of even justice the Apocrypha, the Talmud, the Cabbala, the Targums, and other translations, the Masorah, the Roman Catholic Traditions, and the Apocryphal Gospels, Acts, Epistles, and Revelations, and they are all found wanting. But no other books or documents now extant, save the Holy Bible, have any higher claims to inspiration, than these. And hence we conclude, that the thirty-nine books of the Old Testament, and the twenty-seven of the New, constitute the entire Canon of the Holy Scriptures; and that they are in fact the only safe, proper, and infallible rule of faith and practice.

> "Men's books with heaps of chaff are stored,
> God's Book doth golden grains afford;
> Then leave the chaff and spend thy pains
> In gathering up the golden grains."

PART THIRD.

INTEGRITY OF THE HOLY SCRIPTURES.

CHAPTER I.

SCOPE OF BIBLICAL CRITICISM.

THE third office of Reason in matters pertaining to Divine Revelation, is to decide on the *Integrity* of the Holy Scriptures.* It is not enough to prove that the Bible, as a whole, is of Divine origin; and that the several books of which it is composed, were all written and indorsed by inspired men. We must go still further, and prove also that all the words and phrases of these books are the same that were first recorded by the pen of Inspiration.

For it is a well known fact, illustrated by the entire history of the Greek and Roman classics, that books transcribed and handed down to posterity by uninspired men, are constantly liable to suffer changes. It is estimated that not less than thirty thousand such changes have been made in the six comedies of Terence since their first publication about 150 B. C. And yet,

---

* By the Integrity of the Holy Scriptures, I mean that their several books have been preserved pure and entire; by their Authenticity, that they relate the facts as they really occurred; and by their Genuineness, that they were written by the authors whose names they bear.

says the learned and eloquent Gaussen, "they have been copied a thousand times less often than the New Testament."* Nothing short of a miracle, therefore, could have preserved the books of the Old and the New Testament from the errors and changes to which all documents are liable under similar circumstances.

True, indeed, there has ever been a wonderful providence Providential care of the Sacred Text. over all these sacred books. God has put it into the hearts of his appointed librarians, to have such a care for them as has never been First, of the Old Testament. taken of any other books since time began. "The numbering of the verses, words, and letters of the Old Testament," says the learned Samuel Davidson, "seems to have been an early practice. Separate books and sections were thus counted. The sum total was marked at the end; and the middle letter and verse faithfully given. However laborious and trifling such a task was, it had a good effect on the purity of the text.†" The New Testament Secondly, of the New Testament. was no doubt preserved with equal care. If the primitive Christians would suffer death, as many of them did, rather than deliver up the Scriptures to their persecutors, it is not to be presumed that they would spare any means that might be necessary to preserve, as far as possible, the integrity and purity of the Sacred Text.

But notwithstanding all their care and vigilance, errors Two sources of error. were not unfrequently committed in transcribing these books, sometimes by *design* and more frequently by *accident*. And it now, therefore, belongs to Reason to restore the original text. This she does chiefly through the five following sources of Biblical criticism:

Five sources of Biblical criticism. I. The most ancient versions of the Holy Scriptures.

* Gaussen on Inspiration, p. 196.   † Davidson's Bib. Crit., p. 116.

II. The Manuscripts of the Sacred Text.

III. Parallels or repeated passages.

IV. Quotations made from the Sacred Books.

V. Critical Conjecture, or Evidence arising from the Context.

For a full discussion of this subject, I must refer the reader to " Davidson's Biblical Criticism " and "Horne's Introduction," and "Tragelles on the Printed Text." A few general remarks on each of these topics is all that we have time and space for at present.

Works of refer-
ence.

ANCIENT VERSIONS.

I. GREEK VERSIONS. The oldest known version of any portion of the Bible into any language, is the Greek translation of the Old Testament, commonly called the *Septuagint*, from the Latin word *Septuaginta*, seventy; either because as some *suppose* it was approved by the Jewish Sanhedrim, consisting of seventy members besides the High Priest and his deputy; or because, as the Jews say, it was made by seventy-two translators, under the patronage of Ptolemy Philadelphus, king of Egypt, about 280 B. C. It contains all the canonical books of the Old Testament, with some apocryphal additions. The best manual edition of the Septuagint is that recently published by the Bagsters of London.*

Greek versions.

The Septua-
gint.

The Old Testament was also translated into Greek by Aquila of Pontus, about A. D. 150; by Theodosian of Ephesus, A. D. 160; and by Symmachus of Samaria, A. D. 200. These three translations and the Septuagint were printed in parallel columns by Origen

Other Greek
versions.

---

* See Davidson's Bib. Crit. pp. 162–214; Horne's Introduction, vol. ii, pp. 163–182; Prideaux's Connection, vol. ii, pp. 21–80; and Townley's Bib. Lit., vol. i, pp. 58–64.

about A. D. 230, and together constituted his Tetrapla. The order was, 1. The Septuagint; 2. Aquila; 3. Symmachus; and, 4. Theodosian. To these four he afterward added the original in both Hebrew and Greek letters. These were all likewise printed in parallel columns; and together formed his Hexapla. The order of the Hexapla was as follows: 1. The Hebrew in Hebrew, or rather in Chaldee letters; 2. The Hebrew in Greek letters; 3. Aquila; 4. Symmachus; 5. The Septuagint; and 6. Theodosian. Only fragments of the translations of Aquila, Theodosian, and Symmachus now remain.*

II. THE TARGUMS or CHALDEE VERSIONS. Of these,
Chaldee Versions. eleven are now extant: viz., 1. The Targum of Onkelos on the Law; 2. That of Jonathan Ben Uzziel on the Prophets; 3. That of Pseudo-Jonathan on the Law; 4. The Jerusalem Targum on the Law; 5. The Targum of Rabbi Joseph the Blind, on the Hagiography; 6. An anonymous Targum on the five Megilloth (books or volumes) or books of Ruth, Esther, Ecclesiastes, Song of Solomon, and the Lamentations of Jeremiah; 7. A Targum on the two books of Chronicles; 8. The Jerusalem Targum on the Prophets; and the ninth, tenth, and eleventh, on the book of Esther. The first two are by far the most valuable for the purposes of Biblical criticism; and are generally supposed to have been written before the birth of Christ. The others all belong to a much later period.†

III. THE SAMARITAN VERSION OF THE PENTATEUCH.
Samaritan Pentateuch. Its author and date are both unknown. The Samaritans say, it was made by Nathaniel, a Samaritan priest, who lived about twenty years before Christ. Davidson refers it to a later period.‡

---

* Davidson's Bib. Crit., pp. 215–224; Horne's Introd., vol. ii, pp. 183–186; Townley's Bib. Lit., vol. i, pp. 64–66.

† Davidson's Bib. Crit., pp. 224–239; also Horne's Introd., pp. 157–162.

‡ Davidson's Bib. Crit., pp. 240–242.

IV. THE SYRIAC VERSIONS. One of the most valuable of all the ancient versions is the Peshito (simple, literal) or old Syriac. It contains all the canonical books of the Old Testament; and all Syriac Versions:—The Peshito. also of the New, except the Second Epistle of Peter, the Second and Third of John, the Epistle of Jude and the Revelation. Its origin is unknown. Three opinions are found among the Syrians with regard to it: first, that the Old Testament was translated in the time of Solomon; second, that it was translated by Asa the priest, who was sent back from Assyria to Samaria, about 700 B. C.; third, that both the Old and the New Testament were translated by, or under the supervision of the Apostle Thaddeus, and under the patronage of Abgarus, king of Osrhoene. It is first mentioned by Ephraem, the Syrian, who died A. D. 376. But it was then an *ancient* version; for many of its words had then become antiquated, and needed to be explained, just like the obsolete words of our common English version. Besides, Ephraem calls it *"our"* version: which shows that it was then generally recognized as the received version of the Syrians. And hence Davidson refers it to about the middle of the second century. But Horne thinks that this version was certainly made at the close of the first, or at the beginning of the second century.*

Other Syriac versions were made afterward; the most important of these is the Philoxenian New Testament. The Philoxenian.

V. ARABIC VERSIONS. We have no account of any part of the Scriptures being translated into the Arabic language, before the commencement of . Arabic Versions. the Mahometan era, A. D. 622. After that, several versions were made; the most valuable and celebrated of which

---

* Davidson's, Bib. Crit., pp. 243–254, and 596–630; Horne's Introd., vol. ii, pp. 187–190; also 203; Townley's Bib. Lit., vol. i, pp. 81–83.

is the translation of the Old Testament by Rabbi Saadias Gaon or Hagaon, *the Illustrious,* a learned Jew of Babylon. Its date is given at about A. D. 930. The most valuable edition of the New Testament in Arabic is that of Erpen or Erpenius, printed in 1616.*

VI. LATIN VERSIONS. When and by whom the Old

The Itala or Old Italic Version. and New Testaments were first translated into Latin, is not known. A version called the Itala, or Old Italic, was quoted by Tertullian near the close of the second century; and Horne thinks that the translation was made about the beginning of the same century; Davidson fixes its date at about A. D. 150. All the remaining fragments of this version that could be discovered, were collected together and published at Rome, in one folio, under the sanction of Pope Sixtus, A. D. 1588. A fuller edition of it was afterward printed at Rheims, in three folio volumes, A. D. 1743, and it was afterward republished at Paris, A. D. 1749.†

In A. D. 382, Jerome, at the request of Pope Damasus,

Jerome's Revision of it. commenced a revision of this old Latin version. And it is generally supposed that he completed the entire work. But most of his Old Testament manuscripts were destroyed; so that only the book of Psalms, Job, and his revised New Testament have come down to us. ‡

But it seems that Jerome was not satisfied with a mere

The Vulgate. revision of the Old Testament. For before he had finished it, he commenced a new translation of it from the Hebrew into Latin; and this, together with the revised New Testament, constituted what was then called

---

*Davidson's, Bib. Crit., pp. 255–260. Townley, vol, i, pp. 195, 278, 345. Vol, ii, pp. 227, 448, 463, 466, 476, 534, 565.

† Davidson's Bib. Crit., pp. 261–263; and 687–694. Horne's Introduction, vol. ii, pp. 196, 197.

‡ Davidson's Bib. Crit., pp. 264, 265; and 695–698; Horne's Introd., vol. ii, pp. 197, 198.

his New Version. For some time it was very unpopular: even Augustine was opposed to it. But it rose gradually in public favor; and about the close of the seventh century, it was generally adopted by the Latin churches. Henceforth it was known as the Vulgate or Common Version. In A. D. 802, it was revised by Alcuin, under the patronage of Charlemagne. And after passing through sundry other changes and critical revisions, it was finally canonized in 1546 by the Council of Trent.*

VII. OTHER ANCIENT VERSIONS. According to Davidson, the New Testament was also translated *Other ancient Versions of the New Testament.* into the Sahidic, Coptic, and Basmuric dialects of Egypt, in the third century; into the Ethiopic and Gothic in the fourth; into the Armenian and Syriac in the fifth; into the Gregorian or Iberic in the sixth; and into the Anglo-Saxon in the eighth.†

HEBREW MANUSCRIPTS.

These are of two classes. The first are the *Sacred Copies* or Rolls for the Synagogues; and the second are the *Private* or *Square Copies* made for common use. *Two classes of Hebrew manuscripts.*

The Rolls of the synagogue contain the Pentateuch; the Haphtaroth, or sections of the Prophets appointed to be read; and the book of Esther. *Rolls of the Synagogue.* They are required to be written on clean parchment and in the square Chaldee letters, according to the most exact rules and regulations. When no longer fit for use, they are buried in the earth; or in some other way put out of the reach of profane hands. And hence but few of them have ever come into the possession of Christians.

*Davidson's Bib. Crit., pp. 265–284; and 698–704; Horne, vol. ii, pp. 198–202.

† Davidson's Bib. Crit., pp. 596–704; Horne's Introd., pp. 202–212; and Townley's Bib. Lit., Ancient Versions.

The Private or Square manuscripts, are also prepared ac-
Square manu- cording to very exact rules. But they may be
scripts. written on either paper or parchment; and in
either Chaldee or Rabbinical characters.

With regard to the *number* and the *order* of books in the
Prophets and the Kethubim, there is no uniformity, even
among the highest Jewish authorities. The Talmudists
Number and make twenty-four books, and arrange them as
Order of books
in the Tal- follows: Genesis, Exodus, Leviticus, Numbers,
mud;— Deuteronomy, Joshua, Judges, Samuel, Kings,
Jeremiah, Ezekiel, Isaiah, the Twelve Minor Prophets,
Ruth, Psalms, Job, Proverbs, Ecclesiastes, Song of Solomon, Lamentations, Daniel, Esther, Ezra, and Chronicles.
The Masorites also make twenty-four books, and arrange
in the Maso- them according to the following order: Gene-
rah: sis, Exodus, Leviticus, Numbers, Deuteronomy,
Joshua, Judges, Samuel, Kings, Isaiah, Jeremiah, Ezekiel, Twelve Minor Prophets, Psalms, Job, Proverbs, Ruth,
Canticles, Ecclesiastes, Lamentations, Esther, Daniel, Ezra,
and Chronicles.* The Spanish MSS., and nearly all the
and in the man- Hebrew Bibles printed from them, follow the
uscripts and order of the Masorites, with some slight vari-
Hebrew Bibles. ations in the Kethubim. But the German and
French Bibles and MSS. generally follow the Talmud.
Jerome, Origen, and many other Christian fathers, as well
as some of the most learned of the Jewish Rabbis, make
but twenty-two books, and nearly every one of them has
an order of his own.†

The number of Hebrew MSS. now extant is very great.
Number of He- Dr. Kennicott collated 630 for his critical edi-
brew manu-
scripts collated. tion of the Hebrew Bible; and M. De Rossi

---

* Stuart on the Old Test. Canon, p. 277; and Davidson's Bib. Crit., pp.
330, 331.

† Stuart on the Old Test. Canon, pp. 277, 278.

made use of 479 MSS., besides 288 printed editions, in making out his "*Collection of Various Readings.*" But all the original *autographs* have perished; and it is thought that all existing *apographs* were written between A. D. 1000 and A. D. 1457; when the art of printing became in a great measure a substitute for the art of penmanship. Most of these MSS. contain but a small portion of the Old Testament.

For a description of fifty-three of the oldest and best Hebrew MSS. see "Davidson's Biblical Criticism," chapter xxiv.

GREEK MANUSCRIPTS.

Greek manuscripts are usually divided into *Uncial* and *Cursive;* the former are written in *capital,* and and the latter, in *small* letters. The oldest manuscripts are written in large round or square capitals; and without any accents or division of words. But in the eighth and ninth centuries, the letters were made longer and narrower, and generally inclined a little either to the right or to the left. About the close of the ninth century, the small or cursive letters came into general use.

Two classes of Greek manuscripts.

The number of Greek manuscripts now extant is very great. In his "Introduction to the Critical Study of the Bible," Thomas Hartwell Horne speaks of about 500 that had at that time been collated. But these, he says, are but a small part of all the MSS. that are to be found in public and private libraries. Most of them, however, contain only a part of the New Testament. They are of all forms; and are written on both paper and parchment.

Number of Greek MSS. extant.

Owing to the scarcity of parchment, before the invention of paper,* persons were often induced to obliterate the

---

* According to Montfauçon, cotton-paper was invented about the close

works of ancient writers, in order to transcribe their own
Palimsest man-uscripts. or those of some favorite author in their place.
These manuscripts are called *Codices Palimsesti*
(παλιν—*again* and ψαω—*to rub*) or *Rescripti*.

Critics have discovered a characteristic resemblance be-
Geographical classification of manuscripts. tween manuscripts written in certain localities
and within certain geographical limits. And
on this ground, they are wont to classify them
under certain *Families* or *Recensions:* such, for instance, as
the Latin, Asiatic, Byzantine, and Alexandrine Recensions
of Tischendorf. The Latin Recension is made to embrace
all manuscripts which correspond most fully in all respects
with the writings of the Latin fathers. And in like manner, Biblical critics are accustomed to distinguish and classify
the Asiatic, the Byzantine, and the Alexandrine manuscripts.

The Uncial manuscripts are now commonly represented
Symbols used to represent the Uncial and the Cursive manuscripts. by English and Greek capitals; and the Cursive,
by Arabic numerals. For a description of the
most ancient and valuable manuscripts of both
classes, I must again refer the reader to Davidson and Horne. I will merely introduce a few of them here
for the sake of illustration.

I. *Manuscripts written in large Uncial or capital letters.*

A. The MS. known by this symbol is that which is usu-
The Alexan- drine manu- script. ally called the Alexandrine or Codex Alexan-
drinus. It once belonged to Cyrillis Lucaris,
patriarch of Alexandria, and afterward of Constantinople. In A. D. 1628, he presented it to Charles I,
king of England; and it is now in the British Museum.
It is written on parchment; and consists of four volumes

of the ninth or the beginning of the tenth century. But the mode of
forming paper out of linen rags was not discovered till the twelfth
century. The first paper-mill erected in England is said to have been
at Dartford, in 1588. (Townley's Bib. Lit., vol. i, pp. 41, 42.)

folio; three of which contain the Septuagint text of the Old Testament, and the other contains the New Testament and the Epistle of Clement to the Corinthians. It is not entirely perfect. The first twenty-four chapters of Matthew, and the first five verses of the twenty-fifth are wanting; and also that portion of John's Gospel which is contained between chapters vi: 50, and viii: 52. It is supposed to have been written at Alexandria in Egypt; though its text corresponds more perfectly with the Byzantine or generally received text. Its date has been variously assigned; but it is now pretty generally agreed that it was written in the fifth century.*

B. The Codex Vaticanus is commonly represented by the letter B; but in the Vatican Library, to which it belongs, it is known by the number 1209. Its history is unknown. It is supposed to have been originally brought from Egypt, as its text corresponds most nearly with the Alexandrine. It is written on vellum in quarto form; and contains both the Septuagint Greek of the Old Testament and the original Greek of the New. But in the latter it is deficient from Hebrews ix: 14, to the end of the epistle: and it does not contain the Epistles to Timothy, Titus, and Philemon; nor the Apocalypse. According to Tischendorf and others, it was written in the fourth century; and it is now generally allowed to be *the oldest copy of the New Testament extant, except perhaps the Codex Sinaiticus.*†

C. The Codex Ephræmi or Codex Regius Parisiensis is generally represented by the letter C. It is preserved in the Imperial Library at Paris; and contains several Greek works of Ephraem the Syrian, written over the Greek text of the Old and New Testaments.

Vatican manuscript.

Codex Ephræmi.

* See Horne's Introduction, vol. ii, pp. 66–78; and Davidson's Bib. Crit. 717–720.

† Horne, pp. 73–76; Davidson, pp, 721–727.

The traces of the Sacred text are, however, still visible; and in most places *legible*. It is the purest example extant of the Alexandrine Recension; and is supposed by Tischendorf and others to have been written in the fifth century.*

D. The Codex Bezæ is also called the Codex Cantabri-

Codex Bezæ.

giensis, because it was presented to the University of Cambridge, in England, by the celebrated Theodore Beza, in 1581. It is written on parchment in folio, and contains the four Gospels and the Acts of the Apostles, with a Latin translation: but its lacunæ or omissions are very numerous. The general opinion is, that it was written about the end of the fifth century.†

Cod. Sin. This MS. was discovered by Dr. A. F. C.

Codex Sinaiti-cus.

Tischendorf, in the Convent of St. Catherine at Mount Sinai, in A. D. 1859. He refers it to the fourth century; and thinks it is the oldest MS. extant. It contains all the New Testament, except Mark xvi: 9–20; John viii: 1–11; and sundry other minor passages that have long been regarded by the most eminent critics as spurious. And hence it confirms, to a very remarkable extent, the results of Biblical criticism.‡

The order of Books in this MS. is as follows: Matthew, Mark, Luke, John, Romans, 1 Corinthians, 2 Corinthians, Galatians, Ephesians, Philippians, Colossians, 1 Thessalonians, 2 Thessalonians, Hebrews, 1 Timothy, 2 Timothy, Titus, Philemon, Acts, James, 1 Peter, 2 Peter, 1 John, 2 John, 3 John, Jude, Revelation.

For a description of about thirty more Uncial MSS. see "Davidson's Biblical Criticism," pp. 734–763.

II. *Greek manuscripts written in small or cursive letters.*—

---

* Horne, vol. ii, pp. 89, 90; and Davidson, pp. 727–731.

† Horne, pp. 85–89; and Davidson, pp. 731–734.

‡ See Prolegomena to the Novum Testamentum Græce ex Sinaitico Codice of Tischendorf.

The number prefixed is that by which the MS. is generally known or represented.

1. Codex Basiliensis, B. vi, 27. This MS. is written on parchment, and contains all the New Testa- *Illustrative examples of Cursive MSS.* ment except the Apocalypse. It is supposed to have been written in the tenth century, and preserved in the University of Basel.

69. Leicestrensis. This MS. is written partly on parchment and partly on paper. It contains the entire New Testament, with some gaps; was written in the fourteenth century; and belongs to the Public Library of Leicester.

209. This is a MS. of the fourteenth or fifteenth century, written on parchment in octavo; and contains the whole of the New Testament. It is now in Venice.

After describing more than thirty cursive MSS., Davidson says: "Upward of five hundred cursive MSS. of *Number of such extant.* the Gospels, ranging in date from the tenth to the sixteenth century, have been partially examined. More than two hundred of the same kind contain the Acts and Catholic Epistles; upward of three hundred contain the Pauline Epistles; and one hundred have the Apocalypse. But the list, large as it is, might be much increased: for there are many in the great public libraries of England and the Continent of Europe as yet unknown."*

PARALLEL PASSAGES.

These are divided by Davidson into three classes.

I. Historical sections repeated: such as the *Davidson's classification of parallels.* often-repeated tables of genealogy; the books of Kings and Chronicles, and the four independent Narratives of Matthew, Mark, Luke, and John.

II. Laws, poems, and oracles which have been repeated

---

* Davidson's Bib. Crit., p. 770.

15

by the same author, or by different authors. Compare, for instance, the following passages:

1. Exodus xx: 2–17   and   Deuteronomy v: 6–21.
2. Leviticus xi: 2–19   "   Deuteronomy xiv: 4–18.
3. Psalm xviii: 2–50   "   2 Samuel xxii: 1–51.
4. Psalm cv: 1–15   "   1 Chronicles xvi: 8–22.
5. Isaiah ii: 2–4   "   Micah iv: 1–3.
6. Matt. xxviii: 18–20.   "   Mark xvi: 15–18.
7. 1 Timothy iii: 1–7   "   Titus i: 5–9.

III. Repeated sentences, propositions, and proverbs. Compare, for example:

1. Numbers xxiv: 3, 4   and   Numbers xxiv: 15, 16.
2. Isaiah xxxv: 10   "   Isaiah li: 11.
3. Jeremiah xv: 2   "   Jeremiah xliii: 11.
4. Ezekiel i: 15–21   "   Ezekiel x: 8–17.
5. Proverbs viii: 8   "   Proverbs xx: 22.
6. Luke xxiv: 48–51   "   Acts i: 4–9.

That such comparisons, in connection with other means and sources of Biblical criticism, may often assist us in purifying the text, is very obvious. But great caution is necessary in this, as well indeed as in every other department of this most important and interesting science.

QUOTATIONS.

These may be conveniently classified under the three following heads:

Three classes of quotations.   I. Quotations from the Old Testament by the inspired writers of the New Testament.

II. Quotations from the Old Testament by the Rabbinical fathers.

III. Quotations from both the Old and the New Testament by the Christian fathers.

The examples under each of these are very numerous; and in the hands of the skillful and judicious critic may be of great service in separating the chaff from the wheat; the spurious from that which is genuine.

CRITICAL CONJECTURE.

By this is meant simply a fair and judicious examination of all the *internal* evidence of a passage; or such as may arise out of a just grammatical and logical analysis of the entire context. And hence, as Davidson well remarks, *Critical Conjecture* is very different from *Theological Conjecture.* It must be confessed, however, that the latter has often been mistaken and substituted for the former; and hence this fifth and last source of Biblical criticism should be relied on only in case of necessity: and even then, it should be used with the utmost caution. Indeed, in all such investigations, we should ever remember with the learned and eloquent Gaussen, that Sacred Criticism is merely a Scientific Inquirer, and not a judge; a Historian and not a Soothsayer; a Doorkeeper of the Temple, and not its God.

The proper province and scope of critical conjecture.

Proper scope of Biblical criticism.

We will now take a few examples merely for the sake of illustration.

I. And lead us not into temptation, but deliver us from evil: [for thine is the kingdom, and the power, and the glory, forever. Amen.] (Matt. vi: 13.)

Illustrations. Matt. vi: 13.

The clause contained within the brackets is found,

1. In many ancient versions, such as the Syriac, Arabic, Persian, Ethiopic, Arminian, Gregorian, Gothic, Coptic, and Sahidic.

2. In many Greek MSS.

3. In the writings of many of the Greek fathers.

4. It is consistent with the context.

But it is wanting,

1. In the Old Italic, Vulgate, and some other ancient versions.

2. In some of the most important Greek MSS., such as Cod. Sin. B, D, Z, 1, 17, etc.

3. In the writings of all the Latin and some of the Greek authors.

4. It is much easier to account for its being added as a supplement; than for its omission by so many authorities. And hence it has been generally rejected by the most able critics from Erasmus down to the present time.

II. "And Philip said, if thou believest with all thy heart, thou mayest. And he answered and said, I believe that Jesus Christ is the Son of God." (Acts viii : 37.)

Acts viii: 37.

This verse is found,

1. In the Vulgate and some other ancient versions.

2. In E and ten other cursive MSS. specified by Scholz.

3. In the writings of Irenæus, Jerome, Cyprian, Augustine, and some other Christian fathers.

4. It is certainly in harmony with the context.

But it is wanting,

1. In the Syriac, Coptic, Ethiopic, and several other ancient versions.

2. In Cod. Sin. A, B, C, H, L, and more than forty cursive MSS.

3. In the writings of Chrysostom, and some other Greek fathers.

4. It is easier to account for the insertion of this verse wherever it does occur, than for its omission by so many ancient authorities. And hence it is rejected as spurious by Grotius, Mill, Wetstein, Pearce, Gratz, Tischendorf, Tregelles, Alford, and many other able critics.

III. For there are three that bear record, [in heaven: the Father, the Word, and the Holy Spirit: and these three are one. And there are three that bear witness on earth;] the Spirit, and the water, and the blood; and these three agree in one. (1 John v: 7, 8.)

1 John v: 7, 8.

The words in brackets are wanting,

1. In all the ancient versions.

2. In all Greek manuscripts previous to the sixteenth century.

3. In the writings of all the Greek and many of the Latin fathers.

4. They are not in harmony with the scope of the writer.

And hence they are now rejected as spurious by all our best critics.

CHAPTER II.

HISTORY OF BIBLICAL CRITICISM.

BIBLICAL criticism is a modern science. Its origin, or perhaps we should rather say its embryonic state, may be fixed at about the beginning of the sixteenth century. But according to Davidson and most other eminent critics, it did not attain to its full manhood as a science, till the beginning of the eighteenth century. Since that important epoch in the history of Sacred Literature, the labor bestowed on Biblical criticism has been prodigiously great. This will be best illustrated by a brief notice of the most important editions of the Hebrew Bible and the Greek Testament.

Origin and progress of Biblical criticism.

EDITIONS OF THE HEBREW BIBLE.

I. The first entire *printed* copy of the Hebrew Bible was published at Soncino in Lombardy, A. D. 1488, by Abraham Ben Chayim.*

First printed edition of the Hebrew Bible.

II. The next edition makes no reference to either the time or the place of its publication. De Rossi, supposes that it, too, was published at Soncino.†

The second edition.

III. The third is the Gerson edition, published at Brescia in Lombardy, A. D. 1494. This is the edition from which Luther made his German translation. The copy which he used is still in the Royal Library at Berlin; an object of great interest and curiosity to Protestants.‡

The Gerson edition.

IV. The first edition of the Hebrew Bible, printed and published by Christians, is the famous Complutentian Polyglot. It was commenced in A. D. 1502, under the patronage of Cardinal Ximenes, archbishop of Toledo in Spain : and after the uninterrupted labors of fifteen years, it was finished in 1517. But permission to publish it was not procured from Pope Leo X, till the 22d of March, 1520 : and hence it was not actually published till 1522. It was then first issued from Complutum or Alcala in Spain.

Complutentian Polyglot.

Date and place of its publication.

We learn from the Cardinal's biography, as given by Esprit Flecher, bishop of Nismes, that for this great work he procured seven Hebrew MSS., at a cost of about four thousand crowns in gold, besides the Greek MSS. sent to him from Rome, and many Latin MSS. brought from foreign countries, or procured from the Libraries of Spain; every one of which was at least eight hundred years old. The entire cost of the work is

Means used and expended.

---

* Davidson's Bib. Crit., p. 140.   † Ibid, p. 140.   ‡ Ibid, p. 140.

estimated at more than fifty thousand crowns of gold; or about fifty-four thousand five hundred dollars.

The whole Bible was divided into six parts, comprised in four volumes. The Old Testament contained the Hebrew; the Vulgate Latin; the Greek of the Its contents. Septuagint with a Latin translation; and a Chaldee paraphrase with a similar Latin interpretation. The New Testament contains simply the Greek Text and the Latin Vulgate.*

V. For the next great advance made in Hebrew Sacred literature, we are indebted to Daniel Bomberg. He was a native of Antwerp in Spain, but settled in Ven- Editions of ice, and for many years devoted his press exclus- Daniel Bomberg. ively to Hebrew and Rabbinical literature. He is said to have kept in his employ, as editors, printers, and correctors of his press, about one hundred of the most learned Jews that he could find; and it is estimated, that in printing alone, he spent not less than three or four million crowns of gold.†

By his great exertions and liberality eight editions of the Hebrew Bible were issued from his press : five Contents of his in quarto, and three in folio. His three folio, three Rabbinical editions. otherwise called his three Rabbinical editions, are the most valuable. Besides the Hebrew text, they all contain the most valuable of the Targums, and several Rabbinical commentaries; and the second and third also contain the Masorah.

The first of these was edited by Felix Pratensis, a converted Jew, and published in 1518. The sec- Their editors ond was edited by Rabbi Jacob Ben Chayim, a and date of learned Jew from Tunis in Africa; and pub- publication. lished, A. D. 1525–1526. The third was edited by Corne-

---

* Davidson's Bib. Crit., pp. 141, 142; and Townley's Bib. Lit., vol. i, pp. 549–551.

† Townley's Bib. Lit., vol. ii. p. 151.

lius Adelkind, another erudite Jew; and published, A. D. 1547–1549. " This, on the whole," says Davidson, " is the most copious and most correct Rabbinical Bible extant." And Adam Clarke says, " It is the most useful, the most correct, and the most valuable Hebrew Bible ever published."*

VI. The Gerson, Complutentian, and second edition of
The Antwerp Polyglot. Bomberg, are commonly styled *independent* editions. They were followed by many others of a mixed text. Such, for instance, was the Antwerp Polyglot, of eight volumes folio, published in 1569–1572, by Philip II, King of Spain. It contains the Complutentian text collated with that of Bomberg.†

VII. The Antwerp again was made the basis of the Paris
The Paris Polyglot. Polyglot of ten volumes folio, published in 1645. This edition contains the Hebrew, Samaritan, Chaldee, Syriac, Arabic, Greek, and Latin texts.‡

VIII. The Antwerp was also made the basis of the Lon-
The London Polyglot. don Polyglot of six volumes folio, published in 1657. The editions of Robert Stevens, Christopher Plantin, and several other enterprising publishers, were also taken chiefly from the same text.||

IX. Buxtorf's Rabbinical Bible, published at Basel, in
Buxtorf's two editions. 1618–1619, was formed on the basis of Bomberg's third edition, collated with the Masorah. This and his manual edition of 1611, are both of great value.§

X. The most recent Rabbinical Bible, and in some re-
Simon's Rabbinical Bible. spects the most complete ever published, is the Amsterdam edition, edited by Moses Ben Simon, in four volumes folio, A. D. 1724–1727.¶

---

*Davidson's Bib. Crit., pp. 142–145; and Townley's Bib. Lit., vol. ii, p. 151.

†Davidson, p. 145.   ‡Ibid, p. 146. ||Ibid.   §Ibid.   ¶Ibid, p. 147.

XI. The Hebrew Bible of Rabbi Joseph Athias, of Amsterdam, with a Latin preface by the learned Edition of Joseph Athias. John Leusden, is also worthy of special notice. The first edition of it was published in 1661, and the second in 1667, in two volumes 8vo. The former is the first edition in which the verses were distinguished by Arabic numerals: and for the latter, the States-General presented to the author a chain of gold and a gold medal pendant.*

XII. The edition of Athias was made the basis of that of Opitius, and also that of Van der Hooght. Edition of Opitius. The former was first published at Kiel, in Denmark, 1709. It is one of the most accurate ever printed. Thirty years were spent in its preparation. The edition of Van der Hooght is also of great value. It is particularly distinguished for the beauty of its type; the Van der Hooght's edition. accuracy of its text; and its convenience for ordinary use. It has received the appellation of " *The Textus Receptus* " in Hebrew. It was first published at Amsterdam and Utrecht in 1705; and has been made the basis of many subsequent editions. †

XIII. In 1720, J. H. Michaelis, of Halle, published an edition, in preparing which he compared twenty- Edition of Michaelis. four of the best editions and five MSS. It is generally regarded as a valuable contribution to Sacred literature.‡

XIV. About the middle of the eighteenth century, Dr. Kennicott, of Oxford, encouraged by the liber- Kennicott's edition. ality of the English Government, undertook the work of a more thorough examination of the Hebrew text. He and his colaborers collected together and compared 694 codices; embracing Hebrew MSS., printed editions of the Hebrew Bible, and the most valuable of the Rabbinical

* Townley's Bib. Lit., vol. ii, p. 490.
† Davidson, pp. 149 and 159. ‡ Davidson, p. 150.

works, particularly the Talmud. The first volume of his work was published in 1776; and the second, in 1780. This, on the whole, is one of the most valuable contributions that has ever been made to Biblical criticism; though it failed to meet the expectations of the public. One thing it has fully demonstrated: that there is a very great harmony between existing Hebrew manuscripts and the Masorah. And from all that we know of the veneration which the Jews had for the Sacred Books—a veneration bordering on superstition, we can not but think the Masoretic text is in the main a very correct one. And hence we have reason to believe that the Hebrew text, though still containing many impurities, is far from being as corrupt as many have supposed.*

Present state of the Hebrew text.

XV. Soon after Dr. Kennicott commenced his labors in England, a similar work was undertaken in Italy, by John Bernard de Rossi, Professor of Oriental languages at Parma. His "*Collection of Various Readings*," consisting of four volumes, was published in 1788, to which a supplemental volume was added in 1798. It is a work of great merit.†

Work of De Rossi.

XVI. In 1806, Prof. John Jahn, of Vienna, published an edition of four volumes 8vo. The text is in the main that of Van der Hooght, with the various readings of Kennicott and De Rossi.‡

Jahn's edition.

XVII. In 1831, Dr. Augustus Hahn, of Leipsic, published a manual edition of Van der Hooght's text, with sundry corrections. This with some slight emendations by Isaac Leeser and Joseph Jaquett, is the text-book now generally used in our American Institutions.

Hahn's Manual.

---

* Davidson, pp. 152–155.   † Ibid, pp. 156, 157.   ‡ Ibid, p. 158.

EDITIONS OF THE GREEK TESTAMENT.

I. The first *printed* edition of the entire New Testament was that of the Complutentian Polyglot, under the auspices of Cardinal Ximenes. The work was completed on the 10th of January, 1514; but it was not published till 1522.* <small>First printed edition of the Greek Testament.</small>

II. The first *published* Greek Testament was that of Erasmus, at Basel, in Switzerland, 1516. It contains a Latin translation, based partly on the Vulgate. <small>First published edition.</small>
In preparing this edition, Erasmus used only five MSS., and these were too hastily collated. A second edition was published in 1519; a third in 1522; a fourth in 1527; and a fifth in 1535, all in folio, and from the same press.†

III. From the Complutentian and the Erasmian editions, many others were formed with but slight alterations. Thus, for instance, the Complutentian was made the basis, <small>Editions based chiefly on the Complutentian</small>

1. Of the first two editions of Robert Stephens, published at Paris in 1546 and 1549.

2. The Plantin editions of Antwerp in 1564, 1573, 1574, and 1590.

3. The Antwerp Polyglot in 1571, 1572.

4. The editions of Rapheleng of Leyden, in 1591, 1601, and 1612.

5. The Genevan editions in 1609, 1619, 1620, 1628, and 1632.

6. The New Testament of the Paris Polyglot, by Le Jay in 1645.‡

In like manner the text of Erasmus was followed by John Bebelius, of Basel, in 1524, 1531, and 1535; by Cephaleus,

---

* Tregelles on the Printed Text of the Greek Testament, pp. 1–11; and Davidson, p. 552.

† Tregelles, pp. 19–28.   ‡ Davidson, p. 5 7.

of Strasburgh, in 1524 and 1534; by Robert Stephens in his third edition at Paris in 1550, and in his fourth at Geneva in 1551. This is the first into which the division of verses was introduced. Many other editions followed; some on the basis of the Complutentian; some on the basis of the Erasmian text; and some on that of Stephens.*

Editions based on the Erasmian Text.

IV. The next edition worthy of our special attention is that of Theodore Beza, of Geneva, in 1565. It contains the Greek text of Stephens, amended; the Vulgate; and a Latin translation made by Beza himself. The second edition of this work was published in 1582; the third in 1589; and the fourth in 1598.†

Editions of Beza.

V. In 1624, appeared the first Elzevir edition at Leyden. The name of the editor is unknown; and it is therefore called by the name of the printer. It follows the third edition of Stephens, differing from it only in 145 places. The second edition was issued from the same press, in 1633. This is the best of the Elzevir editions. In its preface, the editor says to the reader: "textum ergo habes nunc ab omnibus receptum. *You have therefore now a text received by all.*" These words were prophetic; for this edition really became the *Editio recepta;* and it contains the *Textus receptus.*

Elzevir editions.

What is now called the *Received Text* has of course been variously modified since 1633; but it is still *substantially* the same as that of the second edition of the Elzevirs. This was taken chiefly from that of Beza; and Beza's from that of Stephens; and Stephens's from the Erasmian and the Complutentian. Hence it is of necessity a very imperfect text.‡

The Textus receptus.

---

* Davidson, pp. 558–561; and Tregelles, pp. 30–32.

† Davidson, p. 562. Tregelles, p. 33.

‡ Davidson, p. 563; and Tregelles, pp. 34, 35.

VI. The Greek Testament of Brian Walton, the very learned and celebrated editor of the London Walton's edition. Polyglot, gave a new impulse to Biblical criticism. It constitutes the fifth volume of that great work; and contains the Greek text with a Latin version: also the Vulgate, Syriac, Arabic, Ethiopic, and in the Gospels the Persic; each with its own translation. The sixth volume contains the various readings of sixteen carefully collated MSS.*

VII. The critical edition of Dr. John Fell, bishop of Oxford, published in 1675, is also a valuable Fell's edition. work. It contains the various readings of one hundred MSS. Here, according to Davidson, ends the infancy of Biblical Criticism; and its manhood begins.†

VIII. In 1707, Dr. John Mill, of Oxford, gave to the world a new edition of the Greek Testament. Edition of John Mill. It was the work of thirty years' hard labor; and was published only fourteen days before the author's death. In it, he brought together all the various readings of previous editions, and added many of his own discovery: amounting in all, it is said, to about thirty thousand. This, for a time, greatly excited the fears of many. They were apprehensive that such investigations would only serve to shake the foundations of the Christian religion. But most of these variations are very trifling and insignificant. And it is now believed, that but few men of modern times, have really done more to strengthen and confirm our faith in the Word of God than John Mill.‡

IX. The first successful attempt to amend the *Received Text*, by a judicious application of accumulated Bengel's edition. materials, was made by John Albert Bengel,

* Davidson, p. 565; see also Townley, vol. ii, p. 445.
† Davidson, p. 566; and Tregelles, p. 40.
‡ Tregelles, pp. 42–48; and Davidson, p. 567.

Abbot of Alpirspach, in Wirtemberg. The first edition of his Greek Testament was published at Tübingen in 1734. Several other editions were afterward printed both at Tübingen and Stutgard.*

X. In 1751, appeared the first edition of John James
Edition of Wetstein. Wetstein, a native of Basel, but then a citizen of Amsterdam. It too was the fruit of thirty years' hard labor. It surpasses all previous editions in the copiousness and value of its various readings, with their respective authorities.†

XI. Preëminent in this department of Sacred Criticism,
Critical works and labors of Griesbach. stands Dr. John James Griesbach, of Halle. His first volume consisting of the first three Gospels synoptically arranged, was published in 1774. His second volume containing John and Acts followed the next year: and before the close of the same year his third volume containing the Epistles and Revelation, was given to the public. In 1777, he published the Gospels and the Acts in their usual order. His labors constitute an important era in the criticism of the Greek Testament. For accuracy, sound judgment, good taste, and critical ability, he excels all his predecessors. Greater reliance can be placed on his references and extracts, than on any that had been before given to the public. ‡

XII. Between 1782 and 1788, Christian Frederic Matthæi,
Matthæi's edition. of Moscow, published at Riga in Russia, a new edition of the Greek Testament, accompanied with the Vulgate. For this work he collated about one hundred MSS. ||

XIII. In 1788, Prof. Birch, of Copenhagen, commenced
Critical labors of Prof. Birch. his publications in Sacred Criticism. His chief merit consists in the collation of one hundred

* Davidson, p. 569.   ‡ Tregelles, pp. 83–91; and Davidson, p. 573.
† Ibid, p. 570. | Davidson, p. 575.

and twenty MSS. His last volume on the Apocalypse, was published in 1800.

XIV. Between 1797 and 1840, several minor editions were published by Knapp, Pittman, Vater, Minor editions Schott, and others. But they all followed with derived from Griesbach's. more or less exactness the great work of Gries-bach; a second edition of which was published at Halle and London in 1796 and 1806; and a third at Berlin by Prof. Schulz, of Breslau, in 1827.*

XV. In 1830, appeared at Leipzic the first volume of the Critical Edition of the New Testament by Dr. Edition of Prof. Martin Augustus Scholz, one of the Roman Cath- Scholz. olic professors at Bonn: and the second volume was published in 1836. More than twelve years of incessant activity were spent by the editor, in collecting material for his work. He personally visited the Royal Library at Paris, and also that of Vienna, Munich, Landshut, Berlin, Treves, London, Geneva, Turin, Milan, that of St. Mark's in Venice, Mute in Sicily, three in Florence, that of Bologna, nine in Rome including the Vatican, that of Naples, and those of the Greek monasteries at Jerusalem, St. Saba, and the Isle of Patmos. At all these places, he compared with the text of Griesbach, whatever ancient versions, manuscripts, and other available materials he could find. No less than 674 MSS. were used in preparing the work; 210 of which were collated by Scholz himself. In some respects he had therefore greater advantages than Griesbach; but he lacked the critical perception and delicate skill of his great predecessor. His work is however, a great improvement on the *Received Text*, and is a much nearer approach to it, than is that of Griesbach.*

XVI. In 1831, Charles Lachmann, of Berlin, published a small manual edition of the Greek Testament. Edition of Lachmann. This was followed in 1842, by the first volume

---

* Davidson, p. 580.   † Ibid, pp. 580–584; and Tregelles, pp. 92–96.

of a larger work; and in 1850 by the second volume. The design of the author was to give the best *historically attested* readings of the first four centuries, especially from *Oriental* sources. And hence the work seems to have been intended rather as a *contribution* to assist in restoring the *original text*, than to serve as *the best representation* of it. In this light, it is of great value.*

XVII. The editions of Tischendorf are all works of merit.

Editions of Tischendorf. The first appeared at Leipzic in 1841; the next three were published at Paris in 1842; and a much improved edition was published at Leipzic in 1849. This or the last edition of Henry Alford, is the best for such as desire to have *but one*.†

XVIII. Dr. S. P. Tregelles of England, has for many

Critical labors aud qualifica- tions of Tregel- les. years been engaged in preparing a large critical edition of the Greek Testament. Only the four Gospels have yet been published. But much is expected from the labors of this very laborious and learned editor. "We believe," says Davidson, "that his accuracy in making collations and faithfully recording them, is superior to that evinced by any of the great editors, Mill, Wetstein, Griesbach, Lachmann, or Tischendorf." This is certainly a very high commendation.‡

Thus, gentle reader, I have endeavored to give you a

Labors expend- ed in Biblical Criticism. miniature sketch of the vast field and history of Biblical Criticism. It is of course very unsatis- factory. But I hope that it is sufficient to give you some idea of the immense labors that have been expended within the last three hundred years, by men of the greatest learning and of the very first order of talents, in their efforts to purify the Sacred Text; and to restore to the Church and to the world the original Hebrew and Greek as they were first

---

* Davidson, p. 585.   † Ibid, p. 589.
‡ Davidson, p. 592. See also Tregelles on the Printed Text, pp. 151–173.

recorded by inspired prophets and apostles. Within this short period of time, every word and even every letter of the entire Bible, and especially of the New Testament, has been examined, and reëxamined; and compared again and again, and again, with manuscripts, and versions, and other documents collected together from all parts of Christendom. And the result is the discovery of perhaps not less than one hundred thousand different readings in existing editions and manuscripts of the Holy Bible. *Probable number of various readings discovered.*

A most fearful result truly! you may be disposed to exclaim; and one which may well excite the fears and alarms of all good and pious men. Well, it is not unreasonable that this should be your first impression. *Impression produced by such.* It was, for a time, the painful impression of even some of the learned editors to whom I have referred in the preceding pages. It was this feeling of alarm that induced the learned and pious Bengel to undertake the great work of revising the Scriptures primarily for his own satisfaction. But after many years of excessive toil and laborious research, he wrote to his friend and disciple Reus, as follows: " Eat simply," says he, "the bread of the Scriptures as it presents itself to thee; and do not distress thy- *Remarks of Bengel.* self at finding here and there a small particle of sand which the millstone may have left in it. Thou mayst then dismiss all those doubts which at one time so horribly tormented myself. If the Holy Scriptures, which have been so often copied, and which have passed so often through the faulty hands of fallible men, were absolutely without variations, the miracle would be so great, that faith in them would no longer be faith. I am astonished, on the contrary, that the result of all these transcriptions has not been a much greater number of different readings." *

* Gaussen on Inspiration, p. 195.

16

The truth is, that most of these various readings practically amount to nothing. They consist simply
in the different arrangement of words, or the
use of one synonyme for another, or one letter
for another, or some other equally unimportant
variation. The proper name David, for instance, is spelled
in four different ways in the Greek MSS. In those that
follow the Elzevir, or Received Text, it is *Δαβιδ*; in P, Q,
and Z, it is *Δαδαδ*; and in A, B, C, D, E, G, L, T, X, etc.,
it is sometimes *Δαυιδ* and sometimes *Δαυειδ*.

Unimportant character of most of these different readings.

I might here multiply such illustrations indefinitely. But
I prefer giving to the reader a few extracts from our highest and best authorities in such matters. The learned
Samuel Davidson says: " Having thus given a
history of the text, printed as well as unprinted,
and having shown the various attempts made to
restore it to its pristine purity, we may add a
few words on the general result obtained. The effect of it
has been to establish the genuineness of the New Testament
text in all important particulars. *No new doctrine has been
elicited by its aid: nor have any historical facts been sum-
moned by it from their obscurity. All the doctrines and duties
of Christianity remain unaffected.*"

Remarks of Davidson: first on what criti- cism has not done.

Hence the question arises, Of what utility has it been to
the world? Why have all this labor and in-
dustry been applied? Have all the researches
of modern criticism been wasted? We believe
they have not. *They have proved one thing—that in the records of inspiration there is no material corruption. They
have shown successfully, that during the lapse of many centuries, the text of Scripture has been preserved with great care;
that it has not been extensively tampered with by daring hands.
It is not very different now from what it was seventeen hundred years ago.* Critics, with all their research, have not

Secondly, on what it has ac- complished.

been able to show that the common text varies essentially from what they now recommend as coming nearest to its earliest form. It is *substantially* the same as the text they propose. Thus criticism has been gradually building a foundation, or rather proving the immovable security of a foundation on which the Christian faith may safely rest. It has taught us to regard the Scriptures as they now are to be Divine in their origin. We may boldly challenge the opponent of the Bible to show that the book has been materially corrupted. Empowered by the fruits of criticism, we may well say that the Scriptures continue essentially the same as when they proceeded from the writers themselves.

Hence none need be alarmed when he hears of the vast collection of various readings accumulated by the collators of MSS. and critical editors. The *Effect of this on our faith.* majority of these are of a trifling kind; resembling differences in the collocation of words and synonymous expressions which writers of different tastes evince. Confiding in the general integrity of our religious records, we can look upon a quarter or half a million of various readings with calmness, since they are so unimportant as not to affect religious belief. We can thank God that we are able to walk without apprehension, over the sacred field he has given us to explore. Our faith in the integrity of his word is neither a blind nor superstitious feeling, when all the results of learning incontestibly show, that the present Scriptures may be regarded as uninjured in their transmission through many ages; and that no effort of infidelity can avail to demonstrate their supposititious character.

Let the illiterate reader of the New Testament also take comfort by learning, that the received text to which he is accustomed, is substantially the same *Encouragement to the illiterate.* as that which men of the greatest learning, the most unwearied research, and the severest studies, have

found in a prodigious heap of documents. Let him go forward with a heart grateful to the God of salvation, who has
put him in possession of the same text as is in the hands of
the great Biblical editors whose names stand out in the literature of the Scriptures.*

　"Of the various readings of the New Testament," says
Mr. Norton, "*nineteen out of twenty*, at least, are
to be dismissed at once from consideration; not
on account of their intrinsic unimportance—that
is a separate consideration—but simply because
they are found in so few authorities, and their origin is so
easily explained, that no critic would regard them as having
any claim to be inserted in the text. Of those which remain, a very great majority are entirely unimportant. They
consist in different modes of spelling; in different tenses of
the same verb or different cases of the same noun, not affecting the essential meaning; in the use of the singular for the
plural, or the plural for the singular, where either one or
the other is equally suitable; in the insertion or omission
of particles, such as ἀν and δε, not affecting the sense, or of
the article in cases equally unimportant; in the introduction
of a proper name, when if not inserted, the personal pronoun is to be understood, or of some other word or words
expressive of a sense which would be distinctly implied without them; in the addition of *Jesus* to *Christ*, or *Christ* to
Jesus; in the substitution of one synonymous or equivalent
term for another; in the transposition of words, leaving their
signification the same; in the use of an uncompounded
verb; or of the same verb compounded with a preposition—
the latter differing from the former only in a shade of meaning. Such various readings, and others equally unimportant, compose far the greater part of all, concerning which
there may be or there has been a question whether they are

Remarks of Mr. Norton on the character of the different readings.

* Davidson's Bib. Crit., pp. 593, 594.

to be admitted into the text or not; and it is therefore obviously of no consequence in which way the question has been or may be determined."*

In these statements, the learned of all schools and classes now acquiesce. Even the bitterest enemies of Christianity have nothing more to say on this point. "They have ceased," says Michaelis, "henceforth to look for any thing from those critical researches which they at first so warmly recommended, because they expected discoveries from them that have never been made."† The learned Eichhorn, for instance, though an uncompromising Rationalist, concedes that "the different readings of the Hebrew manuscripts, collected by Kennicott, hardly offer sufficient interest to compensate for the trouble they cost."‡ But these negative results are just what every Christian had reason to anticipate. And as Gaussen very justly says: "They are of immense value in virtue of their nothingness; and all powerful in virtue of their insignificance."‖

This ground abandoned by infidels.

Remarks of Eichhorn.

Value of these negative results.

Thanks then be to God for his wonderful providential care of the Holy Bible! Since it was written, what changes have occurred in the world! How many thrones, and kingdoms, and empires, and dynasties, and schemes of religion and philosophy have passed away! But *"the word of the Lord endures forever."*

NOTE.—It must be evident to the reader, that the state of the Hebrew text has been much improved by the labors of the Buxtorfs, Athias, Van der Hooght, Michaelis, Kennicott, De Rossi, Hahn, and I may add, through the instrumentality and liberality of the Bagsters, of London, since our common English version was made, in 1611: and also that since that same

Necessity of a revised English version.

* Genuineness of the Gospels, p. 38 (American Edition).
† Michaelis, vol. ii, p. 266.   ‡ Einleitung, 2 Th. S. 700.
‖ Gaussen on Inspiration, p. 169.

important epoch, the Greek text has been still more improved by the joint labors of the Elzevirs, Walton, Fell, Mill, Bengel, Wetstein, Griesbach, Matthæi, Birch, Schulz, Knapp, Tittmann, Scholz, Lachmann, Tischendorf, and Tregelles. And hence it seems to follow, as a matter of course, that our English version should also be brought up to the same standard. For though it is pleasant to know that thousands, we hope indeed millions, of our race have been saved through its instrumentality; and that millions more may be still saved by it; that it in fact contains every thing that is essential to life and godliness; yet it seems but reasonable, that the whole Anglo-Saxon family should have a version of the Holy Scriptures approximating as near as possible to the authentic text of the original Greek and Hebrew; and also in perfect harmony with the present improved state of our own vernacular. We do not want a *New Version*. We simply want a thorough and judicious *revision* of that which we now have. Much of the Old version can never be improved: and this, of course, should never be changed. It is not a small matter to deprive us of even a single word, or sentence, or paragraph which is now embalmed in the religious literature of the whole Anglo-Saxon family, as well as in the hearts and memories of living millions. But there can be no reasonable apology for retaining *known errors* of any kind, in a book, which above all others should serve to develop, and mold, and discipline the understanding, and the affections, and the will of a race, which, under God, must continue to have a powerful influence over the civilization, and liberties, and destiny of the rest of mankind.

PART FOURTH.

INSPIRATION OF THE HOLY SCRIPTURES.

THE fourth province of Reason within the domain of Divine Revelation, is to decide on the *Inspira-* tion of the Holy Scriptures. Fourth prov- ince of Reason.

That the Bible is of Divine origin; that its sixty-six books were all written and often indorsed by inspired men; and that they have suffered no Points already proved. material change during the lapse of intervening centuries, has, I hope, been proved to the entire satisfaction of every candid reader. And if so, this goes very far toward proving also the plenary inspiration of these sacred writings. For it is certainly very unreasonable to suppose that God would supernaturally qualify a few men to *receive* the truth, and then leave them Their bearing on the ques- tion of Inspi- ration. to *communicate* this truth to others, simply by means of their own natural and unassisted faculties.

But as this is a subject of paramount importance, involving many questions of great practical value to every student of the Bible, I have thought it best to devote a few separate chapters to its Reason for considering it separately. special consideration. In doing so, I will as- sume only *the general historical truthfulness of* What assumed in the discus- sion.

these books. This much has certainly been proved beyond all reasonable doubt. And hence it is perfectly legitimate to use the testimony of the original witnesses in settling this controversy. This, I will endeavor to do without prejudice and partiality in the following chapters.

CHAPTER I.

INSPIRATION OF THE OLD TESTAMENT.

Inspiration of the Old Testament proved:

THAT the Old Testament was all given and written by and through the inspiration of the Holy Spirit may be proved,

First, by Old Testament writers.

I. *By the testimony of the writers themselves.* This is very clearly implied in such passages as the following:

Evidence from Deuteronomy.

1. I will raise them up a prophet from among their brethren, like unto thee, and I will put *my words* in his mouth; and he shall speak unto them *all that I shall command him.* And it shall come to pass, that whosoever will not hearken unto *my words* which he shall speak in my name, I will require it of him. (Deuteronomy xviii: 18, 19.)

Joshua.

2. And Joshua said unto the people, *Thus saith the Lord God of Israel,* Your fathers dwelt on the other side of the river (Euphrates) in old time, even Terah, the father of Abraham, and the father of Nahor. (Joshua xxiv: 2.)

Samuel.

3. Now these are the last words of David. David, the son of Jesse, said, And the man who was raised up on high, the anointed of the God of Jacob,

and the sweet psalmist of Israel, said, *The Spirit of the Lord spake by me, and his word was in my tongue.* (2 Samuel xxiii: 1, 2.)

4. *But the word of the Lord came unto Shemaiah,* the man of God, saying: Speak unto Rehoboam the son of Solomon, king of Judah, and unto all the <small>Kings.</small> house of Judah and Benjamin, and to all the remnant of the people, saying, *Thus saith the Lord God,* ye shall not go up nor fight against your brethren, the children of Israel. (1 Kings xii: 22–24.)

5. And it came to pass the same night that *the word of the Lord came to Nathan,* saying, Go and tell David my servant, *Thus saith the Lord,* Thou shalt not <small>Chronicles.</small> build me a house to dwell in. (1 Chronicles xvii: 3, 4.)

6. The *vision* of Isaiah the son of Amoz, which he saw concerning Judah and Jerusalem, in the days of Uzziah, Jotham, Ahaz, and Hezekiah, kings <small>Isaiah.</small> of Judah. Hear, O heavens, and give ear, O earth, *for the Lord hath spoken.* (Isaiah i: 1, 2.)

7. *But the word of the Lord was unto them precept upon precept; precept upon precept; line upon line; line upon line; here a little, and there a little:* that they might go and fall backward, and be broken, and snared, and taken. Wherefore *hear the word of the Lord,* ye scornful men that rule this people which is in Jerusalem. (Isaiah xxviii: 13, 14.)

8. Who is a wise man that may understand this? *and who is he to whom the mouth of the Lord hath spoken, that he may declare it,* for what the land <small>Jeremiah.</small> perisheth, and is burned up like a wilderness, that none passeth through? (Jeremiah ix: 12.)

9. *Hear ye the word which the Lord speaketh unto you, O house of Israel. Thus saith the Lord,* Learn not the way of the heathen, and be not dismayed at the signs of heaven; for the heathen are dismayed at them. (Jeremiah x: 1, 2.)

10. Hear ye and give ear: *for the Lord hath spoken.* (Jeremiah xiii: 15.)

11. And say, *Hear ye the word of the Lord,* O kings of Judah and inhabitants of Jerusalem. *Thus saith the Lord of Hosts, the God of Israel:* Behold, I will bring evil upon this place; the which whosoever heareth, his ears shall tingle. (Jeremiah xix: 3.)

12. *The word of the Lord came expressly unto Ezekiel the priest,* the son of Buzi, in the land of the Chaldeans, by the river Chebar; *and the hand of the Lord was there upon him.* (Ezekiel i: 3.)

Ezekiel.

13. *And he said unto me,* Son of man, go, get thee unto the house of Israel, *and speak with my words unto them.* Moreover he said unto me, Son of Man, *all my words that I shall speak unto thee receive in thy heart, and hear with thy ears. And go, get thee unto them of the captivity,* unto the children of thy people, and speak unto them, and tell them, *Thus saith the Lord God;* whether they will hear or whether they will forbear. (Ezekiel iii: 4, 10, 11.)

14. *The word of the Lord that came unto Hosea,* the son of Beeri, *in the days of Uzziah, Jotham, Ahaz, and Hezekiah, kings of Judah, and in the days of Jeroboam the son of Joash, king of Israel.* (Hosea i: 1.)

Hosea.

15. *The word of the Lord that came to Joel the son of Pethuel.* (Joel i: 1.)

Joel.

16. *Hear this word that the Lord hath spoken against you,* O children of Israel, against the whole family which I brought up from the land of Egypt, saying: You only have I known of all the families of the earth; therefore I will punish you for your iniquities. (Amos iii: 1, 2.)

Amos.

17. *The vision of Obadiah. Thus saith the Lord God* concerning Edom: We have heard a rumor from

Obadiah.

the Lord, and an ambassador is sent among the heathen. (Obadiah i: 1.)

18. *Now the word of the Lord came unto Jonah* the son of Amittai, saying: Arise, go up to Nineveh, that great city, and cry against it; for their wicked- ness is come up before me. (Jonah i: 1, 2.) *Jonah.*

19. *And the word of the Lord came unto Jonah* the second time, saying: Arise, go into Nineveh, that great city, *and preach unto it the preaching that I bid thee.* (Jonah iii: 1, 2.)

20. *The word of the Lord, that came to Micah* the Moras- thite, in the days of Jotham, Ahaz, and Heze- kiah, kings of Judah, which he saw concerning Samaria and Jerusalem. (Micah i: 1.) *Micah.*

21. But they shall sit every man under his vine and un- der his fig-tree; and none shall make them afraid: *for the mouth of the Lord of Hosts hath spoken it.* (Micah iv: 4.)

22. *The word of the Lord which came unto Zephaniah* the son of Cushi, the son of Gedaliah, the son of Amariah, the son of Hizkiah, in the days of Josiah, the son of Amon, king of Judah. (Zephaniah i: 1.) *Zephaniah.*

23. In the second year of Darius the king, in the sixth month, in the first day of the month, *came the word of the Lord by Haggai the prophet,* unto Zerubbabel, the son of Shealtiel, governor of Judah, and to Joshua the son of Josedech, the High-Priest, saying: *Thus speaketh the Lord of Hosts,* saying, This people say, The time is not come, the time that the Lord's house should be built. *Then came the word of the Lord by Haggai the prophet,* say- ing: Is it time for you, O ye, to dwell in your ceiled houses, and this house to lie waste. (Haggai i: 1–4.) *Haggai.*

24. In the eighth month, in the second year of Darius, *came the word of the Lord unto Zechariah* the son of Barachiah, the son of Iddo, the prophet, saying· The Lord hath been sore displeased with your *Zechariah.*

fathers. Therefore say unto them, *Thus saith the Lord of Hosts:* Turn ye unto me, *saith the Lord of Hosts,* and I will turn unto you *saith the Lord of Hosts.* (Zechariah i: 1–3.)

25. *The burden of the word of the Lord to Israel by Mala-chi.* I have loved you, *saith the Lord:* yet ye say, Wherein hast thou loved us? Was not Esau Jacob's brother? *saith the Lord:* yet I loved Jacob, and I hated Esau. (Malachi i: 1, 2.)

> Malachi.

26. Remember ye *the Law of Moses* my servant, *which I commanded unto him in Horeb* for all Israel, with the statutes and judgments. (Malachi iv: 4.)

See also Exodus iv: 3; vii: 1; Numbers xxii: 35; xxiii: 5; Isaiah viii: 11; Jeremiah xvii: 20; xxix: 1–8; xxx: 4; l: 1; li: 12; Daniel viii: 27; x; 8, 27; Nahum i: 1; Habakkuk i: 1; Haggai ii: 1; Zechariah viii: 1–23, *et cetera.*

From this induction of particulars, which might be greatly extended, it is evident that the prophets all claimed to be inspired: and that their office was simply to communicate to others the words and instructions of God, whether they themselves understood them or not. But all the Old Testament is prophecy: and hence it is all inspired.*

> Conclusion from Old Testament evidence.

---

* In common English parlance, the word *prophet* is now generally used to denote one who *predicts* or *foretells.* But this is not in harmony with either Hebrew or Greek usage. The Hebrew word commonly used for prophet is נָבִיא from נָבַע *to boil up like a fountain:* and hence signifies any one who speaks under a Divine influence. And it therefore always implied, among the Hebrews, that the words spoken were not the words of the prophet, but of God. They might convey instruction of any kind and on any subject; and it might relate to either the past, the present, or the future. And hence the books of Joshua, Judges, Samuel, and Kings were all called Prophets or Prophecies by the Jews; as well as Isaiah, Jeremiah, Ezekiel, Hosea, Joel, Amos, Obadiah, Jonah, Micah, Nahum, Habakkuk, Zephaniah, Haggai, Zechariah, and Malachi. The word חֹזֶה *Seer,* from חָזָה *to see,* was also frequently used to denote the same class of persons.

> Scope and functions of the Prophetic office.

II. *The inspiration of the Old Testament may also be proved from the evidence furnished by the writers of the New Testament.* The following passages are deemed entirely sufficient for this purpose.

1. Think not that I am come to destroy *the Law or the Prophets :* I am not come to destroy, but to fulfill. For verily I say unto you, *Till heaven and earth pass away, one jot or one tittle shall in nowise pass from the Law till all be fulfilled.* Whosoever therefore shall break *one of these least commandments,* and shall teach men so, he shall be called the least in the kingdom of heaven : but whosoever shall do and teach them, the same shall be called great in the kingdom of heaven. (Matthew v : 17–19.)

It is evident that by the Law and the Prophets, Christ here means the entire Old Testament : and it is just as evident, that it is here his intention to indorse the Divine origin, the Divine authenticity, the Divine authority, and the Divine inspiration of even its most minute precepts and specifications.

2. Therefore all things whatsoever ye would that men should do to you, do ye also to them: *for this is the Law and the Prophets.* (Matthew vii : 12.)

Here the Law and the Prophets are referred to as containing an authoritative summary of the whole duty of man. This of course implies their Divine origin and inspiration.

3. For all *the Prophets* and *the Law prophesied* until John. (Matthew xi : 13.)

The Greek word προφητης is properly *one who speaks for another;* and especially one who speaks for a god, and interprets his will to man. Thus Apollo is called προφητης Διος *interpreter of Jupiter.* (Æsch. Eum. 19 and Virg. Æn. iii : 252.) The Pythia was called the προφητης or προμαντις of Apollo. (Herod. viii : 36.) And in like manner, the προφητης was the interpreter of the *inspired μαντις.* (Æsch. Ag. 1099.) So also poets are called Μουσων προφηται, interpreters of the Muses. (Plato, Phædr. 262, D.)

In this passage, the Law and the Prophets are again put for the entire Old Testament; and are evidently represented as being the only divinely authorized *interpreters* of God's will, till the coming of John the Baptist.

4. Ye do err not knowing the *Scriptures,* nor the power of God. (Matthew xxii: 29.)

The word *Scriptures* in this connection, as indeed also in most other places where it occurs in the New Testament, denotes all the canonical books of the Old Testament.* And these are here evidently spoken of as a *revelation of God's will and purposes concerning man.* The error of the Sadducees was twofold: they understood neither the infinite power of God, nor his revealed will and purposes in relation to man's destiny.

5. Jesus said unto him, Thou shalt love the Lord thy God with all thy heart, and with all thy soul, and with all thy mind. This is the first and great commandment. And the second is like to it, Thou shalt love thy neighbor as thyself. *On these two commandments hang all the Law and the Prophets.* (Matthew xxii: 37–40.)

6. What think ye of Christ? whose son is he? They say unto him, The son of David. He said unto them, How then doth David *in Spirit* (or by the Spirit) call him Lord? saying: Jehovah said to my Lord, Sit thou on my right hand till I make thy enemies thy footstool. (Matthew xxii: 42–44.)

There is no attempt here to prove that David spoke the truth or that he uttered this sentiment under the influence of the Holy Spirit. This question was settled when the 110th Psalm was placed in the Old Testament Canon, on the authority of inspired men. But the whole force of Christ's remark is evidently based on the following implied argument. All the books of the Old Testament Canon are the inspired words of God. The 110th Psalm is a part of

---

* See Part Second, Chap. I, Sec. II, pp. 161-167.

this Canon. And hence it is inspired; and contains nothing but the truth. And hence it is evident, that in this one
reference of our Saviour, the inspiration of the entire Old
Testament is implied. And the same may be said of nearly
every other allusion that Christ and his Apostles make to
the Hebrew Scriptures.

7. And his father Zacharias *was filled with the Holy Spirit,*
and *prophesied,* saying: Blessed be the Lord God
of Israel; for he hath visited and redeemed his   Luke.
people; and hath raised up an horn of salvation for us in
the house of his servant David; *as he spake by the mouth
of his holy prophets which have been since the world began.*
(Luke i: 67–70.)

8. Abraham said unto him, They have *Moses and the
Prophets;* let them hear them. And he said: Nay, father
Abraham: but if one went unto them from the dead, they
will repent. And he said unto him, *If they hear not Moses
and the Prophets, neither will they be persuaded though one
rose from the dead.* (Luke xvi: 29–31.)

Here again, *Moses* and the *Prophets* are used to denote all
the writings of the Old Testament. And it is evidently
Christ's intention to represent them as the divinely appointed guide of life.

9. Then said he unto them, O fools, and slow of heart to
believe all that the *Prophets* have spoken! Ought not Christ
to have suffered these things and to enter into his glory?
And beginning at *Moses and all the Prophets,* he expounded
unto them *in all the Scriptures* the things concerning himself. (Luke xxiv: 25–27.)

The word *Prophets* in the first clause of this passage, seems
to denote the entire Old Testament, including even the Pentateuch; as the word *Scriptures* certainly does in the last
clause. And both terms are here evidently used for the inspired word of God.

10. And he said unto them, These are the words which I spake unto you, while I was yet with you, that *all things must be fulfilled which were written in the Law of Moses, and in the Prophets, and in the Psalms concerning me.* Then opened he their understanding, that they might understand *the Scriptures.* (Luke xxiv: 44, 45.)

The *Law of Moses*, and the *Prophets*, and the *Psalms* in the 44th verse, evidently comprehend the same writings as does the word *Scriptures* in the 45th verse: and they are each equivalent to the thirty-nine books of the Old Testament. This much is manifest from the context. But whence the necessity that all things written in these books concerning Christ should be fulfilled? Concede that they contain nothing but the inspired words of God; and then all is plain. God is not a man that he should lie; nor is he the son of man that he should repent or change his purpose. His word must and will be fulfilled in all cases. But on any other hypothesis, can any one explain this necessity? Clearly, our Savior here fully indorses the Divine authority and inspiration of the entire Old Testament.

11. Search the *Scriptures :* for in them ye think ye have eternal life; and they are they which testify of me. (John v: 39.)

John.

In what Scriptures did the Jews think they had eternal life? Evidently in the same thirty-nine books that now compose the Canon of the Old Testament. But these were all witnesses for Christ. How so? Evidently because they were all dictated by that Spirit which searches all things; yea even the deep counsels and purposes of Jehovah. Here then we have another proof, that in the New Testament the word *Scripture* or *Scriptures* means simply *the inspired writings :* and, unless restricted by the context, it always comprehends at least the thirty-nine books of the Old Testament.

12. Jesus answered them, Is it not written in your *Law*, I said, Ye are gods? If he called them gods, unto whom the word of God came, *and the Scripture can not be broken;* say ye of Him whom the Father hath sanctified and sent into the world, Thou blasphemest; because I said, I am the Son of God? (John x: 34–36.)

In this instance, as in Romans iii: 19, the word *Law* is manifestly used for the whole of the Old Testament: and so also is the word *Scripture*. But why can not the Old Testament be broken? If it were a work of mere human authority, this might easily be done. But if it is the inspired word of God, it is of course faultless, and sustained by all the authority that Heaven can give it.

13. And he will send Jesus Christ who before was preached unto you; whom the heaven must receive, until the times of restitution of all things, *which God* Acts. *hath spoken by the mouth of all his holy prophets, since the world began. For Moses truly said unto the fathers, A Prophet shall the Lord your God raise up unto you of your brethren, like unto me; him shall ye hear in all things, whatsoever he shall say unto you. And it shall come to pass, that every soul who will not hear that Prophet, shall be destroyed from among the people. Yea and all the Prophets from Samuel and those that follow after, as many as have spoken, have likewise foretold of these days.* (Acts iii: 20–24.)

Here again the evidence of inspiration is clear and satisfactory. According to Peter, it was *God* that spoke through Moses and all the Prophets from Samuel to Malachi, concerning the coming, the sufferings, the resurrection, the reign and the triumphs of the Messiah.

14. And when they had appointed him a day, there came many to him into his lodging; to whom he expounded and testified the Kingdom of God, persuading them concerning Jesus, both *out of the Law of Moses, and out of the Prophets,*

from morning till evening. And some believed the things
which were spoken, and some believed not. And when they
agreed not among themselves, they departed, after that Paul
had spoken one word: *Well spake the Holy Spirit by Isaiah
the prophet unto our fathers,* saying: Go unto this people and
say, Hearing, ye shall hear; and shall not understand. (Acts
xxviii: 23–26.)

15. And that from a child thou hast known the *Holy Scrip-*
tures, which are able to make thee wise unto sal-
Timothy.   vation through faith which is in Christ Jesus.
All Scripture is given by inspiration of God; and is profitable
for doctrine, for reproof, for correction, for instruction in right-
eousness; that the man of God may be perfect, thoroughly fur-
nished unto all good works. (2 Timothy iii: 15–17.)

The word *Scripture* in this connection, evidently means at
least the entire Old Testament. It may perhaps comprehend
also, as in 2 Peter iii: 16, such portions of the New Testament as were then written and in possession of the churches.
But be this as it may, there can be no doubt that it includes,
at least, as usual, the thirty-nine books of the Old Testament.
And as Paul here assures Timothy that they were all inspired,
or given by inspiration of God, this of course puts an end to
the whole controversy.

I am aware that some critics have converted this compound
into a complex proposition; and make it read as follows: "All
Scripture given by inspiration of God is profitable for doctrine, for reproof, for correction," etc. But this is to reject
from the inspired text the conjunction "*and*" (και); a license
which is wholly unwarranted. We are at liberty to *supply*
whatever is clearly implied in the context. But we have no
authority to *reject* any word used by an inspired writer.

16. Knowing this first, that no prophecy of the Scripture
came from private interpretation; for the proph-
Peter.   ecy came not at any time by the will of man; but

holy men of God spoke as they were moved by the Holy Spirit. (2 Peter i: 20–21.)

The word *Scripture* is here evidently used in its ordinary New Testament sense, to denote all the books of the Old Testament. But these books are all prophetic. And as Peter here assures us that all prophecy was given by and through the inspiration of the Holy Spirit, it follows that the entire Old Testament is the product of Divine inspiration.

These evidences might be multiplied indefinitely. But it is not necessary. It is evident from what has already been given, that Christ, and Matthew, and Luke, and John, and Peter, and Paul have all and severally indorsed the entire Old Testament *as the inspired word of God.* This of course is sufficient. Their testimony is to us, and to all others who believe in the Divine origin of the Bible, an end of all controversy.* *(Conclusion from New Testament evidence.)*

CHAPTER II.

INSPIRATION OF THE NEW TESTAMENT.

THAT the New Testament is also the inspired word of God, may be proved,

I. *From the inspiration of the Old Testament.* These two volumes are not separate and independent works. They are together but the development and illustration of one great system. And they are therefore so related, that they must both stand or fall together. Let it be proved, for instance, *(Inspiration of the New Testament proved, first, from its relation to the Old Testament.)*

---

*The following additional references may be of service to those who desire to examine still further the testimony of Christ and his Apostles, touching the inspiration of the Old Testament. Matt. i: 22, 23; ii: 5, 6,

that the earth was created and adorned by Jehovah; and
we need no further proof that Mercury, and Venus, and
Mars, and Jupiter, and Saturn, and Neptune, and indeed all
other parts of the Solar system, are also the workmanship of
the same infinitely glorious and perfect Being. And just so
it is in reference to the Old and New Testaments. If it can
be satisfactorily proved, that any considerable part of either
of them is inspired, then indeed it follows of necessity, that
they are both wholly inspired. But it has already been
proved with all the certainty of moral demonstration, that
the Old Testament was written by holy men of old as they
were moved by the Holy Spirit; and hence it follows just
as certainly, that the New Testament was also dictated by
the self-same Spirit.

II. *The inspiration of the New Testament is further proved
by the promises of Christ to his Apostles; that
they and others should possess the miraculous
gifts of the Holy Spirit.* Such for instance are
the following:

<small>Secondly, from the Promises of Christ.</small>

1. Behold, I send you forth as sheep in the midst of
wolves: be ye therefore wise as serpents, and
harmless as doves. But beware of men: for
they will deliver you up to the councils, and they will
scourge you in their synagogues. And ye shall be brought
before governors and kings for my sake, for a testimony
against them and the Gentiles. *But when they deliver you
up, take no thought how or what ye shall speak: for it shall
be given you in that same hour what ye shall speak. For it
is not ye that speak; but the Spirit of your Father which*

<small>Matthew.</small>

15, and 23; iii: 3; iv: 4, 6, 7, and 10; viii: 17; xii: 17–21; xiii: 35;
xix: 4–6; xxi: 1–5; Mark i: 2, 3; ii: 25, 26; iv: 12; x: 6–9; xiv: 49;
xv: 28; Luke iii: 4; v: 14; John ii: 22; vii: 38; xiii: 18; xvii: 12;
xix: 28; Acts i: 16, 20; ii: 16–21, and 25–31; vii: 35, 37; viii: 28, 32,
33, 35; Romans i: 2; iii: 2, 19, 21; ix: 25–29; x: 19–21; xv: 4, 10, 11,
12· and' *the entire Epistle to the Hebrews.*

speaketh in you. (Matthew x: 16–20. See also Mark xiii: 11; and Luke xxi: 12–15.)

2. I have yet many things to say unto you, but ye can not bear them now. Howbeit, *when He, the Spirit of Truth is come, he will guide you into all* ^John.^ *truth: for he shall not speak of himself; but whatsoever he shall hear, that shall he speak: and he will show you things to come.* He shall glorify me: for he shall receive of mine, and show it unto you. All things that the Father hath are mine: therefore, said I, that he shall take of mine and show it unto you. (John xvi: 12–15. See also xiv: 15–18, and xvi: 7.

3. For John truly baptized in water; but ye shall be baptized in the Holy Spirit not many days hence. *But ye shall receive power after that the Holy* ^Acts.^ *Spirit is come upon you: and ye shall be witnesses unto me, both in Jerusalem, and in all Judea, and in Samaria, and unto the uttermost part of the earth.* (Acts i: 5, 8.)

4. And he said unto them, Go ye into all the world, and preach the Gospel to every creature. He that believeth and is baptized shall be saved: but he ^Mark.^ that believeth not shall be damned. *And these signs shall follow them that believe. In my name they shall cast out demons; they shall speak with new tongues; they shall take up serpents; and if they drink any deadly thing it shall not hurt them; they shall lay hands on the sick, and they shall recover.* (Mark xvi: 15–18.)

It is scarcely necessary to pause here with the view of proving, that these promises of supernatural aid ^The writings as well as the addresses of the Apostles, embraced in these promises.^ to the Apostles, had not reference merely to their verbal instructions and extemporaneous addresses; but also to all their *writings,* as the appointed legislators and plenipotentiaries of the Kingdom of Heaven. The latter, indeed, are even more important

than the former. The effect of their addresses was temporary: but the influence of their writings will endure forever.
And hence it is chiefly through them that the Apostles still
sit on twelve thrones judging the twelve tribes of Israel:*
and it is also in a measure through the same writings, that
Christ will continue with the Apostles and with the Church
over which they still preside, to the end of the world.†

These promises then positively guarantee the inspiration
of all parts of the New Testament, written by
any of the Apostles; that is, of all its books,
save the Memoirs of Luke and Mark. And the
inspiration of even these, is, I think fairly implied, though
not expressed in the aforesaid promises. This, however, falls
more appropriately under our next proposition.

Conclusion from these premises.

III. *The inspiration of the entire New Testament, may also
be legitimately inferred from the miraculous gifts
that were actually bestowed on the Apostles and
others, for the conversion of the world, and the
edification of the Church, until Christianity should
be fully established; the Canon of the New Testament completed; and the evidence of its Divine authenticity perfected.*

*Thirdly, from the gifts actu-
ally bestowed on the Apostles and others.*

That these gifts were actually bestowed on the
Apostles and many of their fellow-laborers, is
proved by the following passages:

Evidence of the bestowment of such gifts.

1. And when the day of Pentecost was fully come, they
were all with one accord in one place. And
suddenly there came a sound from heaven, as of
a rushing mighty wind, and it filled all the house where
they were sitting. And there appeared unto them cloven
tongues like as of fire, and it sat upon each of them. *And
they were all filled with the Holy Spirit; and began to speak
with other tongues as the Spirit gave them utterance.* (Acts
ii: 1–4.)

From Acts.

*Matt. xix: 28.   †Matt. xxviii: 20.

2. Then Philip went down to the city of Samaria, and preached Christ unto them. And the people with one accord gave heed unto those things which Philip spake, *hearing and seeing the miracles which he did. For unclean spirits came out of many that were possessed with them; and many taken with palsies and that were lame were healed. And there was great joy in that city.* (Acts viii: 5–8.)

3. Now when the Apostles who were at Jerusalem, heard that Samaria had received the word of God, they sent unto them Peter and John. Who when they were come down, prayed for them that they might receive the Holy Spirit: for as yet he had fallen upon none of them; only they were baptized in the name of the Lord Jesus. *Then laid they their hands upon them, and they received the Holy Spirit.** (Acts viii: 14–17.)

4. While Peter was speaking these words, *the Holy Spirit fell on all them who heard the word.* And they of the circumcision were astonished, as many as came with Peter: because that *on the Gentiles also was poured out the gift of the Holy Spirit. For they heard them speak with tongues, and magnify God.* (Acts x: 44–46.)

5. But the manifestation of the Spirit is given to every man to profit withal. *For to one is given by the Spirit the word of wisdom; to another, the word* From 1 Corinthians.

---

*That this was the *miraculous* and not the ordinary gift of the Holy Spirit promised to all Christians, seems clear for the following reasons:

1. It was evidently attended with some outward and visible manifestations of power such as occurred on the day of Pentecost. For in the following verse it is said that Simon *saw* that the Holy Spirit was given through the laying on of the Apostles' hands.

2. The ordinary gift of the Holy Spirit is received by every true believer, immediately after his baptism. (See Acts ii: 38.)

3. It was manifestly something that even Philip the Evangelist had not the power to bestow. And hence the necessity that Peter and John should come down to Samaria for this purpose.

of knowledge by the same Spirit; to another, faith by the same Spirit; to another, the gifts of healing by the same Spirit; to another, the working of miracles; to another, prophecy; to another, discerning of spirits; to another, divers kinds of tongues; to another, the interpretation of tongues. But all these worketh that one and the self-same Spirit, dividing to every man severally as he will. (1 Corinthians xii: 7–11.)

Inference from the data thus furnished.
From these and many other similar passages, it appears that miraculous gifts were actually bestowed on the Apostles and many others for the perfecting of the saints, for the work of the ministry, for the edifying of the body of Christ, till they should all come into the unity of the faith and the knowledge of the Son of God, unto a perfect man, unto the measure of the stature of the fullness of Christ.* And this of course furnishes another guarantee not only that the Apostles were inspired, but also that Mark and Luke wrote their Memoirs of Christ and his Apostles, as they were moved by the Holy Spirit. For—

1. God is a God of order; and bestows his gifts when and where and as they are needed. But if it was necessary to confer spiritual gifts on many members of the same congregation, as was certainly done in the church of Corinth, how much more was it necessary to bestow them liberally on such men as Timothy, Titus, Barnabas, Silas, Judas, Philip, Mark, Luke, and other Evangelists who were required to assist the Apostles, not only in setting the churches in order, but also in preaching the Gospel to the heathen.

2. These gifts were actually bestowed on Timothy,† Barnabas,‡ Philip,‖ Silas, and Judas.§ Why then should Mark and Luke be regarded and treated as exceptions?

3. Because these Memoirs were currently circulated among

---

* Ephesians iv: 12, 13.   ‡ Acts xiii: 1.   § Acts xv: 32.
† 2 Timothy i: 6.   ‖ Acts viii: 6.

the brethren, and of course subject to be approved or disapproved by the Apostles or other inspired men, long before the gifts of inspiration ceased in the churches. But, nevertheless, they were from the beginning received by all, as canonical and authentic books. And hence it follows, that they must have been inspired.

IV. *The inspiration of the New Testament may also be proved from the direct testimony of its own inspired writers.* The evidence arising from this source is, of course, wholly incidental. *Fourthly, from the direct testimony of New Testament writers.*
The Apostles were generally known and recognized by those to whom they wrote, as inspired men. And hence, except in a few extraordinary cases, it was not at all necessary that they should attempt to prove either their own inspiration or the inspiration of their writings. But the following incidental remarks will greatly serve to corroborate and strengthen the evidence already submitted.

1. I say the truth in Christ. I lie not, my conscience also bearing me witness *in the Holy Spirit,* that I have great heaviness and continual sorrow in my heart, for my brethren, my kinsmen according to the flesh. (Romans ix: 1–3.) *Testimony of Paul.*

2. And my discourse and my preaching were not arrayed in winning words of wisdom, *but in display of Spirit and might: that your belief might not be brought about by man's wisdom, but by might of God.* Wisdom, however, we speak among the full grown; not, however, a wisdom of this age, nor of the rulers of this age, that are to come to nought; *but we do speak God's wisdom in a mystery, the hidden wisdom, which God fore-appointed before the ages for our glory:* which not one of the rulers of this age has come to know; for had they known it, they would not have crucified the Lord of glory. But we speak—as it is written—*things that eye saw not, and ear heard not, and that entered not into man's heart;*

things that God made ready for those that love him. But to us did God reveal them through his Spirit: for the Spirit searches out all things, even the depths of God. For who of mankind knows the things of the man, but the spirit of the man which is in him? So too the things of God, has no one come to know, but the Spirit of God. We, however, did not receive the spirit of the world, *but the Spirit that is from God, that we may know the things vouchsafed to us by God:* which things we also speak, *not in words taught of man's wisdom, but taught of Spirit, expounding spiritual things by spiritual means.* But a natural man accepts not the things of the Spirit of God; for they are foolishness to him, and he is not able to learn them, because they are spiritually scanned. *But the spiritual man scans them all;* while he himself is scanned by no one. For who learned the Lord's mind that he should instruct him? But *we have Christ's mind.** (1 Corinthians ii: 4–16.)

In this passage, Paul includes with himself the other Apostles and all Evangelists, pastors, and teachers who were endowed with the supernatural gifts of the Holy Spirit. And with respect to them all, he assures us, that even in their choice and use of words, they were under the influence and guidance of that Spirit which searches all things, yea even the deep counsels and purposes of Jehovah. His testimony is therefore really conclusive on the whole matter; and further evidence would seem to be wholly superfluous. But on a subject of so much importance, it is well to have line upon line, and precept upon precept. And I will therefore presume on the indulgence of the reader, while I merely

---

*I quote here from the very literal translation of Thomas Sheldon Green. Dr. James Macknight translates the thirteenth verse as follows: " *Which things also we speak, not in words taught by human wisdom; but in words taught by the Holy Spirit; explaining spiritual things in spiritual words.*"

present, without note or comment, a few more extracts from these sacred writings.

3. If any one thinks himself to be a prophet or spiritual man, let him acknowledge that *the things which I write to you are the commandments of the Lord.* But if any one be ignorant, let him be ignorant. (1 Corinthians xiv: 37.)

4. But I certify you, brethren, that *the Gospel which was preached by me, is not after man. For I neither received it of man; neither was I taught it, but by the revelation of Jesus Christ.* (Galatians i: 11, 12.)

5. Ye are built upon the foundation of the *Apostles* and *Prophets,* Jesus Christ himself being the chief corner-stone. (Ephesians ii: 20.)

6. For this cause I Paul, the prisoner of Jesus Christ for you Gentiles, if ye have heard of the dispensation of the grace of God which is given me to you-ward: how *that by revelation he made known unto me the mystery* (as I wrote afore in few words; whereby, when ye read, ye may understand my knowledge in the mystery of Christ) which in other ages, was not made known unto the sons of men, *as it is now revealed unto his holy Apostles and Prophets by the Spirit;* that the Gentiles should be fellow-heirs, and of the same body, and partakers of his promise in Christ by the Gospel: whereof I was made a minister, according to the gift of the grace of God, given unto me by the effectual working of his power. (Ephesians iii: 1–7.)

7. For this cause also we thank God without ceasing, because when ye received *the word of God which ye heard from us, ye received it not as the word of men, but (as it is in truth) the word of God,* which effectually worketh in you that believe. (1 Thessalonians ii: 13.)

8. For ye know *what commandments we gave you by the Lord Jesus.* For this we say unto you *by the word of the Lord,* that we who are alive and remain unto the coming of

the Lord, shall not anticipate them that are asleep. (1 Thessalonians iv : 2–15.)

9. Of which salvation, the Prophets did inquire and
Testimony of   search diligently, who prophesied of the grace
Peter.   that should come unto you: searching what, or
what manner of time, *the Spirit of Christ that was in them
did signify, when it testified beforehand the sufferings of Christ
and the glory that should follow.   Unto whom it was revealed,
that not unto themselves, but unto us they did minister the
things which are now reported unto you by them that have
preached the Gospel unto you, with the Holy Spirit sent down
from heaven;* which things the angels desire to look into.
(1 Peter i: 10–12.)

10. This second epistle, beloved, I now write unto you;
in both of which I stir up your pure minds by way of re-
membrance: that ye may be mindful of *the words which were
spoken before by the holy Prophets, and of the commandment
of us the Apostles of the Lord and Savior.* (2 Peter iii: 1, 2.)

11. This is he that came by water and blood, even Jesus
Testimony of   Christ; not by water only, but by water and
John.   blood. *And it is the Spirit that beareth witness,
because the Spirit is truth. If ye receive the witness of men,
the witness of God is greater: for this is the witness of God,
which he hath testified of his Son.* (1 John v: 6–9.)

12. *The Revelation of Jesus Christ,* which God gave unto
him to show unto his servants things which must shortly
come to pass: and he sent and signified it by his angel unto
his servant John. *I was in the Spirit,* on the Lord's Day,
and I heard behind me a great voice of a trumpet, saying: I
am Alpha and Omega, the First and the Last: and *what
thou seest, write in a book,* and send it unto the seven churches
which are in Asia: unto Ephesus, and unto Smyrna, and
unto Pergamus, and unto Thyatira, and unto Sardis, and unto
Philadelphia, and unto Laodicea. (Revelation i: 1, 10, 11.)

13. Unto the angel of the Church of Ephesus write: *These things saith He that holdeth the seven stars in his right hand;* who walketh in the midst of the seven golden candlesticks. He that hath an ear let him hear *what the Spirit saith unto the Churches.* (Revelation ii: 1, 7.) See also each of the following letters, addressed to the other six churches.

14. And he said unto me, These sayings are true and faithful. *And the Lord God of the holy Prophets sent his angel to show unto his servants the things which must shortly be done.* Behold I come quickly: *blessed is he that keepeth the sayings of the prophecy of this book.* For I testify unto every man that heareth the words of the prophecy of this book, that *if any man add unto these things, God will add unto him the plagues that are written in this book. And if any man will take away from the words of the book of this prophecy, God will take away his part out of the Book of life, and out of the Holy City, and from the things which are written in this book.* (Revelation xxii: 6, 7, 18, 19.)

Any attempt to explain and to apply this evidence, is, I think, wholly unnecessary. Every thoughtful reader will readily perceive, that in each of the *Conclusion.* preceding extracts, there is at least a clearly implied claim to Divine inspiration: and in some of them this claim is categorically asserted. Even in the last quotation from the Apocalypse, there is a distinction as broad as the heavens, made between that book and all writings of mere human authority. And hence it follows logically, according to all just laws of evidence, that no part of the New Testament is of human invention; but that it was all dictated through the inspired Apostles and Prophets of our Lord and Savior Jesus Christ, by the Spirit of the Living God.

CHAPTER III.

THEORIES OF INSPIRATION.

SECTION I.—FALSE THEORIES OF INSPIRATION.

THAT the entire Bible, consisting of the thirty-nine canon-

The *fact* of Divine Inspiration is now a settled question.

ical books of the Old Testament and the twenty-seven books of the New Testament, is the inspired word of God, has, I think, been clearly and satisfactorily proved by the evidence already submitted: and henceforth we will therefore consider this as an established fact. And if all persons would be satisfied with this result, and simply receive the written word, as they would receive the living and audible voice of Jehovah from the top of Sinai or from the depths of heaven itself, any further discussion of the subject would be wholly unnecessary.

But just here lies the difficulty. Constituted as we now

Necessity of having a true theory on this subject.

are, men will reason and philosophize and speculate on this, as they are wont to do on other subjects: some for one purpose, and some for another; some running to one extreme, and some to that which is the directly opposite. And hence the necessity of having, if possible, a correct theory of inspiration, as far at least as human reason is capable of comprehending the subject.

But first of all it may be well to notice briefly some of

False theories.

the false theories of inspiration. These are very numerous and various. But perhaps the most prominent and important of them may all be regarded as species or modifications of some one of the three following:

I. The first of these is commonly called *the Mechanical Theory of Inspiration*. According to this theory, Mechanical Theory of Inspiration. the writers of the Bible were all the mere passive instruments or penmen of the Holy Spirit: or, at any rate, they did nothing more than act as the mere amanuenses of the Spirit. They are supposed to have merely recorded the words and ideas of the Spirit just as Tertius recorded the words and ideas of Paul in his Epistle to the Romans.

II. Next in order is *the Theory of Natural Inspiration*. This admits of a great many different grades Theory of Natural Inspiration. and shades of meaning. Some make it consist wholly in the natural influence of the subject on the powers and susceptibilities of the human mind: while others concede that it includes also some degree of providential influence. But all of this school seem to think that the inspiration of Isaiah differs but little from that of Homer; and that the inspiration of Paul was essentially the same in kind, as that of Demosthenes.

III. Others again attempt to occupy medium ground on this subject. They concede that the thoughts Theory of Noematical Inspiration. were all suggested by the Holy Spirit; but they insist that, in all cases, the writers were left to express their thoughts in words of their own choice. This for the sake of distinction may be called *the Noematical Theory of Inspiration*.[*]

It is obvious therefore that Reason has something to do in the settlement of this question. And first of First office of Reason in relation to such matters. all, it belongs to her to decide on the proper criteria by means of which every theory should be

[*] From νοος the mind; νοεω to exercise the mind; νοημα a thought; and hence the *noematical*, pertaining to the thoughts.

tested.   This she has already done in many other cases.   In
Proper test of
every theory. every department of science it is now a settled
rule, that *if a proposed theory serves to explain
all the facts and phenomena involved in the case, it should be
accepted as true and valid: but if not, that it should then be
rejected.*   On this principle, the Newtonian or Corpuscular
Theory of Light, was finally abandoned.   It very
Illustration. beautifully accounts for most of the phenomena
of optics.   But because it fails to explain a few of them, it
is now rejected by most Natural Philosophers.   And for the
same reason, they also reject the Franklin Theory of Electricity.

If, then, we accept this rule as a means of testing the aforesaid theories of inspiration, it is very obvious that they must
all be rejected as false and inadequate.   For,

1. The Mechanical Theory fails to account for the *human*
Defects of the
Mechanical
Theory of In-
spiration. *element* that is so very prominent in all the
sacred writings of both the Old and the New
Testament.   If the inspired writers were but
the mere penmen of the Holy Spirit, then indeed we might
expect to find in the Bible, no other varieties and diversities
of style, than such as would naturally arise out of the various
subjects discussed.   The style of Job would in all respects
be the style of David, and Isaiah; and the four narratives
of Matthew, Mark, Luke, and John, would all be characterized by the same modes of thought and style of expression.
But every attentive reader of the Scriptures, knows very well
that this is not the case.   Diversity of style is a marked and
well-defined characteristic of all the Old and New Testament
writers.   The style of Moses differs as much from that of
Isaiah or Paul, as the style of Plato differs from that of
Homer or Demosthenes.   And hence we are constrained to
reject as false, every theory of inspiration which does not

recognize human agency in every book and chapter of the Holy Bible.

2. The Theory of Natural Inspiration is even more absurd and unsatisfactory than the Mechanical Theory. *Defects of the Theory of Natural Inspiration.* It utterly fails to account for those wonderful *revelations* respecting God, the mystery of redemption, and the future history and destiny of mankind which abound throughout the whole Bible. And besides, it is wholly inconsistent with the *promises* of Christ to his Apostles, and the often-repeated declarations of the inspired writers. "It is not ye that speak," says Christ; "but the Spirit of your Father which speaketh in you."* And David says, "The Spirit of the Lord spake by me, and his word was in my tongue."† Such repeated declarations of both Old and New Testament writers are utterly inconsistent with every form and phase of the Theory of Natural Inspiration.

3. Nor does the Noematical Theory meet and satisfy all the requirements of the case. It is evidently inconsistent, *Defects of the Noematical Theory.*

1.) With the promises of Christ to his Apostles. When he first sent them out as the advocates and defenders of the truth, he admonished them to take no thought, either as to the *matter* or the *manner* of their discourses; to have no concern about either the *thoughts* or the *words* of their addresses. For, said he, both the τι and the πως; both the matter and the manner of your arguments and your defenses, shall be given you in the same hour that they become necessary, by the Spirit of your Father.‡

(2.) It is inconsistent with the often-repeated declarations of the inspired Apostles and Prophets. Paul, for instance, assures us that he and his spiritual brethren did not speak the things of God in *words* taught by man's wisdom, but in

---

* Matt. x: 20.   † 2 Samuel xxiii: 2.
‡ Matt. x: 19, 20.

18

words taught by the Holy Spirit; expounding spiritual *things* by spiritual *means* or in spiritual *words*.*

(3.) It is further evident that the force of a whole proposition often depends on the use of a single *word*, or even on some *modification* of a word, which no human sagacity might be able to supply. In Matthew xxii: 32, for instance, Christ founds an important argument on the use of the present tense of the verb *to be*. "I am," said Jehovah, "the God of Abraham, and the God of Isaac, and the God of Jacob." This, he argues, implies that Abraham, and Isaac, and Jacob were still living when God spoke these words unto Moses, about one hundred and ninety-eight years after the so-called natural death of Jacob, and about three hundred and thirty-one years after the death of Abraham. Another very good illustration of this important fact, is found in Galatians iii: 16, in the use of the word *seed* (σπερμα) in the *singular number*.

(4.) The necessity of *verbal* as well as *noematical* inspiration is further evident from the fact that, the Prophets and Apostles often failed to comprehend fully the thoughts that were to be expressed. Like Moses in building the tabernacle, they were constantly employed in setting up types and striking off documents, which they themselves did not and could not, at the time, fully understand. This is evident from many passages in both Testaments. Caiaphas, for instance, did not even apprehend the proper scope of the prophecy which he uttered concerning the death of Christ.† And that the Prophets and even the angels failed to comprehend many of the Oracles of the Old Testament, is clearly taught by Peter in the following brief extract from his first epistle: "*Of which salvation,*" says he, "*the Prophets have inquired and searched diligently, who prophesied of the grace that should come unto you. Searching what or what manner*

---

* 1 Cor. ii: 13.　　　　　　　† John xi: 49–52.

of time, the spirit of Christ which was in them did signify when it testified beforehand the sufferings of Christ, and the glory that should follow. Unto whom it was revealed, that not unto themselves, but unto us they did minister the things, which are now reported unto you, by them that have preached the Gospel unto you with the Holy Spirit sent down from heaven; which things the angels desired to look into." It is therefore evident that every theory of inspiration should be rejected as false and inadequate which does not recognize the agency of the Holy Spirit in every word as well as in every thought of the Holy Bible.*

What I have now said is perhaps sufficient to put the reader on his guard against all false theories of inspiration: and if so, we may now pass to the consideration of the true theory. But as preliminary to this, it may be well to give some explanation of the Natural, the Providential, and the Miraculous, in the Divine administration. This I will endeavor to do in the following section.

SECTION II.—CONSIDERATION OF THE NATURAL, THE PROVIDENTIAL, AND THE MIRACULOUS IN THE DIVINE ADMINISTRATION.

There are three elements in the Divine administration— three ways in which God's power is exercised and manifested—with which every student of the Bible should be very familiar. These are the *Natural*, the *Providential*, and the *Miraculous*. *(The three elements of God's administration.)*

Of these the natural element lies most on the surface, and is therefore most obvious to our senses. It consists in those second causes which God has himself created, and which he has made to operate according to certain fixed and well-defined laws. It con- *(In what the Natural Element consists.)*

* 1 Peter i: 11, 12.

sists in the power which he has himself actually *imparted* to all created things for the good and government of all.

Thus, for instance, he has made every atom of matter a Examples and Illustrations. depository of his power: so that all bodies now actually attract and influence each other, directly as their quantities of matter, and inversely as the squares of their distances. The paper now before me puts forth an influence that actually reaches·to every sun, and moon, and star, and comet in the vast empire of Jehovah.

And hence it is evident, that all the powers of nature are The forces of nature are all *imparted*. but *imparted* powers. They are but the Divine influence treasured up in the depositories of both mind and matter;—of both the material and the immaterial, for the regulation, government, and harmony of the whole created universe.

These powers and forces of nature have all been divinely They are also divinely estimated. estimated and adapted to each other. The mountains were all weighed in scales and the hills in a balance. And the statics and dynamics of each and every planet, were all computed and proportioned according to the constitution and organization of its varied and respective tenantry.

No doubt, then, these natural forces all occupy a very Their proper functions in the Divine administration. important place, and perform a very important part in the Divine administration. They are, as the mathematician would say, the *constant quantities* by means of which God brings about many a result, and works out many a problem in his moral, as well as in his physical government.

But in a complex government such as God exercises over Necessity of *impressed* power, as an element of God's government. his immense universe, *imparted* power is not sufficient. To meet successfully all the wants and contingencies of such an empire as Jehovah's, *impressed* power, or some modifying and regulating force, is also indispensable. It is especially so in the *moral* and spiritual department of the Divine government; and in those physical operations that are most intimately connected with the moral.

And hence it is, that the more abstract physical phenomena are always the most easily explained and accounted for on purely philosophical principles: and that as we approach man, science becomes more and more complex and inexplicable. Suns, moons, and stars, for instance, all seem to move chiefly if not exclusively under the influence of *imparted power* or second causes. And in inert matter these causes are all *fixed quantities:* quantities that can be easily and definitely estimated. And hence the skillful astronomer can easily estimate the exact number and character of all the eclipses and transits that will occur within any given period.

Simplicity of the purely Physical Sciences.

But it is not so in the moral and spiritual department of the Divine government: nor in those links in the chain of causation that serve to connect the physical with the moral; the material with the immaterial. Here there is also of necessity the additional element of *impressed power*. Second causes are not sufficient. *Their influence must often be increased, or diminished, or variously modified, according to the object and purpose of Him who is himself the cause of all causes.*

Complexity of the moral and mixed sciences.

Take, for example, the science of Meteorology. In it, we have the same *imparted forces* or second causes operating from year to year. The earth is the same: its amount of water, and caloric, and electricity is the same; its orbit and its revolutions are the same; and its relations to the sun, and moon, and stars are very nearly the same, during each successive cycle. And reasoning therefore from second causes or imparted forces alone, we would of course be led to infer, *that the resulting*

Illustration from Meteorology.

*phenomena of each successive year, would be ever and invaria-
bly the same:* that during each and every return of the four
seasons of the year, we would have the same amount of rain,
and snow, and hail, and vapor, and cold, and heat, and storm,
and tempest. But our experience gives us a very different
result. It proves to us, that these phenomena are all very
uncertain: and that it is really much easier to estimate all
the eclipses that will occur within the next twelve months,
than to determine, with certainty, the kind of weather that
we will have within the next twelve days.

To the mere Naturalist, this is, of course, wholly inexplicable. But to the Christian philosopher, it is
all plain and obvious. He sees in the benevolent designs and purposes of God, a *reason* for
all these changes and variations. And he sees, moreover, in
God's impressed power, a *cause* sufficient to produce them.
His own Reason enlightened by Revelation, assures him that
the same great and good Being who created the universe,
continues to govern it: and that its successful administration for the *education* of man, and the good of all, must of
necessity often require the controlling and modifying influence of Divine power variously exercised. Sometimes this
may be done through the instrumentality of angels; sometimes, through good or bad men; sometimes, through Satan
and his angels; sometimes, through the laws and ordinances
of the irrational and inanimate creation; and sometimes
through several or all of these agencies and instrumentalities
combined: but in all cases *God himself is the moving cause.*

*Cause and rea-
son of all these
variations.*

Here, then, we have clearly defined the second or providential element of the Divine administration.
It consists in God's *impressed* or modifying
power; as the natural element consists in his
imparted power. It is therefore wholly distinct from the
natural; but nevertheless it always operates in, and by, and

*Difference be-
tween the Nat-
ural and the
Providential.*

through that which is natural; and according to the laws and forces of nature.

And hence we see why it is, that to the superficial observer, the hand of God is never manifest in the workings of his providence. As it always operates, in such cases, according to nature's laws, *The Providential liable to be mistaken for the Natural.* and merely serves to give tone, and energy, and direction to the forces of nature, it is of course wholly invisible to the eye of sense. And to the unreflecting mind, the effect, in most cases, seems to be wholly natural; or owing entirely to the power and influence of second causes.

The imprisonment of Joseph in Egypt, for example, seemed to be wholly and altogether natural. The partiality of his father very naturally excited the jealousy of his brethren; and this again *Illustration from the history of Joseph.* naturally led them to sell him to the Ishmaelites, whose business it was to carry slaves and merchandise into Egypt. The great beauty and amiability of Joseph, in like manner, excited the lust of his mistress; and her disappointment naturally led her to complain to her husband, who in revenge naturally cast Joseph into prison. And this again, as the narrative shows, very naturally prepared the way for his introduction to Pharaoh; and for his promotion to the viceroyalty of Egypt. In all this, therefore, the naturalist sees and recognizes nothing more than the energy and operation of second causes. But the believer in Divine Revelation perceives in every link in this long chain of causation, the rational workings and operations of a special providence: and that too with special reference to the fulfillment of the several promises that God had made to Abraham concerning his posterity.

Sometimes indeed the hand of God becomes more manifest. In some cases the natural vail or covering becomes so very transparent, that *Illustration from the history of Mordecai.*

the hand of Providence is seen through it, working out results that are otherwise wholly inexplicable.   It would puzzle a naturalist, for example, to explain by the mere energy
and operation of second causes, the fall of Haman and the
promotion of Mordecai.*   How did it happen that the purpose of Ahasuerus was so suddenly changed in this critical
case?   Why did his sleep go from him ; and why were the
records of his empire required to be read in his presence?
How did it happen, that the scribe turned to the very page
that contained an account of the fidelity and loyalty of Mordecai?   Why was the king's mind *then*, and for the first
time, so deeply impressed with a sense of gratitude to so
humble a subject; and with a fixed purpose to promote him
to honor and distinction?   And how did it happen that Haman was made the instrument of Mordecai's promotion, and
the cause of his own dishonor and destruction ?

Manifestly such events can be accounted for, only on the
The only ra-
tional way of
explaining
such events.
hypothesis of a *special Providence*: only through
the agency of Him who has at his command all
the powers and resources of nature; and who
can therefore, with the utmost facility, turn the hearts of
kings as the rivers of water are turned, and cause all created
things to work together for the good of his children.   To
Him be glory, and dominion, and power, and thanksgiving
for ever and ever.   Amen.

To this twofold agency, the natural and the providential,
When miracu-
lous power is
exercised.
may therefore be referred most, if not all, the
events that are now occurring in at least this
earthly province of the Divine government.
God is the most exact and particular of all economists.   He
never uses superfluous means for the accomplishment of any
purpose.   If the natural is sufficient, he never uses the providential : and if the natural and providential are sufficient,

* See Esther vi and vii.

he never uses the miraculous. But when these are not sufficient; when the natural and the providential are both inadequate .to his ends and purposes—then, rising above all the
laws, and forces, and formulæ of nature, he simply effects by
his own *immediate* and *direct* agency, whatever   In what it con-
is his will and his purpose. This is what we   sists.
call the miraculous element of the Divine administration.

Sometimes this miraculous power is exercised independ-
ently of all the laws and forces of nature; some-   Modes in which
times in direct opposition to these laws and   miraculous
   power is exer-
forces; but most frequently it is put forth in   cised.
connection with them.

An example of the first mode in which miraculous power
is exercised, is seen in the primitive creation.   Illustration of
Previous to this, there were no second causes.   the first mode.
God alone was, and nothing else beside him. And the first
miracle therefore consisted in giving being and attributes to
nature. God simply spoke, and it was done: he commanded, and it stood fast.

An illustration of the second mode of miraculous agency
is given in the account that we have of the sep-   Illustrations of
aration of the waters of the Red Sea; and of the   the second
   mode.
sun and moon's standing still at the command
of Joshua. The motion of the sun ten degrees backward, as
indicated by the dial of Ahaz,* is also another very remarkable instance of miraculous power, exercised in opposition
to the tremendous powers and forces of nature.

But in most miraculous manifestations, the natural, the
providential, and the miraculous are all united.   Illustration of
And in such cases, the miraculous is but the   the third mode.
supplement of the natural and the providential. As, for instance, in the Noahic deluge. Here the forces of nature
were evidently employed, so far as they could be made

*Isaiah xxxviii: 8.

available by providential agency. The internal fires of the
earth, served, in all probability, to elevate and break up the
fountains of the great deep: and the forces of attraction and
repulsion are still visible in every particle of drift that is
now found on both hemispheres. But the same great, and
good, and Almighty Being that gave new instincts to the
saved animals, was evidently present through the entire
scene, working both providentially and miraculously, as the
circumstances of the case might require. He resolved to
punish an ungodly world; and to change, in some respects,
the course and ordinances of nature; and it was done.

How vast then and how various are the resources of the
Almighty! What folly it is to attempt to set
limits to his power; or to prescribe the mode,
by, and in, and through which it may and it
must be exercised! All the immense powers, and energies
and resources of nature are evidently at his disposal. And
when these are not sufficient, he has but to draw from the
infinite depths and resources of his own Divinity, whatever
is necessary for the accomplishment of his ends and purposes.

Variety and
extent of God's
resources.

Let it then be our wisdom to leave to God the ways, and
means, and modes of his own operations; and
simply to use, with all possible diligence and
prudence, the means of life and happiness with
which he has so highly favored us. Let us remember, that
God has given to us, no *direct* control over either the providential or the miraculous. These are his prerogatives. But
to us he has committed the natural, both physical and moral,
so far as it is necessary in order to promote and to secure
our present and eternal well-being. Let us not then be deceived. God is not mocked. For whatsoever a man sows
that shall he also reap. They that sow to the flesh, shall
of the flesh reap corruption: but they that sow to the Spirit,

In what man's
wisdom and
happiness con-
sist.

shall of the Spirit reap life everlasting. So God has decreed: and so he will certainly bring it to pass.

SECTION III.—THE TRUE THEORY OF INSPIRATION.

From the premises now submitted, it will not be difficult to state in a few words the True Theory of Inspiration, so far as the subject can be understood by our finite reason. The following propositions embrace all that it is really necessary we should understand on this very interesting but difficult subject. *(margin: Statement of the True Theory of Inspiration.)*

I. It is evident that *the Holy Spirit exercised a very special providential and miraculous influence over both the words and the thoughts of the Old and New Testament writers.* The proof of this proposition has already been stated with sufficient fullness. *(margin: Words and thoughts, both inspired.)*

II. But as God never employs unnecessary means in any case; as he never exercises his power providentially when existing natural means are adequate to the end proposed;* nor miraculously when *(margin: Co-existence of the Divine and the human elements.)*

---

*I would not presume to affirm dogmatically that *any* event in the Divine government occurs without the special providence of God. Certain it is that the hairs of our heads are all numbered; that not a sparrow falls to the ground without the care of our Heavenly Father (Matt. x: 29–31); and *(margin: Extent of God's providential agency.)* that every flower that adorns and beautifies our gardens and our landscapes, is a proof and illustration of the special providence of Him who clothes the herbage of the field which to-day is, and to-morrow is cast into the oven for fuel. (Matt. vi: 30.) But as many of the celestial phenomena have been successfully brought within the fixed and definite limits of mathematical formulæ; as eclipses and transits, for example, have been frequently and unerringly calculated, simply on the assumed ground of these *imparted* forces which science has so very definitely estimated; it seems *probable*, that the planets *ordinarily* move solely and exclusively under the influence of natural causes. At all events, this much is evident from God's general administration, that in all his providential

natural and providential means are sufficient for his purpose, it follows in the second place, that in making the Bible what it ought to be, *he used all the learning and talents of the several writers that composed it, so far as these natural means could be made available;* just as he used the forces of nature in producing the Noahic deluge, and as Christ used the five loaves and two fishes in feeding five thousand men. And hence we see that in one sense, every word and every thought of the entire Bible is of God; and in another and subordinate sense, that every word and every thought of the Bible is also of man: and consequently, that the Divine and the human elements coëxist in all parts of the Sacred Scriptures.

III. On the same principle of Divine economy, it also follows, that an *equal degree of inspiration was not always necessary in every case.* To qualify Moses or Paul to reveal the future; or to develop either in type or in fact, the mysteries of redemption, would seem to require a much higher degree of Divine influence than that which was necessary in order to enable him to record unerringly those facts that fell under his own immediate observation.

Different degrees of inspiration.

In both cases, the miraculous aid of the Holy Spirit was indispensable. Without this, no man would have been able to decide infallibly what should, and what should not be recorded; what degree of prominence should be given to one event, and what to another. Who of us, for instance, if left to the guidance of our own erring reason, would ever think of recording the historical events and statistics of the books of Kings and Chronicles, in preference to the discourses that Christ delivered to the two disciples, on his way to Emmaus on the day of his resurrection; or the discourse of Paul to which Luke merely refers in the last chapter of Acts? Mani-

---

dealings with his creatures, he simply uses such means as are adequate to the end proposed.

festly, the miraculous influence of the Holy Spirit was absolutely necessary in all cases, and under all circumstances: but not, I think, in the same degree and to the same extent; if indeed we are at all competent to judge of such matters. Here, as in the ordinary affairs of life, human instrumentality seems to have been employed just so far as it could be used to advantage. But above and beyond all this, the Holy Spirit was ever present, exerting his miraculous power and influence, so as to reveal the whole truth; suppress every error; and in a word, to make such a book as would, in every respect, be perfectly adapted to all the wants and circumstances of mankind. This much was absolutely necessary; and any thing more than this would have been superfluous.

IV. And hence it follows, finally, that *there are no real discrepancies, contradictions, nor errors of any kind in the original Scriptures.* Barring the few remaining unimportant mistakes that have been introduced into the Bible by uninspired transcribers, it is, like its Divine Author, infinitely perfect, and without even a blemish of any kind.

No real contradictions in the Bible.

> "Most wondrous book! bright candle of the Lord!
> Star of eternity! the only star
> By which the bark of man could navigate
> The sea of life, and gain the coast of bliss
> Securely: only star which rose on Time,
> And on its dark and troubled billows, still,
> As generation, drifting swiftly by,
> Succeeded generation, threw a ray
> Of heaven's own light, and to the hills of God,
> The everlasting hills, pointed the sinner's eye."

PART FIFTH.

SACRED HERMENEUTICS AND EXEGESIS.

CHAPTER I.

PRELIMINARY CONSIDERATIONS

SECTION I.—FUNDAMENTAL PRINCIPLES OF INTERPRETATION.

HAVING proved that the Bible is *the word of God;* that it
Fifth Province
of Reason. is *the pure word of God;* that it is *the pure and
inspired word of God;* the next question which
claims our attention, and which requires and involves the
exercise and authority of Reason, is that of its *interpretation.*
How and by what rules is it to be interpreted?—Is it to be
explained grammatically, logically, and historically, as most
other books of like antiquity? Or, like some obscure enigma,
is it to be interpreted by *special* rules, known only to the initiated?

Proof that the
Bible is to be
interpreted as
other books. That the first of these hypotheses is true,
will appear evident from the following considerations:

I. If God has spoken to man at all, he must have spoken
for the purpose and with the design of being understood.
The contradictory of this proposition is a moral absurdity.

II. But if God spoke to man with the design of being
understood, he must, of course, have generally used words

(286)

in their ordinary sense, or according to the *usus loquendi* of the persons addressed. For in no other way short of a miracle could he have conveyed to them his meaning. This is abundantly proved by our intercourse with all foreigners; and especially by our foreign Diplomatic and Missionary operations, and the consequences that have resulted from not using words properly in translating the Scriptures into foreign languages.

III. But it does not follow, that *every word*, must be so used. Every department of science has its own nomenclature; its own system of terminology; and its own list of appropriated words and phrases. Thus, for instance, in Mathematics, the word *line* signifies *length* without breadth or thickness; in the Military Art, it means a certain form of drawing up ships or troops; in Geography, a certain division of the Earth; and in the fisherman's dialect, it means simply a string to catch fish. And just so it is in the Holy Bible. It too has its Divine nomenclature. Many words are used in a special or appropriated sense. Such, for example, are the words εκκλησια church, πρεσβυτερος elder, διαχονος deacon, ευαγγελιστης evangelist, αποστολος apostle, επισχοπος overseer, σαρξ flesh, βαπτισμα immersion, δικαιοσυνη justification, and παλιγγενεσια regeneration. But most Bible terms are used according to the "*usus loquendi*" of the Greeks and Hebrews. And hence it follows, that *every correct system of Biblical interpretation is, in the main, identical with every other correct system of interpretation; and that the Bible should be interpreted by the same general rules and principles as other books of like antiquity.*

Terms used in a special or limited sense.

First Fundamental Principle of Interpretation.

But as the Original Scriptures are wholly from God, and of course perfectly consistent in all their parts, it follows as a second fundamental law and principle of interpretation, *that every part of the Sacred Word*

Second Fundamental Principle.

should be interpreted in harmony with every other part; and that the Bible should in all cases be made its own chief interpreter.

SECTION II.—NATURE AND SCOPE OF BIBLICAL EXEGESIS.

Before we proceed to consider further the rules and principles of Sacred Hermeneutics, I wish to introduce just here, as briefly as I can, the Sixth Province of Reason in matters pertaining to Divine Revelation. This is called Biblical Exegesis; and *consists simply in the proper use and correct application of the aforesaid rules and principles.* A true theory or system is one thing; and its correct application to any practical purpose is a very different thing. It was one problem to discover the laws of universal gravitation; and it was quite a different problem to apply them to the practical explanation of celestial phenomena. The former was the work of Sir Isaac Newton; but the latter was reserved for La Place. And just so it is in the work of Biblical interpretation. The general laws and principles are first discovered and reduced to a science: and afterward they are practically applied in the art of explaining the Holy Bible. The first of these is called *Sacred Hermeneutics;* and the second, as before said, is called *Biblical Exegesis.** In each of these departments, there is ample room for the fullest exercise of the most highly cultivated Reason. But they are very intimately blended together; and it will therefore be most convenient to consider them together in their proper connection.

The Sixth Province of Reason.

Relation of Exegesis to Hermeneutics; and the proper scope of each.

---

*Hermeneutics from ἑρμηνευτικος, skillful in interpreting; ερμηνευς, an interpreter; 'Ερμης, Mercury, the interpreter of Jupiter. Exegesis from εξηγησις, a leading or drawing out; εξηγεομαι, to lead or draw out. Hence Exegesis is simply the art of drawing or bringing out the full meaning of a passage.

SECTION III.—INDUCTIVE AND DEDUCTIVE METHODS OF
EXEGESIS.

First, then, let us briefly consider a few preliminaries with respect to the best *order* and mode of proceeding in this Divine Art. When a chemist wishes to ascertain, with great accuracy, the several properties of any material substance, it is often best to begin with its elements, and to ascertain their several properties and affinities. From elements, he may proceed to the consideration of binaries; and from binaries, to higher and more complex combinations, until he has ascertained the composition and properties of the whole mass. After this, he may, if need be, *reverse* the entire process. He may first resolve the mass into its most complex constituents: and these again into a still lower order; and so on, until he finally reaches the simplest atoms of which the body is composed.

Chemical mode of ascertaining the nature, composition, and properties of any body.

Just so, then, should the Bible student proceed with the study and interpretation of the Holy Scriptures, or any portion of them. After ascertaining, as far as possible, all the *historical circumstances* of time, place, authorship, etc., connected with the composition of any document, he should proceed with its exegesis as follows:

Inductive method of exegesis.

I. He should begin with the consideration of the several words that compose the first sentence. The meaning of these, he should endeavor to ascertain from the best lexicons and other means at his command.

Single words.

II. He should if possible ascertain the meaning of the entire sentence, by carefully examining its syntax, and generalizing the meanings of the several words that compose it.

Sentences.

III. He should proceed in like manner with the several

19

clauses which immediately follow in the course of the com-

Paragraphs. position, and which in any way serve to develop and express the *one* fundamental thought first introduced by the writer. Whenever there is a change of thought, the first paragraph should be closed, and the second should be commenced.

IV. He should endeavor to ascertain very clearly and

Special Scope. definitely, the main thought or design of the writer in the first paragraph. This he can generally do by examining its grammatical and logical construction; and generalizing the meanings of the several sentences that compose it. This is called the *Special Scope* of the paragraph.

V. In like manner he should proceed with each and every succeeding paragraph; until this part of the work is completed.

VI. He should then notice from a careful review of all

Sections. the paragraphs examined and their several scopes, *the second order of breaks,* or the next more important changes of thought, that occur in the course of the treatise or narrative. And by carefully observing the nature of the union that subsists between the several paragraphs that compose each of these higher divisions, and generalizing their several scopes, the reader may generally ascertain without much difficulty the scope of each of these sections.

VII. In like manner he should proceed from Sections to

Chapters, Chapters; from Chapters to Parts; and from
Parts, etc. Parts to the whole Epistle, Book, or Volume. The last or highest generalization will give the main design of the writer; or the object which he had in view in compos-

General Scope. ing the whole work. This is called the *General Scope.*

Deductive Method of Exegesis. This will finish the Inductive process. And now the student may, if he please, reverse the order, and reach the same ends *deductively*. For this purpose, he should

I. Consider all the Historical Circumstances of the work: and especially such as relate to its author; to Historical Circumstances. the party or parties addressed; and to the time, place, and occasion of its composition. If, however, this rule was considered and applied with sufficient care, previous to the *Inductive* process, it may now be passed over.

II. The student should next divide the entire work into its most *Comprehensive Parts*. This he will do, by Parts. carefully noticing as before, the principal subjects of the book, epistle, or narrative, as the case may be.

III. He should then subdivide the first Part, if necessary, into Chapters; and the first Chapters Chapters, Sections, Paragraphs. into Sections; and the first Sections into Paragraphs.

IV. From the special scope of the first paragraph and whatever other helps he may have at his command, he should next proceed to ascertain the Sentences. words, etc. meaning of all the sentences and words that compose it: noticing and considering very carefully all figures of speech; all allusions to any special laws and customs; all parallel passages; and all references of any kind to other parts of Scripture. And in the same way he should proceed with every succeeding sentence and paragraph.

The Inductive Method will generally be found best for the inquirer and investigator; and the Deductive for Proper place and occasion for each Method. the advocate. The former is best suited to the purposes of the Studio; but the latter is generally best adapted to the objects of the Recitation Room and the Pulpit. Very frequently, however, it will be found best to combine both methods.

CHAPTER II.

CONSIDERATION OF HISTORICAL CIRCUMSTANCES.

FROM the aforesaid preliminaries, let us now proceed to

First funda-mental Rule of Biblical Inter-pretation.

consider as briefly as the nature of the case and the importance of the subject will permit, the fundamental Rules of Sacred Hermeneutics, and their application to the objects and purposes of Biblical Exegesis. And first of all, we are required to consider attentively the *Historical Circumstances* of the work or document to be interpreted. These are all briefly comprehended in the following mnemonic hexameter line,

Quis, quid, ubi, quibus auxiliis, cur, quomodo quando;

Summary of historical cir-cumstances.

which, in plain English prose, simply means,

Who, what, where, with what helps, why, how, when.

To the consideration of these particulars, I therefore now invite the attention of the reader.

I. QUIS, WHO? This may relate

Parties repre-sented by the quis, or who.

1. To the writer of the document.
2. To a speaker introduced in the course of the discussion or narrative.

3. To the person or persons addressed.

4. To the person or persons spoken of.

The author of a book may be generally known either

How to ascer-tain the au-thor of a book.

from external evidence, or from internal, or from both. Thus, for instance, all the Christian fathers concede that Paul is the author of the

Epistle to the Romans; and besides, there is abundant evidence in the Epistle itself that it is one of his genuine epistles. And the same may be said of his two Epistles to the Corinthians, two to the Thessalonians, two to Timothy, one to the Galatians, one to the Ephesians, one to the Philippians, one to the Colossians, one to Titus and one to Philemon. The authorship of the Epistle to the Hebrews is not so well sustained by either kind of evidence. But Paul is now generally supposed to be its author.

The names, and character, and circumstances of all the other parties involved in any document may *Means of ascertaining the circumstances of other parties.* also be generally ascertained from the same twofold sources of evidence, the external and the internal. As, for instance, in the testimony of Matthew: he generally informs us whether Christ's discourses were addressed to the Pharisees, the Sadducees, the Herodians, the Publicans, or to his own disciples. And the internal evidence thus furnished by the narrative is greatly strengthened by the testimony of Josephus, Philo, and other writers, touching the character, opinions, and varied circumstances of these several parties.

With respect to the importance of this rule but little need be said. It must be evident to every thought- *Importance of this rule.* ful student of the Bible, that much, very much, may depend on whether the speaker, or the writer, or the person spoken to, or the person spoken of, is a man, or an angel, or a demon: whether he is a natural man or a spiritual man; and whether he is a Jew or a Gentile; a Pharisee or a Sadducee; a Stoic or an Epicurean; a disciple of Plato or a follower of Aristotle. How very different is Christ's discourse to Nicodemus from what it would *Illustrations.* have been had it been addressed to a Gentile ruler or philosopher. How very unlike Paul's other epistles, is his letter to the Hebrews. And how very different is the testimony of Matthew from that of Luke, though they were both evidently designed to prove the same general proposition that Jesus of Nazareth is the Messiah. Indeed it is sometimes impossible to comprehend fully the force, and beauty, and propriety of a passage of Scripture, without a knowledge of the character, education, and prejudices of the parties spoken to or spoken of. Take, for instance, the following words, spoken by Jehovah to Cyrus king of Persia: "Thus saith the Lord to his anointed, to Cyrus, whose right hand I have holden to subdue nations before him. I am the Lord, and there is none else: there is no God beside me. I girded thee, though thou hast not known me: that they may know from the rising of the sun, and from the west, that there is none beside me. I am the Lord and there is none else. *I form the light, and create darkness; I make peace, and create evil:* I the Lord do all these things."*

The general meaning of this sublime and beautiful passage is very plain. Even to one who knows nothing about Cyrus, it must be obvious that its general scope is to declare and set forth the absolute sovereignty of Jehovah. But how much does it add to the force and beauty of these remarks, to know that Cyrus was not only a heathen, but also a *Dualist:* that like most other Persians of that age, he was wont to worship Ormudz *as the author of all light and goodness: and Ahriman as the author of all darkness and penal evil.* And how much more significance is given to Paul's address at Athens, recorded in the seventeenth chapter of Acts, when it is understood that the Epicureans and Stoics, by whom he was chiefly encountered and opposed, were the uncompromising advocates of *chance* and *fatality:* that the former derived all things from the mere fortuitous concourse of atoms; and the latter from an eternal and inexorable necessity over which even the gods had no control!

* Isaiah xlv: 1, 5, 6, 7.

II. QUID, WHAT? The student of the Bible should next carefully consider the nature and character of the part that is to be interpreted. Much may depend on the question, whether it is *poetry* or *prose*, *prophetic* or *didactic*, *devotional* or *argumentative*, *historical* or simply *a narrative of facts given in testimony.* Every species of composition has some peculiarities of style which should be carefully and duly considered by the interpreter. No sane man would think of explaining the sublime odes of Isaiah, as he would the laws and ordinances of the Pentateuch, or the very logical and argumentative epistles of Saint Paul. Poetry, and especially Hebrew poetry, abounds in figures of thought and figures of expression which would be wholly out of place in all historical, didactic, and argumentative prose. Take, for instance, the following address of Lamech to his two wives, Adah and Zillah:

> "Adah and Zillah, hear my voice;
> Ye wives of Lamech, hearken to my speech.
> For I have slain a man for wounding me;
> A young man for hurting me.
> If Cain shall be avenged seven times,
> Certainly, Lamech seventy and seven times."

If this speech of Lamech had been delivered and recorded in prose, it would be reasonable to infer that he had killed two men. But the characteristic *parallelism* * of Hebrew

---

* *Parallelism* is the name given to a peculiar *construction* of sentences; and is one of the chief characteristics of Hebrew poetry. It consists in a certain correspondence of one sentence with another, or one clause or phrase with another. According to Bishop Lowth, there are three species of parallelism: *the Synonymous, the Antithetic,* and *the Synthetic* or *Constructive.*

1. The *Synonymous* parallelism consists in the repetition of the same sentiment in different but equivalent terms; as—
Thou art snared by the words of thy mouth;

poetry does not warrant such an inference. Evidently the man who wounded Lamech and the young man who hurt him were one and the same person.

Similar distinctions and differences abound in all other kinds of composition. But as it may be presumed that most

Thou art caught by the words of thy mouth. (Prov. vi: 2. See Psalm cxiv; Isaiah lx: 1–3; and liii: 1–5.)

2. The *Antithetic* parallelism is the converse of the *Synonymous*. In it one sentiment is opposed to another, forming a very regular and beautiful species of antithesis; as in the following example:

If ye consent and obey,
The good of the land shall ye eat;
But if ye refuse and rebel,
By the sword, shall ye be eaten. (Isaiah i: 19, 20.)

The book of Proverbs abounds in this species of parallelism.

3. The *Synthetic* or *Constructive* parallelism is that species in which the correspondence of the sentences is maintained, by a further development of the main idea expressed in the first member. The following is a beautiful example of this species of parallelism:

The law of Jehovah is perfect, restoring the soul;
The testimony of Jehovah is sure, making wise the simple;
The precepts of Jehovah are right, rejoicing the heart;
The commandment of Jehovah is clear, enlightening the eyes;
The fear of Jehovah is pure, enduring forever;
The judgments of Jehovah are truth, they are just altogether;
More desirable than gold, or than much fine gold,
And sweeter than honey, or the dropping of honey-combs. (Psalm xix: 7–1,)

For other examples of this species of parallelism, see Job xii: 13–16; Psalm cxlviii: 7–13; Isaiah xiv: 4–9; and lviii: 5–8.

To these three species of poetic parallelism, given and illustrated by Bishop Lowth, Bishop Jeb adds a fourth, which he calls *Introverted* parallelism. In it the stanzas are so constructed, that whatever be the number of lines, the first will always be parallel with the last; the second with the last but one; and so on, as military men say, from flank to center; as in the following examples:

My son, if thy heart be wise;
My heart also shall rejoice;
Yea, my reins shall rejoice;
When thy lips speak right things. (Prov. xxiii: 15, 16.)

of my readers are already aware of this, I will pass over the whole matter, with a single caution in reference to the narratives of Matthew, Mark, Luke, and John. I find that most students of the Bible are prone to look upon these as regular histories or biographies of Jesus Christ: and they are often disappointed when they do not find in them a strict regard for chronological order, or such as we have a right to expect in works that are professedly historical. But be it remembered that these narratives are not *histories*. They consist simply of *facts given in evidence to prove that Jesus of Nazareth is the promised Messiah.* "Ye shall receive power," said Jesus Christ to his Apostles, "after that the Holy Spirit is come upon you; and ye shall be WITNESSES unto me, both in Jerusalem, and in all Judea, and in Samaria, and to the uttermost parts of the earth."* And as every witness has a right to give his testimony in whatever order he thinks best, sometimes following one law or principle of suggestion and sometimes another, no one has a right to charge these inspired writers with inconsistencies, discrep-

Neglect of chronological order in the Narratives of Matthew, Mark, Luke, and John.

> The idols of the heathen are silver and gold;
> The work of men's hands;
> They have mouths, but they speak not;
> They have eyes, but they see not;
> They have ears, but they hear not;
> Neither is there any breath in their mouths;
> They who make them are like unto them;
> So are all they who put their trust in them. (Psalm cxxxv: 15–18.)

Bishop Lowth gives three additional principal characteristics of Hebrew poetry:

1. The acrostical or alphabetical commencement of lines and stanzas;

2. The introduction of rare and foreign words and particles; forming a sort of poetic dialect; and,

3. The frequent, and indeed almost constant occurrence of sententious, figurative, and sublime expressions.

Other peculiarities of Hebrew poetry.

* Acts i: 8.

ancies, and contradictions, on the ground that they do not, like Xenophon, Tacitus, Hume, and Gibbon, follow in all cases the exact chronological order of events.

III. UBI, WHERE? To know where a document was written is sometimes of great service in its interpretation. Words and phrases are subject to *geographical changes* as well as to historical. The same words have not always the same meaning in New England and Old England: nor even in Ohio and Kentucky. And every student of literature knows that the many and marked distinctions between the Oriental and the Occidental styles have long been proverbial. The following brief examples may be of service to illustrate some of these differences.

Importance of knowing the birth-place of any document.

1. "The ungodly are not so: but are like the *chaff* which the wind driveth away." (Psalm i: 4.) In Palestine, the threshing-floors were not under cover, as they are with us in the West. They were fixed in the open air and on high places; so that the chaff might be more effectually separated from the wheat by the action of the wind.

Illustrations.

2. "And again I say unto you, it is easier for a *camel* to go through the eye of a needle than for a rich man to enter into the kingdom of God." (Matthew xix: 24.) The camel was the largest animal known in Palestine. And hence a camel's going through the eye of a needle was a proverbial expression among the Jews to denote an impossibility. But in the Chaldean proverb for the same thing, the word *elephant* is used instead of *camel*.

These examples are sufficient to show that locality may have a very great influence on the author's style, figures, allusions, and illustrations: and hence it is always well to know, if possible, the birth-place of every document that is to be interpreted. When

Means of ascertaining where a book was written.

this is not given by the author, it may be generally ascertained from a comparison of the events recorded in the work itself: otherwise we have to depend on external testimony.

IV. QUIBUS AUXILIIS, WITH WHAT HELPS? Under this head are comprehended all the means, instrumentalities, and other circumstances that conspired to bring about any event. In the Noahic deluge, for instance, there was evidently a combination of miraculous, providential, and natural agencies. But the first is wholly ignored by modern Rationalists; and hence they reject as altogether fanciful and absurd, the idea of a universal deluge. On the same ground they deny the infallibility and paramount authority of the Holy Scriptures, and many other matters of vital importance in the scheme and history of redemption. But with his knowledge of the means and resources of Jehovah, the Christian has no difficulty in receiving with all confidence whatever is recorded in the Living Oracles. Does the Holy Spirit say that manna was for a time rained down from heaven; that water flowed copiously from a flinty rock; that the Sun and the Moon stood still at the command of Joshua; that Jonah was three days and three nights in the stomach of the great sea-monster; and that Shadrach, Meshach, and Abednego were unhurt by the lurid flames of Nebuchadnezzar's furnace;—the Christian believes it all with just as much confidence as he believes in the ordinary phenomena of nature. Even the resurrection of the dead is as credible as any other event, when we remember that it is to be brought about by the omnipotent power and energy of Him who in the beginning created the Heavens and the Earth.

V. CUR, WHY? This comprises all the circumstances that served to give being, shape, and character to the document under consideration.

[marginal notes: Circumstances included under the fourth head. Importance of considering these, illustrated. Class of circumstances comprehended under the fifth head.]

They are therefore of great service in enabling us to understand the general scope of a book, or the main
object that the writer had in view in composing
it. This may be ascertained in several ways.
And,

1. Sometimes it is given by the author himself; as in the
following examples:

(1.) Solomon says that his object in writing the Book
of Proverbs was, to make known wisdom and
instruction; and to cause others, and especially
young men, to perceive the words of understanding. (Proverbs i: 1–6.)

(2.) In writing the Book of Ecclesiastes, he avows it as
his purpose, to inquire into the ways and means of happiness.

(3.) In John xx: 31, the beloved disciple has recorded
the object that he had in view in composing his whole narrative. He says, "These things are written that you may
believe that Jesus is the Christ, the Son of God; and that
believing you may have life through his name.

(4.) Paul's object in writing his first letter to Timothy is
given in the fifteenth verse of the third chapter, as follows:
"These things," says he, "I write to you, hoping to come to
you shortly: but if I delay, *that you may know how you ought
to conduct yourself in the house of God, which is the church of
the living God, the pillar and support of the truth.*"

2. When the general scope is not given by the writer, it
may be generally ascertained by reading over the
whole book, and noting, as far as practicable, the
special scope of the several paragraphs, sections,
and chapters of which it is composed. This, the reader may
not in all cases be able to do to his entire satisfaction, without having first obtained a knowledge of the general scope,
and such other helps as a further knowledge of Sacred Her-

meneutics will bring to his aid. But he can generally learn enough from the first and second reading to enable him to determine the general design and object of the writer. It is evident, for example, to every thoughtful and at- Illustration. tentive reader of the Book of Acts, that Luke's object in writing it was not to give a history of Peter, or of Paul, or of the whole Church, as some have hastily inferred; but simply to illustrate the fulfillment of Christ's promises, and to show us how the Apostles acted under the Great Commission, in converting the people and bringing them into congregations for their further instruction and discipline.

3. The general scope of a book or document may often be learned from the *occasion* on which it was writ- Third method. ten; as, for instance,

(1.) We learn from sundry sources, that Jeremiah was sent to prophesy to the Jews when the cup of their Illustrations. iniquity was nearly full. And hence, as we might expect, we find that the general scope of his prophecies is a call and a warning to repentance.

(2.) In like manner, the general scope of many of the Psalms may be inferred from the circumstances under which they were written. The third Psalm, for example, was composed by David when he fled from Jerusalem on account of the rebellion of his son Absalom. And hence we find that its general scope is David's distrust in man and his confidence in God.

VI. Quomodo, how? Under this head or division, are embraced all the circumstances which served in Circumstances relating to the mode or manner of any event. any way to determine the *mode* of any event, or the *manner* in which it was brought about and accomplished. This chapter of circumstances is therefore very nearly allied to those that are embraced under the fourth. And for most practical purposes, it may be best to consider them all under one and the same division.

But sometimes there is an advantage in distinguishing between the *mode* of an event, and the *means* by
which it is accomplished. In all miracles, for
instance, the means are infinite wisdom, power,
and goodness; and may therefore in some degree be appre-
hended by even our finite understanding. But
the *mode* of all miracles is to us, wholly unintel-
ligible. And hence we should never attempt to explain a
miracle. We may readily believe it, and receive it as a fact:
but its mode lies wholly beyond the narrow limits of human
reason and human philosophy. The German and French Rationalists generally invent modes corresponding
with their own fancy; and then they interpret
the Scriptures accordingly. Thus, for example,
they suppose that the mode in which Sennache-
rib's army was destroyed in Judea, was wholly natural, caused
by the poisonous and fatal effects of an east wind called the
Simoom. This is to trifle with the word of God.

Difference be-tween the mode and the means of an event.

Illustration.

Rationalistic mode of Inter-preting all Scripture modes.

VII. QUANDO, WHEN? It is well to ascertain, as near
as possible, the time when any document that
is to be interpreted, was written. This will
often serve, in many ways, to make things plain
which would otherwise be very obscure. Take,
for instance, the conversation of Christ with Nicodemus; or
that which he held with the woman at the well of Samaria;
or his inimitably tender valedictory to his disciples on the
same night on which he was betrayed: how much, how very
much of the point, and the beauty, and the propriety of these
discourses, is derived from the occasion and circumstances
under which they were delivered! And how much pathos
is added to several of Paul's most beautiful epistles, when it
is known and remembered, that they were written while he
was a prisoner at Rome for the Word of God and the testimony of Jesus Christ!

Importance of knowing the time when the book to be in-terpreted was written.

The time may be ascertained in several ways:

1. Sometimes it is expressly given by the author himself. (See Isaiah i: 1; Hosea i: 1; and Amos i: 1.)

Means of ascertaining the date of any document.

2. When the time is not given by the author, it may frequently be ascertained by comparing together sundry events contained in the book itself; or by comparing these with the statements of other authors. For example, it is evident,

(1.) That the Epistle to the Romans was written when Paul was about to visit Jerusalem, to minister to the wants of the poor saints. (Romans xv: 25–27.)

Illustration.

(2.) That this was Paul's last visit to Jerusalem, before he was taken a prisoner to Rome. (Compare Acts xxiv: 17, 18, with xxi: 27.)

(3.) And hence it is highly probable, if indeed not absolutely certain, that the Epistle to the Romans was written by Paul during his three months' residence at Corinth, just before he made the aforesaid visit to Jerusalem. (Acts xx: 1–3.) This then would fix the date of the epistle at about the beginning of the year A. D. 58. For it is generally agreed, that Paul reached Rome about the beginning of A. D. 61. And if so he must have left Cæsarea, about the first of September, A. D. 60. (Acts xxvii: 9.) And as he was for two years a prisoner at Cæsarea, (Acts xxiv: 27,) he must have come to Jerusalem about the last of May, A. D. 58, (Acts xx: 16;) for then was the time of the Pentecost. And hence, his three months' residence in Corinth must have been during the beginning of the same year.

CHAPTER III.

HERMENEUTICS AND EXEGESIS PROPER.

SECTION I.—RULES FOR ASCERTAINING THE MEANING OF SINGLE WORDS AND PHRASES.

First General Rule of single words.

I. *Consult the context.* This may serve to explain the meaning of words in several ways.

Specifications and illustrations.

1. Sometimes the writer himself explains a doubtful or obscure term by an equivalent or synonymous word or expression. *E. g.: Ἐμμανουηλ*, Emmanuel, or from the Hebrew עִמָּנוּאֵל, Immanuel, in Matthew i: 23, is explained to mean *God with us; Ῥαββι*, Rabbi, John i: 38, is made equivalent to *διδασκαλος, teacher; Μεσσια*, Messiah, John i: 42, is translated *the Christ;* and *καταπετασμα*, vail, in Hebrews x: 20, is explained to mean *the flesh of Christ.*

2. Sometimes the subject and predicate of a proposition mutually serve to explain each other. *E. g.:* We say, salt is *good;* the soil is *good;* the house is *good;* our laws are *good;* God is *good.* In all such examples the subject sufficiently defines and explains the predicate. The word *μωραινω* generally means *to be or to make dull;* but in Matthew v: 13, means *to be insipid;* and in Romans i: 22, it means *to become foolish.*

3. Sometimes the antithesis, contrast, or parallelism of words may help to explain and to illustrate their meaning. *E. g.:* In Matthew viii: 22, Jesus said to one of his disciples:

"Follow me; and let the *dead* bury their *dead*." That is evidently, Let those who are dead in trespasses and in sins bury those who are physically dead. This rule is of great assistance to the student of Hebrew poetry.

4. Sometimes the adjuncts of a term enable us to explain its meaning. *E. g.*: Βαπτισμα εν ὑδατι, immersion in water; Βαπτισμα εν τῳ Πνευματι αγιῳ, immersion in the Holy Spirit; Βαπτισμα εν πυρι, immersion in fire. In these examples, the word *immersion* is used with the same signification, but in different senses.

5. Sometimes the meaning of a word can be ascertained from a subjoined example or illustration. *E. g.*: The word πιστις, faith, in Hebrews xi: 1, is beautifully explained and illustrated by the examples that are given in the following parts of the same chapter. In like manner the Acts of the Apostles may be properly regarded as an illustration of the several terms that are used in the Great Commission, Matthew xxviii: 18–20; Mark xvi: 15, 16.

6. Sometimes the meaning of a word can be ascertained from the special scope of a passage in which it occurs. *E. g.*: The word παραπεσοντας, having fallen away, in Hebrews vi: 6, evidently means *having apostatized*. So δικαιοσυνη, justice, or rather the doing what is just and right, in Romans i: 17, means God's *scheme of making men just;* and in Romans iii: 25, it means his *administrative justice*. In all such cases, it is a good, practical rule, to substitute the definition for the word itself. And if it fulfills all the requirements of the context, it is most likely the true meaning of the word in the given passage.

7. Sometimes the general scope of a book or epistle may serve to determine the meaning of a word. *E. g.*: Let it be proposed to determine whether the word *duty* or *happiness* should be supplied in Ecclesiastes xii: 13.

II. *Consult parallel passages, and especially verbal paral-*
20

Second General Rule. *lels*. In doing so it will be well to observe the following order:

1. Consult those that occur in the same book. *E. g.:* The words אֵל גִּבּוֹר in Isaiah ix: 6, are by many Ger-

Proper order of consulting par- allels. man critics supposed to mean simply *the mighty hero*. But in Isaiah x: 21 the same words can apply only to the Deity. The prophet says, "The remnant of Jacob shall return unto *the mighty God*." And hence we infer that the same words have the same meaning in ix: 6; and that the passage should be rendered as follows:

For unto us a child is born; unto us a son is given;
And the government shall be upon his shoulder;
And his name shall be called Wonderful, Counselor,
The mighty God, the Father of the everlasting age,
The Prince of peace.

The word γενεα, generation, in Matthew xxiv: 34, is by some supposed to mean *the race* of the Jews, or the posterity of Abraham according to the flesh. But the same word occurs elsewhere in Matthew, twelve times; and in every instance it means not a *race*, but a *generation*.

2. Consult those that occur in different works of the same author. *E. g.:* In Romans i: 1, Paul calls himself the δουλος, servant, of Jesus Christ; by which term, he meant to convey the idea, that he was not his own, but that he belonged to Christ. This is evident from 1 Corinthians vii: 23: "You have been bought with a price: become not the servants (δουλοι) of men."

3. Consult the works of other authors: always preferring those that were written on the same subject, in the same age, and in the same country. *E. g.:* In Matthew xix: 24, Christ says, "It is easier for a camel to go through the eye of a needle, than for a *rich man* (πλουσιος) to enter into the kingdom of God." But from Mark x: 24, we learn that in Christ's dialect, a rich man is one who *trusts* in his riches.

III. *Consult the etymology of the words to be* *interpreted.* This rule is often of great service in helping us to appreciate the delicate shades of thought designed to be expressed by words that are nearly synonymous. *E. g.:*

1. In Galatians vi: 2, we are exhorted "to bear one another's burdens." And in the fifth verse of the same chapter, it is said, "Every man shall bear his own burden." In the first instance, the burdens spoken of are the cares or weights (τα βαρη) which press heavily on us as matters of business; and from which we may often be either partially or wholly relieved by the assistance of others. But in the second case, the burden (το φορτιον) is the weight of a man's own responsibility, which every man must bear for himself, and from which there is no deliverance.

2. A second example occurs in Romans xi: 15, in the climax expressed by the words ἐλεεω and οἰκτειρω. "I will have mercy (ἐλεεω) on whom I will have mercy; and I will have compassion (οἰκτειρω) on whom I will have compassion." The word ἐλεος simply means pity; but δικτιρμος belongs to the family of the interjection δἰ (oh!) and always implies an *expression* of pity.

3. θειοτη in Romans i: 20 is from the adjective θειος *divine;* and has reference merely to the *attributes* of God, as they are imperfectly revealed to us in the works of nature. But θεοτης, in Colossians ii: 9, is from θεος, *God;* and means the *Divinity,* as it is more perfectly revealed to us in the Bible.

4. The words ἱερόν and ναός are both commonly represented in English by the word *temple.* But the former, from ἱερος, *sacred,* includes the temple proper, and all its courts, porches, and porticos: whereas the latter, from ναιω, *I dwell* or *inhabit,* is simply the temple itself, God's chosen habitation.

5. The two Greek words ζωη and βιος are also always represented in English by the same word *life*. But the former from ζαω, *to live*, means life in contrast with death: and the latter from βιοω, to pass one's life, means (1) the *period* of life; (2) the *means* of life; and (3) the *manner* of life.

6. Μετανοεω from, μετα with, and νοος the mind, implies a thorough change of the whole mind, the intellect, the affections, and the will. But μεταμελομαι, from μετα and μελω, *to be an object of care*, simply denotes *a change of care or anxiety*. It may imply such repentance as needs not to be repented of; or it may simply denote a sorrow that worketh death, as in the case of Judas.

These few examples are sufficient to illustrate the value of Etymology, as a means of ascertaining, in many cases, the exact meaning of words. But at the same time, it is well to remember that great caution is necessary in its application. This is owing to the frequent changes of meaning, to which the words of all living languages are liable. Take, for example, the word *villain*, from the Latin *villanus*. It originally meant simply *a poor serf* attached to the villa or farm of a landlord. But now it means a low, vile, and wicked person. . Or take the word *sycophant* (συχοφαντης, from συχου a fig, and φαινω to show). This originally meant a fig-shower, or an informer against fig-stealers; and hence, in time, it came to signify a tale-bearer; and then a parasite, or an obsequious flatterer. The word archipelago originally meant the great or chief sea, from αρχων *chief*, and πελαγος *sea;* but now it is applied to any and every sea that is filled with islands.

Caution necessary in the application of this Rule.

Illustrations.

For an illustration of the judicious use and application of this rule, see Bengel's Gnomon; and for a very marked instance of its abuse, see Horne Tooke's Diversions of Purley.

Examples of the use and abuse of this rule.

MISCELLANEOUS EXAMPLES.

The following additional examples are given for the purpose of illustrating more fully some of the most important of the preceding rules.

I. The word בָּרָא, *to create*, sometimes means simply to renovate or to make something out of preëxisting substances. Thus, for instance, David says, in Psalm li: x, "*Create* (בְּרָא) in me a clean heart, O God: and renew a right spirit within me." And in Isaiah lxv: 17, Jehovah says, "For behold I *create* (בוֹרֵא) new heavens and a new earth; and the former shall not be remembered or come into mind." And hence some have inferred that this is its meaning in Genesis i: 1. They allege that matter was always in being: and that in the beginning, God simply refitted and rearranged it for the benefit of man. *Meaning of the word בָּרָא create, in Gen. 1: 1.*

But this hypothesis is evidently incorrect, as will appear from the following considerations.

1. The word commonly used in Hebrew, to express a mere formation, or creation in a secondary sense, is not בָּרָא but עָשָׂה. In this sense, the latter occurs in the Hebrew Scriptures, more than twenty-five hundred times; and the former only in a few instances, when great emphasis is required. *Evidence from the use of the word itself.*

2. It is inconsistent with the *context*. The original act of creation, stated in Genesis i: 1, was evidently altogether different and distinct from the arrangements and readjustments that are described in the following verses of the same chapter. And hence, in Genesis ii: 3, both the words בָּרָא and עָשָׂה are used: the former to denote the original act of creation; and the latter the mere formations and modifications that followed it. "And God blessed the seventh day," says Moses, "because that on it he had rested from all his work which God *had created to make*." *Evidence from the context.*

3. It is inconsistent with sundry *parallel passages.* In
John i: 3, for example, it is said, according to
the very literal and exact version of Thomas
Sheldon Green, " All things *came into being*
(εγενετο) through him; and without him, came not one
thing into being, that is in being (γεγονεν)." But matter
is in being. And therefore it was in the beginning, brought
into being by him, according to Genesis i: 1. In Hebrews
xi: 3, we have also evidence to the same effect. " By
faith," says the Apostle, " we understand that the worlds
were framed by the word of God; *so that things which are
seen were not made of things which do appear.*" Or according to Green's version : " By faith we understand that the
worlds have been framed by the word of God; *so that what
is seen, has not come into being from things that meet the view.*"
Hence we conclude, that the word ברא in Genesis i: 1, signifies *creation absolute;* or the bringing into being of that
which had previously no existence in any shape, form, or
condition whatever.

II. In like manner the word יום *day* is sometimes used
for an indefinite period of time; as for instance
in Psalm cx : 3. Here Jehovah is represented
as saying to the Messiah, " Thy people shall be
willing in the *day* of thy power ; in the beauties of holiness,
from the womb of the morning thou hast the dew of thy
youth." The word *day* (יום) in this connection evidently
means the time of Christ's mediatorial reign, or the whole
period of the Christian era. And hence some persons, influenced by geological considerations, have inferred that it
has a similar meaning in the first chapter of Genesis : that
the seven days of the week of creation, or rather of the
week of *renovation,* mean in reality seven long and indefinite geological periods.

But to this hypothesis there are valid objections. For,

1. It is inconsistent with the *context*. The first chapter of Genesis is not a poetical allegory. It is a Evidence from the context. plain and simple narrative of historical events. And in all such composition, it may be laid down as a safe rule of interpretation, that *"the most simple sense is most likely to be the genuine sense."* But who, without a theory to support, would ever think of regarding these seven days as so many indefinite periods?!

It is moreover pretty evident from the narrative itself, that the events described in the first and second verses of this chapter, are not included in the work of the six days of the Adamic renovation. The reader will observe that the work of the second, third, fourth, fifth, and sixth days, is in each case introduced by the very potent and significant phrase, " AND GOD SAID:" and hence it is quite probable, if indeed not quite certain, that the work of the first day was, in like manner, introduced by the first occurrence of this phrase in the third verse. And hence we infer, with a good degree of certainty, from the context,

(1.) That the first verse of Genesis describes creation absolute; or the original generation of all the materials of the physical universe.

(2.) That the second verse has reference to the chaotic state of the earth after the last great cataclysm immediately preceding the Adamic renovation.

(3.) That between these two epochs given in the first and second verses of Genesis, as many ages may have occurred as will satisfy all the demands of Natural Science.

(4.) That when the fullness of time was come, God introduced the *Historic period,* or the Adamic era, by his own omnipotent fiat, as recorded in the third verse of Genesis. " And God said, Let there be light; and there was light."

(5.) And finally, that the entire work of fitting up the earth for the use, comfort, and happiness of man, was com-

pleted within the space of six ordinary days of twenty-four
hours each ; and that on the seventh day of the same length,
God rested from all his works.

2. This view of the matter is also confirmed by sundry

Evidence from parallel passages. *parallel passages.*   Take, for illustration, the
fourth precept of the Decalogue. "Remember,"
said God to Israel, "the *Sabbath day* to keep it
holy. *Six days* shalt thou labor and do all thy work. But
the *seventh day* is the Sabbath of the Lord thy God: in it
thou shalt not do any work, thou, nor thy son, nor thy
daughter, nor thy man-servant, nor thy maid-servant, nor
thy cattle, nor thy stranger, that is within thy gates: *for in
six days, the Lord made heaven and earth, the sea, and all that
in them is ; and rested the seventh day: wherefore the Lord
blessed the Sabbath-day, and hallowed it.*" It is very obvious
that the word *day*, throughout this precept, is used in the
same sense, simply to denote a period of twenty-four hours.
And it is therefore also just as obvious that the six days of
creation were ordinary days of twenty-four hours each.

III. The Hebrew word עוֹלָם and the Greek αιων are each

Meaning of the words עוֹלָם, *αιων,* and *ever-lasting or for-ever.*   equivalent to the English word *everlasting.* They
are all *relative terms*, and may be applied to any
age or period. Thus, for instance, in Exodus
xxi: 6, the word עֹלָם is applied to a period of
service; and simply means, that the servant
should serve his master as long as he lived.   In Exodus
xl: 15, it is applied to the Levitical priesthood ; and means
that it should continue throughout the entire Jews' age, or
while the Old Covenant should endure.   In Genesis xlix:
26, it is applied to the hills ; and comprehends all time: this
is also evidently its meaning in Daniel ii: 44, and many other
passages of Scripture.

From such premises, some have hastily inferred, that these
words always refer to a limited period: and that they never

mean duration without end. But they are always perfectly *exhaustive* of the entire period or cycle to which they are applied. If they refer simply to the period of a man's life, they exhaust it; if to an age, they exhaust it; if to time, they exhaust it; and if to eternity, they in like manner, exhaust it. So that when Christ says, "These shall go away into everlasting punishment ($\epsilon\iota\varsigma$ $\varkappa o\lambda a\sigma\iota\nu$ $a\iota\omega\nu\iota o\nu$), but the righteous into everlasting life ($\epsilon\iota\varsigma$ $\zeta\omega\eta\nu$ $a\iota\omega\nu\iota o\nu$), Matthew xxv: 46, he means, beyond all doubt, life and punishment without end.

IV. In Matthew xii: 31, 32, Christ said to the Pharisees, "All manner of *sin* ($\acute{a}\mu a\rho\tau\iota a$) and blasphemy shall be forgiven unto men: but the blasphemy The unpardonable sin. against the Holy Spirit shall not be forgiven unto men. And whosoever speaketh a word against the Son of Man, it shall be forgiven him: but whosoever speaketh against the Holy Spirit, it shall not be forgiven him, either in the present age or in the age that is to come."

It is generally supposed, and I presume correctly, that in this passage, Christ designs to teach that there is *one sin* among men, and *but one* for which there Various manifestations of it. is no forgiveness.* And it seems to be here identified, at least in some degree, with the blasphemy which the Pharisees had just uttered against the Holy Spirit, in ascribing the miracles of Christ wrought by the Spirit, to Beelzebub. But in Hebrews vi: 4–6, Paul teaches that the sin of apostacy is unpardonable: and in Proverbs i: 24–32, Solomon assures us that the sin of negligence may become unpardonable. How, then, are these statements to be reconciled?

The solution of what has thus appeared, to some persons, to be a very great difficulty, is found in the mean- Mode of reconciling these apparent discrepancies. ing of the word $\acute{a}\mu a\rho\tau\iota a$, *sin*. Ordinarily this word means simply an overt transgression of

* See also 1 John v: 16.

law. But this is not always its meaning. Frequently, it is also used to denote *the sinful, depraved, and wicked state of heart,* that prompts a man to commit such outward acts. This is evidently its meaning in the following passages: "Knowing this, that our old man is crucified with him, that the body of *sin* (ἁμαρτια) might be destroyed, that henceforth we should not serve *sin* (ἁμαρτια): for he that is dead is freed from *sin* (ἁμαρτια). Likewise reckon ye also yourselves dead indeed unto *sin* (ἁμαρτια), but alive unto God through Jesus Christ our Lord. Let not *sin* (ἁμαρτια) therefore reign in your mortal bodies, that ye should obey it in the lusts thereof. Neither yield your members as instruments of unrighteousness unto *sin* (ἁμαρτια).—For *sin* (ἁμαρτια) shall not have dominion over you.—But God be thanked, that though ye were the servants of *sin* (ἁμαρτια), ye have obeyed from the heart that form of doctrine into which ye were delivered. Being then made free from *sin* (ἁμαρτια) ye became the servants of righteousness.—For when ye were the servants of *sin* (ἁμαρτια), ye were free from righteousness.—But now being made free from *sin* (ἁμαρτια) and become the servants of God, ye have your end unto holiness, and the end everlasting life. For the wages of *sin* (ἁμαρτια) is death; but the gift of God is eternal life, through Jesus Christ our Lord." (Romans vi: 6, 7, 11, 12, 13, 14, 17, 18, 20, 22, and 23. See also the whole of the seventh chapter.)

From such passages, which might be greatly multiplied, it is evident, that the word *sin* may denote simply *the depravity or sinfulness of the human heart:* and moreover, that this one sinful state of heart may lead a man to commit many sinful acts. And hence we conclude that the unpardonable sin is In what this *simply such a* DEGREE *of spiritual depravity as* sin consists. *places a man beyond the possibility of being saved.* This, of course, may make itself manifest in many ways. Sometimes it may be seen in a mere Stoical indifference, which all the mercies of God through Christ may not be able to overcome. Sometimes it may be manifested in ascribing the words and works of God to Beelzebub. And sometimes again it may be seen for a long time in the life and character of such men as Julian, the Apostate. But in all cases, it is but *one* and the *same* awfully hard, How it is incurred. corrupt, immovable, and unredeemable state of heart, which the individual has brought upon himself by his own personal transgressions.

SECTION II.—RULES FOR ASCERTAINING THE MEANING OF SENTENCES.

I. *Be careful to ascertain its right construction.* This requires attention, First Rule for sentences.

1. To its ellipsis.

2. To its subject and predicate, with all their primary and secondary adjuncts.

3. To its punctuation.

II. *Consider attentively whether it contains within itself the means of its own explanation.* If it does, these are sufficient. To seek for other means of ex- Second Rule. planation and illustration, is unnecessary, unless in important cases, when it may be well to multiply evidence and arguments for the sake of still greater perspicuity and emphasis. *E. g.:* The third precept of the Decalogue reads as follows: "Thou shalt not take the name of the Lord thy Illustration. God in vain: for the Lord will not hold him guiltless that taketh his name in vain."

This is a compound sentence, the construction of which may be easily understood by all who have studied even the elements of Grammar and Logic. It also contains within itself the means of its own explanation. First, there is given a command, forbidding even all unnecessary and undue familiarity with the name of God. And in the second place, there is a reason assigned for this prohibition: "The Lord will not hold him guiltless, that taketh his name in vain." Such an exegesis, given somewhat in detail, according to circumstances, would be sufficient for all ordinary purposes. But if the persons addressed are young and inexperienced, or if the object of the interpreter is to correct some *habitual* violation of the spirit and letter of this precept,—in either case, it might be well to refer to the context; to make the person or persons addressed feel the awful solemnity of the circumstances under which this precept was given to the Israelites; and furthermore, to refer to such other passages of Scripture as might serve to illustrate the terrible consequences of neglecting this law.

And hence, whenever the meaning of a sentence is not sufficiently clear and obvious from its own construction and a due regard to the meaning of the several words and members that compose it, the next rule to be observed is,

III. *Consult the context;* or the connection in which it

Third Rule. stands. This requires special attention to the two following particulars: first, to *the special*

Two things necessary in order to its proper application. *scope* of the paragraph or passage of which it is a member; and secondly, to *the nature of the union* that subsists between the sentence itself and its

context. Of these we must now speak particularly.

THE SPECIAL SCOPE.

The special scope of a passage may be ascertained in several ways.

1. *It may be ascertained from the preceding context. E. g.:*

First way of ascertaining the special scope of a passage. The special scope of the three parables in the fifteenth chapter of Luke, is easily understood from what is contained in the first two verses. "And all the publicans and sinners came near to hear him. And the Pharisees and Scribes murmured, saying: This man receives sinners and eats with them." This led Christ to speak of God's com- _{Illustration} passion for sinners, and his earnest desire to reclaim and save the *lost*. The oldest son of the third parable resembles the Scribes and Pharisees in *one* respect: he *murmured* at the benevolence of his father.

2. *It may often be ascertained from the following context.* E. g.: In Ecclesiastes x: 1, it is said: "Dead _{The second way.} flies cause the apothecary's ointment to send forth an offensive smell." The design of the writer in this remark is made plain by what follows: "So," says he, "a little folly is more powerful than wisdom and _{Illustration.} honor." That is, a little folly may render offensive the conduct of even the wise and honorable.

3. *It may be ascertained from the general scope.* E. g.: John's object in recording the several miracles and discourses of Christ, may be easily under- _{The third way.} stood from the particular circumstances of each case, taken in connection with the general design of his whole narrative. (See John xx: 30, 31.) _{Illustration.}

NATURE OF THE UNION.

The next step that is necessary in order to a proper examination of the context, is, to notice carefully _{Different kinds of union between a clause and its context.} the nature of the union that subsists between the sentence under consideration, and the several other clauses with which it is connected. This connection is called,

1. *Logical,* when the relation of the clauses is illative. E. g.: The ground is rich, for the trees are flourishing. Become ye holy, for I am holy. _{Logical union.}

With many of them God was not well pleased; for they were overthrown in the wilderness.

In tracing out this connection, all parentheses and digressions must be laid aside. Digressions are longer than parentheses; and are therefore the more liable to mislead the student unless they are carefully considered. The following examples may serve for illustration:

(1.) Romans v: 13–17, inclusive,

(2.) Ephesians iii: 2—iv: 1, inclusive.

(3.) Hebrews v: 11—vi: 20, inclusive.

2. The connection is called *psychological*, when it depends

Psychological union.

on the laws of suggestion, whether primary or secondary; whether objective or subjective. This is beautifully illustrated in many of the discourses of our Savior. (See, for instance, Matthew iv: 19; xvi: 18; John iii: 19; iv: 10; vii: 37–39; ix: 39; x: 1–18.) In all these passages, the law of resemblance or analogy is the bond of union.

3. The connection is called *historical*, when events are

Historical union.

related in their regular chronological order; because this is what we have a right to expect of every historian. This order is commonly followed in the books of Samuel, Kings, and Chronicles.

4. It is called *historico-dogmatic*, when historical events are

Historico-dogmatic union.

regularly introduced for didactic purposes. This very often occurs in the history of the primitive Church. Nothing in its organization or development was laid down by its inspired legislators, as a matter of theory. In most cases, the Holy Spirit suggested to the Apostles, through the force and power of circumstances, the rules that were then necessary, and that are still necessary for its growth, efficiency, and prosperity. This is well illustrated in the appointment

Illustrations.

of the first seven Deacons, (Acts vi: 1–7;) in the sending out of missionaries, (Acts xiii: 1–3;) in an important case of reference from one congregation to another, (Acts xv: 1–31;) in excluding the disorderly from the church, (1 Corinthians v;) and in many other cases of like practical importance.

5. It is called *optical*, when the order of time is neglected, and the past and the future are described as pres- The optical ent realities. This sort of union is very common union. in prophecy. Thus, Isaiah says, "Unto us a child *is born;* unto us a son is given." (Isaiah ix: 6. See also Jeremiah iv: 19–31.)

By these two processes then—namely, that of finding out the special scope of a passage, and that of tracing out the connection that exists between the clause to be interpreted and its other members, the light of the context may be elicited. And this will generally be sufficient to determine the meaning of the sentence, when this can not be ascertained with sufficient clearness from its own construction. I will add a few examples, for the purpose of illustrating more fully this most important rule of Sacred Hermeneutics:

1. In John vi: 53, Jesus says: "Verily, verily, I say unto you; except ye eat the flesh of the Son of Illustrations of Man, and drink his blood, ye have no life in the third General Rule. you." First example.

The object of Christ, in this discourse, is, to draw the minds and the hearts of the people from those created things in which they were wont to trust; and to fix them on himself as their only true and all-sufficient portion. This is the *special scope* of the passage.

The *connection*, in this case, is psychological. The people had recently eaten of the five loaves and two small fishes; and this circumstance suggested to Christ the train of metaphors that follow. This is evident, from the sixty-third verse of the chapter. "It is the Spirit," says Christ, "that quickeneth: the flesh profiteth nothing. The words that I speak unto you, they are spirit and they are life."

It is evident therefore that the words of Christ in the fifty-third verse are figurative: and that it is simply by faith that we are to receive him as the food and portion of our souls. This is made still more obvious by the forty-seventh verse: "Verily, verily, I say unto you, he that believeth into me, has everlasting life." (See also John iii: 36.)

2. Take as a second example 1 Corinthians xv: 29: "For else what shall those do who are baptized for the dead (*ʹυπερ νεκρων*), if the dead rise not at all?"

Second example.

The *scope* of the chapter is to prove the resurrection of the dead: and the *connection* is both logical and psychological. And hence it is evident, that Paul here draws an argument in support of the doctrine of the final resurrection, from the practice of Christian immersion. The typical or symbolical connection between the two is assumed; and on this the Apostle bases his argument. What, says he, does your burial and your resurrection in baptism mean; and of what value is your immersion into Christ, if there is no resurrection from the dead?

3. We will take as a third example Galatians iii: 20: "Now a mediator is not a mediator of one: but God is one."

Third example.

The *object* of the Apostle in this part of his letter, is to show that the eternal inheritance promised to Abraham and to his seed, was intended not for his seed according to the flesh, but for those who were his children by faith and according to the promise: and moreover, that this inheritance is to be enjoyed not through the Law but through the Covenant concerning Christ (*εις χριστον*): and that the Law was simply added to this very comprehensive arrangement, for a mere temporary and specific purpose.

The *connection* is psychological. The law of suggestion

in the case, is the law of contrast. The Law of Moses was given for a temporary purpose: but the Gospel is designed for the eternal good and happiness of all men. The Law was given under circumstances and through instrumentalities that imply some degree of diversity: but God is ever *the one, same, and immutable Jehovah.*

And hence it follows, that if, as is clearly proved by the context, it was once God's purpose to bless through the Gospel, all who are the children of Abraham by faith, then indeed *it is still his purpose:* and moreover, that the law, though given under the most solemn circumstances and for a most important temporary purpose, is not and can not, in any sense, be opposed to the Gospel scheme of Justification by Faith; but on the contrary, it served as a pedagogue to bring to Christ, all who profited by its instructions: so that it was in fact from the beginning but a subordinate part of the Divine plan.

IV. The fourth rule for ascertaining the meaning of a sentence, is as follows: *Consult parallel passages.* Fourth Rule for sentences. That is *real parallels:* passages in which the same *ideas* are expressed in either the same or in different words. The order to be observed under this rule is the Order of applying it. same as that given for verbal parallels.

The following examples will serve to illustrate the importance and the proper use and application of this rule.

1. We will take the first from Isaiah xlix: 7: "Thus saith the Lord, the Redeemer of Israel, and his Holy Illustrations. One, *to him whom man despiseth; to him whom the nation abhorreth;* to a servant of rulers: Kings shall see and arise; and princes shall worship, because of the Lord that is faithful, and the Holy One of Israel, and he shall choose thee."

Of whom is this spoken? Who is he that was despised by man, and abhorred by the nation? The answer to this

21

question is found in Isaiah lii: 13—liii. I have space only to quote the last three verses of the fifty-second chapter, but the reader should also study carefully the whole of the fifty-third; it is but a continuation of the same subject. "Behold my servant shall deal prudently, he shall be exalted and extolled, and be very high. As many were astonished at thee: (his visage was so marred more than any man, and his form more than the sons of men): so shall he sprinkle many nations; the kings shall shut their mouths at him: for that which had not been told them shall they see; and that which they had not heard shall they consider." From this, considered in connection with the next chapter, it is perfectly obvious, that the person previously referred to in the forty-ninth chapter is the Messiah: who at one time was to be despised and rejected by man; but who was soon afterward to be gloriously exalted.

The word נזה signifies, according to Gesenius, (1) to leap for joy, to exult; (2) in Hiphil, to cause to leap for joy; (3) to sprinkle by the spouting or leaping forth of liquids. It is here used in the Hiphil future: and the clause is translated by Gesenius as follows: "So shall he cause many nations to rejoice in himself." This harmonizes well with the context.

2. In Isaiah lxv: 25, it is said: "The wolf and the lamb shall feed together; and the lion shall eat straw like the bullock; and dust shall be the serpent's meat. They shall not hurt nor destroy in all my holy mountain, saith the Lord."

Is this language literal or is it figurative? In Isaiah xi: 6–9, we find a parallel passage, the last verse of which is as follows: "They shall not hurt nor destroy in all my holy mountain: *for the earth shall be full of the knowledge of the Lord as the waters cover the sea.*" This last clause proves beyond all doubt, that the language of the preceding extract is figurative. For powerful as the word of the Lord is to convert human lions, and tigers, and panthers into lambs, it can never change the natural instincts of the beasts of prey.

3. In Genesis xlix: 7, Jacob speaking by the Spirit of prophecy, concerning Simeon and Levi, says: "I will divide them in Jacob, and scatter them in Israel."

This prophecy was literally fulfilled. In Joshua xxi: 1–42, we learn that the Levites occupied as their portion of the land, forty-eight cities scattered among all the Tribes. The Simeonites at first received by lot a part of the inheritance of Judah. (See Joshua xix: 1–9.) But this being too small for them, some went further north, and occupied some of the more central portions of Judah, as Gedor, for example; and others went south to Mount Seir and the country of the Amalekites. (See 1 Chronicles iv: 24–43.) It is therefore very probable that they were scattered still further among the Tribes.

MISCELLANEOUS EXAMPLES.

I. In Matthew xi: 12, Christ said to the multitudes: "From the days of John the Baptist until now the Kingdom of Heaven suffereth violence; and the violent take it by force." *Example illustrative of the commencement of the Kingdom of Heaven.*

The *object* of Christ in the entire paragraph of which this verse is a member, is to commend John to the multitudes: and the *connection* of this clause *Scope of the passage.* with the context is both optical and psychological. The conception in the mind of Christ, which gave *Nature of the union.* bring to the several metaphors used, was that of a city into which a besieging army was resolved to enter. No sooner did John with his mighty voice, announce to the people the near approach of the Kingdom of Heaven, than "Jerusalem and all Judea, and all the region round about Jordan" went out to him, "and were baptized by him in the Jordan confessing their sins." Thus they manifested their confidence in the very near approach of the Kingdom,

and their fixed purpose and determination to enter it as soon as it would really come to hand. But that its existence, at that time, was *ideal* and not *real*, is evident from several considerations.

1. From the fact that John himself was not in the King-dom. For Christ says, in the preceding verse: "He that is least in the Kingdom of Heaven is greater than he." Surely if any one could at that time have entered the Kingdom, John would have done it. And besides, it is difficult to understand how he that was the greatest of all that had ever been born of woman, could be less than the least citizen of the Kingdom, if it was then an existing reality?

2. From the fact, that John himself said: "*The Kingdom of Heaven is at hand.*" (Matthew iii: 2.)

3. From the fact, that Christ proclaimed the same thing. (Matthew iv: 17.)

4. From the fact, that he instructed his disciples to pray: "*Thy Kingdom come.*" (Matthew vi: 10.)

5. From the fact, that the Jewish theocracy, otherwise called the Kingdom of God (Matthew xxi: 43), was not taken out of the way, until its types and shadows were all fulfilled in the great Antitype, and by Him, nailed to the cross. (Colossians ii: 14.) But these two kingdoms, the typical and the antitypical or real, could not exist simulta-neously.

6. From the fact, that Jesus could not be crowned King until after his death, burial, and resurrection. Nor could the Holy Spirit be given, according to the laws and ordi-nances of this most glorious institution, till after Christ was glorified. (John vii: 39.)

7. From the fact, that John never baptized any one *in the name* or by the authority of Jesus Christ: nor did he ever baptize any one *into the name* of the Father, and of the Son,

and of the Holy Spirit. All this was first done, on the day of Pentecost next following the death, burial, and resurrection of Jesus Christ.

8. From the fact, that in Acts xi: 15, the Apostle Peter fixes the same day of Pentecost as the beginning of the Kingdom. His words are: "And as I began to speak, the Holy Spirit fell on them, as on us *at the beginning*." At the beginning of what? Evidently at the beginning of the Kingdom.

From all of which we conclude, that like many of the ancient prophets, Christ in the passage under consideration, simply disregards the idea of time; and contemplates the Kingdom of Heaven as a visible reality, into which the multitudes, under the influence of John's preaching, were striving to enter with a zeal or a species of violence analogous to that of a besieging army. (See, for illustration, the sixtieth chapter of Isaiah.) *Conclusion.*

II. We will take as a second example the following from Matthew xvi: 18: "And I say unto thee that thou art Peter, and upon this rock I will build my church; and the gates of hell shall not prevail against it." *Example illustrative of the Foundation of the Church.*

The *scope* of the paragraph of which this clause is a member, is to reveal the true character of Christ, especially in its relations to the Church: and *Scope of the paragraph.* the *connection* is psychological. It was reserved for Peter to reveal through the Holy Spirit, that Jesus is the Christ, the Son of the living God. And *Nature of the union.* hence there was a beautiful propriety in calling this great and fundamental truth a rock (πετρα); for the twofold reason that it was first suggested by Peter (πετρος), and also because it was to be made the *foundation* of the Christian Church.

The allegation, that Peter himself is the rock, is evidently false for several reasons. *Evidence that Peter is not the foundation.*

1. Because it is inconsistent with the structure of the sentence.   The use of the word πετρα, *a rock*, in-

From the
structure of
the sentence.

stead of πετρος, *a stone*, clearly indicates, that it
was our Savior's intention to express a thought
wholly different from that which was first suggested by the
word πετρος.   Even admitting that these two Greek words
may be sometimes used interchangeably, it does not follow,
that they are so used in this connection. We may use either
thou or *you* to represent a noun in the second person singular.   But it would be a great violation of grammatical propriety, to represent it by each of these in the same sentence.
A change of the pronoun would, in that case, imply also
a change of the antecedent; and of course also of the idea
to be expressed.   And just so in the case under consideration.   The word πετρος means properly *a piece of rock or a
stone:* and the word πετρα means *a rock*, or rather *a mass
of live rock.* They are however sometimes used interchangeably. But this can never be done with propriety in the same
clause or sentence.   In this case, a change of words implies
of necessity a change of ideas.

2. It is inconsistent with the *scope* of the passage.   The

From the scope
of the passage.

object of the Holy Spirit in this connection, is
not to reveal Peter, but Christ to the world.
True indeed, Peter deserved some honor for his agency in
this marvelous revelation: and such honor Christ certainly
confers on him. But he does this, by making him the *doorkeeper*, and not the *foundation* of his Church.

3. It is inconsistent with many parallel passages.   For

From parallel
passages.

instance, in 1 Corinthians iii: 10, 11, Paul says:
"According to the grace of God which is given
unto me, *I have laid the foundation*, and another buildeth
thereon.   But let every man take heed how he buildeth
thereon.   *For other foundation can no man lay, than that is
laid, which is Jesus Christ.*" But it is only by preaching

Christ and him crucified, as Paul did in Corinth, that Christ can be laid as the foundation. And hence there is really no discrepancy between 1 Corinthians iii: 11, and Matthew xvi: 18. And I may further add, that the foundation of the Apostles and Prophets on which the Ephesian Church was builded (Ephesians ii: 20), is the same foundation that is described in these two passages. For the foundation of the Apostles and Prophets is to be found only in their writings. But the *scope* of all these is identical with the confession of Peter, that *Jesus is the Christ, the Son of the living God.*

III. In Matthew xxi: 32, we have the following remarks of Christ, addressed to the Chief Priests and Elders of the Jews: "For John came to you in the way of righteousness, and ye believed him not; but the publicans and the harlots believed him: and ye, when ye had seen it, repented ($\mu\varepsilon\tau\varepsilon\mu\varepsilon\lambda\eta\theta\eta\tau\varepsilon$, *regretted*) not, that ye might believe him." *Example illustrative of Faith and Repentance.*

Throughout the entire Bible, faith is generally represented as preceding both regret and repentance. Faith is described as the antecedent, and repentance as the consequent. But if so, it may be asked, What is the meaning of this passage; and how may it be reconciled with the general teachings and tenor of the Holy Scriptures? *Their relation to each other, as generally represented.*

The whole difficulty is one of our own creation. It arises out of a false assumption on the part of many who have attempted to explain the Bible. Indeed there seems to be a proneness in the human mind, to look upon all the gifts and graces of the Spirit as perfect and full-grown entities from the moment they are received. We seem often to forget, that all Christian graces have a *mutual* and *reflex* influence over each other: and that while faith is of necessity the first of them all, without which every thing else is sinful and *False assumption in the case.* *Their mutual and reflex influence on each other.*

displeasing to God, it nevertheless depends essentially for its subsequent growth on the *reflex* influence of repentance, and the practical exercise of all the other virtues. If the first degree of it leads to a corresponding degree of repentance, this degree of repentance will in like manner serve to produce a second degree of faith; and this again another degree of repentance. So that notwithstanding faith is scripturally, logically, and philosophically the antecedent of repentance, their mutual growth, in all cases, depends, to some extent, on their mutual influence.

And this is just what Christ aims to teach in the passage

Meaning of the passage.

under consideration. The Priests and Elders whom he here reprimands had some degree of faith in God; but when God called on them by his messenger John, to manifest their faith in deeds of repentance and reformation, they refused to hearken. And this refusal on their part was a barrier in their way to higher attainments of faith. Had they repented toward God in whom they did believe, they would also have believed in Christ as the promised Messiah.

IV. The following very profound and interesting passage

Example illustrative of the dependence of Gentile Christians on the Jews.

is found in Romans xi: 16–24: "For if the first fruit be holy, the lump is also holy: and if the root be holy, so are the branches. And if some of the branches be broken off, and thou, being a wild olive tree, wert grafted in among them, and with them partakest of the root and fatness of the Olive Tree, boast not against the branches. But if thou boast, thou bearest not the root, but the root thee. Thou wilt say then, The branches were broken off that I might be grafted in. Well; because of unbelief, they were broken off, and thou standest by faith. Be not high-minded, but fear. For if God spared not the natural branches, take heed lest he also spare not thee. Behold therefore the goodness and the severity of God: on them who fell, severity; but toward thee goodness, if thou continue in his goodness: otherwise thou also shalt be cut off. And they also, if they abide not in unbelief, shall be grafted in: for God is able to graft them in again. For if thou wert cut out of the olive tree which is wild by nature, and were grafted contrary to nature into a good Olive Tree: how much more shall these which are the natural branches, be grafted into their own Olive Tree?"

By many able critics this passage has long been regarded as furnishing conclusive evidence of the general and *essential identity* of the Jewish and Christian churches. And as many infants were, by virtue of their birth and parentage, members of the former; even so, it is confidently inferred, that infants, simply by virtue of their Christian parentage, without any faith or intelligence on their part, may also become members of the latter. *First hypothesis in relation to this passage.*

This is plausible; but wholly at variance with many other portions of Scripture. In Hebrews viii: 6–13, for example, we learn that the covenants or constitutions of these two churches, would differ essentially in several respects: and that among other points of difference, this would be prominent: *that all the subjects of the New Covenant, from the least of them to the greatest, would know the Lord:* whereas, under the Old Covenant, many were always found who could not distinguish their right hand from their left; nor God from Beliel. This therefore is sufficient to disprove the alleged identity of the two churches, and to show the fallaciousness of the given hypothesis. *Evidence of its fallaciousness.*

But one extreme is apt to lead to another. Many in attempting to avoid Scylla have run into Charybdis. This has often proved true in the various attempts that have been made to explain this beautiful passage. Many, apparently for the purpose of avoiding the extreme of the pedobaptists have run into the opposite. They exclude from this beautiful allegory, the Jewish Church *The second hypothesis.*

altogether. They make the good Olive Tree represent the Christian Church exclusively. They allege that the roots, and trunk, and primary branches were composed of the first Jewish converts; and that the Gentiles were not grafted in until after that the Church had become a tree of wide-spreading branches.

This hypothesis has also some apparent ingenuity. But Evidence of its Incorrectness. this is all that can be said in its favor: *for it is utterly inconsistent with the context, and especially with the scope of the passage under consideration.* The object of the Apostle in introducing this allegory, was evidently to make the Gentile Christians feel their dependence on *the Israelites as such;* lest they should be wise in their own conceits. And any hypothesis, therefore, that is inconsistent with this main object of the argument, not to speak of other subordinate matters, is scarcely worthy of a passing notice. Evidently, then, Abraham and his seed according to the flesh, have not only *a place,* but *the first place* in this symbolical representation of God's chosen people. Otherwise, there is neither point, nor logic, nor sense in Paul's reasoning.

How then can this passage be explained in harmony with The obscurity of the argument lies simply in its abstractness. other portions of Scripture, and with the main scope of the Apostle's argument in this connection? The passage is confessedly a difficult one, owing chiefly to the very abstract nature of the argument which it contains. Nothing short of a very high degree of abstraction and generalization would have answered Paul's purpose in this case.

Let us then briefly notice, in the first place, especially for Illustration of the philosophy of common terms. the sake of my junior readers, the philosophy of common terms. And for the sake of illustration, let it be proposed to find a term that may be applied with equal propriety to *a man* or to *a worm.* For this purpose, we first analyze both, and note all their propertics, attributes, and accidents: and we will suppose that as the result of our analysis, in this case, the following elements are discovered:

Man = a, b, c, d, e, f, g, h, i, j, k, l, and m.

Worm = b, l, m, n, o, p, and q.

We next take simply those elements that are common to both, and give to them a common name, canceling and rejecting all others. In this case we find b common to both; and we will let it represent simply *being* or *existence*. We discover moreover, that l and m are common to both. Let the former represent *life*, and the latter *voluntary motion*. To these three elements then, we next give a name, say for instance *animal*, which is equally applicable to a man, and to a worm, and to all other beings having these three properties.

Now let us suppose that the two Churches are in like manner analyzed; and that we have the following results: *Limited identity of the two Churches.*

Jewish Church = a, b, c, d, e, f, g, h, and p.

Christian Church = c, m, n, o, p, q, r, and s.

Here then, for the sake of illustration, we will suppose that there are but two common elements: c and p. Let the latter represent *people*, and the former *chosen* or *covenanted*. To these two elements, we may now give any name that we choose; as for instance, *God's chosen people; God's covenant people; or a good Olive Tree.* If we use the last of these names, as Paul does, then indeed it is evident, not only that it is alike applicable to both Churches, but also that the good and cultivated Olive Tree has its roots in the patriarchs to whom the promises were made; that the trunk and primary branches were composed of members of the Old Covenant; and that the Gentile converts to Christianity must therefore of necessity occupy a very *dependent* position in this symbolical representation of God's elect. This is just what

Paul aims at in the course of his argument, and what he accomplishes in the most effective way possible.

But be it observed, that as in the supposed case of the
Fallacy of rea-
soning from
this partial
identity as if it
were complete.
man and the worm, every thing not otherwise proved to be common, must be eliminated. It will not do to reason from this very partial identity as if it were a complete and perfect identity. It does not follow, because a man and a worm are both animals, that they have therefore both reason, and a will, and a conscience. No more does it follow, because the Jewish and Christian Churches are both included under one symbolical name, that they are therefore in all respects indentical; and that because there were infants in the former, there must therefore of necessity be infants also in the latter. If this is true, it must be proved from other sources, and by other evidence.

SECTION III.—FIGURATIVE LANGUAGE.

The preceding rules are of universal application. They
The preceding
rules are uni-
versal.
serve to determine the meaning of all words and all sentences, whether they be used literally or figuratively. Indeed they furnish the only proper means by which we can determine whether a word, or a sentence, should be taken literally or figuratively. The general
General Rule
relating to lit-
eral and figura-
tive language.
law is, *that all words and sentences should be taken and construed literally: unless this would imply some incongruity or absurdity, or involve a meaning that is inconsistent with the nature of the subject, or with the plain and evident meaning of other portions of Scripture.* But these points can be determined only by a patient con-
Means of deter-
mining these
points.
sideration and judicious application of the preceding rules. Let it be proposed, for example, to determine whether the following passages are to be taken literally or figuratively.

1. "If your enemy is hungry, feed him; if he is thirsty, give him drink: for by so doing, *you will heap coals of fire on his head.*" (Romans xii: 20.)

Illustrations.

"He that *eats my flesh* and *drinks my blood,* has eternal life." (John vi: 54.)

"When thou sittest to eat with a ruler, consider diligently what is before thee; and *put a knife to thy throat,* if thou be a man given to appetite." (Proverbs xxiii: 2.)

In each of these passages, the literal meaning involves a moral absurdity: and the metaphorical meaning is therefore to be preferred.

2. "God came from Teman, and the Holy One from Mount Paran. His glory covered the heavens, and the earth was full of his praise. And his brightness was as the light: he had *horns* coming out of his *hand;* and there was the hiding of his power. Before him went the pestilence; and burning coals went forth at his *feet.*" (Habakkuk iii: 3–5.)

From John iv: 24, we learn that God is *spirit.* And hence all words that ascribe to him human form or physical organs of any kind are to be construed as metaphors; or more particularly, as that species of metaphor which is called *anthropomorphism.*

3. In Genesis vi: 6, it is said: "And it *repented* the Lord that he had made man on the earth; and it *grieved* him at his heart." But in 1 Samuel xv: 29, the prophet assures us that "The Strength of Israel will not repent: for he is not a man that he should repent." In the word *repent* therefore, as it is applied to Jehovah, in Genesis vi: 6, we have another species of metaphor, called *anthropopathy.*

More on this subject would, I think, be unnecessary. By the proper study and application of these rules and principles, the thoughtful student will generally be able to determine, without much difficulty, whether a word or sentence should be construed literally or figuratively. But there are.

a few other matters pertaining to analogical language, on which I wish to add a few words. I refer particularly to *the principle of accommodation; the principle of double reference;* and *the nature, use, and proper interpretation of the allegory and parable.* We will consider these briefly in order.

Other topics pertaining to analogical language.

I. *By the Principle of Accommodation is meant that law and license by which the words of a passage are frequently used in a sense that was not originally intended: but they are applied to some new object, simply on account of their peculiar fitness to describe it.*

Principle of Accommoda- tion.

A beautiful illustration of this principle is found in Romans x: 6–8. But the original words are given in Deuteronomy xxx: 11–14, as follows: "For this commandment which I command thee this day, is not hidden from thee; neither is it far off. It is not in heaven, that thou shouldst say, *Who shall go up for us to heaven, and bring it unto us,* that we may hear it and do it? Neither is it beyond the sea, that thou shouldst say, *Who shall go over the sea for us, and bring it unto us,* that we may hear it and do it? But *the word is very nigh thee; in thy mouth, and in thy heart, that thou mayest do it.*"

Illustration.

In these words, Moses had evidently no other purpose, than simply to remind his brethren, the children of Israel, that they had there and then, *in their possession,* a perfect rule of life: and that it was therefore not necessary for them to travel, as did many of the heathen philosophers, from city to city; and from country to country, in quest of wisdom. The Law in their heart and in their mouth, was to be their guide of life.

But Paul makes use of some of these expressions to illustrate the still greater plainness and simplicity of the Gospel. "But the righteousness which is of faith," he says, "speaketh on this wise: *Say not in thy heart, Who shall ascend into heaven?* that is, to bring Christ down from above: *or who shall descend into the deep?* that is, to bring up Christ again from the dead. But what saith it? *The word is nigh thee, even in thy mouth and in thy heart:* that is the word of faith which we preach; *that if thou wilt confess with thy mouth the Lord Jesus, and shalt believe in thy heart that God hath raised him from the dead, thou shalt be saved.*" (Compare also Psalm xix: 4 with Romans x: 18.)

II. The Principle of Double Reference differs from the Principle of Accommodation, in this respect; that *it always implies an intentional reference to a second object. The words are so selected and the sentences are so framed by the Holy Spirit, that they serve to describe alike both the type and the antitype.* This principle occurs very frequently, especially in the Old Testament. The following may be given as examples and illustrations of it: Principle of Double Reference.

1. Several of God's promises to Abraham. They refer to both the families of which he was made the father and the founder: to his natural and also to his spiritual posterity; to his seed which was according to the flesh, and also to his seed which was according to the promise. (Compare, for instance, Genesis xvii: 4–7 with Romans iv: 11–16.)

2. Many of the Psalms of David. The seventy-second, for example, refers primarily to the reign of Solomon; and secondarily to the reign of Christ.

3. Many of the later prophecies. (Compare, for example, Isaiah vii: 14–16, and also viii: 1–4, with Matthew i: 22, 23; Jeremiah xxxi: 15 with Matthew ii: 17, 18; and Hosea xi: 1 with Matthew ii: 15.)

III. To give a strictly logical definition of an Allegory and a Parable in the present vague state of our religious literature, is not an easy matter. But perhaps the following definitions are as well adapted to the popular mind and as free from metaphysical objections as any that can now be given.

An Allegory (ἀλληγορία from ἀλλος, other, and ἀγορευω, to
Definition of an Allegory. speak) *is a phrase, a sentence, or a discourse, in which the principal subject is described by another which resembles it:* or it is a representation of *one* thing, which is intended to excite in the mind of the reader or hearer the representation of *another* thing. The first or immediate representation is called the *protasis:* and the second or ultimate representation is called the *apodosis.*

A Parable (παραβολη from παρα, beside, and βαλλω, to throw)
Definition of a Parable. *is that species of allegory, in which the protasis is a serious narration, within the limits of probability, and designed to illustrate some moral or religious truth.*

In both of these figures, then, it will be observed, there
Relation on which all allegories are founded. is an *expressed* or *implied* comparison, either *direct* or *indirect.* The object to be explained and illustrated is compared with some other well-known and familiar object which it resembles, or to which it is in some way analogous, for the purpose of expressing a higher degree of perspicuity, or beauty, or energy. And hence it follows that in the interpretation of every allegory, and especially of every parable, three things require our very special attention and consideration:

Objects to be considered in the interpretation of parables and allegories.
1. The illustrating example.
2. The object to be illustrated.
3. The similitude existing between them: or the *tertium comparationis,* as it has been technically called.

From the data thus furnished, the *scope* or main design
How the scope of a parable is to be ascertained. of the parable or allegory, may be generally inferred without much doubt or difficulty. For instance, after the student shall have thus carefully examined the Parable of the Sower in Matthew xiii:

1–9, he will readily perceive that its scope is to show that the fruits of the Gospel or the word preached, *Illustrations.* depend *on the state and condition of the hearts* of those who hear it. And by the same threefold process, he will see that the object of Christ in the Parable of the Darnel of the field (Matthew xiii: 24–30), is simply to warn his disciples and especially the Overseers of his Church, against *an extreme degree of discipline;* or an attempt to discriminate between persons and characters here as God himself will discriminate hereafter.*

I will give with all possible brevity, the scope of a few other parables, as a help and encouragement to such young persons as may desire to make further progress in this very interesting department of Sacred Hermeneutics.

1. *The Parable of the Mustard Seed* (Matthew xiii: 31, 32). *Scope:* The great outward enlargement of *Miscellaneous examples.* the Church. (Compare Daniel ii: 35.)

2. *Parable of the Leaven* (Matthew xiii: 33). *Scope:* The inner workings and assimilating power of the Gospel.

3. *Parable of the Hidden Treasure* (Matthew xiii: 44). *Scope:* The joyful effects of the Kingdom.

4. *Parable of the Pearl of Great Price* (Matthew xiii: 45, 46). *Scope:* The zeal and the sacrifices that should be made in order to secure the blessings of the Kingdom.

5. *Parable of the Drag-net* (Matthew xiii: 47–50). *Scope:* The good and the bad, now nominally existing and living together in the Church, will be finally and forever separated.

---

* Some have hastily inferred from this parable, that all discipline is forbidden as injurious to the growth and prosperity of the Church. But surely it does not follow, because the *darnel* was allowed to remain in the field, that therefore *burdocks, thistles,* and every other kind of noxious weed should also be allowed to remain there to the great injury of the wheat. There is nothing therefore in the parable, that forbids the exercise of church discipline within proper limits. The leper was always to be separated from the camp of Israel. (Leviticus xiii.)

22

6. *Parable of the Unforgiving Servant* (Matthew xviii: 23–35). *Scope:* The imperative and indispensable duty of every one's forgiving the trespasses of his brethren.

7. *Parable of the Laborers in the Vineyard* (Matthew xx: 1–16). *Scope:* All Christians will be rewarded. But this reward will be given not as a matter of debt, but of grace. And hence even those who labor most, if they do so, with the hope and expectation of meriting salvation by their own works of righteousness, will in the end be disappointed, and fail at last of eternal life.

8. *Parable of the Vineyard let out to Husbandmen* (Matthew xxi: 33–44). *Scope:* The Jews to be rejected as a people, on account of their rejecting and killing God's prophets, and finally his own Son.

9. *Parable of the Marriage of the King's Son* (Matthew xxii: 1–14). *Scope:* Call of all classes, both Jews and Gentiles, to a participation of the blessings of the Gospel

10. *Parable of the Ten Virgins* (Matthew xxv: 1–13). *Scope:* Necessity of all the followers of Christ being ever watchful and ready for his coming; whether providential or personal.

11. *Parable of the Talents* (Matthew xxv: 14–30). *Scope:* Christ will hold all men personally responsible for whatever talents he has committed to their charge.

CHAPTER IV.

ANALYSIS OF THE EPISTLE TO THE ROMANS.

HISTORICAL CIRCUMSTANCES.

I WILL merely state these; and leave it to the reader to consider them fully and in detail.

- I. *Quis, who?* Paul was the writer, and the Roman Christians were the persons addressed.
- II. *Quid, what?* Didactic and argumentative prose.
- III. *Ubi, where?* At Corinth.
- IV. *Quibus auxiliis, with what helps?* Paul's own agency; the aid of Tertius as his amanuensis; and the agency of the Holy Spirit.
- V. *Cur, why?* For the edification of the Church of Rome.
- VI. *Quomodo, how?* Naturally, providentially, and miraculously.
- VII. *Quando, when?* A. D. 58.

GENERAL DIVISION OF THE EPISTLE.

PART I.—Introduction. (i: 17.)

PART II.—Argumentative. (i: 18—xi.)

    CHAPTER I.—Justification. (i: 18—v.)

    CHAPTER II.—Sanctification, Redemption, and Glorification. (vi—viii.)

    CHAPTER III.—God's dealings with the Jews as a people. (ix—xi.)

PART III.—Practical. (xii—xv: 13.)
PART IV.—Conclusion. (xv: 14—xvi.)

SPECIAL ANALYSIS.

PART I. INTRODUCTION. (i: 1–17.)

SECTION I. *Paul's Salutation.* (i: 1–7.)

1. Paul's personal relations to Christ. (V. 1.)
2. His official relations to the Gospel. (V. 1.)
3. The origin and proclamation of the Gospel. (V. 1, 2.)
4. This Gospel respects the twofold nature of Christ. (V. 3, 4.)
5. Purpose and object for which Paul had been set apart to the Gospel. (V: 5.)
6. His prayer for all the Roman saints. (V. 7.)

SECTION II. *Paul's deep interest in and for the Church of Rome.* (V. 8–13.)

This he manifests in several ways—

1. By his gratitude to God for their fidelity. (V. 8.)
2. By his prayers in their behalf. (V. 9.)
3. By his great desire to visit them for their edification. (V. 10–13.)

SECTION III. *Paul's great confidence in the Gospel.* (V. 14–17.)

This is shown—

1. By his readiness and willingness to preach it to all. (V. 14, 15.)
2. In his avowed conviction that it is the power of God for the salvation of all true believers. (V. 16, 17.)

PART II. ARGUMENTATIVE. (i: 18—xi.)

CHAPTER I. Justification. (i: 18—v.)

SECTION I. *The Gentiles all condemned on the ground of the Legal Scheme of Justification.* (i : 18–32.)

1. In verse sixteenth, we have Paul's general thesis.
2. In the seventeenth verse, we have given his first sub-thesis. Justification is here taken up merely as the first element of the salvation spoken of in the sixteenth verse.
3. Between the seventeenth and eighteenth verses, there is an ellipsis, in which it is implied,
(1) That there are but two conceivable schemes of Justification ; viz. :
(a) That which is by and through works of law.
(b) That which is by grace, through faith.
(2) It is implied, that though the former is *conceivable,* it is utterly impracticable.
4. From this assumed stand-point, the Apostle now proceeds with his argument. That it is wholly impracticable, he argues,
  I. Because God has clearly revealed and indicated his purpose to punish all transgressors of his law. (V. 18.)
  II. Because that all men, even the heathen, are responsible, through the revelation that God has made to them of himself. (V. 19, 20.)
  III. Because the heathen have all perverted this knowledge; and acted unworthily of the light and privileges they enjoyed. (V. 21, 23.)
  IV. And hence God has abandoned them, and given them up to indulge in the most abominable and degrading vices. (V. 24–32.)

CONCLUSION. *Hence it is implied that all such persons are condemned by law :* and if saved at all, it must be by grace through faith.

SECTION II. *Discussion of some general principles of the Divine government and administration; looking, however, chiefly to the Jews.* (ii : 1–16.)

  I. The man who draws the aforesaid conclusion, is self-condemned. (V. 1.)

  II. God's judgments on all men will be according to TRUTH : *i. e.,* according to all the circumstances and the reality of each case, without any respect of persons. (V. 2.)

IMPLIED OBJECTION. God does not now so judge all men.

  III. True : God is now long-suffering; and to our imperfect reason, perhaps apparently partial. But all this is really for wise and benevolent purposes : he being anxious that all, if possible, should be brought to repentance. And hence he has given us a time of probation. (V. 3–5.)

  IV. But nevertheless, the day is coming when every man will be rewarded according to his works, implying the most exact estimate of all the light and privileges that he enjoyed. (V. 6–12, 16.)

IMPLIED OBJECTION. We Jews have the Law in our possession : besides many other evidences of God's special favor.

  V. True indeed : but it is not merely *having* law, but *obeying* it, that justifies a man and secures the favor of God. For the Gentiles have law as well as the Jews; so that if *having* law justifies a man before God, then indeed the whole Gentile world will be justified. The argument proves too much; and therefore proves nothing. (V. 13–15.)

SECTION III. *The Jews are also all and severally condemned on the ground of the Legal Scheme of Justification.* (ii : 17—iii : 20.)

  I. That the Jews are all transgressors of law, is proved chiefly in two ways:

1. By appealing to their own consciousness. (ii: 17–23.)
2. By the testimony of their own Scriptures. (V. 24.)
   II. IMPLIED INFERENCE. The Jews as well as the Gentiles are therefore all condemned according to law.
   III. IMPLIED OBJECTION. The Jews may expect and claim some special favor, on the ground of their being circumcised.
   IV. ANSWER. (ii: 25–29.)
1. The circumcision of the flesh is a part of the Legal Scheme of Justification; and can of course be of value to any one only as such.
2. The only circumcision that is now of any avail, is the circumcision of the heart. (See also Ephesians i: 14; Philippians iii: 3; Colossians ii: 11.)
   V. Statement and refutation of sundry Jewish objections. (iii: 1–8.)
1. This reasoning seems to give to the Jews no advantage over the Gentiles. (V. 1.)
   ANSWER. Not so: their advantages over the Gentiles are still very great; especially in their having the Oracles of God. (V. 2.)
2. But if some of the Jews have been unfaithful, must God too be unfaithful in fulfilling his promises made absolutely and unconditionally to Abraham? (See, for example, Genesis xvii: 7.)
   ANSWER. Certainly not. God's fidelity must not be called into question, in any event. It is blasphemy to do so: and such objections are not to be considered. (V. 4. See Psalm li: 4.)
3. But as our injustice serves to commend God's scheme of justification by faith, would it not be unjust in God to take vengeance on us? (V. 5.)
   ANSWER. Certainly not: for if this were true, he could judge neither Jews nor Gentiles. (V. 6.)

4. But if God's truth has abounded through my falsehood, why should I be treated as a sinner? Should not my sins be allowed to pass, at least with impunity, as so much good has resulted from them? (V. 7.)

ANSWER. And why not add, in order at once to cap the climax of your wicked speculations, Let us do evil that good may come! (V. 8.)

VI. Amplification and confirmation of the argument against the possibility of being justified by law, drawn from the Scriptures of the Old Testament. (iii: 9–18.)

VII. These Scriptures have all *special* reference to the Jews. (V. 19.)

VIII. GENERAL CONCLUSION: BY WORKS OF LAW THERE-FORE NEITHER JEW NOR GENTILE CAN BE JUSTIFIED. (V. 20.)

SECTION IV. *Exposition of the Gospel Scheme of Justification.* (v: 21–31.)

1. It is of God. (V. 21.)
2. It is without works of law. (V. 21.)
3. It is well sustained by evidence. (V. 21.)
4. It is through the faith of Jesus Christ. (V. 22.)
5. It is provided for all. (V. 22.)
6. It is upon all believers: *i. e.,* it is enjoyed by all such. (V. 22.)
7. It is wholly gratuitous. (V. 24.)
8. It comes to us through the *propitiation* of Christ. (V. 24.)
9. It meets and fully satisfies all the demands of law and justice in our behalf; and vindicates the justice of God's administration and government over man. (V. 25, 26.)
10. It excludes all boasting. (V. 27.)
11. It justifies all, whether Jews or Gentiles, on the same ground. (V. 28–30.)

12. It magnifies God's law, and makes it honorable in the sight of an intelligent, adoring, and admiring universe. (V. 31.)

Section V. *The Case of Abraham.* (iv.)

I. Did not Abraham obtain something on the ground of Legal Justification? (V. 1.)

ANSWER. Nothing whatever; he, like others, was saved by grace through faith. This is proved

(1) By what was said in Romans iii: 27. After a proposition has been once proved, it may afterward be legitimately used in evidence.

(2) By what is recorded in Genesis xv: 6.

II. IMPLIED OBJECTION. But may not Abraham have been justified partly by the Legal and partly by the Gracious Scheme?

ANSWER. Impossible. The two schemes can not be blended together in any case. This is proved,

1. From their own essential and intrinsic difference. (V. 4–6.)

2. From the evidence of Scripture. (Psalm xxxii: 1.)

III. IMPLIED OBJECTION. May not circumcision have been at least a *condition* of Abraham's justification?

ANSWER. Impossible: for he was justified before he was circumcised. (V. 9–12.)

IV. Besides, the fact that Abraham and his seed were made heirs of the world, is a proof that it never was God's purpose to justify men by works of law. (V. 13–17.) This is evident from several considerations.

1. Had it been otherwise, the scheme of justification by grace through faith would have been useless and superfluous.

2. Law always serves to make those living under it, more and more guilty.

3. And hence it follows that the scheme of justification by grace through faith, is the only one that is consistent with God's promise to Abraham.

4. Hence it also follows that all are Abraham's seed, who possess his faith.

  V. Characteristics of Abraham's faith. (V. 18–22.) ·

1. It rested wholly and exclusively on the promises of God.

2. It was very strong and unwavering.

VI. The case of Abraham was recorded for an example and encouragement to us. (V. 23–25.)

SECTION VI. *Fruits and Consequences of being Justified by Faith.* (v : 1–11.)

1. We have peace with God. (V. 1.)

2. We enjoy all the blessings and privileges of the kingdom that now is. (V. 2.)

3. We are enabled to glory in our present tribulations. (V. 3.)

4. We have a well-grounded hope of enjoying still higher honors and privileges. (V. 2, 4–10.)

5. We rejoice in all the attributes and perfections of God, by means of Jesus Christ, through whom we have received all that is necessary in order to our being reconciled to God. (V. 11.)

NOTE.—In the Scheme of Redemption we have

1. The sacrifice of Christ.

2. His offering for sin.

3. The atonement, or the satisfaction rendered by means of this offering to the demands and requirements of law and justice.

4. Propitiation. This respects God alone.

5. Reconciliation. This respects man alone. We loved God because he first loved us. (1 John iv : 19.)

6. Expiation or the forgiveness of sin.

7. Justification; which implies that we are treated and dealt with as just persons; as if we had never sinned.
8. Sanctification, as it respects both our state and our character.
9. The redemption of our bodies from the grave.
10. Glorification in heaven.
11. Everlasting salvation.

The word χαταλλαγη, *reconciliation*, in verse 11th seems to be a "*vox pregnans.*" (See the following section.)

SECTION VII. *The superabounding fullness of this* χαταλλαγη, *or Scheme of Reconciliation, Expiation, Justification, and Redemption that we enjoy through Jesus Christ.* (v: 12–21.) This is shown in two ways.

I. By its power and efficacy in saving *all men,* (even infants and idiots,) *unconditionally,* from all the effects and consequences of Adam's original transgression. (V. 12–19.)

1. All mankind, infants as well as adults, die through Adam, because through him they have all become sinful, (ἁμαρτωλοι.) (V. 12, 18, 19.)

[DIGRESSION.—From the thirteenth to the seventeenth verses inclusive, we have a slight digression from the main line of argument, introduced for the purpose of sustaining and further amplifying the main thought of the twelfth verse. It contains the following subordinate items:

(1) Even during the Patriarchal Age, for example, when mankind were comparatively without law, men died, and even infants and idiots died who had never sinned in their own persons, as did Adam.

(2) And hence it follows that these persons must have all sinned in and through Adam. And hence also it follows that Adam was a type of Christ: for the acts of both had an influence over the entire human race.

(3) But their acts have affected the race very differently. For

(a) The act of Adam brought *death* upon all men; but the act of Christ gives *life* to all men.

(b) The act of Christ reaches far beyond the original sinful act of Adam, and provides for the expiation of many other personal offenses.

(c) It also secures to the redeemed higher degrees of glory, and honor, and happiness than we lost in Adam.]

2. The eighteenth and nineteenth verses stand logically connected with the twelfth. The argument of the Apostle runs thus: As by one act of Adam, the many, *i. e.*, his whole posterity, *without any agency on their part*, were made sinners (ἁμαρτωλοὶ κατεστάθησαν οἱ πολλοί); even so, by one act of Christ, the same persons, without any agency on their part, will be made just (δίκαιοι); and consequently saved from all the effects and consequences of Adam's original transgression. (V. 18, 19.)

NOTE.—The reader will observe that this final and perfect deliverance of our *entire race*, from all the effects of Adam's original transgression, has respect not merely to our bodies, but also to our spirits. For the words ἁμαρτωλοὶ and δίκαιοι are not predicable of matter. And hence this is perhaps the strongest and fullest guarantee given in the whole Bible, that all who die in their infancy, or before they incur the guilt of sin through their own personal transgressions, will be everlastingly saved through the redemption that is in Christ Jesus.

II. The superabounding fullness of this Gospel Scheme of reconciliation and justification, further shown and illustrated by the provisions therein contained for the *conditional* pardon of all our personal transgressions. (V. 20, 21.) The conditions are not here stated, but evidently implied. So that when we stand before the great white throne, it will be, to be judged for the deeds done in our own bodies. (See 2 Corinthians v: 10; Revelation xx: 12, 13.)

CHAPTER II.—SANCTIFICATION, REDEMPTION, AND GLORIFICATION. (vi–viii.)

SECTION I. *The Profession of Christianity implies the necessity of a holy life.* (vi: 1–14.)

I. OBJECTION. This scheme has too much grace in it. It serves as a license and encouragement to sin. (V. 1.)

II. ANSWER. Impossible: the very reverse of this is implied,
1. In our death to sin. (V. 2, 3.)
2. In our resurrection to a *new* life. (V. 4.)
3. In our close and intimate union with Christ. (V. 5.)
4. In the crucifixion of our old man. (V. 6.)
5. In our being delivered from Sin as our master. (V. 7.)
6. In the example of Christ which we have received as our rule of life. (V. 8–11.)

III. Exhortation and encouragement to holiness. (vi: 12–14.

SECTION II. *Our present state of favor furnishes new incentives to holiness.* (vi: 15; vii: 6.)

I. ANTINOMIAN OBJECTION. May we not sin therefore as much as we please because we are not under law but under grace. (V. 15.)

II. ANSWER. Certainly not; for the following reasons:
1. Because this would be inconsistent with our new relations and obligations as the servants of Righteousness. (V. 16–19.)

2. Because the fruits and consequences of Sin, tend always to death: but the fruits of Righteousness tend always to life. (V. 20–23.)

3. Because we were delivered from the Law and placed in our present state of favor for the very purpose of enabling us to become holy. (vii: 1–6.)

SECTION III. *The impossibility of attaining to holiness under law, proved and illustrated, while considering and refuting two Jewish objections.* (vii: 7–25.)

I. OBJECTION FIRST. Is not the tendency of this reasoning to prove that the Law is sinful? (V. 7.)

II. ANSWER. Certainly not. But,

1. The knowledge of sin comes through law. (V. 7.)

2. The Law by attempting to restrain our evil passions, really only serves to excite them, and render them the more active. (V. 8–11.)

3. And hence, although the Law is holy, it really becomes the *occasion* of death, by giving life and energy to sin. (V. 12.)

III. OBJECTION SECOND. Can a good law become the cause of death? (V. 13.)

IV. ANSWER. Certainly not. For,

1. Sin is the *cause* of death. (V. 13.)

2. But, nevertheless, God has allowed Sin to work out this evil result, through a good instrumentality, in order to demonstrate the more impressively, its exceeding sinfulness. (V. 13.)

3. The Law has no power to deliver any one from his state of guilt and bondage under the tyrant Sin. (V. 14–24.)

4. And hence it is impossible for any man to attain to holiness under law, as a rule of justification and sanctification.

NOTE.—In this section, Paul, in imagination, separates himself wholly from the Gospel and all its gracious and
redeeming influences, in order that he may the more
effectually and impressively illustrate the power and
dominion of Sin in the heart of every man, who is without the sustaining grace of God through Jesus Christ
and the quickening and sanctifying influence of the
Holy Spirit.

SECTION IV. *The possibility of attaining to holiness under
the Gospel.* (viii: 1–11.)

Under this head, Paul argues,

   I. That the Gospel has freed us from the rule, power,
and dominion of Sin which is in our members. (V.
1, 2.)

  II. That it has effected this, by and through the sin-
offering of Christ. (V. 3.)

 III. That God's object in all this is to enable us to keep
the requirements of the Law. (V. 4.)

 IV. That the *animus* or mind of the Flesh, under any system, tends always to death: but the *animus* or mind of
the Spirit is always to life and peace. (V. 5–8.)

  V. And hence that if the Spirit of God dwells in us, all is
well. In that case, even this mortal body will finally
become immortal. (V. 9–11.)

SECTION V. *An exhortation to walk according to the Spirit.*
(V. 12–17.)

This the Apostle urges,

   I. On the ground that we have been freed from the flesh.
(V. 12.)

  II. That the consequence of walking according to the flesh
is death. (V. 13.)

III. That the consequence of walking according to the Spirit is life and peace. (V. 13.)

IV. That we are now the sons of God. (V. 14–16.) The evidence of this is threefold:

1. That of our being led by the Spirit of God.

2. That of our having the Spirit of adoption.

3. That of the Spirit, as it testifies with our spirits that we are the children of God. This testimony is given in two ways.

(1) Directly, by and through the written word.

(2) Indirectly, by its effects and fruits in our hearts and lives. (Gal. v: 22.)

V. That we are also the heirs of God, if we faithfully endure sufferings with and for the sake of Christ. (V. 17.)

SECTION IV. *Encouragements to endure sufferings.*
(V. 18–39.)

I. The first of these is drawn from the consideration, that our present sufferings are nothing compared with the glory that awaits us. And in order to heighten and intensify this motive, the Apostle represents this whole Mundane system, as longing and sighing after the glorified state. (V. 18–25.)

II. The second ground of encouragement is drawn from the assistance that is given to us by the Holy Spirit. (V. 26, 27.)

III. From the *purposes* and fore-ordination of God, that all things must work together for the good of those that love him. (V. 28–30.)

IV. From the infinite love, and power, and goodness of God, that are all pledged for the security and final triumphs of his faithful and obedient children. (V. 31–39.)

CHAPTER III. GOD'S DEALINGS WITH THE JEWS AS A
PEOPLE. (ix—xi.)

SECTION I. *The scope of this section is to vindicate God's jus-*
tice and fidelity in rejecting Israel as a nation. (ix: 1–33.)

I. Paul begins the discussion with an expression of his
great sorrow and sympathy for the Jews. (V. 1–5.)
This he felt deeply for two reasons:

1. Because he was once in their condition, an enemy to
Christ and his cause. This was in Paul's estimation
the same as being accursed from God. (V. 3.)

2. Because of their former religious privileges: and their very
important agency and services in the work of redemption.

II. He shows contrary to an objection urged in iii: 3, that
their rejection implies no failure of God's promises to
Abraham respecting his seed, in such passages as Genesis xvii: 7. (V. 6–13.)

1. Because Abraham was the father of two families: the
first according to the flesh; and the second according to
the Spirit and promise of God.

2. That the promises referred to by the Jews, had reference
to the latter, and not to the former of these two families, is proved,

(1) By the rejection of Ishmael.

(2) By the rejection of Esau.

III. OBJECTION. Does not this imply that there is unrighteousness or partiality with God. (V. 14.)

IV. ANSWER. Certainly not. It only implies God's absolute sovereignty, and his right to deal with all sinners
as he wills. (V. 14–18.)

V. OBJECTION. This being the case, God should no longer
find fault: for on this hypothesis, all men are but passive instruments in his hands. (V. 19.)

23

VI. This objection Paul meets and refutes. (V. 19–29.)

1. By showing how very wicked and unbecoming such an objection is. (V. 20, 21.)

2. That God has always exercised his sovereignty in love, and with much forbearance toward even the wicked and undeserving. (V. 22–24.)

3. That the rejection of the Jews on account of their infidelity, and the calling of the Gentiles, had been long and clearly foretold by their own prophets. (V. 25–29.)

VII. The conclusion is therefore, that all who voluntarily accept of justification by faith are saved: and that all others are rejected. Here then is free agency, and here is accountability. (V. 30–33.)

VIII. REMARKS.

1. This whole discussion has reference to man simply as he is—a lost and fallen sinner.

2. All apparently arbitrary distinctions between Jews and Gentiles, had reference merely to certain *temporal* arrangements, designed for the good of *all*.

SECTION II. *The scope of this section is to show the ground on which the Israelites were rejected.* (x: 1–21.)

I. Paul again expresses his sympathy for the Jews. (V. 1.)

II. Their great error was their ignorance of God's scheme of justification by faith. (V. 2, 3.)

III. The end of the law with respect to justification is attainable only through Christ. (V. 4–13.)   For,

1. As has already been proved in the first Chapter of the Second Part, a compliance with the *legal* conditions of justification is impossible. (V. 5.)

2. But the conditions of the Gospel plan, are plain, simple, and accessible to all. (V. 6–13.)

IV. But hence follows the necessity of preaching the Gospel to all. (V. 14–17.)

V. IMPLIED OBJECTION. The Jews should not therefore be rejected nor condemned, until at least after they shall have heard the Gospel.

VI. True, says Paul; but they have already generally heard it

1. Through the preachers of the Gospel. (V. 18.)
2. Through their own prophets. (V. 19–21.)

SECTION III. *Israel's rejection is neither total nor final.* (xi: 1–36.)

I. It is not total. (V. 1–10.)

1. Because Paul himself and many other Jews were saved.
2. But their salvation was of grace.
3. The rest were blinded as their own prophets had predicted.

II. Their rejection is not final. (V. 11–32.) This is rendered probable from the following considerations:

1. Their rejection was for the benefit of the world. (V. 11.)
2. Their conversion would have a powerful influence for good on the whole Gentile world. (V. 12–15.)
3. As a part of them had been saved, it follows that all of them *may* be saved. (V. 16.)
4. This is rendered still more probable, on the ground of their *natural affinity* to the church. (V. 17–24.)
5. The Apostle closes his argument by assuring us, that in the fullness of time, the Israelites will generally be converted to Christ, and saved through him. (V. 25–32.)

III. *Conclusion of the whole argument.* How wonderfully are God's attributes and perfections displayed and illustrated in, and by, and through this Scheme of Redemption! (V. 33–36.)

PART III. EXHORTATIONS AND ENCOURAGEMENTS TO THE FAITHFUL DISCHARGE OF ALL OUR DUTIES. (xii—xv: 13.)

SECTION I. *Our duties to God and to the brotherhood.* (xii: 1–21.)

1. Exhortation to a full personal consecration of ourselves to God. (V. 1, 2.)
II. Exhortation to be humble, and to serve one another, as members of the *one body*. (V. 3–5.)
III. Exhortation to act diligently and faithfully in whatever position or capacity we can be most useful. (V. 6–8.)
IV. Exhortation to cherish certain social virtues, and to discharge faithfully sundry social duties. (V. 9–12.)

SECTION II. *Our duties to Society.* (xiii: 1–14.)

I. An exhortation to respect and obey civil magistrates. (V. 1–7.)
II. An exhortation to so love our neighbor, including our greatest enemies, as to fulfil the whole law. Thus Christians should live above the fear of punishment. (V. 8–10.)
III. An exhortation to higher degrees of holiness, and the prompt and faithful discharge of all the aforesaid social duties, drawn from the advanced period of our Christian life, and the near approach of the eternal day. (V. 11–13.)

SECTION III. *The duties and obligations of Christians to each other, in reference to matters that are in themselves neither right nor wrong; neither good nor evil.* (xix—xv: 13.)

I. The weak in faith should not be harshly condemned. (V. 1–12.)
1. Because *God* has accepted him. (V. 3.)
2. Because it is really not the right nor the prerogative of any one to do so. (V. 4, 10.)

3. Because the weak brother acts conscientiously out of respect to God. (V. 6.)

4. Because our relations and obligations to God, make the
right of private judgment necessary. (V. 7–12.)

II. The liberty of the Gospel should not be used to the injury of others. (V. 13–23.) This would be inconsistent

1. With the law of love. (V. 13–15.)

2. With the honor of religion. (V. 16.)

3. With the object of the Kingdom. (V. 17.)

4. With the duty of mutual edification. (V. 19.)

5. With the rights of conscience. (V. 22, 23.)

III. The duty of mutual forbearance, love, and Christian
unity, still further enforced and illustrated by the example of Christ and the teachings of the Old Testament.
(xv: 1–13.)

PART IV. CONCLUSION. (xv: 14—xvi.)

SECTION I. *Sundry personal matters.* (xv: 14–33.)

I. Paul's great confidence in the Roman brethren. (V. 14.)

II. His reason for writing to them so boldly. (V. 15, 16.)

III. His labors as an Apostle. (V. 17–21.)

IV. His purpose to visit them after his mission to Jerusalem. (V. 22–29.)

V. He requests their prayers in his behalf. (V. 30–32.)

VI. His benediction. (V. 33.)

SECTION II. *Sundry commendations, warnings, and
salutations.* (xvi: 1–27.)

I. Commendation of Phebe. (V. 1, 2.)

II. Salutations addressed to members of the Church of
Rome. (V. 3–16.)

III. Warnings against those who disturb the peace, and
unity, and harmony of the Church. (V. 17–20.)

IV. Salutations of Paul's companions, with his own repeated benediction. (V. 21–24.)

V. Doxology. (V. 25–27.)

CHAPTER V.

ANALYSIS OF THE EPISTLE TO THE HEBREWS.

GENERAL SCOPE.

The main object of Paul in this Epistle, is to persuade his Hebrew brethren in Christ, to persevere in their begun Christian course. For this purpose, he presents to them the many and great obligations they were under to Christ; the many encouragements they had to serve him; and the dreadful consequences of apostasy from him.

The chief danger of the Hebrew Christians arose from the seductive influence of Judaizing teachers. And hence it is, that throughout the whole epistle, there is kept up an almost constant contrast between Judaism and Christianity; and the infinite superiority of the latter, set forth and illustrated by a great variety of the most convincing and persuasive arguments.

SPECIAL ANALYSIS.

The whole epistle may be conveniently divided into the following chapters and subordinate sections:

CHAPTER I. *Motives drawn from the Divine nature, dignity and glory of Christ.* (i—ii: 4.)

In the development of this subject, the following points are made, and more or less fully illustrated:

1. The former revelations had been variously made through the Old Testament prophets, as God's ordinary ambassadors. But the revelation of the Gospel Scheme was made by his own Son. (V. 1.)
2. The Divine glory, and honor, and dignity of this Son. (V. 2, 3.)
3. Amplification of the same thought, by a comparison of Christ with angels. (V. 4–14.)
4. Conclusion from the premises submitted. (ii: 1–4.)

CHAPTER II. *Motives drawn from Christ's identity with us; and his labors, sufferings, and sympathies for us.* (ii: 5–18.)

The leading idea of this chapter, is Christ's *oneness* with us. And the reasons assigned for his assuming our nature are as follows:

1. That he might suffer death for every man. (V. 9.)
2. That he might become our Leader and Captain in the great work of restoring to ransomed man his lost dominion over this world. (V. 5–9.)
3. That he might destroy the works of the devil. (V. 14, 15. Compare 1 John iii: 8.)
4. That having been made perfect through sufferings, he might be better qualified to sympathize with us, and to succor and support us in all our trials and afflictions. (V. 10, 17, 18.)

CHAPTER III. *Motives drawn from the Apostleship of Christ, as the Author and Administrator of the New Institution.* (iii—iv : 13.)

In the discussion and development of this subject, the author draws sundry motives from the following sources:
1. From a comparison of Christ with Moses, the faithful Apostle of the Old Institution. (iii: 1–6.)

2. From a comparison of our pilgrimage under Christ with that of Israel under Moses. (V. 7–19.)
3. From the more perfect and glorious rest, enjoyed under Christ. (iv: 1–10.) ●
4. From the all-searching nature and character of the word of God, by which we are to be judged at the last day. (V. 11–13. See John xii: 48.)

CHAPTER IV. *Motives drawn from the nature and character of Christ's Priesthood.* (iv: 14—v: 10.)

1. From the exalted character, and availing sympathy and intercession of Christ for us, as our High-Priest. (iv: 14–16.)
2. From a further consideration of the same subject, illustrated by a comparison of Christ's priesthood with that of Aaron and Melchisedek. (V. 1–10.)

CHAPTER V. *A Digression,* consisting,

1. Of an admonition to the Hebrew brethren on account of their inexcusable ignorance. (V. 11–14.)
2. Of a warning to them, on account of their danger of apostatizing. (vi: 1–8.)
3. Of an encouragement, on the ground of God's fidelity. (V. 9–20.)

CHAPTER VI. *Motives derived from the superiority of Christ's Priesthood, compared with that of Aaron.* (vii—viii: 5.)

1. From the superiority of Melchisedek's priesthood over that of Aaron; and consequently the superiority of Christ's, which was to that of Melchisedek as the substance is to the shadow. (vii: 1–10.)
2. From the change that was made in the Aaronic or Levitical priesthood. (V. 11–19.)

3. From the oath of God, which was made only in reference to the priesthood of Christ. (V. 20–22.)

4. From the frequent changes in the Levitical priesthood caused by death. (V. 23–25.) From Aaron to Christ, there were sixty-seven High-Priests; and from Aaron to the destruction of Jerusalem, there were eighty-one.

5. From the superior dignity and moral excellence of Christ. (V. 26–28.)

6. Finally and chiefly from the fact that Christ is a High-Priest, not of a typical institution, but of the true Tabernacle. (viii: 1–5.)

CHAPTER VII. *Motives drawn from the superior nature and character of the New Covenant.* (viii: 6–13. Compare Jeremiah xxxi: 31–34.)

1. The New Covenant is faultless; the Old was faulty. (V. 7, 8.)

2. The Old Covenant was written on stone; but the New, on the understanding and the heart. (V. 10.)

3. The subjects of the Old Covenant were not necessarily pious; but all the subjects of the New Covenant must of necessity take Jehovah to be their God. (V. 10.)

4. Most of the subjects of the Old Covenant were introduced into it by a birth of flesh; and they had therefore to learn afterward even the name of God. But all the subjects of the New Covenant are received into it on the confession of their faith; and hence they must all know the Lord, from the least of them to the greatest. (V. 11.)

5. There was nothing in the Old Covenant that could really take away sins; and hence all the sins of the people were again remembered every year, on the day of atonement. But under the New Covenant, the sins of the Christian are remembered no more. (V. 12.)

6. The Old Covenant was abolished when Christ was crucified; but the New will continue while time endures.
(V. 13. See also Daniel ii : 44, and Hebrews xii : 28.)

CHAPTER VIII.—*Motives drawn from the superior offerings,
sacrifices, and services of the New Covenant.* (ix—x: 18.)

Under this head, the Apostle considers,

1. The structure and the arrangement of the Tabernacle and
its furniture. (V. 1–5.)
2. The services of the Tabernacle. (V. 6, 7.)
3. The inefficiency of these services. V. 8–10.)
4. The superiority of Christ's offering. (V. 11–13.) This
is proved chiefly from three considerations:
(1) It procures eternal redemption.
(2) It purifies the consciousness.
(3) It secures for those who accept of it, the eternal inheritance.
5. The necessity of Christ's death. (V. 16–24.) This is
shown and illustrated in two ways:
(1) By the case of a Testator. (V. 16, 17.)
(2) By the typical rites and ceremonies of the Old Covenant. (V. 18–24.)
6. The great contrast between *the one offering of Christ's own
blood*, and the *many* offerings of the blood of Jewish
victims. (V. 25, 26.)
7. The object of Christ's second coming. It will not, in all
respects, be like the reäppearance of the High-Priest
of the Old Covenant, who came out of the Most Holy
Place, merely to *repeat* the same order of things year
by year. Christ's second advent will be without a sin-
offering, to *judge* the world. He will come to bless his
saints; but to take vengeance on them that acknowledge
not God and that obey not the Gospel. (V. 27, 28.)

8. The inefficiency of the Legal sacrifices. They never took away the guilt of sin. They were but shadows; and could therefore procure but a typical and relative pardon. (x: 1–4.)
9. The great efficacy of the Sacrifice of Christ. It procures final pardon. (x: 5–18.)

CHAPTER IX.—*Motives drawn from the superior benefits, rights, honors, privileges, and relations of the subjects of the New Covenant.* (x: 19—ii.)

Under this chapter, we have given,
1. An exhortation to greater diligence in the worship and service of God, drawn from a consideration of the great benefits resulting from the death and intercession of Christ. (V. 19–25.)
2. Admonitions and warnings drawn from the awful consequences of apostasy; on the principle that wherever much is given, much is also required. (V. 26–31.)
3. Encouragements drawn from the previous patient endurance of the Hebrew Christians. (V. 32–34.)
4. Encouragements drawn from the near approach of their deliverance from existing evils. (V. 35–37.)
5. Encouragements drawn from the nature and sustaining influence of their faith. (V. 38, 39.)
(1) The great *subjective* power and influence of faith on the soul: it is the foundation of all our hopes, and the means by and through which we may even now enjoy to some extent the vast resources of the invisible universe. (xi: 1.)
(a) Some *general* illustrations of this important truth. (V. 2, 3.)
(b) Various *personal* illustrations of this. (V. 4–37.)
(2) The superior privileges and advantages of the Christian, with regard to the *object* of his faith. Christ the *promised* Savior has now actually come. (V. 38, 39.)

6. Exhortations and encouragements drawn from the contemplated presence and observation of a great multitude of victorious spectators. (xii: 1.)
7. Exhortation drawn from the example of Christ. (V. 2–4.)
8. From the design of all Divine chastisements. (V. 5–13.)
9. From the dangers and consequences of apostasy. (V. 14–17.)
10. From the greater and more encouraging privileges of the Christian dispensation. (V. 18–24.)
11. From the greater obligations that now rest on the subjects of the New Covenant. (V. 25–27.)
12. From the stability of Christ's Kingdom. (V. 28, 29.)

CHAPTER X.—*Exhortations to various practical duties.*
(xiii: 1–19.)

1. To continue in brotherly love. (V. 1.)
2. To be hospitable. (V. 2.)
3. To sympathize with those that are in bonds and afflictions. (V. 3.)
4. To be faithful in the marriage relation. (V. 4.)
5. To be content and confiding. (V. 5, 6.)
6. To imitate the fidelity of their teachers. (V. 7.)
7. To be stable in doctrine. (V. 8–15.)
8. To be benevolent. (V. 16.)
9. To submit to their rulers. (V. 17.)
10. To pray for the Apostle and his co-workers. (V. 18, 19.)

CHAPTER XI.—*Conclusion of the Epistle.* (V. 20–25.)

1. Benediction. (V. 20, 21.)
2. Admonition. (V. 22.)
3. Timothy's release. (V. 23.)
4. Salutations. (V. 24, 25.)

PART SIXTH.

THE LAST AND HIGHEST FUNCTION OF REASON.

The last and, perhaps I might say, the highest function of Reason in matters pertaining to Divine Revelation, is *to cordially and fully acquiesce in the fitness, the wisdom, and the correctness of whatever God has clearly revealed.* His authority is supreme. From it, there is no appeal. And hence to refuse to submit to it in any case, and under any circumstances, is most irrational and absurd.

If Reason is not fully satisfied with the entire chain of evidence, she may reëxamine it. She may, if she pleases, again consider each of the questions, Whether the Bible is the word of God: whether it is the pure word of God: whether it is the pure and inspired word of God: whether the Principles of interpretation are all founded in truth: and finally, she may examine and see with the most rigid and scrutinizing exactness, whether the Rules and Principles have all been correctly and judiciously applied in the course of the exegesis. But all these points having been found correct, and having been conceded, then indeed REASON HAS NO ALTERNATIVE LEFT BUT TO CORDIALLY AND FULLY ACQUIESCE IN THE TRUTHFULNESS AND PARAMOUNT AUTHORITY OF EVERY ORACLE THAT BEARS THE SEAL AND STAMP OF GOD'S OWN INSPIRATION.

(865)

We have no right to reject it on the ground that we can not comprehend it: or that we can not reconcile it with our preconceived notions and opinions. No sane man so reasons in any other department of knowledge, science, and literature. On the contrary, we all receive *as facts,* in other branches of learning, many things that we do not and that we can not comprehend. We believe, for instance, that the sun holds the earth in its orbit, and regulates its motions: but does any living astronomer profess to comprehend fully the philosophy of these phenomena? We believe, that food received into the stomach is converted into all the various cells and tissues of the body: but does any physiologist, however learned, presume to understand fully and perfectly these mysterious processes? We feel perfectly sure that the soul dwells within the body as its clay tabernacle: that it preserves it; moves it; gives tone, energy, beauty, and vitality to it: but has any metaphysician ever pretended to explain how it accomplishes all these results? These and ten thousand other phenomena equally mysterious are now received *as facts* by every man of ordinary intelligence: not because we fully understand them; but simply because no one can any longer reasonably doubt the evidence of their reality.

Whether Revelation may be rejected on the ground of its incomprehensibility.

Illustrations.

And just so it is with respect to many things contained in the Holy Bible. No philosopher can explain them: but even the child may, on the evidence submitted, believe and receive them as the real and veritable oracles of that Spirit which searches all things, yea even the deep counsels and purposes of Jehovah. Such, for instance, are the following:

The mysteries of Revelation are confessedly great and numerous.

1. The fact that God has existed from all eternity. (Genesis i: 1; Deut. xxxiii: 27; John i: 1, 2; Acts xv: 18.)

Illustrative examples.

2. The fact, that the Father, the Son, and the Holy Spirit are the One ever-living and true God. (John x: 30; xiv: 9–11; Acts v: 3, 4; Matthew xxviii: 19.)

3. The fact, that in the beginning, God created all things out of nothing. (Gen. i: 1; John i: 1–3.)

4. The fact that at the bidding of Joshua, he caused the sun and the moon to stand still; and that in the administration of his government, he has often from the beginning wrought many other miracles. (See, for instance, the inspired account that we have given of the mission of Moses and of Christ.)

5. The fact, that all persons are *by nature* (φυσει) the children of wrath. (Ephesians ii: 3.)

6. The fact, that by one act of disobedience, on the part of the first Adam, all men, including infants and idiots, have, without any agency on their part, been constituted *sinners;* (ἁμαρτωλοι κατεσταθησαν ὁι πολλοὶ). (Romans v: 19.)

7. The fact, that by one act of obedience on the part of the second Adam, the Lord of life and glory, all mankind, without exception, will, in like manner, be rendered *just,* so far as it respects the guilt of Adam's sin. (δικαιοι καταστα- θησονται ὁι πολλοὶ.) (Romans v: 19.)

8. The fact, that by and through the death and mediation of Christ, all men may be justified and saved from all their personal sins, on the conditions of faith and obedience prescribed in the Gospel. (Mark xvi: 16; Acts ii: 38; 2 Peter i: 5–11; 1 John i: 9.)

9. The fact, that the Holy Spirit really and truly dwells in the hearts of all the children of God. (John vii: 39; Acts ii: 38; Romans viii: 9–11; 1 Corinthians vi: 19; and Galatians iv: 6.)

10. The fact, that the spirits of the redeemed can, without their organs of sense, be in a state of conscious activity and enjoyment, while separated from their bodies, between their

death and the resurrection. (Luke xvi: 19–31; 2 Corinthians v: 1–10; Philippians i: 21–26; Revelations iv: 8—v: 10.)

11. The fact, that the disembodied spirits of the wicked are, during the same interval, in a state of misery and torment. (Luke xvi: 19–31; 1 Peter iii: 19.)

12. The fact, that the bodies of all, both old and young, both saints and sinners, will be raised from the dead and reünited to their spirits, forever and ever, by the omnipotent voice of our glorious and adorable Immanuel. (John v: 28, 29; 1 Corinthians xv; Revelations xx: 12–15.)

13. The fact, that after death and throughout eternal ages, there will be no change of *state* on the part of either the righteous or the wicked. As death leaves us, so will the judgment find us; and as the judgment leaves us, so will we ever be throughout the endless cycles of eternity. (Daniel xii: 13; Matthew xxv: 46; Luke xvi: 26; xx: 36; 1 Thessalonians iv: 17; Revelations xxii: 11.)

These and many other lessons clearly taught in the Holy

The foundation of our faith in all such matters.

Bible, are not *contrary* to Reason; but they are *above* Reason; that is, human Reason. Such knowledge is too high for us: too strange to be fully comprehended by finite mortals. We can understand them only in part; but the evidence on which they rest as the Oracles of God, is clear and satisfactory. This is enough. It places our faith just where it ought to rest; and indeed where all genuine faith must ever rest: ON THE INFALLIBLE AUTHORITY OF THE WORD OF GOD.

And hence we conclude that *the paramount duty of every*

Conclusion.

man is, first, to ascertain what God has revealed in his Holy Word: and secondly, to receive it and to obey it as the living voice of Jehovah.

O Lord, open thou our eyes and our hearts, that we may behold wondrous things out of thy Law.

PART SEVENTH.

SUPPLEMENTARY.

CHAPTER I.

THE BIBLE AS A MEANS OF EDUCATION.

"KNOWLEDGE is power," says Lord Bacon. And hence the more knowlédge a man has, other things being equal, the better he is prepared both to do good and to receive good. *A knowledge of all matters desirable.*

But no man can study every thing. For such a work, life is too short; and our capacities are too limited. And hence the necessity of being very select in our studies: of prosecuting merely such *Why this is not, at present, attainable.* branches of learning, as will best serve to fit and prepare us for the great ends and objects of life. A knowledge of the Chinese language, for example, may be of very great importance to a missionary or *The proper course for every student.* to an ambassador who expects to labor for some years among the citizens of the Celestial Empire; but it would not be of very much service to our Kentucky merchants, farmers, and mechanics. And just so it is with most other branches of secular learning. They are of great importance to some; and of but comparatively little consequence to others.

24 .

But there is one book that should be carefully, prayer-fully, and constantly studied by all men, what-ever may be their rank or their position in Society: I mean, of course, THE HOLY BIBLE. This follows of necessity from the chief end and object of life. We live in a wide world: a world in which there are a great many objects to be accomplished. And hence a di-vision of labor is necessary to success. Some men should cultivate the soil; some should engage in commercial pur-suits; some should attend to the civil wants and interests of society; and others again should act as the physicians and the educators of mankind. But there is one common calling to which all others are subordinate: one common object for which every man should labor from his cradle to his grave: and that is *to get such an education as will best qualify him to glorify God and to enjoy him forever.*

Reason why the Bible should be studied by all.

Without stopping to define just now what an education is, it may be conveniently regarded and consid-ered as a threefold process: viz., the acquiring process; the developing process; and the form-ative process; in all of which the study of the Bible is of paramount importance. This I will endeavor to show in the following sections.

Threefold pro-cess of educa-tion.

SECTION I.—THE ACQUIRING PROCESS.

This consists in the acquisition of useful knowledge: and especially of that knowledge that will best qual-ify us for all the great ends and purposes of our existence. In this department, the knowledge of God, the knowledge of man, and the knowlege of the way of life and happiness stand preëminent. So taught Confucius, Zoroaster, Thales, Pythago-

In what the Acquiring Pro-cess consists.

Opinions of ancient philos-ophers.

ras, Socrates, Plato, Aristotle, Zeno, Cato, Cicero, and nearly all of the most eminent of the ancient philoso- *Their failure to acquire this knowledge.* phers, as well as the Prophets and Apostles. And for the attainment of this knowledge, many of them labored with a zeal that is worthy of all commendation; but with very little success:

> "For self to self, and God to man revealed
> Are themes to Nature's eye forever sealed."

It was reserved for that Spirit that searches all things, yea even the deep counsels and purposes of Jehovah, to reveal to man these great mysteries. This it *Where and by whom revealed.* has done in the Holy Bible. Those things which were concealed from ancient sages, God has, in this wonderful volume, revealed unto babes. So that a child who now sits at the feet of Jesus, may really know vastly more of these sublime themes, than the greatest of naturalists: for they are spiritually discerned.

I know, the Heavens declare the glory of God; and the firmament showeth forth his handiwork. I am *Knowledge of God among the heathen.* well aware that all nature is, to the believer, but an expression of the infinite wisdom, and power, and goodness of God. But I am also aware, that it is a well-attested historical fact, that "the world by wisdom knew not God:" and that in nearly every place where the light of the Bible has not been enjoyed, Polytheism has been the popular belief.

And the same may be said in substance of man himself, and of the only possible efficient scheme of life *Their knowledge of man and of the Gospel.* and happiness. After all that has been learned from the light of nature, it is a well-known historical fact, that the origin of man; the present state and condition of man; and the destinies of man, are still mysteries to all who are without the knowledge of the Holy Scriptures.

And where in all the revelations of nature and the learned discussions of heathen philosophy, is the name of JESUS to be found? And where, save in and from the Bible, can we learn any thing of that SCHEME OF REDEMPTION of which he is the Author and the Finisher; and which is really the only scheme known under the whole heavens or given among men, whereby poor sinners may be saved and made heirs of immortality?! Manifestly, the knowledge of the Bible is of paramount importance to *every man*. This will become more and more evident as we proceed with the consideration of the two remaining elements of education.

SECTION II.—THE DEVELOPING PROCESS.

This consists in the full and perfect development of all the
In what the Developing Process consists. *powers and susceptibilities of man's entire nature, in harmony with their relations to each other, and also in harmony with all the relations that man himself sustains to the entire universe.*

To do this, it is necessary that every faculty be exercised
How this may be done. on its own corresponding and appropriate objects: that is, on objects suited to its own nature and capacity. The eye could never be developed without light; nor the ear without sound; nor the lungs without an atmosphere; nor the heart without purified blood. We must, then, in the first place, have an object divinely adapted to the development of each faculty: and in the second place, said faculty must be duly exercised on it, or by means of it.

But where shall we find objects corresponding with all the
These objects found partly in our College Curriculums. faculties of the human soul? Can they be found in the curriculum of studies that has been very generally adopted by our oldest and most influential Literary Institutions? No doubt many of them can. There is much in the Greek and Roman Classics; in the

science of Mathematics; in the department of Metaphysics; and in every branch of Natural Philosophy and Natural History, to improve the memory; to cultivate the taste; to expand the intellect; and to mature the judgment. But how much is there in all these to cultivate the heart; to educate our emotional nature; and especially to develop and to strengthen in due proportion our moral and religious powers and susceptibilities?

I am aware that almost every branch of science and literature has some tendency this way. I know that the morally beautiful is to be found in some of the poems of Homer and in the orations of Demosthenes and Cicero, as well as in every branch of Natural Science. But I also know, that in the whole created universe there is really nothing which in this respect is fully adequate *Their chief deficiency.* to meet and to satisfy all the wants of the human soul. The Earth finds an object of attraction in every planet, in every comet, in every star, and even in every particle of matter however small and however remote. But the Sun only has power to regulate its motions, and to preserve the harmony of our mundane system. And just so our hearts tend to cluster around ten thousand lovely and beautiful objects in both nature and art: but God himself is the only object in the wide universe that can fill the vast capacity of the human soul; that can satisfy all *The only satisfying portion of the human soul.* its desires after happiness; and that can properly excite, develop, strengthen, and regulate all its moral and religious powers and susceptibilities. And to attempt to accomplish all these ends in any other way and by any other means, is like attempting

"To satisfy the ocean with a drop;
To marry Immortality to Death:
And with the unsubstantial shade of time,
To fill the embrace of all eternity."

"My flesh and my heart fail," says the Psalmist, "but God is the strength of my heart and my portion forever."*

Every rational system of education, then, must begin and end with the study of God. It is not enough to teach our children that it is their *duty* to remember their Creator in the days of their youth.

The study of God an essential element in every system of education.

We must help them to do this. We must lead them to such views and conceptions of God, as will enable them to love him with all their hearts, and soul, and mind, and strength. In this way, and in this way only can we properly develop, cultivate, and educate their benevolent affections; and restore to LOVE its supremacy and empire in the government of the human soul.

But *how* may this be done? is now the great question. I say *now:* for there was a time when it was not a question; when the glory of God shone as directly and as naturally into the deep recesses of the human soul, as the rays of light now penetrate the lenses of the eye: when God and man spoke, face to face, as friend to friend.

Man's intercourse with God in Eden.

Then was the Golden Age of humanity. Then it was, that all the faculties of the human soul were duly and properly exercised on their own corresponding and appropriate objects: and man's whole nature was developed according to the most exact laws and principles of Divine harmony. The empire of Love was then supreme; and every other passion and emotion was kept in perfect subordination to this all-permeating and governing principle of the human soul.

Happy results and consequences of this union and communion.

But sin separated man from his Maker. It interposed a dark and thick cloud between the parties. God no longer appeared to man in his true character. His glory was obscured; and the Divine love-

Effects and consequences of sin.

*Psalms lxxiii: 26.

liness of his whole nature was perverted through the influence of a false medium.   There was no longer an object adequate to the proper development and discipline of man's moral and religious faculties.   Love was no longer duly and properly exercised.   It became, as a consequence, weak and powerless.   And selfishness—supreme selfishness, stimulated and excited by ambition, envy, jealousy, hatred, and revenge, took possession of the human heart!

It is chiefly owing to man's having fallen into this preternatural condition, that his education has become *Present difficulty of educating mankind.* a problem of so much difficulty.   Even under the most favorable circumstances, the full, perfect, and harmonious development of all the powers and susceptibilities of the human soul, would have been a question worthy of the most exalted genius.   Who, then, is now sufficient for these things, since human nature has become a wreck by sin?   Since all its passions have been preternaturally excited?   Since the heart itself has become more like a Hydra, pouring out its venom from a thousand serpentine heads, than like that Divine image in which it was originally created? and since the great source of all moral light and moral influence has been veiled from the eyes of mortals?!

No wonder that, under such circumstances, the whole heathen world has been so badly educated.   No *Practical evidences of this.* wonder, that the most favored and enlightened nations of antiquity, degenerated even under the instruction of a Socrates, a Plato, an Aristotle, and a Cicero.   No wonder that woman has been enslaved; and that the world has been so long governed by a set of intellectually-educated, but heartless monsters.   The light and heat of the Divine effulgence, are just as necessary to the development and proper education of the human heart, as are the rays of the Sun to the healthful and perfect development of the rose, the lily, or the pink. Without them, no fallen son or daughter of humanity, was ever yet properly educated, and from the nature of the case, as it now stands, it is utterly impossible that any one ever can be.

What, then, was to be done for man—fallen as he was

Man's educa-
tion not to be
abandoned. from his primitive glory? Must he forever remain uneducated? Must the Godlike powers of his moral nature remain forever undeveloped for want of some proper object on which they might be exercised? This was not consistent with either the will or the purposes of God concerning man.

Shall the veil, then, be removed? Shall the unclouded

Nor the full-
orbed glories
of the Divine
splendor to be
enjoyed. splendors of the Divine glory be again allowed to shine forth with all their dazzling brilliancy into the dark, cold, and chilly recesses of the human soul? Impossible. This would have been inconsistent with both the glory of God and the happiness of man. "Thou canst not see my face; for there shall no one see me and live,"* was the reply of Jehovah to one of the meekest, the holiest, and the best of men.

The case of man was therefore most peculiar. The eyes of his understanding were diseased. The retina of his moral vision had become morbidly sensitive. He was not in a condition to bear the full and open blaze of God's glory; and yet he really needed more of such Divine influences on his soul, than he had ever felt even in the groves and bowers of Eden. The problem was therefore one of extreme difficulty.

But nothing is too hard for the Almighty: nothing is too

Solution of the
Problem. profound for infinite wisdom. And the question was therefore finally solved, no doubt to the entire satisfaction and profound astonishment of all the higher created intelligences. The awful majesty of Jehovah was concealed; and those rays of glory which reflected most of

---

* Exodus xxxiii: 20.

his love, and his mercy, and his benevolence, and his philanthropy, were concentrated and brought to a focus of tran-
scendental power, in the person of Jesus of Nazareth, our
Immanuel, and the Divine Shekinah of the New Institution. Thence they were, by the Holy Spirit, reflected and
transmitted to the sacred pages of the Holy Bible: so that
looking into it, we can now, with open face, behold as in a
mirror, the glory of the Lord; until under its transforming
influence, we are changed from glory to glory even as by the
Spirit of the Lord.*

The Bible, then, is in this respect a substitute for the more
direct original displays of God's glory. It contains the only manifestation of his philanthropy, The Bible is
that is at all adequate to eradicate the selfishness therefore essential to our spir-
and deep-rooted enmity of the human heart; and itual development.
to enable us to love Him who first loved us.† And hence it
follows, that the study of the Holy Scriptures, is just as necessary to the proper and rational development of the human
soul, in harmony with its relations to the universe, as food is
to the healthful development of the body; and as the rains,
dews, and sunshine of heaven, are to the growth and fra-
grance of the rose of Sharon and the lily of the valley.

Whether, then, the Bible should be taught and studied in
our families, our Sunday-schools, our common It should be
schools, our academies, our female seminaries, made a Text-
Book in every
our colleges and our universities, as a means of department of
moral discipline and spiritual development, is education.
not a question of mere expediency or metaphysical specula-
tion. It is not a matter of mere Protestant, Catholic, or
Jewish prejudice. It is a question which has its origin in
the wants and deep-seated principles of the human soul: and
which involves man's highest interests for time and for eternity.

* 2 Corinthians iii: 18.   † Colossians i: 20–22, and 1 John iv: 19.

And hence no other Divine precept was ever expressed
Divine direc-
tions on this
subject. with more point, emphasis, and particularity,
than that which expresses and enforces the duty
of training and educating our children in the
very words, and through the instrumentality of the Living
Oracles. *"These words which I command thee this day,"*
said God to his ancient people, *"shall be in thine heart; and
thou shalt diligently teach them to thy children; and shalt talk
of them when thou sittest in thy house, and when thou walkest
by the way, when thou liest down and when thou risest up.
And thou shalt bind them for a sign on thy hand; and they
shall be as frontlets between thine eyes.   And thou shalt write
them on the posts of thy house, and on thy gates."* *

SECTION III.—The Formative Process.

This consists in the formation of such HABITS *of thought,*
In what the
Formative Pro-
cess consists. *and feeling, and action, as are essential to the
perfection of our own character; and as will best
enable us to discharge with facility and pleasure,
all the duties and obligations that we owe to God and to society.*

It is of course very closely connected with the developing
It is simulta-
neous with the
Acquiring and
Developing
Processes. process.   Indeed, it is only in theory that we
can separate them.   While our latent powers,
energies, and susceptibilities are being brought
out from the deep recesses of our being, by each
one's being exercised on its own appropriate objects, they
all, at the same time, receive a particular cast: they are, as
it were, molded in the types of the educator.   They are
either brought into a state of more active and sympathetic
harmony; or they are perverted, and peradventure even
crushed beneath the fetters of the most tyrannical, inexorable, and oppressive despotism.

---

*Deuteronomy vi: 6–9.

This is so very obvious, that it scarcely needs any illustration. It is a matter of daily consciousness, with *Formation of habits.* every youth, that the performance of any one action, begets in his system, an increased facility for its repetition. This again strengthens the same tendency: and so on, till a corresponding *habit* is formed. We all know with what fear and trembling we made our first essay *Illustration.* in the simple art of chirography. To form even the first letter in the alphabet, required, at that time, a very considerable effort. But now, since a habit has been formed, we make it almost unconsciously: provided, however, that our chirographic organs have received the *proper* training and discipline.

This is a very simple and familiar illustration of the force and power of habit, over all the faculties of the *The very plastic nature of the infant mind.* body, soul, and spirit of man. So plastic, indeed, is the infant constitution, that it, may be easily cast into almost any mold whatever. I do not of course by this remark, intend to indorse the very absurd dogma, that "Man is a mere creature of circumstances." Certainly not. Such a hypothesis has no foundation whatever in fact. There is evidently in the mind of every man, a *natural* affinity for truth; just as there is in his body, a natural tendency to assume the upright position. But we all know that the human frame has, in its infancy, been distorted into a thousand hideous forms: and we are just as painfully conscious, that the infant mind has, as often, been cast into false systems of politics, philosophy, morality, and religion. The present chart of the civilized world is a melancholy illustration of this fact.

How exceedingly important, then, it is, that *Importance of conducting this process properly, and by the use of the proper means* during the process of education, all the faculties of every youth, should not only be fully developed, but also so molded, trained, and disciplined in the truth, as to form *habits* in har-

mony with his own nature and with all the relations that he
sustains to the entire universe.   This is a matter on which
there is no room for exaggeration.   Here it is, that all the
powers and resources of language become utterly bankrupt;
and every attempt at hyperbole, falls far short of expressing
the simple, eternal realities and consequences that are involved in the education of every son and daughter of our
fallen race.

Here, then, the study of the Bible again becomes a matter
of infinite importance to every man.   He who
made man, and who knows what is in man, made
the Bible also for man; and especially for his intellectual, moral, and religious discipline.   Of course, then, it
is perfectly adapted to this end.   And all that is now wanting is simply this, that it be properly used as a book of instruction, correction, and discipline by all parents and other
educators of youth.   Let this be done, and soon

The study of
the Bible essen-
tial in this pro-
cess.

"The wolf also shall dwell with the lamb,
    And the leopard shall lie down with the kid;
    And the calf, and the young lion, and the fatling together;
        And a little child shall lead them.
    And the cow and the bear shall feed;
    Their young ones shall lie down together:
    And the lion shall eat straw like the ox.
And the sucking child shall play on the hole of the asp,
And the weaned child shall put his hand on the cocka-
    trice's den.
They shall not hurt nor destroy in all my holy mountain:
FOR THE EARTH SHALL BE FULL OF THE KNOWLEDGE
    OF THE LORD,
AS THE WATERS COVER THE SEA."   (Isaiah xi: 7–9.)

Happy results
and conse-
quences of its
proper use.

CHAPTER II.

QUALIFICATIONS OF THE BIBLE STUDENT.

OUR next theme is the necessary and proper Qualifications of the Bible student. These may be conveniently considered under three heads: viz., the Intellectual, the Moral, and the Literary.

Three kinds of qualifications pertaining to the Bible student.

SECTION I.—INTELLECTUAL QUALIFICATIONS.

I will omit, in this discussion, the consideration of the distinct elementary faculties: such as Perception, Memory, Imagination, Judgment, and Intuition: and merely say a few words on those *happy combinations of these faculties,* and *those peculiar habits of mind,* that most serve to qualify the student of the Bible for a correct and practical understanding of the Sacred Volume. These may perhaps be all generically comprehended under what we usually call GOOD COMMON SENSE.

In what these chiefly consist.

But what is Good Common Sense? This is not strictly a fixed quantity, as a mathematician would say. It admits of some variations, according to circumstances. But I presume, that it will always be found, on analysis, to comprehend two very different powers and capacities of the understanding. *The first of these is intellectual acumen;* or the power to discriminate between things that differ. And *the second is intellectual expansion;*

Two elements of common sense.

or the power to comprehend all the parts and elements of one united whole in their true and proper relations to each other. An excess or deficiency of either of these elements is apt to unbalance the mind and lead to error.

These, then, are the two intellectual qualifications that

Two things necessary in order to understand the Bible.

should be most earnestly sought for by every student of the Holy Scriptures. The Bible, if comprehended at all, must be understood; first, with respect to its elements; and secondly, with respect to the one grand and comprehensive scheme of redemption which pervades the whole volume, and extends from its alpha to its omega. Those who fail at either of these points, can never be safe interpreters of the Living Oracles.

SECTION II.—Moral Qualifications.

The first of these is a profound reverence for the Bible. We

First Moral Qualification.

should never separate God from his word: but in all cases, and under all circumstances, we should approach the Bible as we would approach its Divine Author. To read it as we read a heathen classic, is of but little use; perhaps often an injury.

The second moral qualification of the Bible student is an

Second Moral Qualification.

honest and sincere desire to know the truth. It is not enough to go to the Bible for proof-texts. We must go to it for the truth, at all risks and at all hazards. This may indeed sometimes prove ruinous to our preconceived systems of philosophy and theology: but be it so.

This desire should also be accompanied with an honest pur-

Third Qualification.

pose and determination to obey the truth. Otherwise, the study of the Bible may only serve to blunt the sensibilities, and to harden the moral and religious affections. Such is often the case with the man who is accustomed to witness the effects of poverty and distress, without making any effort to relieve them. And hence Christ says: *"If any man will do his (God's) will, he shall know of the doctrine, whether it be of God or whether I speak of myself."** We should, then, tremble, when we feel ourselves in any measure disposed to trifle with any of God's commandments.

SECTION III.—LITERARY QUALIFICATIONS.

These are very numerous and various. For although the Bible is, in some respects, one of the most simple and intelligible of all books, it is, in other respects, the most profound volume that was ever written. And hence it really requires more learning to understand the Bible *perfectly* than to understand any other book extant. And consequently the man who has the most knowledge, other things being equal, is always best qualified to understand and interpret the Living Oracles.

Amount of learning necessary to understand the Bible.

But, nevertheless, there are certainly some branches of science and literature that are of *special* importance to every man who desires to understand for himself the Holy Bible. Such, for instance, are the following:

Branches of most importance.

I. *A thorough knowledge of his own vernacular.* This is absolutely necessary in order to carry on successfully any train of thought whatever. We may *think* as the infant must think without language: but we can never reason without it. And unless we become master of it, it is very apt to become master of us. The literature of the world is full of illustrations on this point.

A knowledge of one's own vernacular.

II. *A critical knowledge of the original Greek and Hebrew* will be of great service to the student of the Holy Bible, in several ways.

A knowledge of Greek and Hebrew.

*John vii: 17.

1. It will enable him to understand the *meaning* of many obscure passages. *E. g.:* In Mark xvi: 15, Christ said to his Apostles: "Go into all the world and preach (κηρυξατε) the Gospel to every creature." And in Acts viii: 4: "They that were scattered abroad (on account of the persecution) went every-where preaching (ευαγγελιζομενοι) the word." Κηρυσσω means to preach or to proclaim by authority; and ευαγγελιζω means simply to announce or proclaim good news.

2. It will greatly assist him in comprehending the *beauties* of many portions of the Bible. *E. g.:* In Psalm c: 1, we have this exhortation: "Make a joyful noise unto the Lord, all ye lands." This is certainly very beautiful; but not so beautiful as the original is to the Hebrew ear. Every Hebrew scholar sees at once in the word הָרִיעוּ (R. רִיעַ, to make a loud noise) an allusion to the sounding of the Jubilee trumpet.

Another very good illustration occurs in 2 Peter i: 5: "Besides this," says the Apostle, "giving all diligence, *add* to your faith, virtue; and to virtue, knowledge," etc. Here the word used for *add* is not προστιθημι or επιφερω, but επιχορηγεω, to *furnish besides or in addition*, from επι, *on*, and χορηγος, a chorus-leader: and this again from, χορος, *a dance*, and αγω, *to lead*. In the use of this word, then, the Greek scholar at once recognizes an allusion to the ancient Drama, in which the χορηγος, or chorus-leader, led the way, taking by the hand the next in order; the second in like manner led the third; the third, the fourth; and so on, until the entire chorus appeared on the stage.

3. It will greatly strengthen his faith, and give him a becoming confidence in the correctness of his own conclusions. This is no doubt the common experience of all critical students of the original Greek and Hebrew Scriptures.

III. *A general knowledge of history.* This will greatly General History. assist him in understanding many portions of the Sacred Scriptures; particularly the prophecies: and at the same time furnish him with a fund of the most simple and appropriate illustrations.

IV. *A knowledge of Ancient Geography.* This will assist the Bible student in fixing the locality of events. Ancient And besides it is well to remember, that no other Geography. class of names are more liable to vary in the extent of their meaning. The word *Asia,* for instance, in the days of Homer, referred only to a very small district in the south-west portion of Asia Minor; in the time of Paul, it embraced the entire western part of Asia Minor, of which Ephesus was the capital; and now it is applied to a continent. The words *Europe, Africa,* and many other geographical terms, have passed through similar changes. And hence in any given case, it is necessary to understand the *historical* meaning of such words.

V. *A knowledge of the different systems of Chronology is also essential to a correct understanding of many* Ancient sys- *portions of the Holy Scriptures.* It would puzzle tems of Chro- an American, for instance, without any knowl- nology. edge of Jewish Chronology, to understand how it was that *"the early rain"* could fall about the first of November; and *"the latter rain,"* about the middle of March. But when he is informed that the civil year of the Jews commenced about the autumnal equinox, the mystery is solved.

VI. *A knowledge of Archæology or of Sacred and Profane Antiquities.* This will very greatly assist the Archæology. student in understanding the many *references* and *allusions* that are made by the Sacred writers. *E. g.*: In Matthew v: 21, 22, there is an allusion to the inferior courts, composed in the time of Josephus of seven judges; to the Sanhedrim, composed of seventy judges, besides the High-Priest and his deputy; and also to a still higher tribunal. For at that time, the Sanhedrim had no power to put any man to death. (John xviii: 31.) In Hebrews xii: 1, Paul refers to the Grecian foot-races.

25

VII. *A knowledge of Mental Science.* This will be of
Mental Philos-
ophy.
service to the student in many ways: and especially in the study of man's powers, capacities,
and responsibilities; and the secret springs and workings of
the human heart.

VIII. The last subject that I shall name for the present,
Physical Sci-
ences.
is *a knowledge of the Physical Sciences and of
God's physical government.* If God is the Author of both Nature and Revelation, it is reasonable to suppose that these two volumes would mutually serve to explain
and to illustrate each other. And such we find to be the case
in fact. The points of resemblance and analogy that exist
between these two expressions of the Divine will and character, are just as full and complete as the nature of the case
and the subjects will permit. (See Butler's Analogy.)

CHAPTER III.

HELLENISTIC GREEK.

SECTION I.—Its History.

About a century before the beginning of the Christian
Decline and
death of the
Hebrew Lan-
guage.
Era, the Hebrew ceased to be a living language.
Indeed, from the time of the captivity, the *common people* seem to have rapidly changed their
own vernacular for the Chaldee (Nehemiah vii: 8); though
the Hebrew was certainly used by the *learned,* especially in
writing, till after the time of the Maccabees.

But about one hundred years before Christ, the Hebrew
The Jews' ver-
nacular in the
time of Christ.
was wholly superseded, both in speech and in
writing, by that corrupt Aramæan dialect, com-

monly called the Syro-Chaldaic. This was therefore the vernacular dialect of both Christ and his Apostles.

Why, then, was not this new dialect of the old Hebrew, made the medium of communicating to the world, the Gospel of our Lord and Savior Jesus Christ? The testimony of the Fathers is full and explicit to this effect: that all the writers of the New Testament wrote in Greek, *The New Testament written in Greek.* with perhaps the exception of Matthew. He seems to have written in both the Aramæan and the Greek: first, in the Aramæan, for the sake of his Hebrew brethren in Palestine; and afterward in Greek, for the benefit of his Hellenistic brethren who were scattered abroad. But why was this? Why did God prefer the Greek to the vernacular of Christ and his Apostles in giving to mankind a revelation of his will and his purposes of mercy? Chiefly, I presume, for two reasons: *Reasons for this.*

1. Because the Greek was in all respects a more perfect language than the Aramæan.

2. Because, through the conquests of Alexander the Great, and the constant intercourse between the Greeks and the Romans, the Greek language had, for about three hundred years, been the common medium of communication throughout the whole civilized world.

But the Greek of which I now speak, was not the Greek of Plato and Demosthenes. By the conquests *Origin of the Common or Hellenic Dialect.* of Alexander the Great, the hitherto independent States of Greece were all fused into *one empire.* And as a consequence, their various dialects were all fused into one Common or Hellenic Dialect ($\dot{\eta}$ $\varkappa o\iota\nu\eta$ or $\dot{\eta}$ $'E\lambda\lambda\eta\nu\iota\varkappa\eta$ $\delta\iota\alpha\lambda\varepsilon\varkappa\tau o\varsigma$); having for its basis the ancient Attic; but being, at the same time, very greatly modified by the Ionic and the Æolic; and even still more by the Doric, which was the prevailing dialect of Macedonia.

Out of this Common Dialect was formed, at an early

period of its history, by and through Hebrew and Aramæan influence, that variety of the language, which since the time of Scaliger (1550), has been generally known as Hellenistic Greek; *i. e.*, the Greek spoken and written by those who were, by birth, Jews or Israelites. The purest specimens of this dialect now extant are found in the Septuagint, the Apocrypha, and the New Testament. It is distinguished by many peculiarities; the most important of which, I will briefly notice in the next section.*

Origin of Hellenistic Greek.

SECTION II.—CHARACTERISTICS OF HELLENISTIC GREEK.

Characteristics of Hellenistic Greek:

The chief peculiarities of Hellenistic Greek may be briefly summed up as follows:

Transferred words and phrases.

I. *It contains many words and phrases, which are never found in the classic authors.* E. g.:

1. Αββα, *father;* Chal. אַבָּא; Heb. אָב. (Mark xiv: 36; Romans viii: 15; Galatians iv: 6.)

2. Αβαδδων, Heb. אֲבַדּוֹן, *destruction,* (Revelation ix: 11;) Greek απολλυων. The usual word for *destroyer* in Hebrew is מַשְׁחִית, Sept. ὁ ολοθρευων. (Exodus xii: 23.)

3. Αμην, Heb. אָמֵן; properly an adjective, *true, faithful:* also as an adverb, *truly.*

4. Αχελδαμα, Aramæan חֲקַל, *a field,* and דְּמָא, *blood.* (Acts i: 19.)

5. Αρμαγεδδων, *Armageddon,* Heb. הַר, *a mountain,* and מְגִדּוֹ, *Megiddo.* (Revelations xvi: 16.)

6. Βηθεσδα, *Bethesda,* Aram. בֵּית, *house,* and חִסְדָּא, *mercy.* (John v: 2.)

7. Βηθανια, *Bethany;* Heb. בֵּית, *a house,* and הִינִי, *dates.*

8. Παραδεισος, *Paradise;* Heb. פֻּרְדֵּם from the Sanscrit *paredeca, a pleasure garden.*

* For a full discussion of these matters, see Winer's Grammar of the New Testament Diction.

9. Γεεννα, *Gehenna*, Heb. גַּיְא, *a valley*, and הִנֹּם, *Hinnom:* used as a symbol of Hell. (Matthew v: 22.)

10. Σατανας or σαταν, *Satan;* Heb. שָׂטָן, *an adversary;* Gr. ὁ διαβολος.

All such words are mere Oriental terms in Greek letters. And hence their meaning must be sought for, not in the Greek, but in the language or dialect from which they are taken.

II. *The second characteristic of Hellenistic Greek consists in the use of many words and phrases of Greek origin;* Greek words *but which are, nevertheless, used in a sense that is* used in a Hebrew or Christian sense. *either wholly or partially different from that which* *was usually given to them by profane writers* E. g.:

1. Ἑις, *one*, in the sense of τις or πρωτος; like the Heb. אֶחָד (Genesis i: 5.) Thus in Matthew viii: 19, we have ἑις γραμματευς, *one scribe*, for τις γραμματευς, *a certain scribe*.

2. Πασα σαρξ, *all flesh*. In classic Greek this means simply *"the whole flesh"* of a man or an animal, as the case may be. But in Hellenistic Greek it means *all mankind*. (Acts ii: 17.) Heb. כָּל־בָּשָׂר.

3. So οὐ πασα σαρξ, Heb. לֹא כָל־בָּשָׂר, means *"no flesh;"* no part of mankind. (Matthew xxiv: 22; 1 Corinthians i: 29.) The negative particle, in such cases, qualifies the *verb* and not the adjective. Hence the phrase in 1 John ii: 19, ὁτι ουχ εισι παντες εξ ἡμων, should be translated *"that none of them are of us."*

4. Ἁιμα εχχειν, *to pour out blood*. In classic Greek, this means simply *" to shed blood:"* but in Hellenistic Greek, it means, *"to kill"* or *"to put to death."* The reason of this is found in the Jewish sacrificial formula שָׁפַךְ דָּם, Sept. ἁιμα εχχει; because to shed the blood of a victim for sacrifice was equivalent to taking its life.

5. The word ὄνομα, *name*, is more expressive in Hellenistic Greek than it is in either the Hellenic or the classic.

In the latter it was a mere arbitrary *sign* of the person so designated. But in the former, it was also expressive of the attributes and characteristics of the person referred to. And hence in Hebrew and Hellenistic Greek the words שֵׁם and ὄνομα (*name*) are each made equivalent to the person which it represents. The expression, "Calling on the *name* of the Lord" is equivalent to calling on the Lord himself.

6. The word σκανδαλον is used in Hellenic Greek for the older classic form σκανδαληθρον to denote the stick in a trap to which the bait is fastened: *i. e.*, the trap-spring. But in the Septuagint, it is used for מִכְשׁוֹל, *an offense, a snare, a stumbling-block*. And hence in the New Testament, σκανδαλιζω means *to stumble*, or *to cause to stumble*.

7. The word σπλαγχνα in Hellenic and classic Greek, means simply the intestines. But in Hellenistic Greek, it is used for the Hebrew word רַחֲמִים, *bowels, mercies, affections;* from רחם, *to love*.

In all such cases, we must go to the Hebrew and not to the Greek for the meaning.

III. *The chief and most important characteristic of Hellen-*
A leaning and approximation to the Hebrew construction. *istic Greek, consists in a marked and sensible approximation or leaning to the Hebrew style and construction, whenever the Hebrew idiom differs from that of the Greek.* This may be seen in such cases as the following:

1. In the frequent use of prepositions to express what the Greeks were wont to express simply by means of cases. *E. g.*, ἀθωος απο του αἱματος for ἀθωος του αἱματος, *I am innocent of the blood.* (Matthew xxvii: 24.) Ὁμολογησω εν αυτῳ for ὁμολογησω αυτῳ, "*I will confess him.*" (Matthew x: 32.) The cause of this difference is, that the Hebrews had no case-endings: and hence they were compelled to resort more frequently than

the Greeks to the use of prepositions, in order to express clearly the relations of words to each other.

2. In the use of fewer conjunctions. In both the Septuagint and the New Testament *και* is often used Paucity of for *αλλα, καιπερ* or *καιτοι* : and *γαρ* or *ουν* is used Conjunctions. for *επει,* *ὡστε,* or *ὁτι.* This again is owing to the Hebrew custom of expressing many relations by the same conjunction.

3. In the use of nouns for adjectives. *E. g.: Sons of God* for *godly men; sons of Belial* for *wicked men;* Nouns for *newness of life* for *a new life.* Adjectives.

4. In the frequent use of the possessive case of Personal Pronouns instead of the Possessive Adjective Genitive case Pronouns. *E. g., σου* for *σος, ση, σον; μου* or of Personal *εμου* for *εμος, εμη, εμον; αὐτου* or *αὐτης* for *ὁς* or Pronouns. *ἑος, ἡ, ὁν; ἡμων* for *ἡμετερος; ὑμων* for *ὑμετερος; αὐτων* for *σφος* or *σφετερος.* This arises from the Jewish habit of using personal suffixes.

5. In the use of the Personal Pronoun after the Relative to express more particularly its person, num- Personal Pro- ber, and gender. The Hebrews had but one noun after the Relative Pronoun; and it was indeclinable. And Relative. hence the necessity of expressing its person, number, and gender by an additional Personal Pronoun. This construction occurs very frequently in the Septuagint, and occasionally in the New Testament. *E. g., ἡ γη εφ' ἡς συ κατοικεις επ' αυτης,* "the land whereon thou liest, *upon it.*" (Genesis xxviii : 23.) *Οὑ τῷ μώλωπι αὐτου ἰάθητε,* by whose stripes of him ye were healed.

6. In the uses of the tenses of verbs. The Hebrews had but two tenses: the Preterite and the Future. Tenses of verbs. And they had no Potential, Optative, or Subjunctive mood. All that the Greeks expressed by these moods, the Hebrews attempted to express by their Future tense; generally lengthened in the first person, and short-

ened in the second and third. And hence it is, that in Hellenistic Greek, the Future Indicative is often put for any tense of the Optative, Potential, or Subjunctive mood. *E. g.*: In Matthew xii: 31, 32, it is said: πασα ἁμαρτια και βλασφημια αφεθησεται τοις ανθρωποις, κ. τ. λ. Here the Future Indicative passive of the verb ἀφιημι is evidently used for the Present Potential. The meaning is, "All sin and blasphemy *may be* forgiven men." In Romans vi: 5, the Future Indicative εσομεθα is put for the Imperfect Optative ἐίημεν. The meaning is, "We *should be* in the likeness of his resurrection."

7. In the use of the Nominative Case Absolute instead of any other case, after the government has been once clearly indicated in a preceding word or clause. *E. g.*, ἐις τον τοπον τον πονηρον τοπον· τοπος ὀυ ὀυ σπειρεται. "Into this place, this evil place: a place where seed is not sown." (Numbers xx: 5.) Και το ὄρος εκαιετο πυρι εως του ὀυρανου, σκοτος, γνοφος, θυελλα. "And the mountain burned with fire, even to the midst of heaven: (*with*) darkness, and a black cloud, and a tempest." (Deuteronomy iv: 11.) These are not solecisms but Hebraisms. By this construction, great emphasis is given to the words put in the Nominative Case Absolute.

Nominative Case Absolute.

From the preceding examples, then, it is evident that we have given in the New Testament, three distinct elements, viz., the Greek, the Hebrew, and the Christian. The words and letters are Greek; the idiom is a mixture of the Greek and Hebrew; and the thoughts are Christian.

Three elements of the New Testament.

CHAPTER IV.

FAITH AND INFIDELITY.

SECTION I.—FAITH.

" For with the HEART, *man believeth unto righteousness."* (Romans x: 10.)

THERE is, perhaps, no truth more fully illustrated in the whole Bible, than that God requires every man to do something, as a test of his loyalty, and also as a condition of *enjoying* that salvation which Christ has purchased with his own blood. Almost every page of the Living Oracles contains some precept that is to be obeyed, in order to the enjoyment of some blessing that is promised. Even in Eden, Adam was required to abstain from the fruit of the Tree of Knowledge, as a condition of his having free and continued access to the Tree of Life. So, too, were the Israelites in the wilderness required to be obedient in all things, as a condition of their entering the Promised Land. And, in like manner, Christ offers rest to all who are weary and heavy-laden, on condition that they come to him; take his yoke upon them; and continue to learn of him.*

Blessings promised conditionally.

What these terms and conditions of enjoyment are, can, of course, be learned only from the Holy Bible. It is the only revelation that God has ever made to fallen man, on the subject of his salvation

The conditions of salvation, revealed only in the Bible.

* Matthew xi: 28–30.

from sin. On this point, nature is a perfect blank; and all human philosophy is as silent as the grave. And hence it follows, that to the Bible, and the Bible alone, we must ever look for all the terms and conditions on which life and immortality have been offered to guilty man.

Some of these are in their nature and character, *positive*:

Two kinds of stipulated conditions: the Positive, and the Natural or Moral.

that is, they depend wholly on God's *legislative* appointments; and may therefore be changed, by Divine authority, according to circumstances. The offering of sacrifices, for example, was, for many years, made the duty of every patriarch. He was required to offer frequently bleeding victims both for himself and for his family. But the law of Moses restricted this privilege to the house of Aaron. None but the priests, under the Sinaic covenant, could legally officiate at the altar.* And since the advent of the Messiah, the legal custom of offering animal sacrifices has been wholly abolished. Spiritual sacrifices are the only kind that is now required.†

Other conditions are immutable. They are founded on God's *creative* appointments and arrangements: they depend on the nature of things and on the moral relations that man sustains to his Creator: and they are therefore essentially the same in all ages and under all circumstances. *Faith* is

Faith, a natural and essential condition.

one of these natural and essential conditions. And hence it has always been required as a condition and means of salvation. It was required in the Patriarchal Age; it was required in the Jewish Age; and it is still required in the Christian Age. And so it ever must and it ever will be required of all who would enjoy the great salvation. "For he that comes to God *must believe* that he is; and that he is the rewarder of them that diligently seek him."‡

* Numbers iii: 10 and xviii: 3.   ‡ Hebrews xi: 6.
† 1 Peter ii: 5.

But it is important to observe just here, that God never requires of any man, what is impossible. If he requires us to behold his glory in the firmament, it is because he has given to us both light and the powers of vision. If he requires us to hearken to the sweet melodies of nature, it is because he has given us an atmosphere to conduct sound to our ears, and auditory nerves to communicate it to the sensorium. And just so, if he requires us to believe, it is because he has endowed us with the necessary faculties, and given us, at the same time, the most reliable and indubitable testimony. This is a matter which Christ himself places beyond all doubt. In speaking of his rejection by the Jews, he says: "If I had not come and spoken unto them, they had not had sin; but now," he adds, "they have no cloak for their sin." And again he says: "If I had not done among them the works which no other man did, they had not had sin; but now they have both seen and hated both me and my Father."*

The first thing, then, that God requires of every man who hears the Gospel, is evidently to study it; and to weigh well the evidences of its Divine authenticity. It is here that every successful attempt at reformation must begin. For without testimony there is no faith; and without faith, it is impossible to please God in any thing, "for whatever is not of faith is sin."†

We can not, then, study the Bible too diligently. We can not too earnestly impress it on the tender minds and hearts of the rising generation. We can not sacrifice too much in our efforts to send it to the benighted nations of the earth; to those that are perishing through the ignorance that is in them. It is the germ of immortality, which, when planted in the soul, buds, and blossoms, and brings forth the peaceable fruits of righteousness and love.

Faith attainable.

First requisite in order to faith.

---

*John xv: 22, 24.   †Romans xiv: 23.

I wish, however, to say here very emphatically, that
This alone not sufficient. something more than the mere study of God's word, is essential to the perfection and consummation of our faith. A man may read his Bible more or less every day; and he may study, with much care and logical precision, the varied and multiplied evidences of its genuineness, its authenticity, its integrity, and its inspiration; and still he may come far short of the faith that the Gospel requires. For as the Spirit itself testifies, "It is with the *heart* that man believeth unto righteousness."

It is not my purpose to give here an analysis of the powers and susceptibilities of the human mind; nor to go into a logical or metaphysical disquisition respecting the intellect and the heart of man. This is not necessary for my present purpose. My readers, no doubt, all sufficiently understand this matter. They know that it belongs to the intellect to think; and to the heart to feel. They know that the former is the seat of perception, memory, imagination, and reason; and that the latter is the seat of the emotions, the affections, and the desires.

They know, moreover, that *these two faculties of the mind do not always act in concert and harmony with each other;* that the intellect, for example, is often exercised on one object, while the heart is firmly fixed on something else. Of this all are conscious. And many, at least, are also conscious, that this distraction of mind occurs more frequently on the subject of religion than on any thing else. God has so multiplied the evidences of Christianity, that a man in this country might about as well attempt to shut out the light of the sun from his eyes, as to shut out the light of the Gospel from his understanding. These evidences are seen in the Bible itself; they are seen in profane history; they are seen in the fulfillment of prophecy; they are seen in the effects of the Gospel on society; they are seen every-where. And hence it is, that almost every intelligent person in this country is willing and ready to give an intellectual assent to the Divine authenticity of the Christian religion. But how many of us believe with all our *hearts?* Ah, this is the question.

Before any man can do this, *his heart must be set free from its earthly attachments, and allowed to accompany his understanding in the investigation of the truth.* Second requisite in order to Faith. This is the one thing needful, so far as it respects human agency. When this is done, we may say that all is done. The intellect, then, immediately conveys the truth to the heart; the heart then influences and directs the will; the will controls the hand; the hand opens the purse; and the purse, properly directed, sets in motion the whole machinery of society for the glory of God and the good of humanity. And hence it is, that the true believer has no compromise to make with God. He never stops to inquire how much he must do, or how little he may do, in order to get to Heaven. His only question is, "Lord, what will thou have me to do?" When this is ascertained, he no longer confers with flesh and blood.

> "Through floods and flames, if Jesus lead,
> He'll follow where he goes."

To set our hearts free, then, from all the undue and evil influences that the world, the flesh, and the devil, have thrown around them, is evidently the second, and, I may add, the paramount duty of every man who hears the Gospel of the grace of God; as it is also an essential condition of that faith which works by love, and which purifies the soul. I do not say that it is made the duty of any man to do this Possibility of doing this. simply by his own unaided efforts; nor do I say that any man, whatever may be his capacity, can do all this, solely in and of himself. In this respect, we have no ability to do any thing. "Without me," says Christ, "ye can not do nothing."* We can not even live a single moment without him. But nevertheless, he has allowed us to have some agency in the preservation of our own lives as well as in the lives of others. And just so it is with respect to the discipline and government of our hearts. We can never control and purify them by our devices. But with the proper use of the means that God has himself provided, and with the gracious assistance that he has promised to give us, we may all do so, and do so most effectually, if we will.

It is only necessary to change our circumstances, and to place ourselves under the influence of Divine grace, in order to feel a corresponding change in our whole mental and moral constitution. How often, for example, have we felt that our hearts were being gradually weaned from the world and its vanities, while we were attending a protracted meeting; while we were listening to the pleadings of the sanctuary, or to the songs of Zion, or to the prayers of God's children? Under these circumstances, we have felt that it is good to be with Jesus; and like Peter, James, and John, when they saw his glory on the Mount of Transfiguration, we may, perhaps, have wished for tabernacles in some secluded spot, where we might be permitted to remain with him forever.

Way and means of accomplishing it.

· But oh, how very different are the influences of this vain world! When we neglect, even for a short time, the ordinances of God, and allow our affections to be absorbed in the things of time and sense, how very hard and insensible our hearts soon become; and how greatly changed is the appearance of every thing else, both within us, and around us! The heavens above us seem to lose much of their brightness; the Church, too, loses many of her charms and

* John xv: 5.

attractions; and Jesus himself, it may be, is no longer to us the one altogether lovely. And all this, be it remembered, has been brought about by a change of circumstances which are in a great measure under our own control. O, yes, we have an agency in these matters. Otherwise, God would never have said to each of us, "Son, give me thy heart;" * otherwise, he would never have commanded us "to watch over our hearts with all diligence." †

Let us then, dear reader, give good heed to these admonitions. Let us ever remember that it is not a mere cold assent of the understanding that will save us from our sins; that will serve to make us pure and holy; that will unite us to God as the children of his adoption; and that will give us a title clear to mansions in the skies. O, no; it is with the *heart,* as well as with the understanding, that man believeth unto righteousness. It is this *living* principle, that, through the agency of the Holy Spirit, fills the soul with love, and joy, and peace, and long-suffering, and gentleness, and goodness, and fidelity, and meekness, and temperance. It is this, that prepares us for the solemn hour of death; and that, through the infinite grace of God, gives us an abundant entrance into the everlasting kingdom of our Lord and Savior Jesus Christ.

Nature and influence of a living Faith.

While, then, God is giving us life and reason, and while he is aiding us and warning us, by his Spirit and by his providence, let us all be more diligent in turning our hearts from the unsatisfying vanities of this world, to him, who, of God, has become unto us wisdom, and righteousness, and sanctification, and redemption; so that when he who is our life shall appear, we also may appear with him in glory.

Admonition to seek for it.

* Proverbs xxiii: 26.　　　† Proverbs iv: 23.

SECTION II.—FORMALISM.

"Having a form of godliness; but denying the power thereof."
(2 Timothy iii: 5.)

Faith, says Paul, comes by hearing the word of God; that

Origin and
prevalence of a
living Faith.

is, by and through the careful study and critical examination of the testimony that God has given to mankind, in his Holy Oracles, concerning his only and well-beloved Son. And hence, as I endeavored to show in the preceding section, it always begins with the understanding. Afterward, it reaches and permeates the heart; and through the heart, it influences and controls the will. And thus it is, that it finally brings our whole persons, with all their attributes and accidents, under the dominion and government of our blessed and adorable Redeemer.

And hence it is, that *the faith of the Gospel always implies*

Always implies
obedience.

the obedience of the Gospel. When Paul says, for example, that the Gospel is the power of God for salvation to every one that believes it; he does not mean to say that it is the power of God for salvation to every one that merely yields an intellectual assent to the truth of the proposition, that Jesus of Nazareth is the Messiah, the Son of the living God. Nay verily: for he says afterward, in the same letter, that *it is with the heart that man believes unto righteousness.** And in his letter to the Hebrews, he says, that it was by and through this ever-active, vivifying, and fruit-bearing principle, that Noah was moved to build an ark for the saving of his house; that Abraham was induced to offer his son Isaac upon the altar; and that many of the other ancient worthies were enabled to work righteousness, obtain promises, stop the mouths of lions, quench the violence of fire, escape the edge of the sword, gain strength in weak-

*Romans x: 10.

ness, become valiant in fight, and put to flight the armies of the aliens.*

It is evident, then, as Sir Humphrey Davy well remarks, that " Faith is one of the greatest and best gifts that God has ever bestowed on man." As a means of enjoyment, nothing else will compare with it. It is the eye of the soul that enables it to perceive and to appropriate the beauties and the glories of the spiritual universe. It is the ear that fills the soul with the melodies of heaven. It is the taste that gives us a relish for the bread and the water of eternal life. It is the olfactory sense that regales us with the sweet odors of Paradise. It is the spiritual touch that brings us into direct contact with the invisible world; that fills the heart with peace, and love, and joy; that brings us into the enjoyment of a whole universe of pleasure that lies far away beyond the regions of mortal sense. And it is, in a word, as Paul testifies, the substance or foundation of all our hopes, and the demonstration and realization of things that are unseen.†

Faith as a means of enjoyment.

No wonder, then, that infidelity is every-where regarded and represented in the Bible, as one of the greatest evils that can possibly befall any man. True indeed, it is a mere *negation*. It is the mere absence of faith; just as darkness is the absence of light; and just as cold is the absence of heat. But nevertheless, it has, on every one that is subject to it, a very positive influence for evil. It deprives the soul of all the happiness that faith imparts to it; and finally, it consigns both soul and body to the blackness of darkness forever and ever.

Relation of Infidelity to Faith.

It is not, however, as some seem to suppose, a fixed and definite negation. Like its prototype darkness, it has every possible grade and shade of intensity, from the first decline of faith, to its absolute extinction in

Its shades and variations.

* Hebrews xi.   † Hebrews xi: 1.
26

the human soul. And hence it is, that it is so very difficult to describe this Chameleon or Proteus-like negation; to
enumerate and classify its phases; and to treat of it with
any degree of logical precision and accuracy. And indeed
it is not often necessary to do this. The best way to remove
darkness from a room, is to fill it with light. And the best
way to remove all infidelity from the soul, is to fill it with
faith which comes to us through the multiplied evidences
of God's love.

But sometimes there is an advantage in looking at the
negative, as well as at the positive side of a question. And there are certainly some prominent
features and forms of infidelity which all persons
should endeavor to understand. If a knowledge of them
does not serve directly to promote and to increase our happiness; it may do so indirectly, by guarding us against the
snares and vices into which they are ever prone to betray
the unwary. If it does not fill the soul with the joys of the
redeemed, it may at least help to save it from the agonies of
the damned. To the very brief consideration, then, of some
of the most prominent and popular forms of infidelity, I now
respectfully invite the attention and consideration of my
readers.

Advantage of understanding its Forms and Phases.

The first of these is that to which the Apostle refers in our
introductory quotation from his second letter to
Timothy. It is commonly called Formalism;
and as its name implies, *it consists in having the
mere form of godliness without its power.* It is the body of
religion, or rather, it is its lifeless carcass without its soul.
It is a disease of the *heart.*

First grade or species of Infi- delity.

As a form of infidelity, it is peculiar to no time or place.
Wherever true religion has prevailed, there
Formalism has, to some extent, prevailed also.

Instances of it.

The ancient Hebrews were often charged with it;* so too were the Pharisees.† But it is in the Church of Rome, that Formalism has received its fullest and most complete development. And it is probable, that it is to this phase of it, that Paul particularly alludes in his letter to Timothy.‡ But be this as it may, one thing is very certain, that Formalism is not now confined to the Catholics. It exists, to a most alarming extent, among all classes of Protestants. Indeed it would be difficult to give a more perfect description of modern Christendom, than the Apostle has given in this short paragraph. These are certainly perilous times. There is also now a great amount of selfishness in the Church, and covetousness. Many who profess to be the followers of Jesus, are " boasters, proud, blasphemers, disobedient to parents, unthankful, unholy, without natural affection, truce-breakers, false accusers, incontinent, fierce, despisers of those that are good, traitors, heady, high-minded, lovers of pleasure more than lovers of God; having a *form* of godliness, but *denying the power thereof.*"

But wherever Formalism exists, whether among Jews or Gentiles, Catholics or Protestants, it always proceeds from one and the same cause; it may always be traced back to one and the same source. *It is, in all cases, a compromise between conflicting principles; between the natural tendency of the soul to worship God, and the preternatural alienation of the heart from him.* The fact is manifest, that mankind will worship something; and it is, moreover, just as manifest, that they will worship this real or imaginary divinity, whatever it may be, under some material form, or through some material medium. Such is man's nature, and such is his history. But under the full blaze of Christianity, men are almost compelled to assent to

Source and origin of Formalism.

---

* Isaiah i: 10–15, and xxix: 13, 14.   ‡ 2 Timothy iii: 1–5.
† Matthew xxiii: 23–28.

the claims of its evidence. They concede that it is from God; and many are constrained to accept and to adopt its *form* of worship. But the misfortune is, that in many cases, their *hearts* are not in it. Their spirits do not lay hold of it, and appropriate it as a means of union, communion, and fellow-ship with God, through Christ. Like the ancient Israelites, many of us are still prone to worship God with our lips, while our hearts are far from him.*

And hence it is evident that Formalism, wherever found, is utterly worthless. We might as well attempt to satisfy the appetite, and to supply the wants of the body, with the mere pictures or shadows of bread and water, as to satisfy the desires of the soul with the empty forms and ceremonies of any system of religion. So teaches the Holy Bible.† So teaches all sound philosophy, and so teaches all human experience.

Why it is worse than useless.

Indeed, a merely formal profession of religion is always worse than useless. I know of no condition that is so much to be dreaded as that of the formalist; as that of the man who is nominally alive in the Church, but who is really dead in spirit. O, it is bad enough to go down into perdition under any circumstances; even amidst the errors and dark-ness of heathen superstition. But to hear the awful anath-ema, "Depart, ye cursed, into everlasting fire," after we have been baptized into the sacred name of the Father, and of the Son, and of the Holy Spirit; after we have had our names inscribed on the rolls of the Church, and been al-lowed to participate in all her rites and ordinances—this, it seems to me, is the very consummation of human woe! O, wretched state of deep despair, how can any one endure it!

The very thought of such a state seems to us dreadful and horrible in the extreme. But it is rendered doubly so, from the reflection that many of us

Our danger and encourage-ments.

* Isaiah xxix: 13, 14.   † Isaiah i: 10–15, and John iv: 24.

will, in all probability, have to endure it, *unless we amend our lives.* O, brethren, what a contrast there is between the cold and heartless formality of our lives, and the standard of piety and practical godliness that is required by the Holy Scriptures!

But let us not, however, be discouraged. God our Father loves us and pities us. Christ, our elder Brother, has died for us; nay more, he lives for us; and he has sent his Holy Spirit to comfort us, and to help our infirmities. We have, moreover, the blessed Bible to guide us. And all that is now necessary, and that is now required of us, is, that we give up our *hearts* to God, that we be united to Christ; that we believe in him, and love him and serve him with all our hearts, and with all our souls, and with all our strength, and with all our understanding.

Let us do this, and then all will be well. For then, indeed, we can say with Paul, that all things are ours, whether Paul, or Apollos, or Cephas, or the world, or life, or death, or things present, or things to come; all are ours, and we are Christ's, and Christ is God's. Then, indeed, life, with all its cares and labors, will be but a pleasure to us; and death itself will be but a calm sleep, a state of sweet repose, from which we will finally wake up to partake of the joys, and honors, and pleasures of God's everlasting kingdom. There, there is rest for the weary soul; there, there is fullness of joy; and there, there are pleasures for evermore.

SECTION III.—INDIFFERENTISM.

"Because sentence against an evil work is not executed speedily, therefore the heart of the sons of men is fully set in them to do evil." (Ecclesiastes viii: 11.)

There is in the natural world, or under the the physical government of God, a very close connection between cause and effect: between the transgression of a law, and the in-

Connection be-
tween the
transgression
of law and the
penalty (1) in
God's physical
government.

fliction of the penalty that God has connected
with it, and that he has made consequent upon
it. No man can thrust his hand into the fire,
and not be burned instantly. No one can pro-
ject himself from a lofty eminence, under the
influence of gravitation, without being at once dashed into
pieces.

But under the present administration of God's moral gov-

(2) In his moral
government.

ernment, the case is somewhat different. Here,
the penalty is often, in a great measure, suspended for a time. And hence it is that the liar, the thief,
the profane swearer, and even the murderer, may escape
the full measure of their desert, for weeks, and months, and
years together.

This is no doubt a most benevolent arrangement. Indeed,

Reason of this
difference.

*it is the only arrangement that is possible under
our present state of probation.* God is now long-
suffering; not being willing that any should perish, but that
all should be brought to reformation. But like every other
Divine blessing, this forbearance of God has been miscon-
strued and misinterpreted by thousands, to their own ruin
and condemnation. Because sentence against their evil deeds

Effect of this
delay.

is not executed speedily, their hearts are fully
set in them to do evil. Some of them seem to
imagine that there is really no such thing as a moral government over the universe. They suppose that every thing
happens merely as a matter of chance or accident. Others
seem to admit the existence of God's moral government.
But then they allege, that its administration is altogether
uncertain and capricious. They seem to think, indeed, that
it is a matter purely arbitrary with God, whether he should
punish any one; or whether he should permit all transgressions of his law to pass with impunity. Others, again, sup-

pose that God is so very kind, merciful, and benevolent, that he will surely make all his creatures happy in some way.

The tendency of all such theories and speculations is very obvious. Though differing much in their details, they all lead to the same ruinous consequences. They all serve to weaken, if not indeed to destroy, our sense of responsibility to God; and, of course, to make us indifferent to the claims of the Divine government.

This, then, is the second stage or form of infidelity, to which I wish to call the attention of my readers. The Second grade or first, as I have explained it, is called Formal- species of Infi-delity. ism. It consists in a form of godliness, without its power. But the species of infidelity, now under consideration, has neither the form nor the power of godliness. *It consists in the denial of man's responsibility; and in the consequent indifference which all who are under its influence show with respect to the claims of the Divine government.* And hence, for the sake of distinction, we shall call it *Indifferentism.*

This is, perhaps, the most common form and species of infidelity known in this country. It is not like Formalism, confined to professors of religion; Its prevalence. nor, like Atheism, is it limited to non-professors. On the contrary, it pervades, more or less, all classes of society. It is owing to its influence, for example, that many neglect the command to search the Scriptures; to believe on the Lord Jesus Christ; to repent of their sins; to confess the name of Jesus; and to be baptized into the name of the Father, and of the Son, and of the Holy Spirit. And it is for the same reason, viz., the influence of this species of infidelity on the soul, that a large number of those who enter the Church, give no farther diligence to make their calling and their election sure. Most of this latter class of persons have no intention of rebelling against God. They never expect to hear the anathema, " Depart, ye cursed, into everlasting fire." But for the reason assigned, they have become stupidly and alarmingly indifferent, with respect to the one thing needful.

Their error consists not so much in denying the Divine

False assumption on which it rests. authenticity of the Holy Scriptures, as in practically neglecting what is therein contained.

Like the ancient Sadducees, they err in not understanding the Scriptures, nor the power of God. And hence it is, that their whole system (if indeed views so vague, so heterogeneous, and so discordant, can be called a system) rests on a false assumption. They assume, contrary to all evidence, that the world is now in its natural and normal condition; that the Divine administration is the same now that it ever was, and that it ever will be. And hence they infer, that as many escape here the just reward of their deeds, so it is probable that many will in like manner escape it hereafter.

This assumption, however, is plainly in opposition to

Twofold evidence of its incorrectness. *both the light of nature and the evidences of Divine Revelation.* Conscience makes no separation between the crime and its just and merited

punishment. And though this is often partially done under

Testimony of conscience. the present administration of God's moral government; the Bible assures us that it is owing entirely to God's forbearance and long-suffering toward mankind in their present state of probation; feeling anxious, as he does, that as many as possible should be brought to repentance. But the same authority also assures us, that the period of our probation is limited; and that, at its close, all men will be strictly and impartially judged for the deeds done in the body :* so that every man shall finally have to give an account of himself to God.†

And hence it follows that the connection between moral

* Romans ii: 1–16.   † Romans xiv: 12.

causes and their effects, in other parts of God's universe, may be as close and as intimate as the connection that exists between physical causes and their effects. And this may be the case even in our own world, whenever our state of probation shall have ended.

But, after all, the most convincing and satisfactory way of settling this question is by an appeal to the Divine administration itself. For although, as I have said, it has been somewhat modified by the circumstances of man's preternatural condition, there is, nevertheless, enough in it to prove, beyond the possibility of a doubt, that all men are held responsible for every thought, and every word, and every action of their lives. And to this source of evidence, I therefore now respectfully invite the attention of my readers. *(margin: Evidence from the actual administration of God's government.)*

What, then, let me ask, has God done for the punishment of transgressors? What has he done to suppress rebellion; to maintain the honor of his throne and the majesty of his government? What has he done by way of vindicating the rights of his subjects, and for the purpose of promoting peace, happiness, and prosperity, throughout his vast dominions?

Or, perhaps, I should rather speak in the first place of what he has not done. And judging from his works and from his Word, I presume that my readers will all concede that *God has never inflicted any unnecessary pain or suffering on any of his creatures.* A being that has displayed so much benevolence in all the works of creation and providence, and that so loved even a rebellious world as to give his own Son for its redemption, would certainly inflict no unnecessary pain on any thing. And if so, it follows, *that whatever penalties men or angels have endured, have resulted from a necessity as profound as the being of Jehovah, and as fixed as the throne of his holiness.* *(margin: All existing suffering a necessity.)*

This, then, being conceded, as I presume it will be, by every thoughtful and reflecting person, I again ask, what has God done in the way of punishing transgressors of his law, and for the purpose of showing to the universe that his moral creatures are responsible to him for all their actions?

He has done much—very much; enough, one would think, to silence all vain speculators; and to secure the most perfect allegiance from every man who has an eye to see, an ear to hear, and a heart to understand the revelations of his will. He has cast angels out of heaven and thrust them down to hell. "The angels," says Jude, "who kept not their first estate, but left their own habitation, he has reserved in everlasting chains, under darkness, unto the judgment of the great day."* And all this, be it remembered, he has done from the *necessities* of his own nature and government; and with a full appreciation of all that these fallen seraphs will have to endure throughout the endless cycles of eternity.

But angels have suffered.

How, then, O impenitent sinner, do you expect to escape the righteous judgments of God? If God spared not an angel, a favorite angel, perhaps at that time, or rather previous to that time, the archangel, why do you imagine, O rebellious man, that you will escape the execution of his just and righteous vengeance?

But perhaps Satan whispers to you that you are not an angel, but a man: and that to man God has always shown peculiar favor; and therefore, that after all, you will not surely die.

If this is the ground of your hope, then let me remind you that this same arch-deceiver made a similar suggestion to our first parents in Eden; and that that evil insinuation has deprived mankind

All men have suffered on account of Adam's sin.

* Jude, verse 6.

of the pleasure of Paradise; that it has separated them from
the Fountain of life and happiness; that it has infused the
poison of sin into their whole constitution; and that it has
affected their body, soul, and spirit, with ten thousand mal-
adies; that it has laid one hundred and forty generations in
the dust of death; that it has clothed the Earth with mourning, and cursed the very ground from which we seek our
daily bread. And remember, moreover, that it has done
all this, by simply inducing man to sin; by leading him to
disobey his Maker; to eat

> "Of that forbidden tree, whose mortal taste
> Brought death into the world, and all our woe."

Now, if one sin, and that, too, in the estimation of most
skeptics, quite a venial sin, has done all this,—has brought all
this ruin upon mankind, *under the government and administration of a just, and righteous, and merciful God,* then I ask,
O sinner, what must be the legitimate and *necessary* consequences of all the sins that any one of us has committed,
unless indeed they be washed away through the efficacy of
that blood which alone can take away our sins! You that
make a mock of sin; that speak of it as a light and trivial
matter, *go to the death-bed of the old, of the young, and behold what sin has done. Go into the grave-yards and cemeteries
of Earth—go among the skeletons and scattered fragments of
the dead, and behold what sin has done. Lift up the curtain
that separates Earth from Hades; the visible from the invisible; look upon the agonizing souls of the damned, and behold
what sin has done.*

But, it may be said, that much of this is the consequence
of the sin committed before the promise was made that the
Seed of the woman should bruise the head of the Serpent;
that we now, however, live under a dispensation of peculiar
favor and mercy; and consequently, that we may still rea-

sonably hope for some other way of escape than through the obedience that the Gospel requires.

If any of my readers are disposed to build on so uncertain a foundation, then let me refer you to the his-

All have suffered for their personal sins. tory of the deluge; to the overthrow of Sodom and Gomorrah, and the other cities of the plain. Let me refer you to the history of God's chosen people; to their punishment in the wilderness and in Canaan; to their captivity in Assyria and Babylon; to their subjugation by the Romans; to the destruction of their city and their temple; and to their captivity and oppression in all nations for the last eighteen hundred years. Let me remind you of the ruins of Assyria, Babylon, Egypt, Greece, and Rome; and of the woes pronounced by our benevolent Redeemer on those cities in which most of his mighty works were done, because they repented not. "Woe," said he, "unto thee Chorazin; woe unto thee Bethsaida; for if the mighty works which have been done in you had been done in Tyre and Sidon, they would have repented long ago, in sackcloth and ashes. But I say unto you, it will be more tolerable for Tyre and Sidon on the day of judgment than for you. And thou, Capernaum, which art exalted unto heaven, shalt be brought down to hell. For if the mighty works which have been done in thee, had been done in Sodom, it would have remained until this day. But I say unto you, that it will be more tolerable for the land of Sodom in the day of judgment than for you." *

This does not sound much like universal salvation. This is not a license to continue in sin, because grace has abounded. But it is a very plain illustration of a principle that has ever been recognized and adopted by all just governments, human and Divine: that wherever much is given, there much should also be required.

* Matt. xi: 21-24.

What, then, careless and impenitent sinner, will be your doom, when all men shall be judged according to this principle for the deeds done in the body? When the inhabitants of Chorazin, Bethsaida, and Capernaum shall be banished with an everlasting destruction from the presence of the Lord, where will you stand? You have enjoyed, it may be, the full evidence of our Savior's mission. You live under the full-orbed glory of the Sun of Righteousness. There is now no obstacle in the way of your obedience; no enemy to terrify you; no persecuting arm to bind you to the stake. You have an open Bible; and in it you have all things pertaining to life and godliness. What, then, must *of necessity* be your portion, if you neglect this great salvation?

I acknowledge, with thankfulness, that the Gospel is a dispensation of mercy; that Jesus Christ has, by the grace of God, tasted death for every man; that God has set him forth as a propitiation for our sins, to demonstrate his righteousness in passing by the sins committed, both before and after the coming of the Messiah; and also to open up a new and living way through which God's mercy might freely flow to penitent sinners.

But, while the gift of Jesus Christ is the fullest exhibition of God's love to the world, *it is also at the same time the very highest demonstration of his justice, and of the absolute inflexibility of that law which would be satisfied with a sacrifice of no less value.* The death of Christ, an evidence of man's responsibility. It presents to us a view of the majesty, the purity, and the holiness of the Divine government, which has called forth the admiration of angels. It enables us to understand why it is that the heavens and the earth should pass away rather than that one jot or tittle of the law should fail; and why it is that the Gospel is a savor of life unto life, or of death unto death, to all who hear it. And while it is said that Jesus Christ has become the author of eternal salvation to all them that *obey* him, we can now comprehend why the Spirit should add that the same merciful Savior shall be revealed from Heaven in flaming fire, taking vengeance on them that do not acknowledge God, and that *obey not* the Gospel of his grace.

Better, then, O careless sinner, that you had never been born; that you had never heard of Jesus; that you had lived in some dark recess of this sin-stained earth, where the light of the Sun of Righteousness has never shone, than that you should live and die in this land of Bibles neglecting the solemn warnings, admonitions, and precepts of the Gospel.

This, then, is a subject in which every man has a deep and abiding personal interest. It is a matter that concerns us all for time and for eternity. If it does not, like the known love of God, fill the soul directly with heavenly peace and holy joy, it may do so at least indirectly, by restraining us from the commission of many crimes that might otherwise lead to our ruin. If it takes away all hope from the willfully and pertinaciously disobedient, it, at the same time, gives to the humble, consistent, obedient followers of the Lord Jesus Christ, a pledge of safety and security that never could be enjoyed under a Government that is carelessly and imperfectly administered. To all such, it is an anchor of the soul, sure and steadfast.

Practical importance of this subject.

SECTION IV.—Spiritualism.

"Beware, lest any man spoil you through philosophy and vain deceit, after the tradition of men, after the rudiments of the world, and not after Christ." (Colossians ii: 8.)

Guide of inferior animals. It is a fact generally conceded by students of nature, that God has given to all animals inferior to man, a perfect guide. They have all in the gift of instinct a perfect rule of action. Under the influence of this mysterious principle, every species perfectly fulfills the object of its existence. Thus, for example, the bee constructs its comb, and distills its honey, with a degree of accuracy that baffles the skill of the most profound mathematician and the most skillful chemist. And just so it is with most other species of animals, whether living on earth, in air, or in water. They all work with the most perfect accuracy in accomplishing the object for which they were created.*

But to man God has given no such natural powers or faculties. The infant is the most helpless and de- Man, destitute pendent creature on earth. It learns every thing of such a guide. by the slow process of experience; and even as it grows up to manhood, it is wont to commit the most serious blunders and mistakes in the gravest, as well as in the most common concerns of life. Thus, for instance, while all bees are laboring incessantly toward one and the same end, one man is pursuing wealth as his chief good; another is seeking after power; another, after political or military distinction; another, after knowledge; and a few only are earnestly striving to attain to celestial honor, and glory, and immortality.

The reason of this distinction between man and the inferior animals, has long been a question with naturalists. But it is a question to which the natural man has never given a satisfactory answer; though it is a subject of which he has often sorely complained. The elder Pliny, after contemplating and examining this subject as far as the Reflections of light of nature and philosophy could carry him, the elder Pliny. concludes his reflections in the following melancholy strain: "A being," says he, "full of contradictions, man is the most wretched of creatures; since the other creatures have no wants transcending the bounds of their nature. Man is full of desires and wants that reach to infinity; and which can never

* Parker's Discourse on Religion, p. 186.

be satisfied. His nature is a lie, uniting the greatest poverty with the greatest pride. Among these so great evils, the best thing that God has bestowed on man is the power to take his own life."

The light of Divine revelation is, therefore, necessary to

The Scripture solution of the difficulty. the solution of this problem. With its aid, all is plain, clear and satisfactory. In it we are taught that God designed that he himself should be man's guide; and that for this purpose, and with this view, he formed him after his own image, and after his own likeness. And for a time, it seems that he admitted him into his own immediate presence, and spoke to him with all the kindness, and love, and familiarity of a father. That was the golden age of humanity, when God conducted Adam and his lovely bride through the green pastures of Eden, and led them beside its still waters.

But soon sin broke off this happy union. It very soon interrupted the familiar and agreeable intercourse that originally existed between man and his Creator. God no longer conversed with him, face to face, as friend to friend. He very justly and very benevolently withdrew his presence from erring man. But even then he did not leave mankind without a guide. He gave us the Bible—the Holy Bible—to lead and direct us in the way of holiness; till readmitted into the presence of our God, we shall see as we are seen, and know even as also we are known.

Happy, then, is the man that makes the Bible the guide of

The Bible, man's guide of life. his life. It has already conducted millions of our race within the vail, whither the forerunner has for us entered, even Jesus who is made a High Priest forever, after the order of Melchisedek. And, guided by its precepts, many others are still on their way to glory. Wherever its influence is felt, like the river of God, it gives life and health to every thing.

> "Blessed flowers do spring where 'er it flows,
> And deserts blossom as the rose."

How glorious, then, and how delightful, would be the effects and consequences, if all men would take the Bible as the guide of their lives! How soon would enmity be removed from the human heart; how soon would man be reconciled to his Maker, and peace and good-will abound among all the tribes and families of this sin-stained earth.

But poor, weak, fallen man has ever been prone to seek a guide of his own. Deceived by his disordered affections, his blinded reason, and many false analogies, he has always been inclined to follow the instincts of his own perverse nature as the guide of his life. This is the rule that was generally adopted by the ancient philosophers; and it is the same rule that is now followed by the modern Spiritualists. This class of religious sophists maintain that *every man has a guide of life within himself; a guide that is as unerring in its object, as is the instinct of any species of animals; a religious guide, by means of which the mind takes as direct cognizance of God, and of our relations, duties, and obligations to him, as it takes of things material through the medium of the senses.**

Guide of ancient philosophers and modern Spiritualists.

This is the fundamental and characteristic doctrine of the Parker school in America, and of the Newman school in England. It is also held by many of the so-called philosophers of France and Germany. The power or faculty of which they thus speak, is variously designated, as the Reason, the Pure Reason, the Intuitive Faculty, etc. But by whatever name they may see fit to call it, they all agree with Theodore Parker, that its office is to give us direct knowledge of all that is essential in religion. *They maintain that Christianity proper, or religion absolute, consists in a system of spiritual philosophy founded in the nature of things; and that the mind perceives*

Fundamental Principle of modern Spiritualists.

* Parker's Discourse on Religion, pp. 159, 209.

27

it intuitively, just as it perceives color by means of the eye; and sound, through the medium of the ear. *

The absurd consequences of this theory are very obvious. If all true religion is but a system of spiritual philosophy, founded in the nature of things; and if this is really perceived and enjoyed by all men simply through the exercise of Reason or the Intuitive Faculty; then, of course, it follows that we need neither a Bible nor a Redeemer. And this indeed is the avowed creed of the most distinguished advocates of modern Spiritualism. Theodore Parker, in his Discourse on Religion, says: "Our theology," meaning Christianity as it is taught in most modern churches, "*has two great idols—the BIBLE and CHRIST.*" † These Mr. Parker and his colleagues would cast to the moles and to the bats, just as they would cast aside the carved images of pagan worship. And with them they would, of course, reject as old wives' fables, all that is taught in the Bible respecting the fall of man; the incarnation of Christ; his atonement for sin; his resurrection from the dead; his ascension into heaven; and his glorious reign over all the created powers and principalities of the entire universe. This is the religion of many of the self-styled philosophers of England, as well as of continental Europe. And this is one of the boasted reforms that are now spreading like a moral pestilence over our own once prosperous and happy country.

Their views of Christ and the Bible.

· To refute all the errors of this pretended scheme of philosophy within the narrow limits of one short article, is, of course, practically impossible. To do this would require the space and labors of at least a very respectable octavo. But to attempt this would only be a work of supererogation. It would be giving far more time and attention to the system than it really merits. And I will, therefore, for the

* Parker's Discourse on Religion, pp. 6, 33, 34, 372. † Ibid, p. 369.

present at least, confine my remarks to a single point. *I
mean the very bald and naked hypothesis or as-*   The System, a
sumption on which the whole system rests. Remove   baseless hy-
this, and the scheme falls like the baseless fabric   pothesis.
of a vision.

How, then, let me ask, does Mr. Parker know that there
is no difference, except in words, between Natural and Revealed Religion? How does he know that there is a *natural*
supply for all our spiritual and corporeal wants? How does
he know that there is a *natural* connection between God and
the soul, just as there is between light and the eye; between
sound and the ear; between food and the palate; between
truth and the intellect; and between beauty and the imagination?* How did Mr. Parker make this great discovery?
Was it by means of this Intuitive Faculty, which he says is
possessed by all men? If so, then why do not all men make
the same discovery? Why do men differ so much   Opposed to the
in their views of God, and of their relations, du- experience and
                                                    observation of
ties, and obligations to him? They do not so   mankind.
differ in their views of color, sound, taste, touch, and odors.
All the world will say, with Messrs. Parker, Newman, and
Mackay, that the sky is blue; that grass is green; and that
flowers are variegated. But not one in a thousand, or even
in ten thousand, will agree with them in their religious philosophy. Why is this? If there is but one absolute religion,
and all men are able to perceive it naturally and intuitively,
then, I ask, why do men entertain so very different views
concerning it? Why does the Atheist, for example, say,
There is no God? Why did the ancient Hebrews worship
but one; the Persians, two; and the Greeks, thirty thousand?
Surely there must be something wrong in this hypothesis.
*A theory that is opposed to the experience of all mankind must
be false.* And such a theory is modern Spiritualism.

* Parker's Discourse, p. 160.

But our objections to Mr. Parker's theory of religion do not rest wholly on observation. *It is as much opposed to the consciousness of mankind,* as it is to their experience. How many, for instance, will acknowledge that they are conscious of having such a faculty as that described by Mr. Parker? and of having such a knowledge of Divine things through it, as his theory implies? We are all conscious that we have the faculties of seeing, hearing, feeling, tasting, smelling, judging, reasoning, and willing. Or, to speak more accurately, we are conscious of those states of mind that necessarily imply the existence and exercise of these faculties. But how many will acknowledge that they are conscious, either directly or indirectly, of possessing a faculty by means of which they intuitively know God, and the absolute or only true system of religion? None, I apprehend, but a few visionary fanatics, whose minds the god of this world has blinded, lest the light of the glorious gospel of the grace of God should shine into them.

Ah, no; these are not the matters of which we are conscious. We are all conscious that we are sinners; and that we need to be pardoned. But how to attain to the blessed state of that man whose iniquities are forgiven and whose sins are covered—this is a question that no powers of the human mind, unassisted by Revelation, have ever yet answered. It is the Bible, fully authenticated by many infallible proofs, that reveals God to man, and man to himself. It is the Bible that teaches us that God so loved the world, even when it was dead in trespasses and in sins, that he gave his only-begotten Son, that whosoever believeth in him should not perish, but have everlasting life. It is the Bible that makes known to us God's plan of enlightening, justifying, sanctifying, and redeeming our poor fallen race; of making us holy here, and everlastingly happy hereafter.

Opposed to the consciousness of mankind.

The Bible alone, meets the religious wants of mankind.

Let us all, then, beware lest any man spoil us through philosophy and vain deceit, after the tradition of men, after the rudiments of the world, and not after Christ. *Let us cling to our Bibles as the wisdom of God and the power of God, through Christ.* They will guide us like a pillar of cloud by day, and like a pillar of fire by night, till, having crossed the Jordan, we shall enter that blessed land, where we shall see as we are seen; and where we shall know even as also we are known. "Blessed are they that do his commandments, that they may have a right to the tree of life, and may enter in through the gates into the city."

Hence it is our only practical guide in religion.

SECTION V.—NATURALISM.

"Beware, lest any man spoil you through philosophy and vain deceit, after the tradition of men, after the rudiments of the world, and not after Christ." (Colossians ii: 8.)

It is very obvious, that in the creation of the universe, God has established certain laws for its regulation and its government. Every creature, whether in heaven or on earth, whether material or immaterial, has been made subject to law. Thus, for instance, the little seed, as it is developed into the vine, or the oak, or the cedar, does not grow up at random, without form and proportion. Nay, verily. Its entire development, from its first buddings to the ripening of its fruit, is in harmony with the most exact, definite, and unchangeable laws. The size of the flower, its form, its color, and its chemical constitution, are matters that are almost as fixed and as definite as are the properties of a triangle, a square, or a circle. And just so it is with every species of the animal and of the mineral kingdom. Water is always composed of hydrogen

Evidence of the existence of natural laws.

and oxygen united in the ratio of one to eight. And all the chemists of earth can not combine these elements so as to form water in any other proportion. Observe, too, with what regularity the heavenly bodies move under the laws and influence of gravitation. We all anticipate with confidence the ordinary changes of day and night, summer and winter, seed-time and harvest. And the astronomer foretells, with the most unerring certainty, the rarer and more extraordinary phenomena of eclipses and transits, even for coming ages. And thus it is that the heavens declare the glory of God, and that the earth shows forth his handiwork.

Nor is this all. God has not only placed every creature under law, but he has also, to a certain extent, *Natural powers: what they are.* made it a depository of his power. It is true, indeed, that all power is of God. The powers that be, whether intellectual, or moral, or political, or religious, or physical, are all, in a certain sense, ordained of God. And thus it is that he creates and establishes what we call *second causes.* The mind of man, for example, has in itself no inherent or absolute power. But, nevertheless, God has endowed every man with a certain amount of power and energy, which he uses, in a great measure, according to his own will and pleasure. The sun has no inherent power in and of itself. But God has given to it an influence that is sufficient to keep all the planets of the solar system in their own proper orbits.

This is certainly a beautiful arrangement. It detracts *Beauty of this arrangement.* nothing from the glory, or power, or wisdom, or goodness of the Creator. On the contrary, to the eye of all enlightened reason, it but serves to illustrate more and more fully his infinite perfections.

But all men have not this faith. And some of them have not even the perspicacity that is necessary to enable them to look up through and beyond these second causes to Him who is himself the cause of all causes. *They see, or think they see, in those delegated laws and powers of* nature, *enough to regulate and govern the whole* created *universe. And hence it is that they sepa-* rate *God wholly and entirely from his works. They allow him to have no longer any care or concern in the government of things celestial, terrestrial, or infernal.*

Fundamental principle of Naturalism.

Second causes are now, in their judgment, abundantly adequate and sufficient for all practical purposes. Indeed, some would go so far as to say, "There is no God," no First Cause. But it is of Naturalism, and not of Atheism, that I now speak. And the Naturalist professes to recognize in nature the foot-prints of the Creator. He admits that there are evidences of design all around him. But he sees no evidence of God's presence in existing phenomena; nor of his energy or power in the present operations of nature. And hence he infers, that nature is a sort of a self-adjusting machine, and that God has retired from any and all participation in its government.

The *consequences* of this theory are numerous; and some of them are pernicious and ruinous in the ex- treme. Carried out to its legitimate results, it

Its evil tendencies.

of course ignores every thing that is supernatural in the administration of the universe. Miracles are impossible, for the simple reason, that there is no power left either to suspend, or to change, or in any way to modify any of nature's laws. Divine providence is also discarded and ignored by the very conditions of the hypothesis. And hence it follows that prayer, intercession, and all other religious observances, are to be regarded as wholly superstitious and altogether worthless. The Bible, too, according to this theory, is a myth, if not a falsehood; and philosophy is the only rational guide of life.

Such is the form of infidelity that is now taught and industriously propagated by many of the most popular writers

Popular works imbued with Naturalism. on both sides of the Atlantic. Combe's "Constitution of Man" is deeply imbued with it: and so, too, I regret to say, are many of the more recent and popular works, on almost every department of Natural Science.

But all such writing indicates a very partial and superficial view of nature. There is really nothing in the whole scheme of the universe, that, when properly understood, has the slightest bearing in favor of Naturalism. But, on the contrary, there

Geology is opposed to Naturalism. is much that is evidently opposed to it. *Geology is all against it.* The mountains and valleys around us are witnesses, not only that God has from the beginning exercised a special care over the world, but also that at several different epochs of the earth's history, he interposed *miraculously,* and actually created many new species of both vegetables and animals. Professor Hitchcock says: "*If we take only those larger groups of animals and plants, whose almost entire distinctions from one another has been established beyond all doubt, we shall find at least five nearly complete organic revolutions on the globe.*" *

This, then, is a complete refutation of Naturalism. These facts prove conclusively, that God has never forsaken the earth; that from the beginning, he has watched over it, and taken care of it: and, furthermore, that he has even worked miracles, whenever the occasion and the circumstances required that he should do so. This, I say, is evident from the facts reported by all Geologists. *For as the universe originated in miracles, so unquestionably did every species of animals and plants originate in miracle.* Second causes may indeed greatly influence and modify both animals and vegetables. But all the laws and powers of nature never did and never can give birth to a new species of either. And hence it is that *the*

---

* Hitchcock's Elementary Geology, p. 196.

appearance of a new species of either animals or vegetables, just as clearly indicates the presence and energy of the Creator, as the fall of an apple indicates the existence of gravitation.

Geology, then, is clearly opposed to this infidel hypothesis. And, I think, it may be affirmed with Meteorology is equal certainty, that *the science of Meteorology* opposed to it. *is also opposed to it.* For consider why it is, that the phenomena of each year are not invariably and uniformly the same. Why have we not the same amount of rain, and snow, and hail, and frost, and vapor, during each and every successive year? The laws of nature are the same; and so are also the second causes that serve to produce these phenomena. The same earth still exists from age to age. The same quantity of water and the same atmosphere continually surrounds it. The sun, too, is the same. Its relative positions to the earth, are the same throughout the successive days and nights of every year. The same amount of heat, and light, and electricity would therefore seem to be evolved during each successive year, causing the same or an equal amount of evaporation. And yet the quantity of rain, and snow, and hail, varies from year to year.

Why is this? There must be a variable power or energy some place. And if it is not in nature, it must be in the power that is providentially exercised, by the Author of nature. If it is not in the energy which God has *imparted* to the ordinances of nature, it must be in the energy which he himself puts forth, and providentially exercises in and through these ordinances. A man, for instance, may impart a certain amount of energy to a clock by suspending weights to the machinery. But he may very greatly increase this energy by laying his own hands upon the weights. In this case he works no miracle. No law of nature, nor even of the piece of machinery, is changed or suspended. Nor does the agent exercise his power against, above, or in any way contrary to the laws and forces of nature. He merely, by his own personal agency, adds to the force and energy of causes already acting in harmony with the established laws of nature.

This is human providence. And when God so acts, it is Divine Providence. This energy he can, of course, increase or diminish at pleasure. And hence, it seems to me, is produced the astonishing variety that we every-where witness amidst the unchanging laws and forces of nature. And hence it is, that God, without working a miracle, sometimes gives us plenty of corn, and wine, filling our hearts with food and gladness; and again, when he withholds the rains, and the dews, and the sunshine of heaven, the flowers fade, crops die, and the whole face of nature seems to languish.

And hence it is, also, that Meteorology has never yet been reduced to a science. It is a very remarkable fact, that while the astronomer can foretell the exact time and duration of all the eclipses that will occur within the lapse of many centuries, he can not tell with any degree of certainty what kind of weather we will have to-morrow.

And the same is true, in some measure, of the phenomena of human life. The art of healing is still a matter of experiment. All the skill, and knowledge, and experience of six thousand years, have so far failed to reduce medicine to a science. This is certainly a very remarkable fact. And it does seem to me, that this of itself is a refutation of Naturalism.

The phenomena of life and health are opposed to it.

But as I do not wish to multiply arguments and illustrations, I will only say finally, that *the Bible is opposed to Naturalism.* I assume here, of course, that the Bible is true. And in doing so, I am fully sustained by the common practice of mankind. The mechanic does not think it necessary, to prove that the square

The Bible is opposed to it.

described on the hypothenuse of a right-angled triangle, is equivalent to the sum of the squares described on the other two sides, every time that he attempts to square a building. It is enough for him to know that this truth has been once demonstrated to the entire satisfaction of all competent judges.

But we have proved the Divine origin and plenary inspiration of all parts of the Bible, I hope, to the entire satisfaction of the reader, in the first four parts of this treatise. This is enough. We may now reason from the Holy Scriptures, as we would reason from the *demonstrated* propositions of Geometry.

It being conceded, then, that the Bible is the Divinely inspired word of God, it is an easy matter to dispose of this *infidel hypothesis*. Almost every page of the Bible is against it. Almost every page of the Bible shows, that God is ever present in all his works, directing, controlling, and governing all things for his own glory, and also for the greatest good and happiness of the whole creation. . Let us take one or two cases, for the present, merely by way of illustration. Let us take, for instance, the history of Joseph. How think you, courteous reader, the Naturalist would, on his hypothesis, explain this remarkable chapter of Sacred History? How, without the presence and agency of God, could he account, not for one event merely, nor for two, but for all the events that led to the promotion of Joseph; to the enslavement of the Israelites; and to their final exodus from Egypt, according to the promises which God had before made to Abraham? On his hypothesis, how could the Naturalist explain the eventful biography of Moses, or of Mordecai, or of Daniel? How could he account for the emancipation of Israel by Cyrus, and their restoration to their own land? And above all, how could he explain the history of our Redeemer, and the fulfillment of the many prophecies that relate to his birth, his early education, his ministry, his death, his resurrection, his ascension, and his glorious reign and government?

But it is unnecessary to multiply arguments and illustrations. The problem is solved, and the truth fully revealed, in the few inimitable words of our blessed Redeemer, in which he assures us that *God takes care of every thing; that he clothes the lily; feeds the young ravens; allows not a sparrow to fall to the ground without his knowledge and care; and that, in a word, he numbers the very hairs of our heads.* This is enough. This is a foundation broad enough and strong enough on which to rest our faith and hopes forever.

Let us, then, "beware lest any man spoil us through philosophy and vain deceit, after the traditions of men, after the rudiments of the world, and not after Christ." And let us ever rejoice that in God we live, and move, and have our being; and that in him, and through him, and to him, are all things; to whom be glory forever and ever. Amen.

Conclusion.

SECTION VI.—PANTHEISM.

"Beware, lest any man spoil you through philosophy and vain deceit, after the tradition of men; after the rudiments of the world; and not after Christ. (Colossians ii: 8.)

One of the first forms of idolatry known and practiced among men, was the worship of the heavenly bodies. The great influence of some of these bodies, and especially of the Sun and Moon, upon the Earth, was observed by many of the ancient philosophers. They observed, too, that these bodies were continually changing their position in relation to the Earth, and some of them in relation to each other. And hence many inferred that the stars and planets were living beings

Notions of ancient astrologers.

endowed with the power of locomotion; that they were in fact real divinities, each one of which was constantly exerting an influence on the fortunes and destinies of mankind.

But modern science has completely exploded these notions of ancient astrologers. By the aid of the tele- *Revelations of modern science.* scope, the calculus, and other' means of investigation, it has been discovered that these bodies are composed of inert matter; that they are but parts of one great system, called the universe; and that their motions and influences are all essential to the stability and harmony of the one grand and universal scheme.

This, to the eye of enlightened reason, is a most convincing and glorious demonstration of the unity *Proof of the Divine unity.* of the Godhead. If creation is a unit, so also is its Creator a unit. If all created things are but parts of one stupendous whole, then indeed it follows that to us there is but one God, the Jehovah Elohim, who in the beginning created, out of nothing, the heavens and the earth, the seas and the fountains of water.

This seems to me to be a fair and legitimate conclusion from the premises. But all men do not think so. As we have no direct sensible evidence of God's existence, some have thought and argued that it is more reasonable and more rational *to transform all the innumerable* *Origin of Pantheism.* *imaginary divinities of the ancients into one divinity;* to merely change Polytheism into Pantheism; and thus to identify God and the universe.

Indeed this is not, strictly speaking, a modern notion. It has always prevailed in India: and it is sub- *Prevalence of Pantheism.* stantially the same doctrine that was taught by Pythagoras, in his celebrated school at Crotona, about 500 years B. C. But it was reserved for Germany to bolster up this monstrous absurdity by all the lights and evidence of modern science. The attempt was first made by Benedict de Spinoza, an apostate Jew of Amsterdam, about the middle of the seventeenth century. And more recently this system has been defended and variously modified by Fichte, Schelling, Hegel, Strauss, and other German philosophers. And even now, in the year 1867, while we are anxiously endeavoring to mold the minds and the hearts of the rising generation in the Holy Bible, many of the Professors in the German and French Universities, are laboring to disseminate this form of infidelity among all ranks and classes of European society.

I do not feel, therefore, that I need offer any apology for introducing to the notice of my readers, even so absurd a scheme of the philosophy of religion as that of Pantheism. If some of the most profound thinkers of Europe have been deceived by its plausible pretensions, the American youth may not be wholly out of danger; they, too, may be deluded by its undue assumptions, and by the pretensions of science falsely so-called. *Indeed, all history proves, that without a knowledge of Divine Revelation, a man may be induced to believe almost any religious creed, and to worship almost any idol.* He must, and he will worship something. If he can not worship the Creator, he will worship the creature, even in its lowest and most degraded forms. If his soul does not find rest in the religion of Jesus, he will seek it in Spiritualism, Pantheism, or any thing else. And hence it is important to guard the young against all the prevaling forms of Infidelity, and especially to expose their errors, by frequently contrasting them with the very plain, simple, and rational truths of the Scheme of Redemption, as these are revealed and presented to us in the Living Oracles.

I trust, then, that I shall have the attention and indulgence of my readers, while with this object in view, I attempt to discuss, very briefly, the claims of even so absurd a system as Pantheism.

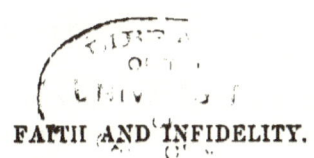
This whole scheme, then, as I have said, is nothing more nor less than Polytheism generalized. *It simply reduces the universe to a unit. This unit is God; and God, of course, is the universe.* This one dogma is the basis of the whole system.

<small>Its fundamental Principle.</small>

But from this assumption, there follow of necessity many very grave and serious consequences. These, of course, constitute a part of the scheme, and must stand or fall with it. It may therefore be interesting and instructive to notice a few of these very briefly, by way of illustration.

<small>Some of its subordinate Principles.</small>

In the first place, then, it is evident, that, on this hypothesis, *God is not a person but a thing, a mere thing, having no self-government and no self-control. He makes nothing; and he does nothing. But he is himself subject to constant changes and modifications, owing simply to the inherent, eternal, and immutable laws of his own nature.* And hence we see why it is, and how it is, that Strauss and other Pantheists argue so confidently against the possibility of all miracles. On their assumption, a miracle is indeed an evident impossibility. Admit their premises, and their conclusion follows of necessity.

<small>Character of its Divinity.</small>

Another consequence of these premises is *the denial of man's personality, freedom of will, and immortality.* If the universe is God, and God is the universe, then indeed, properly speaking, man has not even individuality, and much less has he personality. He is a mere mode or manifestation of the Divine existence;—a phenomenon that appears for a little while, and then vanishes forever. Like bubbles that rise from the ocean, and float and glitter for a few moments on its surface, and are then lost forever in the abyss of waters; even so, by a fatal necessity, man rises for a little while out of the abyss of the Divine essence; appears for a few days in the beauty of youth and the glory

<small>Character of its Humanity.</small>

of manhood; and then sinks into a state of unconsciousness—forever absorbed and lost in the fullness of the Divine existence. And this is the repose of Pantheism. This is its heaven. This is its boasted glory and felicity.

One more thought, and I have done with this part of my subject. It is evident that *Pantheism obliterates all moral distinctions; all supposed differences between right and wrong, between moral good and evil.* It is incredible to suppose that one part of a Divinity under the dominion of an absolute necessity, can ever transgress against another part. As well might we suppose that the human hand would transgress against the human foot: or that the head would violate its moral obligations to the heart. But this is impossible; for the simple reason, that no such moral obligations exist or can exist between different parts of the human body. And just so it is on the Pantheistic hypothesis; there being no moral relations, there can, of course, be no moral obligations; and where there are no moral obligations, there can be no moral wrongs or injuries inflicted.

Its Moral Code.

Many other consequences of a similar and equally absurd nature, necessarily follow from the assumptions of Pantheism. But the points already explained and illustrated are sufficient for our present purpose. And I simply wish now, in conclusion, to say a few things in relation to the merits of the whole system.

Proofs of its fallaciousness.

1. And the first remark that I wish to make is, that *the evidence of design, taken from the structure and mechanism of the universe, is all against it.* No man in his senses thinks of identifying a watch and its maker. The evidence of design seen in its structure and arrangement, is proof positive to all sober-minded persons, that it had a designer. And just so it is in the vast empire of nature. The nicely-adjusted mechanism of the heavens, and the more delicately-wrought struct-

From the structure of the universe, and the evidence of the Bible.

ure of every species of vegetables and animals, clearly indicate to every sound and well-balanced mind, that the universe is not eternal; that it did not make itself; and that it is not the result of chance; but that, as the Bible assures us, "In the beginning God created the heavens and the earth" out of nothing. In this respect, then, the evidence of Nature and the evidence of Divine Revelation harmonize most perfectly. And the evidence of both is irreconcilably opposed to all the claims and assumptions of Pantheism.

2. My second argument against this modern scheme of infidelity, is derived from *the evidence of our own consciousness.* We are all conscious of our own individuality; of our own personal identity; and of our ability to will, and generally to act as we please. We need no evidence beyond that of our own consciousness to prove that we think, and feel, and act for ourselves. Any scheme of philosophy, therefore, that makes man a mere passive machine, or that ignores the highest principles and attributes of his nature, by reducing him to a mere phenomenon or mode of the Divine existence, must be false, if there is any reliance to be placed in the evidence of our own senses and consciousness. And if we can not rely upon these witnesses, then most assuredly we can rely upon nothing. Then, indeed, Pantheism, and every other ism, becomes a mere chimera of the brain, and universal skepticism is the inevitable result.

Let not, then, the youth of our country be deceived by such wild and extravagant speculations. "Evil communications corrupt good manners." How much more rational and consistent with the testimony of our own consciousness, is the account which God has given us in the Holy Bible, respecting man's powers and capabilities. After Jehovah Elohim had created every thing else pertaining to this world;

28

after he had filled its mountains and its valleys with coal, and iron, and other precious minerals for the good of man; after he had covered its surface with fruits, and flowers, and all kinds of herbage; after he had filled the water with fishes, the air with birds, and land surface with quadrupeds, he said within himself: "Let us make man in our own image, after our likeness; and let them have dominion over the fish of the sea, and over the fowl of the air, and over the cattle, and over all the earth, and over every creeping thing that creepeth upon the earth. So God created man in his own image; in the image of God created he him; a male and a female created he them." This is the first lesson that God has taught us concerning man. And the second is that in which he informs us that by the abuse of this freedom, man sinned, and thus brought death into the world and all our woe. *Indeed, in every chapter of the Holy Bible, man is represented, just as he appears within the domain of his own consciousness, as a voluntary agent, free in all cases to refuse the evil and to choose the good.* Here, then, again we have the most perfect and entire harmony between Nature and Revelation; and as in the first instance, they are both in opposition to the claims and assumptions of Pantheism.

3. Another objection to this hypothesis is, that *it is irreconcilably opposed to the dictates of conscience, or to the impulses of man's moral nature.* If it is true, as Pantheism always implies, and as it sometimes affirms, that human actions have no moral qualities; that they are *but* the legitimate effects of causes as immutable as the Divine nature; and that they are therefore all equally good or bad—then, I ask, whence and for what purpose is this inward monitor that we call Conscience? Why was this lying witness ever placed within the human breast to torment man by its falsehood? Why does a man feel remorse for one action, and the highest degree of com-

From the office of Conscience, in connection with the Bible.

placency on account of another? Surely there must be something wrong just here. Surely there must be some error in a scheme which is so contrary to every man's experience and to every principle of human government and social order. And what must be still more perplexing to the Pantheist, is the very remarkable fact, that here again the testimony of Nature corresponds exactly with the testimony of Divine Revelation, and that both these witnesses are opposed to his favorite hypothesis.

My fourth objection to Pantheism is, that *it is opposed to some of the strongest natural desires of the human heart; and particularly to man's desire to live forever; to preserve his own personal identity amidst the wreck of matter and the crush of worlds.*

From the natural desires of the human heart, and the evidences of the Bible.

That this is true of every man I presume no one doubts. I can conceive of nothing but the fear of everlasting torment that could induce any man to desire annihilation, or to seek for eternal absorption in the Divine essence. But why was the desire to live and to preserve our own personality ever implanted in the human breast, if it is not to be gratified; if, in a few days or years, we must all sink into a state of absolute unconsciousness, never again to see the light of heaven, nor to hear the sweet melodies of nature; nor to feel one more emotion of sympathy, or of friendship, or of love? Surely a theory must be greatly at fault which is so contrary to nature, and which is so directly opposed to many of the strongest and most elevating impulses of the human soul.

How much more rational and consistent is the doctrine of Divine Revelation. How consonant with our desires and our happiness is the assurance given in that blessed volume that man was made for immortality; that though in Adam all die, yet that in Christ Jesus all shall be made alive; that the hour is coming when all that are in their graves

shall hear the voice of our Savior, and shall come forth—
they that have done good to the resurrection of life; to a
state of honor, and glory, and immortality in the presence
of our God.   There, there will be fullness of joy, and there,
there will be pleasure forevermore.

> "No chilling winds, nor poisonous breath
> Can reach that healthful shore;
> Sickness and sorrow, pain and death,
> Are felt and feared no more."

    "Beware," then, my dear readers, "lest any man spoil you
Admonition. through philosophy and vain deceit; after the
tradition of men; after the rudiments of the
world; and not after Christ."   O, never give up your Bibles
for any such baseless and unsatisfactory hypothesis as Spiritualism, or Naturalism, or Pantheism.   They have not the
shadow of evidence to support them, and they can only fill
the soul with darkness and doubting.   But the Bible is full
of light, full of joy, and full of comfort.   Follow its precepts and they will lead you safely through your earthly
pilgrimage; through the dark valley of the shadow of death;
and finally through the gates into the everlasting city of
our God.

SECTION VII.—ATHEISM.

"The fool hath said in his heart, There is no God."
(Psalm xiv: 1.)

    This is Atheism: the greatest extreme of infidelity; the
The last and greatest ex-
treme of Infi-
delity. most monstrous and absurd negation that was
ever uttered by human lips.   All other forms
of infidelity concede something to Christianity
but Atheism concedes nothing.   It dogmatically obliterates
from the Bible, as a falsehood, every thing that is said in it

respecting God, and Christ, and the Holy Spirit, and the Scheme of Redemption.

It is true, there is one form of Atheism, now perhaps more commonly called *Secularism*, which does not go sc far in its affirmations. It is rather more modest and unassuming in its pretensions. It is satisfied with doubting in regard to these matters. It does not pretend to decide positively whether there is or is not a God. There may be, or there may not be. This is a matter that does not concern the Secularist. It is enough for him, he thinks, to attend to the affairs of this world: to things of the present life. All beyond this, he regards as uncertain and unimportant. And hence his motto is the old Epicurean maxim revived: " Let us eat and drink ; for to-morrow we die." *Characteristics of Secularism.*

But the Atheist of which David here speaks, dogmatically affirms that there is no God; no Christ, no Holy Spirit, and no redemption from death and the grave. With him, nature is every thing; and every thing is nature. Whether the universe is eternal, as Aristotle taught; or whether it is the work of chance—the mere product of matter in motion, as many of the disciples of Epicurus supposed ; or whether it is the result of an infinite series of developments from primordial and uncreated monads, as most modern Atheists affirm, may indeed be a question. On this, and also on many other kindred subjects, some of the most enlightened of the school still entertain doubts. But that there is no God ; no moral government over the universe ; and no future state of rewards and punishments, are matters clear as sunshine, if we may believe the testimony of such men as Diagoras, Bion, and Lucian among the ancients ; and d'Holbach and Comte among the moderns. *Pretensions of Dogmatic Atheism.*

I presume, then, that I need not consume more time in explaining what Atheism is. It is all summed up and told in the affirmation of the fool, *"There is no God."* But as young persons particularly are very liable to be misled by the mere authority of names, I wish, for their sake, to say a few things on the merits of this so-called system of infidelity.

And in the first place, I wish all my readers, and particu-

Folly and ab-
surdity of these
pretensions.

larly the young, to consider how very reckless and unauthorized is this assertion of the Atheist. *How does he know that there is no God?* Has he seen all the parts of the universe? Has he explored its infinite dimensions; and does he comprehend every thing pertaining to its structure and organization—material and immaterial? You see, at once, that nothing short of infinite knowledge can justify any one in making this assertion. And yet it is made by a creature that does not know himself: that does not know the powers and capacities of his own soul: that does not comprehend many things pertaining to the little clay tabernacle in which his spirit has its present abode :—a being to whom every blade of grass, and every leaf of the forest, and every particle of the earth is a mystery :—a being who does not know one in a hundred of the creatures that inhabit this world; and who knows almost nothing of the ten thousand times ten thousand other worlds that compose the vast empire of Jehovah.

What would you think of the man who would stand up in a court of justice, and testify that there is no gold, nor silver, nor iron, nor copper in the moon; though he has never set a foot upon its surface, nor examined a single particle of the vast masses of which it is composed? How much would such testimony weigh with the court and jury? And yet that testimony would be reasonable compared with the dogmatical assertion made by any man, however learned, that there is no God.

There is also another circumstance, which I think detracts very much from the force and credibility of this assertion. You observe that it is not given as a logical deduction from

premises, either d ıly or unduly assumed.   On the contrary,
it springs from the common source of all infidel-   Source of Athe-
ity, *the desire of the heart.*   The fool hath said,   ism.
not in his reason, nor in his understanding, *but in his heart,*
"There is no God."   He first wishes it were so; and then he
believes it to be so.   Such, I think, is the testimony of all
infidel experience; and such is certainly the testimony of
that Spirit that tries the hearts and reins of the children of
men.   In speaking of Gentile idolaters and Atheists, Paul
says, by the Spirit: *"And even as they did not like to retain
God in their knowledge, God gave them over to a reprobate
mind—i. e., to a mind void of judgment—to do those things
which were not becoming."* *

It is not, then, because men are forced by any fair course
of reasoning, that they become Atheists; but it is because,
that *not liking* to retain God in their knowledge, and *loving*
darkness rather than the light, God has given them over to
believe a lie, that they all may be damned who obey not the
truth, but have pleasure in unrighteousness.

And hence you see, in the third place, *the bitter fruits and
consequences of Atheism.*   "As they did not like   Evil conse-
to retain God in their knowledge," says the   quences of
Apostle; or, in other words, as they desired to   Atheism.
become Atheists, God gave them up to this disposition of
mind.   And the consequence was, that they became immoral
and impious just in proportion as they advanced   Illustrations.
in Atheism.   "Being filled with all unrighteousness, fornication, wickedness, covetousness, maliciousness;
being full of envy, murder, deceit, malignity;" and at the
same time they became "detractors, backbiters, haters of
God, despiteful, proud, boasters, inventors of evil things, disobedient to parents, without understanding, covenant break-
ers, without natural affection, implacable, unmerciful." †

*Romans i: 28.   † Romans i 28–32.

It was a question of dispute among the ancients, whethei

Question among ancient philosophers.

a community, leavened throughout with atheist-ical principles, could possibly, subsist. But as a majority of both statesmen and philosophers were always on the negative side of this question, the experiment was never practically made and fairly tested, till the time of the French Revolution. True, indeed, the natural and necessary tendencies of this form of infidelity, were very plainly indicated long before that ever-memorable epoch. This was particularly the case, during the decline of the Greek Republics and the Roman Empire. But in A. D.

Solved by the French Revolution.

1793, the reign of Atheism commenced in France; and with it commenced, simultaneously, the Reign of Terror. France was like the troubled sea: it was, in fact, a sea of blood. For a time, every species of iniquity prevailed to a most alarming extent. But in a little while, there was a re-action in the public mind. The people soon recoiled from a system so impious and so horrible. And the very same convention that had publicly disowned the Most High, ignored his au thority, and proclaimed death to be an eternal sleep, wa compelled, by the immense increase of crime, to revoke their edicts; acknowledge the immortality of the soul; and bow though reluctantly, to the government of the King eternal immortal, and invisible. Surely, then, a system of such ten-

Inference.

dencies can not be a system of truth. Let us either make the tree good, and its fruit good; or else, let us make the tree corrupt, and its fruit corrupt; for the tree is known by its fruit.

How beautifully and how gloriously Christianity contrasts,

Contrast be-tween Atheism and Christian-ity.

in this respect, with this form of infidelity. Its fruits are all light, and life, and love. Its tendencies are all, "Glory to God in the highest; and on earth, peace and good-will to all men." .

I am aware that much wickedness has been committed in the name of Christianity. I know that "adultery, fornication, uncleanness, lasciviousness, idolatry, witchcraft, hatred, variance, emulations, wrath, strife, seditions, heresies, envyings, murders, drunkenness, revellings, and such like," have been practiced and tolerated within the very pale of the so-called Church of Jesus Christ. But I also know that *these crimes have no proper connection with Christianity.* They are the legitimate offspring of infidelity; and can never, with any propriety, be ascribed to the teachings and workings of that blessed Spirit, whose fruits are all "love, and joy, and peace, and long-suffering, and gentleness, and goodness, and fidelity, and meekness, and temperance." Let these virtues become universal, and the very highest state of civilization of which the human race are susceptible, will soon become universal. Man will cease to hate and to annoy his fellow-man; and all the kindreds, tribes, and families of the Earth will be united in one harmonious and delightful brotherhood.

My fourth ground of objection to Atheism is, that *it is directly opposed to the evidence of design and contrivance so clearly and so abundantly manifested in every department of nature.* If it is true, that every effect must have had a cause, that every design implies a designer, then verily this great universe must have had an Almighty Framer and Architect. Let any man, for example, carefully examine the structure and the mechanism of the human eye, and he will say, with Newton, that the study of this one organ is a cure for Atheism, if indeed it is a curable malady. Or let him look up to those beautiful stars—

> "That nightly roll,
> And shed their light from pole to pole,
> Forever singing as they shine;
> The hand that made us is Divine."

(margin note: Evidence of design versus Atheism.)

and he will be constrained to say with David, "The heavens declare the glory of God, and the earth showeth forth his handiwork."

I do not say, that without the aid of Divine Revelation, any man could have derived a correct knowledge of the character and attributes of Jehovah from the mere works of nature. This is not the question before us. There is a difference as wide as the poles between *the discovery* and *the proof* of a proposition. And it is therefore enough for our present purpose, that the truth respecting God's existence and character, first communicated to Adam and Noah by direct revelation, and afterward transmitted to their posterity by oral and written tradition, is now corroborated and sustained by the light of all nature: so that 'God's eternal power and Divinity are now clearly seen, being understood by the things that are made."* This, it would seem, ought to be sufficient. If the heavens and the earth, the seas and fountains of water, with all their varied and multiplied tenantry, are opposed to Atheism, then what farther need have we of witnesses? Surely we might rest the matter just here, and allow the voice of nature, which is now distinctly heard in all the earth, to proclaim its Maker's praise.

But, after all, it is in the Bible, and from the Bible, and

The Bible *versus* Atheism.

through the Bible, that we have most convincing and satisfactory evidence against Atheism and every other species and form of infidelity. Indeed, this evidence is perfectly overwhelming. We need no other. And the man who is not convinced by this, would not be persuaded though one witness or one thousand witnesses should rise from the dead, to testify to the world the existence of God, and the glorious realities of the spiritual universe.

* Romans i: 20.

How, for example, can the Atheist, or the Pantheist, or the Naturalist, or the Spiritualist, account for the *fact*, that the promise made by God in Paradise, that the seed of the woman should bruise the head of the serpent, has been so exactly fulfilled in the person of Jesus of Nazareth? How can he account for the *fact*, that the prophecy of Noah respecting his three sons and their posterity, has been illustrated and confirmed by the history of more than four thousand years? How can he account for the *fact*, that in and through the seed of Abraham, all the nations of the earth have been blessed? How can he account for the *fact*, that Jesus appeared as the Shiloh or Prince of peace, just a little while before the scepter departed from Judah, and that to him has since been the gathering of the people? How can he account for the *fact*, that every type of Moses has its exact counterpart in the Christian Institution; and that without the latter, the former would be as empty, and as worthless, and as inexplicable, as a shadow without a substance? How can he account for the *fact*, that just at the beginning of the seventieth week after the date of the decree to restore and to build Jerusalem, the Messiah appeared: confirmed the covenant with many for one week, or part of a week; and that in the midst of the week, he was put to death as a malefactor, though acknowledged by most modern skeptics to be the greatest and best reformer that ever lived? How can he account for the *fact*, that soon after this, as predicted by Daniel, the city of Jerusalem was swept away as by a flood; that the Jews were then scattered among all the nations; and that their present condition, as well as their history for the last eighteen hundred years, exactly corresponds to what Moses and Christ predicted concerning them? How can he account for the *fact*, that soon after the death of Christ, as has been acknowledged even by Tacitus and other profane

Illustrations.

historians, a new Institution was founded by his few humble and despised followers; that this Institution has flourished despite the opposition, and hatred, and malice of Jews and Gentiles; that it now claims as its advocates and supporters the most enlightened, the purest, and the best portions of the human race; and that, judging from the signs of the times, this Institution or kingdom, which was at first indeed but as a grain of mustard-seed, or like a little stone cut out of a mountain without hands, is itself likely to become a great mountain, and fill the whole earth? How can he account for the *fact*, that the Bible, composed as it was by so many authors, and under so great a diversity of time, place, and other circumstances, should be perfectly harmonious within itself and correspond so exactly with the most recent developments of modern science in any and every department of nature to which it refers? And finally, how can he account for the *fact*, that when the doctrines and sentiments of this Blessed Volume, are received into the head and heart of any man, and developed in his life, they change his whole nature, character, and disposition; filling his heart with love, and peace, and joy; and, at the same time, inspiring him with an earnest desire to do good to all men as he may have opportunity?

Ah, my dear readers, there is but one way to answer these and ten thousand other questions of like import; and that is by conceding the fact that the Lord God Omnipotent reigneth, and that the Bible is a revelation of his will to fallen man.

Conclusion from these facts.

And after all, this is just what every good man desires. To the morally impure and corrupt, the idea of God's presence and government, is of course full of terror and remorse. For to all such, God is a consuming fire. But to the pure in heart, nothing can be more delightful and consoling than this thought. To know

Consolation to the pure in heart.

that though we are weak, and erring, and helpless, yet that our Father is omnipotent; omniscient and omnipresent; kind, and merciful, and good; and that if we are only faithful and obedient for a little while, he will cleanse us from all our sins, purify our hearts, and lead us safely through the dark valley of the shadow of death, to the joys, and honors, and pleasures of his everlasting kingdom;—this, I say, is just what every child of God desires. And nothing short of this can ever satisfy the desires of the human soul. "Beware, then, lest any man spoil you through philosophy and vain deceit, after the tradition of men, after the rudiments of the world, and not after Christ."

THE END.